SOPHOCLES: AN INTERPRETATION

SOPHOCLES

AN INTERPRETATION

R. P. WINNINGTON-INGRAM

*Emeritus Professor of Greek Language and Literature in the
University of London (King's College)*

CAMBRIDGE UNIVERSITY PRESS

CAMBRIDGE

LONDON · NEW YORK · NEW ROCHELLE

MELBOURNE · SYDNEY

Published by the Press Syndicate of the University of Cambridge
The Pitt Building, Trumpington Street, Cambridge CB2 1RP
32 East 57th Street, New York, NY 10022, USA
296 Beaconsfield Parade, Middle Park, Melbourne 3206, Australia

First published 1980

Printed in Great Britain by The Alden Press, Oxford

Library of Congress Cataloguing in Publication Data

Winnington-Ingram, Reginald Pepys, 1904–
Sophocles: an interpretation.

Bibliography: p.
1. Sophocles — Criticism and interpretation
I. Title.
PA4417.W55   882'.01   79-50511

ISBN 0 521 22672 4 hard cover

ISBN 0 521 29684 6 paperback

CONTENTS

PREFACE

The main function of criticism is the interpretation of individual works of art; and it is a primary concern of this book, by detailed study, to interpret the seven extant tragedies of Sophocles, each in its own unique form, quality and theme. Amid their variety, however, resides an elusive unity, Sophocles, being a dramatist whose mind and vision are characteristic and, throughout a long career, remarkably consistent. 'Sophoclean' is not an empty term, hard as it may be to define, controversial as the tragic vision of this tragedian may be. It is, therefore, my further aim to inject some (more or less) new ideas or emphases into the general criticism of the author. This double aim has determined the form, in some ways unusual, of the book.

It is addressed, primarily, to those who are already familiar with the plays, but this does not mean classical scholars only. Except for footnotes, virtually all Greek is translated or paraphrased or, in the case of some words having thematic importance, transliterated. The classical scholar will demand, rightly, that the problems of a difficult text be faced: they are generally discussed in the footnotes which proliferate, and which the non-specialist will, rightly, disregard. The detailed arguments in the main body of the work will need no apology for those who agree that interpretation must be closely based upon the actual words of the poet.

I have read fairly widely in the modern critical literature of this author, but cannot claim to have covered its vast range. I cite liberally in footnotes works where some point of view receives cogent expression, but there may be many unacknowledged debts. One debt is obvious and outstanding, which is to Jebb's great series of editions. I pay tribute also to the careful scholarship of Bowra, to the zest of Perrotta, to the sharp insights of Reinhardt, to the lucid analyses of

Linforth. Among living scholars, I owe more to Kitto and Knox than may always appear: to Kitto for that sense of form which is as essential to the critic of Greek poetry as it is to the musician, to both for the dispersal of much cant and cliché.

On all seven plays I lectured at one or other of the three London colleges in which I have taught: Birkbeck, Westfield, and King's. This book is a direct product of those lectures. If I indulged myself by exploring the plays in greater detail than the circumstances demanded, the patience of my undergraduate audiences was exemplary. A graduate seminar in the University of Texas at Austin caused me to rewrite an earlier draft on *Ajax;* and this I did in the congenial environment of the Institute for Advanced Study at Princeton, to which I offer my warmest thanks. I am grateful to friends for criticism and encouragement: to Professor Thomas Gould and Professor A. A. Long who, respectively, read and commented upon earlier drafts of Chapters 10 and 7; above all, to Mrs P. E. Easterling who saw every chapter in draft and had the great kindness to read the proofs. Along with my gratitude, I absolve them from all responsibility. To my wife, who has endured some tedium, I owe, as so much else, my title. Finally, it is no formality if I thank the staff of the Press for their skill and consideration.

London, July 1979   R. P. WINNINGTON-INGRAM

BIBLIOGRAPHY OF
SHORT TITLES

Adams: S. M. Adams, *Sophocles the playwright* (Toronto 1957)

Adkins, *MR:* A. W. H. Adkins, *Merit and responsibility* (Oxford 1960)

Adkins, *MV:* A. W. H. Adkins, *Moral values and political behaviour in ancient Greece* (London 1972)

Alt:K. Alt, 'Schicksal und φύσις im *Philoktet* des Sophokles', *Hermes* 89 (1961) 141–74

Anderson: M. J. Anderson (ed.), *Classical drama and its influence* (London 1965)

Avery: H. C. Avery, 'Heracles, Philoctetes, Neoptolemus', *Hermes* 93 (1965) 279–97

Beck: A. Beck, 'Der Empfang Ioles', *Hermes* 81 (1953) 10–21

Biggs: Penelope Biggs, 'The disease theme in Sophocles' *Ajax, Philoctetes* and *Trachiniae*', *CP* 61 (1966) 223–35

Bowra: C. M. Bowra, *Sophoclean tragedy* (Oxford 1944)

Burian: P. Burian, 'Suppliant and saviour: Oedipus at Colonus', *Phoenix* 28 (1974) 408–29

Cameron: Alister Cameron, *The identity of Oedipus the King* (New York and London 1968)

Campbell, *Paral.:* L. Campbell, *Paralipomena Sophoclea* (London 1907, reprint Hildesheim 1969)

Coleman: R. Coleman, 'The role of the chorus in Sophocles' *Antigone*', *PCPS* 18 (1972) 4–27

Dain–Mazon: A. Dain & P. Mazon, *Sophocle*, 3 vols. (Paris 1955–60)

Davidson: J. P. Davidson, 'The parodos of Sophocles' *Ajax*', *BICS* 22 (1975) 163–77

Dawe: R. D. Dawe (ed.), *Sophoclis tragoediae* I (*Aj., El., O.T.*) (Teubner, Leipzig 1975)

Dawe, *STS:* R. D. Dawe, *Studies on the text of Sophocles* I (Leiden 1973)

Dirlmeier: F. Dirlmeier, 'Der Aias des Sophokles', *NJ* I (1938) 297–319 = *Ausgewählte Schriften* (Heidelberg 1970) 13–30

Dodds, *GI:* E. R. Dodds, *The Greeks and the irrational* (Berkeley & Los Angeles 1951)

Dover, *GPM:* K. J. Dover, *Greek popular morality in the time of Plato and Aristotle* (Oxford 1974)

Easterling, *Ant.:* P. E. Easterling, 'The second stasimon of *Antigone*', *Dionysiaca* (ed. R. D. Dawe et al.) (Cambridge 1978)

Easterling, *BICS:* P. E. Easterling, 'Sophocles, *Trachiniae*', *BICS* 15 (1968) 58–69

Easterling, *ICS:* P. E. Easterling, '*Philoctetes* and modern criticism', *Illinois Class. Stud.* 3 (1978) 27–39

Easterling, *PCPS:* P. E. Easterling, 'Oedipus and Polynices', *PCPS* 13 (1967) 1–13

Ehrenberg: V. L. Ehrenberg, *Sophocles and Pericles* (Oxford 1954)

Erbse: H. Erbse, 'Neoptolemus und Philoktetes bei Sophokles', *Hermes* 94 (1966) 177–201

Errandonea, *SO:* I. Errandonea, 'Das 4. Stasimon der "Antigone" von Sophokles', *SO* 30 (1953) 16–26

Fraenkel, *Sem.: Due seminari romani di Eduard Fraenkel (Sussidi eruditi* 28 – Rome 1977)

Fraenkel, *MH:* E. Fraenkel, 'Zwei Aias-szenen hinter der Bühne', *MH* 24 (1967) 79–86

von Fritz: K. von Fritz, 'Zur Interpretation des Aias', *RhM* 83 (1934) 113–28 = *Antike und moderne Tragödie* (Berlin 1962) 241–55

Garvie: A. F. Garvie, 'Deceit, violence, and persuasion in the *Philoctetes*' in *Studi classici in onore di Quintino Cataudella* I (Catania 1972) 213–26

Gellie: G. H. Gellie, *Sophocles: a reading* (Melbourne 1972)

Goheen: R. F. Goheen, *The imagery of Sophocles' Antigone* (Princeton 1951)

Gould (1) and (2): Thomas Gould, 'The innocence of Oedipus: the philosophers on Oedipus the King', (1) *Arion* 4 (1965) 363–86, 582–611; (2) *Arion* 5 (1966) 478–525

Hinds: A. E. Hinds, 'The prophecy of Helenus in Sophocles' *Philoctetes*', *CQ* 17 (1967) 169–80

Jebb: R. C. Jebb, editions of all seven plays (Cambridge 1883–96)

Johansen: H. Friis Johansen, 'Sophocles, 1939–1959', *Lustrum* 7 (1962) 94–342

Johansen, *C&M:* H. Friis Johansen, 'Die Elektra des Sophokles', *C&M* 25 (1964) 8–32

J. Jones: John Jones, *On Aristotle and Greek tragedy* (London 1962)

Kaibel: G. Kaibel (ed.), *Sophocles Elektra* (Leipzig 1896)

Kamerbeek: J. C. Kamerbeek, editions of *Aj.* (1953). *Trach.* (1959), *O. T.* (1967), *El.* (1974) (Leiden)

Kells: (ed.) J. H. Kells, *Sophocles Electra* (Cambridge 1973)

Kells, *BICS:* J. H. Kells, 'Problems of interpretation in the Antigone', *BICS* 10 (1963) 47–64

Kirkwood, *HSA:* G. M. Kirkwood, 'Homer and Sophocles' *Ajax*', in Anderson (ed.) 51–70

Kirkwood, *SSD:* G. M. Kirkwood, *A study of Sophoclean drama* (Ithaca, N.Y. 1958)

Kitto: *FMD:* H. D. F. Kitto, *Form and meaning in drama* (London 1956)

Kitto, *GT:* H. D. F. Kitto, *Greek tragedy* (London 1939, 3rd ed. 1961)

Kitto, *Poiesis:* H. D. F. Kitto, *Poiesis: structure and thought* (Berkeley & Los Angeles 1966)

Kitto, *SDP:* H. D. F. Kitto, *Sophocles, dramatist and philosopher* (London 1958)

Knapp: C. Knapp, 'A point of interpretation of the *Antigone* of Sophocles', *AJP* 37 (1916) 300–16

Knox, *HS:* B. M. W. Knox, 'The *Ajax* of Sophocles', *HSCP* 65 (1961) 1–37

Knox, *HT:* B. M. W. Knox, *The heroic temper: studies in Sophoclean tragedy* (Berkeley & Los Angeles 1964)

Knox, *OTh:* B. M. W. Knox, *Oedipus at Thebes* (New Haven 1957)

Lattimore, *PGT:* R. Lattimore, *The poetry of Greek tragedy* (Baltimore 1958)

Lattimore, *SPGT:* R. Lattimore, *Story patterns in Greek tragedy* (London 1964)

Lesky, *TD:* A. Lesky, *Die tragische Dichtung der Hellenen* (Göttingen 1956, 3rd ed. 1972)

Letters: F. J. H. Letters, *The life and work of Sophocles* (London 1953)

Levy: C. S. Levy, 'Antigone's motives: a suggested interpretation', *TAPA* 94 (1963) 137–44

Linforth (1951): I. M. Linforth, 'Religion and drama in "Oedipus at Colonus"'. *U.Cal. Publ. in Class. Phil.* 14 (1951) 75–191

Linforth (1951): I. M. Linforth, 'The pyre on Mount Oeta in Sophocles' *Trachiniae*', *U. Cal. Publ. in Class. Phil.* 14 (1951) 255–67

Linforth (1956): I. M. Linforth, 'Philoctetes: the play and the man', *U. Cal. Publ. in Class. Phil.* 15 (1956) 95–156

Linforth (1961): I. M. Linforth, 'Antigone and Creon', *U. Cal. Publ. in Class. Phil.* 15 (1961) 183–259

Linforth (1963): I. M. Linforth, 'Electra's day in the tragedy of Sophocles', *U. Cal. Publ. in Class. Phil.* 19 (1963) 89–126

Lloyd-Jones, *JZ*: H. Lloyd-Jones, *The justice of Zeus* (Berkeley & Los Angeles 1971)

Long: A. A. Long, *Language and thought in Sophocles* (London 1968)

Méautis: G. Méautis, *Sophocle: essai sur le héros tragique* (Neuchâtel 1940, 2nd ed. Paris 1957)

Müller (1): G. Müller, 'Überlegungen zum Chor der Antigone', *Hermes* 89 (1961) 398–422

Müller (2): G. Müller, *Sophokles Antigone* (Heidelberg 1967)

Müller, *OT*: G. Müller, 'Das zweite Stasimon des König Ödipus', *Hermes* 95 (1967) 269–91

Musurillo: H. Musurillo, *The light and the darkness* (Leiden 1967)

O'Brien: M. J. O'Brien (ed.), *Twentieth-century interpretations of Oedipus Rex* (Englewood Cliffs, N.J. 1968)

Pearson: A. C. Pearson, *The fragments of Sophocles*, 3 vols. (Cambridge 1917)

Perrotta: G. Perrotta, *Sofocle* (Milan 1935)

Podlecki, *TAPA*: A. J. Podlecki, 'Creon and Herodotus', *TAPA* 97 (1966) 359–71

Poe: J. P. Poe, *Heroism and divine justice in Sophocles' Philoctetes* (*Mnem.* Suppl. 34 – Leiden 1974)

Pohlenz: M. Pohlenz, *Die griechische Tragödie* (2nd ed. Göttingen 1954)

Reinhardt: K. Reinhardt, *Sophokles* (Frankfurt 1933, 3rd ed. 1947; Eng. transl., Oxford 1979)

Robinson: D. B. Robinson, 'Topics in Sophocles' *Philoctetes*', *CQ* 19 (1969) 34–56

de Romilly: J. de Romilly, *Time in Greek tragedy* (Ithaca, N.Y. 1968)

de Romilly, *CA*: J. de Romilly, *La crainte et l'angoisse dans le théâtre d'Eschyle* (Paris 1958)

Ronnet: G. Ronnet, *Sophocle, poète tragique* (Paris 1969)

Rose: P. W. Rose, 'Sophocles' *Philoctetes* and the teachings of the sophists', *HSCP* 80 (1976) 49–105

Rosenmeyer, *MT*: T. G. Rosenmeyer, '*Ajax*: tragedy and time', *The masks of tragedy* (Berkeley 1961) 155–98

Rosenmeyer, *Phoenix*: T. G. Rosenmeyer, 'The wrath of Oedipus', *Phoenix* 6 (1952) 92–112

Seale: D. Seale, 'The element of surprise in Sophocles' *Philoctetes*', *BICS* 19 (1972) 94–102

Schadewaldt: W. Schadewaldt, 'Sophocles, Aias und Antigone', *Neue Wege zur Antike* 8 (1929) 61–117

Segal, *Arion:* C. P. Segal, 'Sophocles' praise of man and the conflicts of the *Antigone*', *Arion* 3.2 (1964) 46–66

Segal, *Hermes:* C. P. Segal, 'Philoctetes and the imperishable piety', *Hermes* 105 (1977) 133–58

Segal, *TAPA:* C. P. Segal, 'The Electra of Sophocles', *TAPA*97 (1966) 473–545

Segal, *YCS:* C. P. Segal, 'Sophocles' Trachiniae: Myth, poetry, and heroic values', *YCS* 25 (1977) 99–158

Sheppard: J. T. Sheppard, *The Oedipus Tyrannus of Sophocles* (Cambridge 1920)

Sicherl (1): M. Sicherl, 'Die Tragik des Aias', *Hermes* 98 (1970) 14–37

Sicherl (2): M. Sicherl, 'The tragic issue in Sophocles' *Ajax*', *YCS* 25 (1977) 67–98

Simpson: M. Simpson, 'Sophocles' Ajax: his madness and transformation', *Arethusa* 2 (1969) 88–103

Stanford: W. B. Stanford (ed.), *Sophocles Ajax* (London 1963)

Steidle: W. Steidle, *Studien zum antiken Drama* (Munich 1968) 169–92

Stinton: T. C. W. Stinton, 'Notes on Greek tragedy, 1', *JHS* 96 (1976) 121–45

Taplin: O. Taplin, 'Significant actions in Sophocles' *Philoctetes*', *GRBS* 12 (1971) 25–44

Torrance: R. M. Torrance, 'Sophocles: some bearings', *HSCP* 69 (1965) 269–327

Vickers: Brian Vickers, *Towards Greek tragedy* (London 1973)

Vidal-Naquet: P. Vidal-Naquet, 'Le *Philoctète* de Sophocle et l'éphébie', in J.-P. Vernant & P. Vidal-Naquet, *Mythe et tragédie en Grèce ancienne* (Paris 1973) 159–84

Waldock: A. J. A. Waldock, *Sophocles the dramatist* (Cambridge 1951)

Webster, *IS:* T. B. L. Webster, *An introduction to Sophocles* (Oxford 1936, 2nd ed. 1969)

Whitman: C. H. Whitman, *Sophocles: a study of heroic humanism* (Cambridge, Mass. 1951)

Woodard (1) and (2): T. M. Woodard, '*Electra* by Sophocles: the dialectical design', Part I, *HSCP* 68 (1964) 163–205; Part II, *HSCP* 70 (1965) 195–233

CHAPTER ONE

Introductory

Interest in Sophocles is unabating. If it was marked in the periods which followed the two world wars, yet now, when the second war has been over for more than thirty years, books and articles on Sophocles still flow from the presses. There is clearly a fascination here – a sense of relevance, if one may use a modish word. From all this scholarly and critical activity – and much of it has been of quality – one ought not to expect or even desire that a consensus should emerge any more than from the critical study of Shakespeare. The range of opinion, however, has been and still is fantastically wide. There are orthodoxies and dogmas, but they conflict. There is conflict over the interpretation of individual tragedies and over the tragic thought of Sophocles in general.

A complete survey would be tedious. We have been asked to look at Sophocles in many different guises: the virtuoso playwright, unconcerned with ideas or consistency or character; the portraitist; a Homeric, or aristocratic, or conservative, Sophocles turning his back on the contemporary world or confronting it with paradigms of a lost heroism; a pious Sophocles, the outcome of whose plays must always reflect well upon the gods; an acceptant Sophocles, but also, by contrast, one whose heroes rightly arraign the gods. On the critical stage they have had their entrances and their exits and their reappearances with a change of mask and costume; and we seem to look in vain for the face behind the mask. No dramatist perhaps has stamped his mark more strongly upon his plays, yet without obtruding his personality or advertising his personal views. That is part of the trouble.

Seven tragedies have survived, spanning some forty years or more.

Despite an uncertain chronology,[1] we can trace developments in technique: Sophocles did not write *Philoctetes* and *Oedipus Coloneus* in quite the same way that he wrote *Ajax* and *Antigone;* in the later plays there is more flexibility of form and, to employ a dangerous word, more regard for realism. The Athenian audience had changed, in its tastes and its demands, and Euripides had been at work. It is a futile exercise to ask whether both dramatists had reacted independently to the change or whether, since each knew what the other was doing, there was a mutual influence. One can play with the idea of the two fellow-craftsmen meeting in the agora and discussing, as they would do, not justice and the gods but stichomythia, messenger speeches and 'gods from the machine'; one may think to discern cases in which Sophocles, in his unobtrusive way, is showing that he can handle a technical problem with greater skill than Euripides! His way is unobtrusive, and he is in general as concerned to conceal cleverness as the other to display it. Hence an impression of conservatism. Yet take the two *Electras.* Euripides innovates boldly with his 'married' Electra, his transference of the action to a cottage in the country which necessitated ways of bringing Aegisthus and Clytemnestra within range of murder. But Sophocles, adhering closely to tradition and convention, postpones the recognition and so transforms the drama – a stroke as brilliant and (one presumes) original as the more obvious innovations of Euripides.

To trace developments in thought is more difficult, and here comparisons with Euripides are perhaps less helpful. Sophocles was the older by some fifteen years, but the early plays of both are lost, their extant works belonging, broadly, to the same period. There could have been mutual reaction and an interplay of ideas, a negative – if not a positive – influence. This has often been suspected but is never demonstrable. There were common subjects, common themes, but a different cast of mind. It is not that Euripides lacked roots in traditional thought, but no critic would have written of him what Dodds writes of Sophocles, that he was 'the last great exponent of the archaic world-view'.[2] It is not that Sophocles lacked acquaintance

---

[1] On chronology see App. G below. The most serious doubts arise over the dating of *Trachiniae* and *Electra*, but the former is likely to be relatively early and the latter relatively late.

[2] Dodds, *GI* 49. On traditional modes of thought in Euripides, see Lloyd-Jones, *JZ* 147ff.

with contemporary thought,[3] but, just as his technical originality is concealed and not paraded, so he is quite unconcerned to appear in the van of intellectual progress. Hence, again, that impression we gain of conservatism which may or may not be illusory but is confirmed by the persistence throughout his work of certain basic notions, themselves highly traditional – the breach between divine and human nature, between divine and human knowledge, between appearance and reality, which is indeed a main source of that irony so pervasive a feature of his theatre.

If comparisons with Euripides are, except in technical matters, rather unhelpful, it may be different with Aeschylus. *Antigone* certainly – and *Ajax* probably – are relatively early plays (though Sophocles had been producing tragedies for more than a quarter of a century before *Antigone*) and in point of time stand closer, though not close, to Aeschylus. Some critics, not without justification, have found Aeschylean modes of thought in *Ajax*; and it could well be, though it may be vain to say so, that, if we possessed the *Hoplon krisis,* we might have a better understanding of the Sophoclean play. It will be argued below that *Antigone,* with the contrasted tragedies of two central figures, is a fundamental document for the relationship of Aeschylean and Sophoclean tragic thought. These being relatively early plays, we might suppose that the influence of Aeschylus thins out or disappears as the career of Sophocles advances. Yet, when we turn to later plays – to *Electra*[4] and to *Oedipus Coloneus,* they will be found to stand in a significant relation to the Oresteian trilogy. Every critic works on assumptions derived from study of his author: I have been led to assume that, from first to last, Sophocles was reacting, one way or another, to the influence of that great predecessor who had shown how the categories and formulations of traditional Greek thought could convey a profound vision of a tragic world.[5]

It is partly for this reason that I have included chapters on Fate and on Furies[6] which deal substantially with the Aeschylean background.

---

[3] Cf. Long 166f.

[4] The play is certainly later – and could be considerably later – than 420.

[5] Cf. my 'Tragedy and Greek archaic thought' in Anderson (ed.) 31–50. The virtues of this tradition are eloquently presented in the last paragraph of Lloyd-Jones, *JZ.*

[6] In principle it is preferable to use the Greek word Erinyes, and I do so generally and especially when discussing texts where it occurs. Sometimes, however, it has seemed convenient to use the Latinate equivalent for these goddesses of many

For the most part, however, the book consists of detailed studies of
the extant plays. Not all these studies are upon the same lines or upon
the same scale, but each of them seeks to relate interpretation closely
to the text. There is always a certain arrogance in supposing that one's
careful study of a text will reveal things which others have missed or
from which they have failed to draw the right conclusions. A scholar
has, however, no right to inflict his views upon the world, unless he
sincerely believes that he has something new to say; and he will be
rash to believe this unless his views are firmly based upon the words of
his author. Those words are the ultimate evidence. The more careful a
writer the poet the better the evidence; and there is reason to suppose
that Sophocles was a very careful and controlled writer who did not
use words at random, even small words in short speeches, while his
long speeches, even where they are most emotional, are dense with
thought and carefully structured. For, like the other tragedians, he
was working in a formal tradition which demanded the imposition of
a shape upon the subject-matter. Thus form too is a criterion: the
form of the play, the scene, the ode, the speech, the sentence. Why has
the poet shaped this or that element, large or small, in this particular
way? Why has he made his personages to say this and not that?

To say or to sing. The lyric features in Sophocles – odes and
kommoi[7] – have not been neglected by scholars, their close relationship to context has been observed and discussed. It may be, however,
that their structural and thematic importance has not always been
given its due weight.[8] To take a couple of examples: the Second
Stasimon of *Oedipus Tyrannus* is a notorious problem. Why, for
instance, is the Chorus made to raise the issue of tyranny? Is Oedipus,
or do they think him to be, a 'tyrant' or on the way to become one?
And is his destruction related to his 'tyranny'? If so how? And if not
what does this signify? The problem has been assailed from many
directions, some rather tangential to the main themes of the play. Yet
the ode is symmetrically constructed, dove-tailed into the structure,
packed with traditional religion and morality. Placed centrally and at

names (cf. *O.C.* 42f.), and, since their nature is discussed at length, there should be
no danger of misconstruction.

[7] For convenience I have, like others, used this term to cover all lyric features in
which the Chorus is joined by one or more singing actors, though it should
properly refer only to laments (cf. Arist. *Poet.* 1452b24).

[8] Lloyd-Jones, *JZ* 115, speaks of 'the too prevalent habit of treating the choral lyrics
as an unimportant element in Sophoclean drama'.

a crucial point of the action, it should, if it can be rightly interpreted, have crucial significance for the understanding of Oedipus and his fate. If this ode has always been taken very seriously, the First Stasimon of *Ajax* is often dismissed cursorily as the distressed reaction (which it is) of a chorus in perplexity, given its due as a fine lyric utterance (which it is), but neglected as a clue to the understanding of Ajax and *Ajax*. Yet it brings into relation two themes – of time and of madness – which run throughout the first phase of the play. These odes, and some other lyric features, are closely examined below. (In one or two cases, where such an analysis would hold up the argument, it has been placed in an appendix.) In contrast with the relatively rational, not to say rhetorical, processes of dialogue, the subtleties of the lyric mode and style are elusive; the critic who tries to seize the aesthetics of a phrase or image, to detect overtones and undertones, runs the usual dangers of subjectivity and over-interpretation. These risks are better faced than abandon a vital kind of evidence. The more closely these lyric features are studied, the clearer it becomes that here too the art of Sophocles was under a masterly control.

Aristotle defined a tragedy as the imitation (or representation) of a 'serious' action, and much of the *Poetics* is concerned with situation and plot; in an earlier chapter, he distinguished tragedy from comedy as 'imitating' men 'better' than ordinary.[9] The second way of looking at it could be Platonic, since Plato was much disturbed by the tragic mode of representing heroes: it could even be popular, since what the audience might particularly remember was the great figures upon the stage. We too, when we think of Sophocles, think of imposing figures such as Ajax, Antigone, Oedipus, and Electra; and it is no wonder that some critics have regarded the creation of such figures as his paramount interest. He was, however, writing tragedies and not assembling a portrait-gallery; his figures exist for the purpose of expressing a tragic vision of the world in action. It was the great service of Aristotle to stress the cardinal importance of action

---

[9] Aristotle, *Poetics* 1449b24; 1448a16–18. John Jones, in his justly admired book, *On Aristotle and Greek tragedy*, maintains that the notion of 'tragic hero' has been foisted on to Aristotle by later critics. I should prefer to say that, having inherited such a way of looking at plays, he strove to get away from it – not with entire success, since he keeps returning to a theme which obviously interested and exercised him, namely, the definition of the right sort of *person* to be 'imitated', cf. e.g. 1454b8ff.; 1460b33f.

(*praxis*). There is action, and there is character; the relation between
the two – and the whole question of the nature and limitations of
characterization in Greek tragedy – have been the matter of lively
debate. That Sophocles preserved an even balance between character
and action is – or deserves to be – a commonplace of Sophoclean
criticism. But what does 'character' in Sophocles mean? What does it
amount to? Since much of what follows will be concerned with
'character' in one degree or another, it may be useful to face this
question now in a preliminary way.

And perhaps the first thing to be said is this: we do not have to
search for 'character' in Sophocles, since his whole theatre is
dominated throughout by a concern with states of mind. States of
mind are psychological phenomena; a stable and persistent state of
mind is a character. In Sophoclean tragedy the vocabulary of mind
meets us at every point: *phrenes, phronein, nous, gnome,* and other
words. The personages are aware of their states of mind and comment
on them;[10] those states are the subject of judgements and controversy.
In what do *phronein, eu phronein, sophronein,* consist? *sophrosune*
(whatever place we give it in the Sophoclean scheme) is a state of
mind and not a course of conduct, though it governs conduct.[11]
States of mind have a past: if they determine action in the future, they
have themselves been determined in the process of time by heredity,
by situation, by experience, by things done and suffered. The work of
time is a constant preoccupation of the dramatist. It is from the womb
of time that events, often long prophesied, come to birth: no less
important is the part played by time in the genesis of mental states.
The first half of *Ajax,* from Prologos to suicide, is not only a dramatic
exploration of the hero's mind but also an account of how it came to
be what is was. The minds of Electra and Philoctetes are shown no less
to be moulded by their pasts.

There is a sense, then, in which Sophoclean drama is highly
psychological. Psychology has become an emotive word in this
connection; and there are good reasons for this in the excesses of
earlier critics who assumed that it was a primary purpose of the Greek

[10] Cf. H. Diller, *WS* 69 (1956) 74ff.
[11] Conversely, *hubris* is a mode of behaviour, but arises out of a state of mind. Since
the man who is *sophron* will not act hubristically and the man who acts hubristically cannot be *sophron, hubris* and *sophrosune* can, with due reserve, be regarded as
antithetical.

dramatists to depict character as such and that any failure on their part to provide fully fleshed 'characters' recognizable by the standards of ordinary life was a deficiency which should not be imputed to them until every effort had been made on their behalf. Reactions tend to run to extremes: hence those denials that fifth-century Greeks possessed a concept of the unitary personality at all or, alternatively, that the tragedians cared to preserve even a semblance of consistency in their portrayal of personality.[12] On the whole, the more sensible critics today recognize that there is a core of unity and consistency in the characters of Greek tragedy and that, in this form of drama at any rate, our responses depend upon a feeling that these are human-beings not altogether unlike ourselves whose emotions follow paths which are not beyond our comprehension.[13]

This takes us some way, but not very far. In the case of Aeschylus perhaps we do not go much farther than to say that he has provided that minimal degree of character and motivation which is required in order to account for the action. How far do we go with Sophocles?

[12] Cf. Tycho Wilamowitz-Moellendorff, *Die dramatische Technik des Sophokles* (Berlin 1917). For a sympathetic, if critical, account of this work see H. Lloyd-Jones, *CQ* 22 (1972) 214–28. For a representative – and highly intelligent – post-Wilamowitz reaction see Schadewaldt 61ff., esp. 63–9.

[13] Characterization in Greek tragedy might be easier to discuss, if there were any clear understanding of the means by which dramatists cause a character to 'live' upon the stage. Serious and effective drama can be written with characters ranging from mere abstractions to highly complex and 'life-like' individuals. The extent, however, to which the personage is imposed upon the audience seems not to vary directly with the complexity of his characterization. Bringing a character to 'life' may be a trade-secret not divulged, but may have something to do with giving him a characteristic 'tone of voice' (a notion I believe to be derived from Stoll, the Shakespearian scholar). Aeschylus' Clytemnestra is a good example. She is not built up with an accumulation of traits; her characterization is little more than an unfolding of the implications of the first statement made about her in the play: 'the woman's heart of manly counsel' exercising 'mastery'. And yet, when we hear her say: ἔστιν θάλασσα· τίς δέ νιν κατασβέσει;, we feel that no one but Clytemnestra could have spoken those words. Clytemnestra is the supreme achievement of Aeschylus in that line, but Eteocles in *Septem* (nine years earlier), simpler in conception, closer to being defined by status (son and king), yet imposes himself in an impressive way from the beginning, so that we accept him as a person, we believe in him during the traffic of the stage.

Characterization in Aeschylus is too big a matter to be dealt with ἐκ παρέργου. Cf. P. E. Easterling, 'Presentation of character in Aeschylus', *G&R* 20 (1973) 3–19, and some sensible remarks by K. J. Dover, *JHS* 93 (1973) 69. On characterization in Greek tragedy in general, C. Garton, *JHS* 77 (1957) 247–54, is an outstandingly valuable contribution.

We must wait and see what we find, relying more upon texts than upon dogmas. A recent writer has, however, presented us with a useful way of looking at the problem.[14] Sophocles builds down and he builds up; he builds down from the traditional situation and the mental attitudes which the action implies, and he builds up from observation of human life in such a way as to create credibility and encourage emotional response. The building-down is not, however, just a matter of exhibiting a unitary *ethos* (which has been a popular way of looking at Sophoclean character). Ajax is proud, but virtually all heroes are proud: Ajax has a special degree of pride, the quality and causation of which are essential to the action. Nor is the process of building-up a matter of introducing psychological peculiarities for their own sake.[15] Indeed it is within that large area between 'unitary *ethos*' and psychological niceties that Sophoclean characterization lies. We must take what we find. We should not wave our antennae, delve into our egos, or read ingeniously between the lines: we should, however, read the lines, and read them carefully. We should not be frightened by a dogma into dismissing the natural interpretation of a text.

Nor need we expect the observation of human nature to play the same part in the portrayal of every character or in every kind of play. When towards the end of his career, Sophocles decided to write a play about Philoctetes left alone on a desert island and to introduce the young Neoptolemus as the tool of Odysseus, he faced and met a double challenge. He had, by an effort of sympathetic imagination, to picture the mind of a heroic person in a situation which no normal man encounters; he had to enter into the mind of an adolescent in a situation which, despite the heroic setting, was not too remote from common experience. In both areas he drew upon his knowledge of human nature and human life; in both cases, character and action are inextricably intertwined.

Consideration of Sophoclean drama is bound to be focused to a very considerable extent upon the great personages who dominate his plays, who are human, yet have a stature above that of ordinary men, through whom and through whose destinies he expresses his tragic

---

[14] Gellie 212f.
[15] Easterling, 'Character in Sophocles', *G&R* 24 (1977) 124, draws a useful distinction between idiosyncrasy and individuality.

thought about men and the gods. For their destinies are in one way or another god-given; and the world of Sophocles is, like that of Aeschylus, inhabited and ordered by gods of power. When, however, we come to ask how the nature and fate of a Sophoclean hero are related to the divine ordering of the world, the interpreters provide us with a variety – even a confusion – of views. As one writer has well put it:[16] 'Answers range from the most pious justification of the ways of God to a radically anti-religious hero-worship.'

Sophocles has been seen by some as the prophet of *sophrosune*,[17] concerned to teach through his plays a lesson in modesty, the recognition of human status, the poverty of human power and knowledge; his heroes suffer in order that this lesson may be taught and learnt, by others if not by them. Now, if one thing is certain, one generalization valid, it is that the Sophoclean hero is not himself *sophron* in any ordinary sense of the word. A man or woman of excess, an extremist, obstinate, inaccessible to argument, he refuses to compromise with the conditions of human life.[18] Be *sophron* and, in a tragedy of Sophocles, you may hope to play Creon in the *Tyrannus* or at best Odysseus in *Ajax;* your place in the chorus is assured; you can be Ismene but not Antigone, Chrysothemis but not Electra, Deianira but only if, at the fatal moment, relaxing your *sophrosune,* you abandon the 'salutary state of mind' that keeps you safe. The greatness of these figures is, surely, bound up with their failure to conform to conventional standards of moderation. In what does their 'heroism' consist, if not in their very extremism and refusal to compromise? In ordinary life we seek, so far as lies in our power, to keep ourselves remote from tragedy, but we also stay remote from greatness, aspiring to the condition of a Creon and not an Oedipus. In Sophocles it often seems as though greatness – at least this kind of greatness – attracts disaster by a kind of natural law which may have little to do with justice as

---

[16] H. Friis Johansen, in his indispensable survey, 'Sophocles 1939–1959', *Lustrum* 1962/7, 152.

[17] The definition – not to say the translation – of *sophron/sophronein/sophrosune* is notoriously difficult, so wide is the semantic field. They can connote chastity or common sense, be opposed to indiscipline, sheer madness or mere ill-judgement. *Sophrosune* is moderation, self-control, prudence, sanity, good sense, mental balance. The first element in the compound *(σω-)* is often felt: such a state of mind is both sound and salutary. The theme is carefully examined by Helen North in her *Sophrosyne: self-knowledge and self-restraint in Greek literature* (Ithaca, N.Y., 1966).

[18] Cf. Knox, *HT* passim.

justice is commonly understood. We ask if the gods are just and, if so, what kind of justice they administer.

Tragedy is disquieting. Terrible things happen: they are terrible in themselves, and they happen to people with whom our emotions, though not necessarily without ambivalence, have been engaged by the dramatist. It is natural to seek comfort somewhere.[19] But where, in Sophocles, do we look? We can look to the heroes; and this raises the first of two primary and interrelated issues, which is the nature of heroism and its place in the world. No one can deny their greatness. Do we say, then, that they are supremely admirable, destroyed in a world which does not deserve them? That they show their greatness above all in the moment of defeat? There is no theme, perhaps, in literary criticism which involves a greater temptation towards sentimentality. The heroes are prepared to sacrifice everything, even life, to their principles, to the maintenance of their standards. It is, then, essential to enquire what, precisely, those principles and standards are; and much of the examination which follows is concerned with just that question. Whatever they may be, they lead to tragedy.

There is a second issue: there are the gods. They are powerful and rule us. Justly? Do we say that, despite appearances, they order everything for the best? That they have some kind of good-will towards men from which we can draw comfort? Or was Hyllus right to speak of unfeeling gods?[20] For what principles and standards do *they* stand? Could there be a dreadful kinship between heroes and gods, jointly productive of tragedy?

Finally, there is pity. If Hyllus arraigned the gods as pitiless, he claimed pity – sympathy – from his companions. If the theatre of Sophocles is full of suffering, it is full of pity, but it is not the pity of the gods. There is the pity of those characters who are capable of it; and there is the poet's own pity which is dominant and all-embracing. One is led to ask what the status of pity may be in a tragic world. We will return to these questions when the individual plays have been examined.

---

[19] Why we derive pleasure from the presentation on the stage of such terrible happenings has never, to my knowledge, been satisfactorily explained, certainly not by Aristotle with his ingenious doctrine of *katharsis*.

[20] *Trach.* 1264ff., on which see pp. 73f. below.

CHAPTER TWO

The mind of Ajax

After the death of Achilles his arms were awarded not to Ajax, who thought them his due, but to Odysseus. Ajax nursed his injured pride and then went out by night to avenge himself upon Odysseus and the Atridae and all the Greeks who had insulted him. But Athena, the patron of Odysseus, sent a mad delusion upon him so that he wreaked his vengeance upon flocks and herds, taking animals for men. Some he killed, but the ram he thought to be Odysseus was reserved for torture. When he came to his senses and realized what he had done, he saw nothing for it but to take his own life. The Atridae then forbade him to be buried. Despite the protests of his brother Teucer, this inhuman decree would have been carried out, if it had not been for the generosity of Odysseus who secured his burial.

That, in broad outline, is the story told in the *Ajax* of Sophocles. It has its revolting aspects and the main character is, on the bare facts as stated, neither attractive nor laudable. If the grimness is offset by the pathos of Tecmessa, by the loyalty of Teucer perhaps, and certainly by the generosity of Odysseus, Ajax, on the other hand, seems to earn his disastrous fate by his own conduct. Towards the gods he is arrogant; towards men he is treacherous and cruel, going out by night to attack and kill the Greeks, torturing a ram in the belief that it was Odysseus. Yet the interpretation of the play and of its central figure is vexed. And one could wonder at first why this should be, and why the play should not be taken as a simple story of *hubris* punished.

It is in fact easy, if inadequate, to interpret *Ajax* on these lines, following a critical method which, so far as it goes, is unexceptionable. One observes the form of the play, the careful balance of opening and close, the role of Odysseus. The play opens with him: he is invited by the goddess Athena to gloat over his deluded enemy but refuses to do so; the play ends with him persuading a reluctant Agamemnon to allow the burial of Ajax. In both scenes he is the man who understands the limits of human status,[1] who knows how human beings should behave. He is wise (1374); he is *sophron* and by his *sophrosune* earns the love of the gods. The words with which Athena brings the Prologos to a close sound like a motto: 'The gods love the sound of mind (the moderate, the modest, τοὺς σώφρονας), and they hate the bad' (132f.). Is this not the motto of the play?[2]

Enclosed within this frame we see an arrogant Ajax and then, after his suicide, the corresponding arrogance of lesser men. Nor does this line of interpretation need to depend upon the opening and closing scenes. At the play's central point, and at a moment of crisis, we have the reported words of a prophet. Ajax has left the stage bent on suicide, but having convinced Tecmessa and the Chorus that he will be reconciled to the Atridae. Between his exit and his re-entry, a messenger arrives to announce the return of Teucer and to give a strict injunction that Ajax should not be permitted to leave his hut. This was the advice of the prophet Calchas (and its significance must be considered later). But Calchas had also given an explanation of the disaster which had befallen Ajax. He had incurred the wrath of Athena by his arrogance. Twice, in overweening terms, he had rejected the help of heaven. Though a mortal man, he had had more than mortal thoughts.[3] The implications, moral and theological, are the same as those of the words of Athena already quoted, commending a moral attitude exemplified by Odysseus. Some critics[4] have

---

[1] 121–6, cf. 1365.

[2] 'The end of the prologue comes so emphatically and with so clear a message from man and goddess that we cannot but accept it as given *ex cathedra* by the poet' (Bowra 38). Contr. H. Diller, 'Menschendarstellung und Handlungsführung bei Sophokles', *Antike und Abendland* 6 (1957) 158 = *Sophokles*, ed. H. Diller (Wege der Forschung, 45, Darmstadt 1967) 193: 'Aber es wird im Verlauf des Dramas und gerade in der Schlussszene deutlich, dass Athenas Lehre selbst in der menschlichen Form, die Odysseus ihr gegeben hat, nicht das letzte Wort bleiben kann, dass sie sich wandelt in dem Masse, wie Aias' Wesen immer klarer zum Vorschein kommt.'

[3] οὐ κατ' ἄνθρωπον φρονῶν (777), cf. 760 f. (ὅστις ... μὴ κατ' ἄνθρωπον φρονῇ).

[4] E.g. Lattimore, *PGT* 73: 'Sophocles sometimes writes as if he had been reading the handbooks on Attic tragedy and suddenly realised that he had left something out, namely, the theory of *hamartia*, or of pride and punishment, or of *hybris*, or what you will.' Adams 35 (on the *hubris*): 'Was *that* all it was?' Rosenmeyer, *MT*, 183 'It would appear that Sophocles cites [these incidents] remarkably late in the proceedings, and with a minimum of emphasis ... The timing, the scope, and,

indeed sought to discount the words of Calchas. But it is difficult to see how Sophocles could have made them more impressive, from the moment Calchas steps out of the circle of the princes, separating himself from the Atridae, and grasps the hand of Teucer in friendship. The earnestness of his benevolent counsel is matched by the authority of his pronouncements; the formality of the structure is appropriate to the speaker and to his words. The two examples of arrogance, shocking of themselves, are enclosed within a twofold reference to 'more than mortal thoughts' (761, 777). The whole intervention of Calchas is enclosed within a twofold reference to his superior prophetic insight (746, 783). The formality is Aeschylean, to match what might be considered Aeschylean thought.[5]

Why then – why, given all this, should critics not only disparage the importance of the words of Calchas but reject a whole interpretation of the play which is prima facie attractive? The answer is complex and not limited to the obvious inadequacy of an account which gives Odysseus the fine role and makes it appear as though Ajax only existed in order to enhance the virtues of Odysseus.[6] We run up here against a problem of the first moment and the greatest difficulty, which is the nature of the Sophoclean hero (if it is legitimate to use the term) and the attitude towards him to which Sophocles invites his audience.

Something has been said already, near the end of the last chapter, about this problem.[7] In what light are we intended to regard these Sophoclean heroes and, for that matter, the gods by whom their destinies are controlled? The views of interpreters are diverse. At one extreme stand the pietists, at the other are ranged the 'hero-worshippers', with every variety of compromise in between. Now, if *Ajax* is the easiest play to interpret in terms of *hubris* and *sophrosune*, so Ajax is of all the heroes (with one possible exception) the most difficult for the hero-worshipper to worship (though the feat has been per-

___

not the least, the source of the information conspire to play down the importance of the crimes, for Calchas is not, in this play at any rate, an entirely reputable informant.' Why ever not? Contr. Fraenkel, *Sem.* 8 (on 127).

[5] The archaic ring-composition is carried still further: 756f. are balanced by 778f.; the first boast of Ajax is preceded by ὑψικόμπως (766) and followed by ἐκόμπει (770). See pp. 40f.

[6] Cf. Lattimore, *PGT* 80.

[7] See pp. 8ff. above.

formed).[8] Yet he shares with a majority of those heroes characteristics which have been skilfully analysed by Bernard Knox. Ajax is – or should be – a problem. Some critics seem to have argued, almost syllogistically, as follows. Ajax is a Sophoclean hero; Sophoclean heroes, for all their faults, are admirable; therefore we must find something not merely tremendous but admirable in Ajax. To put it another way, Ajax is great;[9] we must find greatness in him other than his great size, his great courage, his great capacity as a fighting-man. What can we do for Ajax? We can play down his impiety; we can play up his sense of grievance; and we can endow him with insight before he dies. We can even strain a point and make him *sophron*.

We can play down his impiety, his arrogance. On this something has been said already. It is methodologically unsound (a phrase calculated to strike terror into the heart of any modern scholar), since it amounts to disregarding something which is given prominence in the text, just because it happens to be inconvenient. In fact, the actual instances which Calchas gives of Ajax's vainglorious rejection of divine help merely confirm an impression we have already received in the Prologos, where his tone to Athena is dismissive and almost patronizing.[10] Pride before the gods is, naturally, matched – and over-matched – by pride towards his fellow-men. 'Speak no great word', sings the Chorus at one point. Sure enough, a few lines later, Ajax sings: 'I will speak out a great word'[11] and boasts that he is a man whose peer Troy never saw come from the land of Hellas (421ff.). Greek heroes indeed spoke freely of their merits and achievements, but every member of the audience will have known an Attic drinking-

[8] I know that I am begging a question here. Critical reactions to Ajax have varied widely. Perrotta 160: 'Sofocle ha amato questo suo eroe.' Letters 137: 'The truth is, this hero has practically no virtues but his heroism.' 'This heroic criminal of terrible grandeur' (Torrance 273, in a well-balanced statement).

[9] On μέγας in this play, see n. 35 below.

[10] This, perhaps, rather than an 'offhand and hearty familiarity' (Kirkwood, HSA67). Ajax, in his final speech, going straight to the supreme authority, does not mention Athena. See n. 99 below.

[11] μηδὲν μέγ' εἴπῃς (386); ἔπος ἐξερῶ μέγ' (422). 422 is not said with direct reference to 386, which serves however to alert the audience to this theme. It is not indeed quite clear what, specifically, the Chorus has in mind. The scholiast refers to El. 830, also following a cry of lamentation (see Jebb's note for various parallels). Kamerbeek and Stanford refer to 362 (εὔφημα φώνει, after Ajax's συνδάϊξον): that was a matter of making ate worse, so that perhaps here the wish expressed by him at 384 strikes the Chorus as outrageous for one in his condition. The theme was prepared at 127f.

song which said that Ajax was the best of the Greeks that came to Troy *after Achilles* (μετ᾽ Ἀχιλλέα).[12] This is the tenour of the *Iliad* and of the whole post-Homeric tradition; and it is what Odysseus says towards the end of the play (1341). Ajax fails to make the exception. A small point it might seem, but it is only one of several instances which could be quoted of a megalomaniac pride.[13]

If critics can play down the arrogance and impiety of Ajax, they can play up his sense of grievance – not its importance in the motivation of Ajax, which cannot be over-stressed, but its extenuating value. We are, one hopes, long past the day when figures in Greek tragedy were judged by Christian or even by Platonic standards. We are right to see Ajax against the background of a morality established in the heroic age and surviving tenaciously in the popular standards of the fifth century. For Greeks did not cease to be preoccupied with personal prestige because city-states had come into being. We know that they were – and continued to be – emulous and proud and preoccupied with their honour. Still, the ideal conditions for the operation of a code of heroic self-sufficiency, if they had ever existed, had passed away by the later fifth century. Knox writes as follows:[14] 'Ajax is presented to us in this play as the last of the heroes. His death is the death of the old Homeric (and especially Achillean) individual ethos which had for centuries of aristocratic rule served as the dominant ideal of man's nobility and action, but which by the fifth century had been successfully challenged and largely superseded.' This is a not unrewarding line of interpretation, and we shall return to it. Certainly Ajax is presented to us throughout in terms of the heroic morality; and Knox goes on to say that 'this is the function of the wealth of Homeric reminiscence which editors have noted in the language of the play'. The Homeric echoes are certain, though not of course surprising in view of the subject-matter. It may, however, be doubted whether the relationship of the Sophoclean Ajax to Homer is quite so straightforward as Knox's words might suggest.

---

[12] *Scolia anonyma* 15 Diehl=Page, *PMG* 898. Cf. C. M. Bowra, *Greek lyric poetry*[2] (Oxford 1961) 379, who cites *Iliad* 2.768f. and Alcaeus fr. 387 LP (on which see Page, *Sappho and Alcaeus* (Oxford 1955) 285).

[13] But is it such a small point? Cf. S. N. Lawall's brief but illuminating article 'Sophocles' Ajax: *aristos* . . . after Achilles', *CJ* 54 (1958/59) 291ff., and see n. 52 below.

[14] Knox, *HS*20f.

One can well imagine that, when writing *Ajax*, Sophocles steeped
himself in those parts of the *Iliad* which dealt with the hero and there
are clear signs that he had done so.[15] He would remember – and could
count on his audience remembering – the silence of Ajax in the
Nekuia and his prayer to Zeus in *Iliad* 17, his speech to Achilles in *Iliad*
9, his preoccupation with *aidos*, his duel with Hector and the
exchange of gifts. In point of characterization, there were hints that
could be neglected, or taken up and developed. It is perhaps fair to say
there is little in the Sophoclean Ajax which is not present, in the germ,
in the Ajax of Homer. But in the development there is both similarity
and difference; and the difference may be more significant than the
similarity. The Sophoclean Ajax is a new creation, which we may
compare with Homer's, but more profitably perhaps with the total
picture of heroism and its attitudes which we gain from the epic.

Actually, the most striking Homeric reminiscence is of a passage in
Homer that does not deal with Ajax. In writing the scene between
Ajax and Tecmessa Sophocles reminds his audience in the most
deliberate and specific way of the farewell between Hector and
Andromache in *Iliad* 6.[16] There is a threefold echo. (i) At 501ff.
Tecmessa imagines the scornful words which will be spoken of the
fallen hero's concubine. In *Iliad* 6 it is Hector who puts words – words
of respect – into the mouths of enemies. Hector's heart is torn with
imaginative compassion; Ajax makes no response to the plea of
Tecmessa. (ii) In *Iliad* 6 Hector stretched out his arms for his son, but
Astyanax was frightened by the crested helmet. Father and mother
laugh, and Hector lays the helmet on the ground. Ajax (545ff.)
demands of his infant son that he show no fear of the slaughtered
animals, but be already schooled in the harsh ways of his father. (iii)
Both heroes wish for their sons: Hector that people may say 'He is a
far better man than his father', Ajax that his son may be more
fortunate than his father, but like him in all else 'and he would prove
no coward' (550f.). Lattimore comments that these echoes are 'just off
key and to the disadvantage of Ajax'.[17] Is this unfair?

---

[15] This would account for the fact that several echoes of Homeric language come
from passages where Ajax is either speaking or present in the immediate context.
137: for πληγὴ Διός Stanford cites *Il.* 14.414 (of a thunderbolt, but in an
Ajax-passage) and 13.812 (where Ajax is speaking). 147: for αἴθωνι σιδήρῳ, cf.
among other passages, 4.485 (of a wainwright, but the passage is about Ajax).
242: for λιγυρᾷ μάστιγι, cf. 11.532. See also n. 74.

[16] See Perrotta 144–7.   [17] *PGT* 68.

Hector is perhaps the most attractive of Homeric heroes; sensitive to his honour, but also in all human relationships, he dies in defence of his home and country. What then of Achilles? (Knox speaks of the Achillean ethos.) He, and his whole career, loom in the background of the play. The disposal of his arms precipitates the tragic action. It is in regard to him that Ajax makes his greatest boast. Surely Greeks bred on Homer were likely to make a comparison between the way in which Achilles acted in the *Iliad* and the way in which Ajax acts in our play. Both heroes were injured in the pride by which they lived; both were deprived of a *geras*; both withdrew from the battle and brooded. When Achilles sulked in his tent, the consequences were bad enough (and badly regarded): many Greeks lost their lives, and Achilles lost his friend. But finally he was reconciled to Agamemnon and returned to the battle. It is true that, in hot blood, he was about to draw his sword upon the Greek leader. The point is that he did not.[18] Ajax brooded and then, deliberately, went out by night to murder the Atridae – and not only the Atridae. He went out by night, treacherously, and this is much stressed (in the text, though not always by modern interpreters). Perhaps Sophocles had not forgotten the prayer of the Homeric Ajax, which was his most famous utterance. He prayed to Zeus (*Il.* 17.646f.): 'Make light, and grant that we may see; slay us at least in the light, since such is your pleasure.' In the play he goes out by night, craftily, to kill his former friends one by one as they slept. νύκτωρ ἐφ᾽ ὑμᾶς δόλιος ὁρμᾶται μόνος (47).[19] Stealth and cunning were not entirely alien to the heroic world, though more to be expected from an Odysseus than from an Ajax.[20]

---

[18] It is true that at 1029f. Sophocles gives us the grimmer figure of an Achilles who tortures a still living Hector (cf. Kamerbeek ad loc., Jebb's appendix on 1028–39), but it is with the Iliadic Achilles that the audience would be likely to compare Ajax.

[19] Ajax is much characterized with adjectives in the play (cf. Knox, *HS* 21 and n. 103). At 217 the word-order (cf. Stanford ad loc.) produces a curious effect as though νύκτερος was a descriptive epithet (which could be added to δεινός, μέγας, ὠμοκρατής, θούριος, κλεινός, αἴθων – all in this part of the play). Cf. Davidson 166.

[20] Cf. von Fritz 248: 'Das Nächtliche, Heimliche seiner Beginnens zeigt, ohne dass ihm selbst dies noch zum Bewusstsein kommt, wieweit er schon aus der Bahn seines bisherigen Lebens einer freien offenem Rittertums geworfen ist.' Cf. A. Roveri, 'Il prologo dell' *Aiace* di Sofocle', *Vichiana* 1 (1964) 39. On *dolos* in Homer, see M. Detienne & J.-P. Vernant, *Les ruses d'intelligence: la Métis des grecs* (Paris 1974), ch. 1. In Sophocles, cf. *Phil.* 90f., *Trach.* 269ff. and, for *Electra*, p. 335 below.

The more closely one looks at the Sophoclean Ajax the more gaps seem to open up between him and the typical Homeric hero. The greatest gap is this, and it is revealed by Calchas. Ajax was confident that he could win without the gods and spurned the help of Athena in battle. Nothing could be less characteristically Homeric.[21] Divine help was the way in which the hero accounted for his moments of superior prowess, as for his sudden insights; and the poet dramatizes this conviction in the form of actual appearances of gods. When Achilles refrained from attacking Agamemnon, it was Athena that checked him; and it was with the aid of Athena that he overcame Hector. Ajax – and Ajax alone, the Sophoclean Ajax, feels that it would derogate from his prestige to accept help from a god.[22]

Ajax rejects – and we shall see it is not his only rejection – that sense of dependence upon the gods by which the pride of a Homeric hero is normally mitigated. So far, then, from lapsing into 'text-book' theology, Sophocles may have given us, through the words of Calchas, a significant clue to the nature of his hero and the understanding of the dramatic action. One might formulate as follows.

How did it come about that a great hero – a supreme embodiment of *arete* – launched this outrageous attack upon his former friends? The answer lies in injured pride, and the brooding over injured pride, but it is not a complete answer. The answer lies, certainly, in the heroic code of values, but also in a hero who carried this ideal – or an aspect of this ideal – to a point so extreme that it falls, one might say, outside the range of normal humanity. To say that he carried it to its logical conclusion might imply that he acted rationally. It might also imply that the code had itself a logic free from contradictions. It was not, however, a logical construction, but rather a collection of emotional attitudes and socially conditioned imperatives which might – and did – conflict with one another. It was a hard code for men living dangerously in competition, but it contained mitigations of its own

---

[21] Cf. P. Chantraine, *Fondation Hardt Entretiens* I (Vandoeuvres–Genève 1954) 48–50.

[22] In the *Iliad* Ajax is never shown as aided specifically by any god: 'he never prays for victory or thanks the gods when they voluntarily help him' (Stanford xxxix, cf. Lattimore, *SPG T* 61 n.7, Kirkwood, *HSA* 61f.). This may be one of the hints that Sophocles has developed, though it should not be over-stressed. Oddly enough, alone of Homeric heroes, it was the other Ajax who boasted, in a context of shipwreck not war, that he needed no help from the gods, cf. Pohlenz, (1st ed.), Erläuterungen 49; Dirlmeier 307.

hardness. At every point we see Ajax – the Sophoclean Ajax – rejecting anything which might mitigate his fierce concentration upon the pursuit, the maintenance, and the restoration, of his prestige. We shall see him reject the appeals of Tecmessa, though they are appeals to which a hero might respond:[23] respect for aged parents, pity for the weak, and above all the claims of gratitude for services done. There is one other curious and interesting rejection. Ajax committed suicide upon the sword of Hector. (Three times our attention is drawn to the fact.)[24] This sword he had received in an exchange of gifts after the abortive duel in *Iliad* 7; and now he feels that he did ill to exchange gifts with Hector and quotes a proverb that the gifts of enemies are no good gifts. But such an exchange was part of the courtesies of heroic warfare, mitigations of a brutal business. Ajax wishes he had had no part in them and speaks of Hector in terms of an extreme personal animosity which is unrelated to the Homeric facts. Achilles had a personal enmity towards Hector for the killing of Patroclus. But why should Ajax speak so? In *Iliad* 7 (303ff.) the Homeric Ajax partakes in the exchange and then, happy to have had the advantage in the duel, goes off to dine with Agamemnon. Why should the Sophoclean Ajax speak so? Except that for him the rivalry of champions in battle, each staking his prestige, was so deadly a matter that no mitigation was desirable, no relationship possible other than an extreme of enmity?[25]

Ajax, then, is not just the typical Homeric, the Achillean, hero, but rather one who carries the implications of the heroic code to the extreme possible point, as no one in Homer, and perhaps no one in real life, ever did. Such extremism, such (in a sense) idealism, is characteristic of Sophoclean heroes; and in it their greatness lies. Ajax is *megas*. Is that all we can say?

Some pages back, the word 'megalomaniac' was used. *Megalomania* is

---

[23] See below.
[24] 661–3; 817f.; 1027ff. See also n. 98 below.
[25] δυσμενεστάτου (662), ξένων ἐμοὶ μάλιστα μισηθέντος, ἐχθίστου θ᾽ὁρᾶν (817f.). The language (esp. ὁρᾶν) hardly comports with Stanford's rationalization: 'because Ajax has come to realise that Hector's friendship-gift is going to cause his death, Hector has come to be the most hated' of all his *xenoi*. Ajax and Hector met in conflict several times, with varying outcome, but (apart from Hector's abusive epithets at *Iliad* 13.824) there is no indication of a particular animosity. Cf. Kitto, *Poiesis* 180.

Greek of sorts, though not the Greek of Sophocles.[26] But if he had
known the term, he could not have combined the themes of greatness
and madness more intricately than he has done in this play. The theme
of madness and sanity, of sense and sickness of mind, pervades the first
half of the play, but, until recently, it had not been adequately
investigated.[27] Perhaps there is still something more to be said about
it.

Ajax of course was mad. Athena sent him mad, and during the
Prologos he is brought out and shown to us mad. His madness was the
delusion which she cast upon him,[28] when he had already reached the
generals' quarters, so that his murderous fury was diverted upon the
flocks and herds. It was an action which did not make sense (40), until
it was explained by Athena, who describes it in terms of sickness (59,
66 νόσοις, νόσον) and madness (59 μανιάσιν) and a wandering mind
(59 φοιτῶντα). Odysseus shrinks from seeing Ajax in his mad state
(μεμηνότα), though, as he says, he would never have shrunk from him
sane (φρονοῦντα, 81f.).[29] That, broadly, is the position in the Prologos: a mad Ajax, subject to a crude delusion. But there are hints of
other things. We learn about the Judgement of the Arms (100) and the
resentment of Ajax, and the notion of atimia is introduced for the first
time (98). When Ajax returns into his hut, Odysseus pities him, 'since
he has been yoked to an evil ruin' (ἄτῃ), and regards him as an
example of the transitoriness of human fortune (125f.). In what does

[26] Though, oddly enough, μεγαλομανής occurs in the scholia to Ajax 143, in the
    sense of 'greatly mad'.
[27] Two quotations will show the importance of clarifying these questions. 'L'Aiace
    e il dramma di Aiace savio, non dell' Aiace folle del prologo' (Perrotta 138). 'The
    intervention of the goddess makes no difference; his attempt at wholesale murder
    was not the act of a sane man' (L. Pearson, Popular ethics in ancient Greece
    (Stanford, Cal. 1962) 192). Recently we have had a brief but valuable study by
    Penelope Biggs, to which I shall refer. See also Simpson. Some of the evidence is
    handled by Vandvik, who maintains that Ajax is quite literally insane through-
    out the play and so not responsible for his actions. This hardly does justice to the
    subtlety and insight with which Sophocles has developed the theme of mental
    sickness.
[28] At 51f. I take τῆς ἀνηκέστου χαρᾶς after ἀπείργω. Cf. BICS 26 (1979) 1f., where I
    also put forward a suggestion that δύσφορος (there and at 643) may be an instance
    of that medical language which is not infrequent in Sophocles. See Knox, OTh
    139ff., who gives Hippocratic references for δύσφορος (n. 106 on p. 245) in
    connection with O.T. 87.
[29] Critics have made heavy weather of the 'cowardice' of Odysseus, surely a very
    natural human reaction to a madman.

the *ate* consist? In his mad delusion? Or in something else? Athena, contrasting the present state of Ajax with his former excellence in thought and action,[30] finds an instance of the great power of the gods. Neither in her words (118–20) nor in those of Odysseus is there any necessary moral implication or reference beyond the current situation. But Athena ends the scene with a sermon against proud words and over-confidence. And she must be thinking of Ajax, when she says that 'the gods love the sound of mind (τοὺς σώφρονας), but hate the bad'. Within its wide semantic range, *sophrosune* can be contrasted with *mania*, as sanity with madness, but she cannot now be thinking of the delusion she herself has sent upon Ajax. Of what, then, is she thinking?[31] It is left a mystery, so far as the prologue goes. An act of Ajax seems at first to make no sense and is then explained by a mad delusion put upon him by a goddess. But we are taken back a stage: to the Judgement of the Arms, to the resentment of Ajax, and to his attack upon the Greeks. He is not *phronōn*, because he is mad; he is not *sophron*, but this appears to be for some other reason. The state of the *phrenes* of Ajax is a cardinal point.[32]

Sailors of Ajax now enter as the Chorus.[33] They have heard the rumour about his attack on the herds. Two possible explanations occur to them: either their master has been driven out of his mind by a divine force, or else it is all a malicious story. Clearly they hanker after the latter alternative, which dominates the anapaests of the Coryphaeus, but the former remains in their minds and returns when they break into song. In those anapaests the loyalty and dismay (and confidence) of the sailors are expressed at a length which might seem

30 119f.: τούτου τίς ἄν σοι τἀνδρὸς ἢ προνούστερος|ἢ δρᾶν ἀμείνων ηὑρέθη τὰ καίρια; What value do we place on this tribute, endorsed by Odysseus? Cf. Kirkwood, *HSA*61f. The main point is no doubt 'that Ajax has in the past shown himself no fool, in contrast with his present mad folly'. (Ajax himself commends the πρόνοια of Tecmessa at 536.) We are meant to envisage Ajax, prior to the Judgement of the Arms, as a man of apparent good sense and mental balance, as he is in Homer. It is not until later we discover that he was, in some sense, ἄνους from the beginning (763): see below. To say that Athena's words are 'a barefaced mockery of the truth' (Rosenmeyer, *MT* 172ff.) is a gross exaggeration.

31 When she speaks in such proverbial (and Aeschylean?) terms, using an instance (ἢ μακροῦ πλούτου βάθει, 130) irrelevant to Ajax. For other instances of 'irrelevant' wealth in Sophocles, see p. 170 n. 52.

32 Perrotta rightly stresses (e.g. 129, 135, 161) the importance of the *mind* of Ajax, though he does not see it quite as I do.

33 For a careful examination of the Parodos, see J. F. Davidson, *BICS* 22 (1975) 163–77.

tedious, if there were not a point to be made. The point is an insistence
on the theme of greatness; and it is perhaps twofold. There is the
contrast between the great and the small (154–61);[34] and it is a regular
function of the Sophoclean chorus, as of minor characters, to represent the ordinary man who is not, like the heroes, exposed to the
stresses and perils of greatness. But, principally, the purpose of the
insistence on the word *megas*[35] is to insist upon the greatness of Ajax.
Not only his greatness, but the force of the powers arrayed against
him.[36] The princes too are great (189, 225), but so also is the power of
rumour spread among the people (142, 173, 226). Great though these
are, he is still greater. Or so the Chorus believes. They believe that he
has only to show himself in order to reduce his enemies to a cowering
silence (167ff.).[37]

Yet the rumour could be true; and, if true, it could only be that a
god was responsible. Artemis perhaps or Ares repaying a slight. (Ajax
then might slight the gods, and the gods might react to a slight upon
their honour like Ajax himself?) Some such explanation is required,
since 'never in your right mind (φρενόθεν γε), son of Telamon, would
you have gone astray – so far astray as to fall upon the flocks. For it
could be that a sickness from heaven has come (ἥκοι γὰρ ἂν θεία
νόσος)' (182–5).[38] They prefer, however, to believe that the rumour is
false; they immediately call on Zeus and Apollo to avert, not the
sickness, but – and it is a striking *para prosdokian* – the false report; and

---

[34] That they constitute a community prepares a theme which will be important: see
below.

[35] The word μέγας occurs thirty-six times in the play – far more frequently than in
any other extant play of Sophocles, which is not surprising in view of the subject
and of the fact that this is a Homeric epithet for Ajax. But the occurrences are not
spread evenly through the play. The word occurs thirteen times between 139 and
241; nine times in the Parodos, seven of them in the anapaests, including four in 8
lines. There are careless (as well as designed) repetitions in all the plays (cf. L.
Massa Positano, *L'unità dell' Aiace di Sofocle* (Naples 1946) 140 n. 1), but not on
this scale; and this would seem to be an early example of a technique not
uncharacteristic of the poet. The word μέγας and the notion of greatness are
meant to sink into the minds of the audience. Cf. Stanford xxvii n. 37 (his count
is too small); Knox, *HS* 21; Davidson 175 n. 12.

[36] The point is made by Stanford on 224–6.

[37] 167–70 ~ 139f. (one of the numerous examples of ring-composition in this play).

[38] The twofold γάρ (183, 185) is explained by Kamerbeek, following Denniston 64
(6) (contr. Dawe, *STS* 133); and, with Campbell, he rightly interprets the
potential force of ἥκοι ἄν – a hypothesis relating to the past, a *possible* explanation
of what has happened.

once more they urge Ajax to arise and quench the *hubris* of his enemies which is spreading like a forest-fire.

Their appeal is answered, not by the great, but by the weak – not by Ajax, but by Tecmessa. Chorus and Tecmessa, each knows something which the other does not know, and, when their knowledge is combined, it becomes terribly clear that Ajax had indeed attacked the flocks. The audience knew this; what the audience did not know and now learns from Tecmessa is that Ajax, who had been mad, is now sane – or at least that is how Tecmessa sees it. This does not become clear at once.[39] When the Chorus sing of their terror of involvement (245ff.), they still think Ajax mad,[40] until Tecmessa states in clear terms that the gale is over and that he is now – φρόνιμος (259), he is in his right mind. Surely we are bound to recall what the Chorus sang at 182 – that never in his right mind (φρενόθεν) would he have gone so far astray. We have seen Ajax mad; we shall see him 'sane' and can judge the quality of his sanity.

Tecmessa's narrative of the night's work is preceded by a short dialogue in which she seeks to convince the Chorus that Ajax's new state of sanity is worse than his state of madness, more distressing for him and so also for them. She speaks to correct a sudden burst of optimism on their part; simple-minded and self-centred, they think their fortunes will be mended now that their master has recovered his wits (263f.). The argument is highly formal and rather strained in expression.[41] A conclusion is reached at 269 which controverts 263;

---

39 The aorist participles at 207 and 216 do not in themselvs imply that the mental sickness is over; and Tecmessa uses historic presents to describe the torture of the animals (239, 242).

40 This is the implication of ἄπλατος (256). Cf. H. Diller (op. cit. n. 2) 193: 'Mit Aias in seinem Wahn war eine menschliche Kommunikation ja nicht möglich.' It will be a question whether he is any more 'approachable' in his 'sanity'.

41 Torrance 276: 'an emphatic, if rather awkward exchange'. The subject of πέπαυται is Ajax (cf. 279), of εὐτυχεῖν the Chorus (contr. their fears at 245ff.). At 269 the case for Hermann's νοσοῦντος (adopted by Pearson and Dawe) is almost overwhelming. It is not enough to say, in defence of νοσοῦντες, that it displays Tecmessa's identification with the fortunes of Ajax: she shares his *ate* but not his *nosos*. The objection to the received reading is that it blurs two distinctions on which the structure of thought is based: (i) the distinction between Ajax and his friends (ἀνὴρ ἐκεῖνος, αὐτός, κεῖνος ~ ἡμᾶς, ἡμεῖς), so that ἡμεῖς at 269 should *not* include Ajax (which it must if νοσοῦντες is read); and (ii) the distinction between Ajax sick and Ajax sound, the Chorus and Tecmessa being sound all along (cf. 273). With νοσοῦντος, 269 is Tecmessa's answer to 263: they thought the end of Ajax's sickness meant prosperity for them; she argues that it means disaster (cf.

the Chorus fail to follow, and Tecmessa explains at greater length.
The passage may appear frigid and not to advance the drama in
proportion to its length.

Yet it has its value, quite apart from the contrast it brings out
between the insight and devotion of Tecmessa, the obtuseness and
self-interest of the Chorus. It advances one theme and introduces
another. The new theme, though already adumbrated in the Parodos,
is that of community, of social environment; and it is of the first
importance.[42] For Ajax's problem is a social problem, his situation is
– or should be – social. There is a wider and a narrower environment.
The wider environment is that of the Greek army as a whole, with
which he is at odds, from which he has deliberately severed himself.
And there is the inner circle: Tecmessa and his child, the absent
Teucer, his loyal and dependent sailors. (It will be noted that the
whole action, from the entry of the Chorus up to the suicide of Ajax,
is played within this inner circle, only the speech of the Messenger
coming from the larger world outside.) The members of this inner
circle are all deeply involved; and they are anxious to help, Tecmessa
passionately, the sailors within the limits of their emotional capacity
(and dramatic role).[43] But it becomes clear that Ajax has hardly more
contact with his immediate than with his remoter environment. It is
not for nothing that writer after writer has described the four long
speeches of Ajax as monologues or soliloquies. Is this the typical
isolation of the Sophoclean hero? Is it the difficulty which a heroic

---

Ant. 17 for a contrast of εὐτυχεῖν with ἀτᾶσθαι). It is of course because she enters
into the feelings of Ajax that she sees it in this light. Cf. A. C. Pearson, *PCPS* 21
(1922) 21.

[42] Note the pleonasm of 267: ξυνών as well as the correlative κοινὸς ἐν κοινοῖσι.
ξυνών is repeated at 273; κοινός is picked up by κοινωνός (284), which also relates
to 283. The limits of the Chorus's capacity for sympathetic participation are
perhaps shown by a comparison of 283 and 255. The extent to which Ajax is
himself participant in a community of feeling (267) is the important issue. ξύνειμι
is a common word in Sophocles, cf. Pearson on fr. 950: of 31 instances (excluding
fragments) 7 occur in *Ajax*. Turn to 337f. (where Dawe's παροῦσι . . . ξυνών,
STS 139, is attractive). Is Ajax with *them*? Or consorting in his own mind with
his old νοσήματα? Turn to 610f. Is Ajax with them or with his θεία μανία? On this
see p. 33 below.

[43] The Chorus is addressed by Tecmessa as ναὸς ἀρωγοὶ τῆς Αἴαντος(201), by Ajax
as γένος ναίας ἀρωγὸν τέχνας (357) – 'a fulsome periphrasis for "sailors" (but also
reflecting Ajax's need for help, ἀρωγή)' (Stanford). Tecmessa asks them to help
(ἀρήξατε, 329) – with their persuasions (the reading λόγοις is almost necessary
here?).

figure finds in communicating with lesser men who do not understand heroism? Or is it something more? Perhaps there is a relationship between this and that other theme which, as I have said, is
promoted during the exchange.

For one may suspect that its main point and purpose lies in its
development of the *nosos*-theme, in the contrast between sickness and
soundness of mind (*nosein* and *phronein*), in Tecmessa's insistence that
Ajax is now sane. And the same may be true of the final comment of
the Coryphaeus. 'I agree', he says, 'and fear that some stroke has come
from a god. How else, if now that he has ceased to be ill, he is not a
whit more cheerful than when he was sick?' (278–80). The reference
to a divine stroke refers back to the 'stroke of Zeus' (πληγὴ Διός) at
137 and the 'divine sickness' (θεία νόσος) of 185. Of the alternative
hypotheses one is now ruled out: the rumour has been confirmed and
therefore Ajax had acted so inexplicably because some god had sent
him mad. The mental process of the Coryphaeus is less important
than the insistence on the mental state of Ajax.[44]

The main feature of Tecmessa's narrative is the torturing of the
animals and particularly of the animal which is a substitute for
Odysseus. It is the third time the scene has been described at more or
less length; if all three descriptions are strictly relevant where they
occur, the fact that there are three gives great emphasis to the theme.
In each case it is brought out that he took beasts for men; and the
natural implication is that what he did to beasts he would have done
to men.[45] Tecmessa goes on to tell how Ajax gradually came to his

[44] The Chorus, not for the first or the last time, is obtuse, but an obtuse Chorus
must have a train of thought. Why, then, is Ajax's present state of gloom
evidence for the divine origin of the madness which is now supposed to have
passed? If they had been prepared to face facts, they must have realized that Ajax
had humiliated himself by his mad actions and, if they knew their master, that
this was bound to have an appalling effect upon his mind. They might have said
that a sickness which led to such a result must have come from the gods. But the
Coryphaeus shies away and merely argues on the basis (apparently) that, after an
ordinary sickness, once you are rid of it you feel better, you begin to enjoy
yourself again; therefore this was no ordinary sickness but a stroke from the
gods. His use of εὐφραίνεται is quite amazing, coming after Tecmessa's argument
that Ajax had had pleasure in his sickness (266, 272), grief at his recovery (267,
275). Cf. 105 (ἥδιστος), after 79; 114 (τέρψις).

[45] Indignantly rejected by Ronnet 106: 'Ajax voulait tuer ses ennemis, non les
torturer: la rage de tortionnaire qu'il manifeste dans le prologue exprime sans
doute sous la forme la plus instinctive sa soif de vengeance, mais précisément
parce que la raison est absente, la scène se situe en deçà de l'humain.' It is open to

senses (ἔμφρων, 306, echoes φρόνιμος, 259) She describes his loud cries of lamentation which were followed by silent dejection and by the refusal of food and drink – symptoms of disease. As the Coryphaeus says, he is like one possessed;[46] and immediately his cry is heard (333). Is Ajax sick or sound, then? Is he sane or mad? Again, there is puzzlement on the part of the Chorus. It is as though the Coryphaeus said to Tecmessa: 'You have told us that Ajax is sane (φρόνιμος). Well, to judge by his wild cries, if not sick, he is in distress through association with the products of his sickness.' Then Ajax speaks, and speaks sense, asking for Teucer (342f.).[47] 'It seems that the man is sane (φρονεῖν).' The puzzlement of the Chorus, the almost pedantic attempts of the Coryphaeus to determine whether Ajax is sick or sound, lack interest or importance in themselves: what is important is that the audience should be invited to consider the state of the hero's mind.[48]

This they can now judge by his own words.[49] First he expresses his mental agony in lyric stanzas which are among the most tense and moving in Greek tragedy; then he speaks, and tells of his resolve to die. Tecmessa pleads with him, but he ignores her pleas and sends for his young son (and there is that famous passage to which reference has already been made). She pleads again, and again he is stubborn. He returns into his hut, clearly determined upon suicide.

us to believe this – the matter cannot be proved one way or the other; and those critics – and they exist – who play down the murderous attack itself will wish to believe it. At 300 the phrase ἐν ποίμναις πίτνων is repeated from 185, where it was put in evidence that Ajax was not in his right mind. It does not follow from this, though it may be suggested by it, that, if he had been sane, he would have tortured, as well as killed, men. Rosenmeyer, *MT* 177ff. has some interesting remarks on Ajax's butchery of the cattle as the acting-out of a fantasy 'as truthful as the reality he wakes up to' and on the 'man–beast identity'.

[46] 331 f.: 'By διαπεφοιβάσθαι the Chorus mean that a malign power has taken *permanent possession* of his mind. The mental trouble outlasts the frenzy (279f.)' (Jebb). Stanford speaks of Cassandra, mere exclamations followed by wild words; and Mr James Dee pointed out to me that Ajax, like Cassandra, sings in dochmiacs. But there are intervening trimeters (342f.), which adds to the confusion of the Chorus!

[47] On 337f. see Stanford's note and n. 42 above. On 339–43 see Fraenkel, *Sem.* 12f.

[48] Biggs 224 speaks of 'the chorus' confusion as to when he is "in his right mind"'.

[49] And it will be observed that the Coryphaeus still swings between the poles of Ajax νοσῶν and Ajax φρονῶν. At 344 he is φρονῶν, because he calls (in trimeters) for Teucer, but his first lyric stanza evokes the comment that 'no sane mind is here' (ἀφροντίστως ἔχει, 355). 371, with φρόνησον εὖ, is better given to Tecmessa (see Kamerbeek and Stanford).

The keynote is of course humiliation, the keyword *atimos*. Ajax wakes from his delusion to find himself humiliated – this great warrior who has exercised his valour upon harmless animals. Not only so, but what seems to rankle even more, he has let his human enemies slip through his hands; and we come to realize that, if he had shed the blood of the Atridae and tortured Odysseus, he would have been perfectly satisfied with such exploits for the restoration of his heroic honour. It is a striking feature of this scene that the madness – the literal madness of Ajax which up to this point has so much dominated the play – drops into the background and is seen by him less as a humiliation in itself than as a frustration – a divine intervention which had allowed the base to escape the vengeance of a better man (455f.).[50] The stress is throughout upon the Judgement of the Arms and upon the hatred for the Greek leaders which this has bred in Ajax. Never at any point in the play does Ajax display a shadow of doubt that to kill the Atridae and Odysseus had been the right thing for him to do. He has tried to restore his honour; a goddess has frustrated him; one course only remains.[51]

This train of thought and emotion, adumbrated in song, is given calmer exposition in the speech which follows. His song had ended, after his proud boast (to be not merely the equal but the superior of Achilles), on the note of *atimos* (426); and to this word the first section of his speech works round (440). If he finds a true omen of lamentation in his name, it is because he, the son of a hero who had won glory and the prize of valour in the land of Troy, equal to his father in strength and achievements, is dishonoured by the Greeks and ruined. How dishonoured? Because the arms of Achilles had been awarded,

---

[50] Biggs 224 (on 447ff.): 'The sane Ajax regrets not the planned attack, but the missed aim.' The relationship between 367 and 303f. is worth noting. In his madness Ajax had mocked and (as he thought) outraged his enemies; now he finds himself mocked and outraged. He uses of Athena the word ($\alpha i \kappa i \zeta \epsilon \iota$, 402) which she had herself used of his torturing the animals (65). It is precisely this mockery of an enemy which Odysseus rejects (79, contr. 961, 969). This theme is well investigated by G. Grossmann, 'Das Lachen des Aias', *MH* 25 (1968) 65–85, who makes the illuminating comment that ' "Unmenschlichkeit" ist ein Vorrecht der allmächtigen Götter' (84).

[51] The decision to kill himself was taken when he was still in the hut? Cf. 326. Why does he call for his son and for Teucer, if not that he is going to die? His lyrics are obsessed with death, with the impossibility of a continued life. This is not to say that, from 457 ($\kappa \alpha i \nu \hat{\nu} \nu \tau i \chi \rho \dot{\eta} \delta \rho \hat{\alpha} \nu$;), he does not go over the argument again in his own mind.

by the jobbery of the Atridae, to a rascal and not to him, whereas, if
Achilles, living, had had to adjudicate the disposal of his arms on
grounds of valour, none but Ajax would have laid hands on them. (Is
there not something vaguely unpleasant about Ajax, even in hypothesis, seizing greedily upon the arms of a living Achilles? Something
that echoes his boast?)[52] 'If my eyes and wits, distracted, had not
sprung away from my intention, they [the Atridae] would never have
rigged a vote against another man.' 'And now what should I do?'
(457).

He must die. It is, however, worth sparing a moment to consider
the courses which he rejected. Return home across the Aegean? No,
he could not go back without a prize to face his father who had won
the garland of fair repute. But note how he speaks of leaving the
Atridae alone (μόνους, 461). As Stanford puts it: 'Ajax characteristically assumes that whoever is without *him* is truly alone.' Launch a
single-handed attack (for Ajax to be alone, that is another matter)
upon the fortifications of Troy? But note the expression μόνος μόνοις.
'In single combats', says Stanford, 'i.e. a series of μονομαχίαι.' This
surely does less than justice to the grandiose conception of Ajax, who
thinks of himself as taking on the whole might of Troy. These courses
he rejects in favour of suicide. 'The man of noble race must either live
nobly (καλῶς) or be nobly dead. That is all' (479f.).

The comment of the Chorus is most significant: 'No one will say
that this is a spurious word which you have spoken, but it comes from
your own mind (τῆς σαυτοῦ φρενός).' And we should remember how
they said that Ajax in his right mind (φρενόθεν) would never have

---

[52] Clearly one should not attach too much weight to this. But the statement (which
precedes the reference to the Atridae) is the more extraordinary the more one
thinks of it. One might even say it supplies the personal mention of Achilles so
strikingly absent from 421–6. Does κράτος ἀριστείας, followed by ἔμαρψεν,
convey the idea of a forcible seizure of the status of *aristos* (which Ajax had in
effect made by his words at 423–6)? It is dangerous to speculate about matters
which are, more or less, outside the drama, such as the feelings of Ajax about
Achilles (upon which Homer is not evidence, any more than he is for the
relationship of Ajax and Menelaus). Did Ajax resent the primacy of Achilles and
the fact that for ten years he had lived and fought under the shadow of a greater
warrior? At any rate Lawall (op. cit. n. 13) 292, seems perfectly justified in calling
this a 'preliminary frustration' which made it 'all the more important to him that
he acquire Achilles' arms upon his death'. Cf. the interesting remarks of M. M.
Willcock, BICS 20 (1973) 4, on the Homeric Ajax. 'This is Ajax' fate – to be
second.'

attacked the flocks. No, but to attack the Atridae and, having failed, to kill himself – that is a true expression of the mind of Ajax.

'Still', says the Coryphaeus, 'stop' (which is futile, because it means to stop being Ajax); 'let your friends sway your purposes (γνώμης); give up these thoughts (φροντίδας).' No friend has a greater claim upon Ajax than his faithful concubine. The speech she now makes is complex in structure and dense in thought. It deserves careful examination as a piece of rhetoric, but we are concerned primarily with the grounds of her appeal and the response – or lack of response – which they evoke. The speech falls into two parts, dividing at 505–6. The first half deals mainly with her own plight but ends with an appeal directed towards the honour of Ajax which will suffer, if his concubine falls into menial slavery; the appeal is the more forcible because she can associate his son with it (499). The last line (505) contains the powerful word 'shameful' (αἰσχρά), and ends with 'family' (γένει), which acts as a lead into her next appeal. Hardly less powerful as a word is *aidesai* (506, 507);[53] hardly less powerful as a motive is it that he should respect his father and mother and not abandon them in their old age. Next she returns to his son and to herself, moving into a field of softer emotion. When she bids him pity (οἴκτιρε, 510)[54] his infant son who will be brought up by cruel guardians, it is the plight of the child and not his own honour on which the appeal is based. If pity for the weak was not unknown or unregarded in the heroic world, one may doubt if it was an essential component of *eugeneia*. In her own case, she goes on to plead the obligation created by the conferment of joy and claims that he who forgets a benefit has lost the status of a *eugenes aner*. It is Ajax's word (480), of which she gives, one might say, a 'persuasive' redefinition.[55] The sense of obligation was indeed strong in the heroic world. And it may be worth noting how similar – how ironically similar – is the language with which Teucer (at 1266ff.) castigates the ingratitude of

---

[53] For αἰδώς as a mark of the Homeric Ajax, see Stanford xxxiii and n. 47. The contexts are of course military.

[54] The syntax of 510–13 is debated (see the editors). The εἰ-clause should preferably be taken with οἴκτιρε, the relative clause ὅσον κακόν κτλ. being loosely attached: 'so great an evil is it . . .'. τοῦτο must refer to the plight of the child, which Tecmessa thus represents, characteristically, as foremost among the evils she herself may expect. κἀμοί then leads into 514ff.

[55] On 'persuasive definitions' cf. Adkins, *MR* 38ff. (who cites for the expression C. L. Stevenson, *Mind* 1938, 331ff.).

the Greeks.[56] But that was in the martial context. How much could it be expected that the mutual obligations of a sexual relationship would weigh – and weigh with an Ajax? If they weighed with Hector, they could not outweigh the claims of his honour.[57] Did they weigh with Ajax at all? Was this, the narrowest and most intimate of all communities, an environment to which he still belonged? For there is one further point to notice in the speech: that Tecmessa's plea has returned upon itself, that she has reverted to the theme of relationship. If she speaks at the end of the pleasure she had given him, not only does she tell in the first half how she had come to his bed (ξυνῆλθον, 491) but appeals to him by that bed in which he had been joined to her (συνηλλάχθης, 493). (The repetition of the prefix is not accidental.) He was joined to her as she to him: that the sexual relationship lacked its ideal symmetry is Tecmessa's tragedy as it was Deianira's.[58]

'Pity your son', said Tecmessa. 'I could wish you to have pity as I have' says the Coryphaeus (525f.). And Ajax sends for his son, though his tone is hard and impatient. As we have seen already, the presence of the child serves to show him as a man so much harder than Hector. Serves only this? We come to an area in which opinions differ greatly, and in which it is not easy to avoid dependence upon subjective impressions. What capacity for pity, for affection, did this Ajax possess? Did he love Tecmessa? Did he love his son? In what degree if at all were his actions influenced by such softer emotions?[59]

One thing we can say with certainty about Eurysaces: that his father looks upon him in the light of *eugeneia* and of a male succession – one who is to follow Ajax in a career of heroism as Ajax had

---

[56] Note especially χάρις, διαρρεῖ (cf. ἀπορρεῖ, 523), μνῆστιν. Ajax, the man of war, rejects the appeal of Tecmessa: the pleasure of their relationship means little to him in comparison with warlike matters and to respect it is not part of his code of honour. It is ironical therefore that his warlike services to the Greeks should not evoke a lasting χάρις, that their memory too should fade.

[57] Andromache was a wife, Tecmessa a slave-concubine. But too much need not be made of this distinction. If she calls herself δούλη (489), by contrast with her birth, she refers to her state as a ζῆλος (503), by contrast with λατρεία. Ajax intends that Eurysaces shall be accepted as a legitimate heir and perform the functions of one (567ff.), which implies perhaps a kind of status for his mother. See also n. 63.

[58] There seems to be a relationship between 489f. and 492f., in respect of the divine and human factors. The gods have willed her slavery, but Zeus Ephestios protects it; Ajax has taken her by violence (χειρί), but she has become his bedfellow so that she has a claim upon him.

[59] The issue arises again in the Deception Speech, on which see p. 48.

followed Telamon, to succeed like Telamon where Ajax, through lack of fortune, had failed (550f., 556f.). For this destiny he must be schooled – and be preserved. And it becomes clear that the appeals of Tecmessa have not gone unregarded, in respect of Eurysaces and in respect of Ajax's parents. The former will play the part of son to Telamon and Eriboea; the protection of Eurysaces himself against the fears of Tecmessa is entrusted to Teucer (562ff.). Ajax's confidence that Teucer can be an effective protector is unrealistic, as the subsequent action shows, and perhaps characteristic. No less so is the confident disposal of his arms, the famous shield to Eurysaces, the rest to be buried with him, when it will be a question whether Ajax is to be buried at all – a question resolved not by Teucer but by Odysseus. Ajax is self-centred in a world he does not fully understand. He seems to regard his half-brother, who had fought by his side in so many Homeric battles, as a lesser self, but still capable of proving an adequate substitute. Is it too much to suggest that his son too he regards primarily as an extension of himself?[60]

It is true that for a moment (552ff.) he is touched by envy of his son's untroubled infancy: not only so, but he uses eight words which evoke a poetic vision of childhood and three which show regard for Tecmessa (558f.). At this point there is indeed a striking alternation of toughness and tenderness.[61] And for this there is some dramaturgical necessity: it must not be too certain that Ajax will remain inflexible, if the dramatic effect of the famous Deception Speech (646ff.) is to succeed; the apparent softening of Ajax in the following scene must be prepared. To what extent there is also a revelation of character – to what extent, that is, Ajax feels not only envy but pity and a conflict between tough and tender emotions in himself – must be a matter of individual judgement. We have no reason to assert that there is no such conflict.[62]

---

[60] On the self-centredness of Heracles in the *Trachiniae,* who also seems to regard his son as a mere extension of himself, see p. 84.

[61] 545–51 tough; 552–5 tender; 556–7 tough; 558–9 tender; 560ff. tough.

[62] 552–5 are not easy. 554b (not in Stobaeus) is deleted by editors, but Dawe adds a warning that it may have replaced a genuine verse, presumably because he saw that the connection of thought between 554 and 555 is not quite satisfactory without some mediating notion. There is perhaps, as Kamerbeek sees, a case for retaining 554b. Ajax is preoccupied with his own state of mind (hence $\zeta\eta\lambda o\hat{v}\nu$). The sense of 554 is complete in itself, but it has only to be spoken to raise a question. How can $\tau\grave{o}$ $\phi\rho o\nu\epsilon\hat{\iota}\nu$ $\mu\eta\delta\acute{e}\nu$ be commended? Is it not a $\kappa\alpha\kappa\acute{o}\nu$? If so,

Three words for Tecmessa does not seem much.[63] When he
addresses her – and for the last time in the play – the words are cold,
impatient, impersonal and (in part) proverbial. He tells her to be
sophron.[64] She implores him to be softened (μαλάσσου), and he replies,
as he leaves the stage: 'I think you have the mind (φρονεῖν) of a fool, if
you suppose that at this late hour (ἄρτι) you can school my character
(ἦθος)' (594f.). *ethos* is a settled disposition, the product of nature and
nurture. Is it indeed reasonable to suppose that Ajax can change now?
Can he take back the word that was spoken from his true mind
(481f.)? If his closing words look back to the comment – and the
appeal – of the Coryphaeus which marked the end of the first half of
the scene, they also lead into the choral ode which follows.[65]

It is the first regular choral ode – the first stasimon; and it is the longest
and most elaborate in the play. It comes at an important climax,
which is also a point of rest. Till now there has been almost continuous exposition, which has been, in one aspect, an investigation of
the mind of Ajax, in terms of sickness and sanity. The ode has two
dominant themes; and one of them is disease. The other theme is time.
How, if at all, are the two related? The song demands close analysis,
for it is one of the most complex and subtle in the whole of Sophocles,
not to be dismissed in a short paragraph as a more or less appropriate

   however, it is at least ἀνώδυνον, until true knowledge of joy and sorrow comes.
   The state of a young child, it was also that of the deluded Ajax. Does this pass
   through his mind? Should it pass through ours?
      If 552–7 are self-centred, what of 558f.? Which have something of the same
   poetic quality as *Trach.* 144ff., where so different a character as Deianira envies
   the carefree virgins of the Chorus (in a similar context of joy and sorrow, cf.
   129ff.). μητρὶ τῇδε χαρμονήν. And so welcome to Ajax, for her sake? A joy in
   parenthood which he might (like Hector) share if he lived? Or is it the mother's
   joy only, the father's concern being with the matters of 550f. and 556f.?
63 What will happen to Tecmessa? It goes without saying that she will accompany
   her infant son to Salamis? But what goes without saying tends to go without
   dramatic effect. If one is to believe that Ajax is deeply concerned for Tecmessa at
   this point of the play, it is better to go the whole hog (with Adams 33) and take
   the very harshness of Ajax as evidence 'that he has been moved to the depth of his
   being, that only his iron will prevents him from breaking' – if one can believe it.
64 σωφρονεῖν καλόν (586): see Stanford ad loc. The use of φρενί in the preceding line
   may or may not be accidental.
65 Contrary to a widely held view, Tecmessa probably does *not* enter the hut with
   Ajax, cf. Gellie 281 n. 9; Sicherl (2) n. 101. Fraenkel, *MH* 79f. revives the view
   that 650ff. refer to conversations which have taken place off-stage between the
   acts, but this unfortunate idea is rightly rejected by Sicherl.

choral reaction filling the time till Ajax reappears. It does indeed express the limited, even obtuse, attitudes of this limited and obtuse Chorus, but Sophocles uses it to tell us things about Ajax which are beyond the comprehension of the singers.

Str. α΄. The war-weary sailors are preoccupied with time.[66] Time has grown old; the months have been countless; the singers are worn down with time, and there is no prospect but the evil fate of death. Yet all the while there abides Salamis their home, glorious, happy, ever visible to the eyes of men, ever resistant to the waves that break upon it. There could be no finer symbol of the permanence of nature and the impermanence of man.[67]

Ant. α΄. From time to disease. As though the troubles of the strophe were not enough to wrestle with,[68] the sailors have with them an Ajax hard to cure (δυσθεράπευτος), since he dwells, alas, with a heaven-sent madness (θείᾳ μανίᾳ). They say 'hard to cure' rather than 'incurable', for they take it as their function to apply such therapy as will restore him to a mood which is not suicidal. (At no point in the ode do they recognize the inevitability of his death.) This is a function of friends (330), and he is with them (ξύνεστιν). But in what sense and in what degree? He is with them, yet keeping company (ξύναυλος) with a mental sickness.[69] And this mental sickness was sent by a god. Their notion of *theia mania* had shifted, as we saw; what began as an explanation of his attack on the cattle has now become descriptive of the suicidal mood which derived from the Judgement of the Arms

---

[66] On the textual problems of 602–5 see the editors. One simple point: χρόνῳ (605) is not to be touched. So far from indicating corruption (so Stanford), χρόνῳ after χρόνος is a deliberate repetition, a characteristic Sophoclean accumulation of significant words. παλαιὸς . . . χρόνος is striking and (as Stanford suggests) could be an echo of Aesch. *Agam.* 983–5. Hermann's μηνῶν for μήλων is highly probable (cf. *Phil.* 721), to be taken after ἀνήριθμος, the meaning of which is fixed by ἀναρίθμητος in 646 (cf. 1186). There is no reason at all why ἀνήριθμος, as an expression of time, should not agree with the subject ἐγώ: the use of such expressions applied adjectivally to persons seems to be highly idiomatic and reveals a Greek way of looking at time as a function of him who experiences it. (Cf. *O.C.* 441, with Jebb's note, and probably *Trach.* 164f.; Plato, *Rep.* 614b, Theocritus 2.157; the familiar use of χρόνιος; and many other examples.)

[67] ἔτι: 'with an anxious regard for the future' (Stanford, cf. Kamerbeek). ἀίδηλον Ἅιδαν: probably, as Stanford suggests, an etymological pun; and with the darkness of death contr. περίφαντος of Salamis.

[68] For the metaphorical use of ἔφεδρος (610) see Jebb.

[69] The repetition of ξυν- is far from careless. Which association is the more significant?

and his frustrated vengeance.[70] What follows should be important.

What follows is a contrast of times. (And we shall see that the second antistrophe also involves a contrast of times.) They contrast Ajax as he now is with the mighty warrior that Salamis (for Salamis is still in their minds and should be in ours) sent forth to Troy (πρὶν δή ποτε). But now (νῦν δ' αὖ) 'he is pastured in the solitude of his own mind (φρενὸς οἰοβώτας) and has proved a great grief to his friends (φίλοις)'.[71] Once more the *phren* of Ajax. 'Never in his right mind (φρενόθεν)' would he have attacked the animals. 'No one can say that these words' (the determination to suicide) 'did not come from your own mind' (τῆς σαυτοῦ φρενός). Ajax *phronimos*; Ajax mad. Now his 'madness' is described as a brooding in the solitude of his own mind. The contrast of 'then' and 'now' is not quite specific: there is an unexpressed term, which is Ajax inside and outside the community. Then the fierce warrior acclaimed for his exploits, and bringing joy to his friends; now cut off from human society, even from his friends, consorting only with his sick mind. What was implied is made explicit in the words which follow, with a third expression of time (τὰ πρὶν ἔργα). We return to the past, but to a more recent past. For how had this come about? Because his heroic achievements had been rejected by those who should have been his friends, because of the Judgement of the Arms. 'The former works of his hands, works of the greatest *arete*' had counted for nothing. The diagnosis of the Chorus is really quite simple.[72] Prior to the Judgement of the Arms, Ajax was the embodiment of *arete*, the ideal hero; then, cheated of his prize and of his vengeance, he cuts himself off from society and determines to die. Note that the Chorus is still confused about madness and sanity. (Is the suicidal mood the true expression of his heroic mind? Or is it a madness inflicted by the gods?) Note the scheme of times. For it is a main function of this ode to widen the time-perspective. This is a

---

[70] On the shift between 185 and 278–80, see p. 25 above. But why is his present state a θεία μανία? See p. 42 below.

[71] Biggs 225: 'The *nyn d'au* misses the real problem of Ajax: for he is the same man he was when he left Salamis, and his particular kind of "great soul" can only react to the given circumstances with this self-alienation.'

[72] The explanation is repeated, after the death of Ajax, at 933–5: on the stanza (925–35) as a whole, see p. 163 n. 31 below. For a modern re-statement see Biggs 226: 'The "real" disease dates from the award of the arms; it is the loss of *eukleia* that has forced this heroic nature to its logical outcome.' The explanation has truth, but is incomplete: it needs to be complemented by the fourth stanza of this ode and by the messenger's speech: see pp. 36ff. and 41 below.

process which has already been carried some way. The action of the play began at a particular point of time, on a particular night when Ajax went out and performed his extraordinary action. But almost immediately we are taken back to the Judgement of the Arms from which the subsequent action is seen to flow. Before that, what? The weary years of the Trojan War, sung with such feeling by the chorus, which were yet the years of the glory of Ajax. And before that? The hero's son setting out from Salamis for the war.

Str. β'. The aged mother of Ajax will surely utter no piteous nightingale-lament, but the shrill tones of a dirge; she will beat her breast and tear her hair.[73] She will, that is, act as one mourning the dead. The Chorus does not, however, say: 'when she hears that Ajax is dead', but 'when she hears that he is fatally sick in mind' (or, with a different reading, 'sick of a sickness that devours his mind').[74] The Chorus cannot see or will not say that he is bound to kill himself; and there is a dramatic reason for this, since later they are to be deceived into believing that he intends to live. If the references to sickness and to the mind of Ajax pick up the disease-theme from the preceding stanza, the reference to the great age of Eriboea reminds us of the long span of time since Ajax left Salamis.[75]

Ant. β'. The opening connects closely with the strophe. 'Better hidden in Hades is the man who is sick with folly.' The Chorus cannot mean that Ajax would be better dead (though that is what Ajax thinks), since his death is what above all they fear. They mean that his mother may well lament as for the dead, since the condition of her son is worse than that of the dead, sick as he is – and sick μάταν.[76] Then once again, as in the first antistrophe, we have the contrast of present

---

[73] Text and interpretation of 628–31 are disputed, but the general sense must be as stated.

[74] 626: φρενομόρως, -μώρως codd. φρενοβόρως Dindorf. One cannot have much confidence in the form φρενομόρως, and Dindorf's suggestion is attractive, cf. θυμοβόρος at Iliad 7.210, 301. This could be another case in which a word from an Ajax-passage has stuck in the poet's mind (see n. 15 above).

[75] The bold form of expression (παλαιᾷ . . . ἁμέρᾳ) recalls the παλαιὸς . . . χρόνος of 600: more insistence on time. One may hanker after Nauck's σύντροφος, but, since the metrical argument is not compelling, hesitate to change the ἔντροφος of the tradition. (It is the theme of nurture which is significant.)

[76] μάταν is generally, and I suppose rightly, taken to indicate madness: Jebb cites Aristophanes, Peace 95. Otherwise it might describe a sickness which does not respond to diagnosis and treatment, cf. δυσθεράπευτος (609). Linforth's useful discussion of the adverb, (1951) 188f., hardly settles the matter.

and past. There is a reference to his paternal descent and to his supreme *arete* (the text is here uncertain);[77] 'no longer', however, 'does he abide firm in the temper to which he was bred, but keeps company outside it' (οὐκέτι συντρόφοις ὀργαῖς ἔμπεδος, ἀλλ᾽ ἐκτὸς ὁμιλεῖ, 639f.). The Chorus is seeking to describe a madman – a man who is 'beside himself'; and they do so by saying that he has departed from his σύντροφοι ὀργαί.[78] But how can they say this? The Coryphaeus himself, when Ajax first hinted at suicide, said that he was speaking 'from his true mind' (481f.). Ajax scoffed at Tecmessa for thinking that she could school his *ethos;* and what is *ethos* but the 'temper to which you have been bred'? Is this a slip on the part of Sophocles? Or an irrelevant obtuseness on the part of the Chorus? Or an instance of their normal confusion in this matter of sickness and sanity? They will not see that Ajax is being true to himself. They will not recognize that either he is not mad or, if his impulse to suicide *is,* in some sense, madness, then he must have been in some sense 'mad' all along? When, in the time-scheme, did his 'madness' begin? The Chorus, in the first antistrophe, had no doubt (any more than some modern scholars) that it began with the Judgement of the Arms. Unless Sophocles has been very careless in his use of language, there is a difference between the two antistrophes, and it may be significant.

In both stanzas the Chorus attempt a lyric description of the diseased state of the hero's mind; in both he is seen as having placed himself outside a certain range. In the earlier stanza he is outside human society, confined within the limits of his own mind, which is true and important and (as they see it) something which has taken place since the Judgement of the Arms. In the later stanza he is ranging outside his σύντροφοι ὀργαί, which is untrue on the testimony of the Coryphaeus himself. The temper in which he reacted to the Judgement of the Arms had already been bred in him, and he was faithful to it. Are we reading too much into a few words? The stanza is not over yet.

The Chorus apostrophizes the father of Ajax and sings of the terrible news that he too is to hear. These lines (641ff.) correspond to the passage about Eriboea in the strophe (and the first lines of the antistrophe); and between them the Eriboea and Telamon passages

---

[77] See the editors and H. Lloyd-Jones, *JHS* 76 (1956) 112. ἄριστος or ἄριστα is certain, and the general trend is clear.
[78] See Stanford on 639–40.

enclose the references to the breeding of Ajax and to the temper from which he is supposed to have departed. As in the case of the mother, the Chorus does not speak of death: it is of his son's 'intolerable doom' (δύσφορον ἄταν) the father is to learn. The word *ate* has been frequently used[79] of the present disastrous state of Ajax. It could presumably refer to death, but, if we turn to 848 (which is also about the parents of Ajax) we find his *atai* distinguished from his death. The *ate* is the *nosos* (as it should be to correspond to *nosounta* in the strophe). It is called δύσφορος, which may merely mean 'intolerable', but the word occurred at 51 in connection with his madness and could be a term of medicine.[80] The father, then, must hear of the disastrous mental sickness of his son – 'a disaster of such kind as, apart from him, no *aion* of the Aeacidae has yet nurtured (ἔθρεψεν)'. The language of the closing phrase has been much discussed. Interpreters have wished to understand the statement simply as referring to a disaster which has supervened at a certain point of (comparatively recent) time, namely, the Judgement and the consequences flowing from it. The word αἰών must, accordingly, be taken in the sense of 'lot'; and it is true that it belongs, marginally, to the wide vocabulary of fate. Normally, however, it is used of the life-span of a human-being, and the Sophoclean passages quoted in support of the meaning 'lot' or 'destiny in life' all seem on examination to indicate the character or quality of a continuing, and often a long, stretch of time.[81] The verb τρέφειν must, on this understanding, be taken as a mere synonym for ἔχειν; and, very common as it is in Sophocles, it sometimes seems to mean little – though always something – more than that.[82] But immediately after the expression συντρόφοις ὀργαῖς (639), unless Sophocles is to be

---

[79] 123, 195, 269, 307, 363, 384.

[80] See n. 28 above.

[81] *Trach.* 34 (where this reference to the αἰών of Heracles balances an implied reference to the αἰών of Deianira at 2); *Phil.* 179 (of the disease-stricken life of Philoctetes, cf. 173). Both *O.C.* 1736 and Eur. *Andromache* 1215 refer to a stretch of life. For *aion* as part of the vocabulary of fate, see ch. 7 p. 151.

[82] Half-an-hour with Ellendt makes this clear; and, though he uses expressions like 'ut plerumque commode interpreteris ἔχειν', his own amplifications generally reveal how misleading this is. Apart from cases where the word means 'rear' or 'nurture' or 'cherish' or 'increase', a frequent connotation is that of a quality or mode of life (e.g. *Ajax* 503). At *Phil.* 795 the object of the verb is νόσον and the whole point resides in its long continuance. C. Moussy, *Recherches sur τρέφω* (Paris 1969) 70–2, has reservations about the equation with ἔχω, but does not go into much detail.

convicted of careless writing, one would prefer not to depart too far
from the normal implications of *trephein,* which implies a process. It is
surely methodologically unsound, in an ode so full of time, to take
two words which naturally imply a process (of time and in time) and
to assume for both an unusual and diluted sense, merely in order to
eliminate a notion fundamental to the ode. But if the words mean
what they seem to say, then the poet is suggesting, through the
subtleties of his lyric diction, that the *nosos,* which was the *ate* of Ajax,
is a long-continuing, long-fostered disease, bound up (as the Chorus
fail to see) with his σύντροφοι ὀργαί; that it is something which has
grown with Ajax during his life-span, something that his life has bred.

The two leading themes of the ode fall together: disease and time,
disease fostered throughout a long process of time, in a receding
perspective stretching out behind the Judgement of the Arms. The
language, and the transitions of thought, are those of lyric poetry,
subtle and elusive. How, then, can we clinch the argument in less
ambiguous terms? By turning to the Messenger's speech and the
words of Calchas.

In reviewing and interpreting a play, it is seldom desirable to depart
from the dramatic sequence. At the end of the ode Ajax appears
sword in hand and makes a long speech. It opens with famous words
about time, which must surely relate to the themes of the ode. But the
interpretation of the speech is highly controversial. I am not thinking
so much of the old – and now somewhat outmoded – controversy
about the intentions of Ajax, since most critics now agree that he has
never abandoned the intention to kill himself. The controversy – and
it is crucial to an understanding of the play – ranges upon a different
level and concerns the mind of Ajax, the thoughts that pass through
his mind as he approaches his death, the degree of insight into the
processes of the world which the high poetry of Sophocles enables
him to express. It may be convenient, therefore, to postpone consideration, until we have examined, not only the Messenger's speech
which follows it, but also the final speech of Ajax before his suicide.

Ajax has said that he will yield to the gods and respect the Atridae;
the gloom of the Chorus turns to rapturous joy (693ff.). Ajax has
forgotten his troubles again (711); he has returned to reverence and
the due observance of custom; he has undergone a change of mind
(μετανεγνώσθη) away from his wrath against the Atridae and his great

quarrels.[83] This was contrary to all expectation (ἐξ ἀέλπτων, cf. 648), and it was the work of time. (Had not Ajax said that time is the master of all things and that in the long course of time there is nothing that cannot be expected?) It is characteristic of the Chorus (and perhaps a reflection through them of the mind of Ajax) to assume that it is enough if Ajax forgoes his wrath, to forget that, if it takes two to make a quarrel, it takes two to make it up. The opening lines of the Messenger's speech remind us of the realities.[84] It should be noted that, towards the end of the song, we find a small cluster of occurrences of the word *megas* (713f., 718). Those who can must believe that this is accidental. Most notably, the epithet is given to Time.[85] Where the word occurred so frequently in the Parodos, we saw that it was used of the great Ajax, but also of the great forces ranged against him. Perhaps the question is here: does great time work for Ajax or against him? Time also enters into the Messenger's speech.

It enters in a twofold connection. The Messenger reports the strange fact, revealed by Calchas, that it is for this one day alone that Ajax will be pursued by the wrath of Athena. The prophet had been insistent: if Ajax is to live, then by every possible device he must be kept indoors during the day now visible, this present day (κατ' ἦμαρ τοὐμφανὲς τὸ νῦν τόδε, 753). The warning is repeated at 778: 'If he is alive this day, then with the help of god we may prove his saviours.'[86] This is the crucial day, the day of tragedy, the day which, as Athena herself said, tilts the scales of all human things and lifts them up again (131f.). It is a narrow point of time. Having said that it was only for this day that Ajax would be pursued by the wrath of Athena, the

---

[83] Cf. 735f., 743. See B. M. W. Knox, *GRBS* 7 (1966) 217.

[84] 721ff. 744 seems to show the same naïvety on the part of the Chorus in another connection: just as Ajax has merely to abandon *his* wrath against the Atridae (718) for all to be well, so too he has (as they think) dropped his wrath against the gods, as shown by the making of sacrifices (711ff.). We are about to learn what caused the wrath of the gods against *him*.

731f. are of course necessary to the plot: Teucer must not be killed. They may however also suggest, not that it was unfair to penalize Teucer for his brother's madness, but that there was still scope for a reasonable diplomatic settlement (Ajax was still an asset to the Greek army), but one of course which it would have been psychologically impossible for Ajax to accept.

[85] Again at 933, also from the Chorus (see p. 163 n. 31). They sing of time as μέγας, not (like Ajax at 646) as μακρός: the span of time since the Judgement of the Arms was *not* long.

[86] M. W. Wigodsky's interpretation of these lines, in *Hermes* 90 (1962) 149–58, is adequately criticized by Stanford, 'Addenda to notes' 237f.

prophet went on to expound the causes of that wrath. Ajax knew that he was in some sense the victim of Athena (401ff.), but he saw her simply as frustrating his vengeance on the Greeks. That Athena was in some sense against Ajax has always been clear. But was this more than the act of a protective goddess saving Odysseus? Only her closing words give us the right to say so (127ff.); and their implications have never been quite clear – until Calchas makes them clear.

In doing so, Calchas takes us back in time; and this is the second way in which time enters into the speech. He begins by generalizing about the heavy misfortunes which the gods send on one who, having the physical nature of a man, yet has more than mortal thoughts. He goes on to apply his theme to the case of Ajax, about whom he tells two stories; first his proud answer, when his father bade him seek the mastery, but ever seek it with the help of (a) god; then his proud rejection of Athena's help in battle.[87] The first saying is described as a boast: with the formality, the archaic ring-composition,[88] character-istic of the whole passage it is preceded by ὑψικόμπως (766) and followed by ἐκόμπει (770). It is boastful; it is also senseless (ἀφρόνως, 766), and Ajax himself is called ἄνους (763): 'foolish', 'lacking in right mind'. The state of the mind of Ajax has been a point of cardinal importance throughout the play. In the last choral ode, it appeared (at least in the first antistrophe) that the Judgement of the Arms was the turning-point, the event which threw the mind of Ajax off the track, though the second antistrophe is so phrased as to hint that his mental trouble had a longer time-span. Now, by Calchas, we are taken back, not only to the battles of the Trojan War to see Ajax, in the period of his heroism, rejecting (so un-Homerically) the help of Athena, but still further, to the time of his departure from Salamis (cf. 613). The time is marked with some emphasis (ἀπ' οἴκων εὐθὺς ἐξορμώμενος, 762). The interlocutor is Telamon, who may well stand as a represen-tative of the heroic ideal (as indeed he is seen by Ajax) and so a touchstone of the normality of his son.[89] The receding perspective,

[87]

πάτερ, θεοῖς μὲν κἂν ὁ μηδὲν ὢν ὁμοῦ
κράτος κατακτήσαιτ'· ἐγὼ δὲ καὶ δίχα
κείνων πέποιθα τοῦτ' ἐπισπάσειν κλέος.   (767–9)

ἄνασσα, τοῖς ἄλλοισιν Ἀργείων πέλας
ἴστω, καθ' ἡμᾶς δ' οὔποτ' ἐκρήξει μάχη.   (774f.)

[88] See p. 13 above.

[89] Reinhardt, 38, suggests that this may have been prompted by *Iliad* 9.252ff.

then, is now carried back to the furthest relevant point, to show us an Ajax already abnormal, already *aphron* and *anous,* already megalomaniac, before ever he leaves home for Troy.

Already mad? It is a matter of terms. Many modern critics, like the Chorus, have seen the Judgement of the Arms as a turning-point. And rightly. So far as we can read a past situation from the text of the play, we are meant to think of Ajax, prior to the Judgement, as to all appearance a normal Homeric hero of high grade, glorying in his reputation, accepting (so far as we are permitted to speculate) the fact that that reputation stood second to Achilles; undisciplined only in the prejudiced eye of a Menelaus (1067); a man of sense (119f.) as well as a man of phenomenal strength and courage. Then how did it come about that he reacted with such abnormal violence to the affront of the Judgement? Went 'mad' and launched his murderous night-attack upon the Greeks at large? Because the award was spurious? We have no right to say so, though Ajax must believe it.[90] Because now, with the death of Achilles, was the opportunity for him to win the unchallenged supremacy in *arete* and therefore his disappointment was the more bitter?[91] Perhaps. But why was he so unhinged? Because the seeds of madness were already in him, evidenced by an abnormal megalomaniac pride.

It was a very proper function for a spokesman of the divine world, by widening the time-scale, to correct the short-sighted vision of the Chorus. But perhaps we have not exhausted the significance of his prophetic insight, in relation to time. The backward glance in time is enclosed (and this is another instance of the extreme formality of the speech) between two references to the crisis of the present day. Though the arrogance of Ajax is of more than ten years' growth, the wrath of Athena will pursue him for this day alone, and, if he still lives on this day, there is hope that he can be saved. Why for this day alone? Is this a sign of the compassion of the gods? But what other evidence have we, in this or in other plays of Sophocles, that the gods can be compassionate towards those who have offended them? Or is it

(Peleus' farewell to Achilles). Peleus' remarks are indeed very interesting in relation to heroic ethics: Achilles will be *honoured* for restraining his θυμός, refraining from ἔρις, and showing φιλοφροσύνη (to his φίλοι of course). Cf. Lloyd-Jones, *JZ* 16. The passages are alike in that both fathers, in the different contexts, urge upon their sons a limitation of heroic individualistic pride.

[90] Cf. von Fritz 148.

[91] See nn. 13 and 52.

simply an arbitrary dramatic datum used to obvious dramatic effect? This could indeed be the sole explanation. Still, in a play so much concerned with time, one is loth to believe that the dramatist has used time so casually.

We now know what caused the wrath of Athena: it was the more than mortal thoughts of Ajax as shown by his rejection of divine aid; it was his mortal self-sufficiency. But how did, does and will, her wrath manifest itself? As Ajax saw it,[92] her wrath had shown itself in the madness which sent him against the cattle, humiliating and frustrating him. But in what danger does he now stand from the wrath of Athena? What will he escape if he remains at home, fail to escape if he goes out alone? These are questions which must be asked; and the answer to both must be suicide. The suicidal impulse of Ajax was presented by the Chorus in terms which had once been used of his sheer delusion. It is a *nosos*, a *mania*, a *theia mania*. Sent, then, by what god? If all the gods were offended by his arrogance, it is Athena who is primarily interested and dramatically relevant. It was Athena that sent the one madness – the delusion – upon him: now it seems that she may be responsible for the other. (If the Chorus could be wrong to see it as *theia mania*, Calchas cannot be wrong in speaking of the wrath of Athena.) That the suicidal mood of Ajax should be at one and the same time the natural working of his mind and character and a product of the divine wrath involves no contradiction in terms of Greek archaic thought as used and moulded by Sochocles.[93] There is no contradiction, because divine power and mental process are, from Homer onwards, intimately connected, because passions are the work of gods, because the pathological intensity with which Ajax reacts to an injury done to his pride is the nemesis appropriate to that pride. If the suicide of Ajax will be the work of divine wrath, then, no less, if he refrains from suicide, it can be represented as a cessation of that wrath. The wrath will cease to drive him, if, and only if, he remains at home; and if he lasts out the day.

Sophocles knew from Homer (and from Aeschylus) how to see events upon two levels, human and divine. If Ajax goes out, he will be

---

[92] Cf. 450–3: ἐμβαλοῦσα λυσσώδη νόσον, | ὥστ᾽ ἐν τοιοῖσδε χεῖρας αἱμάξαι βοτοῖς. At 654–6 he speaks of purifying these λύματα as a means of ridding himself from the heavy wrath of the goddess (μῆνιν βαρεῖαν . . . θεᾶς).

[93] No more contradiction than when Oedipus saw Apollo as responsible for the deliberate act by which he blinded himself, cf. O.T. 1329ff., on which see p. 175 below.

alone, and his last chance will have gone, for it is only his friends, who, if it could be done at all, could restore this mind, now ranging solitary, to human social life.[94] If he needs friends, he also needs time. When the Chorus believed that Ajax had indeed softened, they said, echoing his own words, that great time quenches everything (714).[95] Certainly Sophocles knew, when he wrote *Oedipus Coloneus*, that even the strongest passions die down in time (*O.C.* 437ff.). Time could work even for Ajax, as it had worked against him in the long nurture of his pride. But time must be given time. Is it conceivable that Ajax, whom time has made what he is, will allow time for time to do its softening work? Not, surely, now that he has gone out alone with his sword to the sea-shore. The limit placed upon the operation of the divine wrath can be of no benefit to him.[96]

Ajax is bent on death, as Tecmessa now knows (812). When she and the sailors have left in search of him, he reappears, still sword in hand. He fixes it point upwards in the ground, stands back, and speaks. He is now alone, about to take leave of the world, and we can be sure that what he now says is a true expression of his mind. It is an amazing, and at the end a deeply moving, speech. It would be the wrong speech, if some interpretations of the *Trugrede* were correct. All the more important, therefore, to examine closely its content and its tone. And Lattimore's words will provide the starting-point. 'The death is enacted, like the blinding of Oedipus, in an atmosphere of unreason, barbarism, primitive passion, where logic cannot reach, whose force we feel but can never quite account for nor understand.'[97]

Unreason, where logic cannot reach. The point is paradoxically made by the carefully chosen words of the first sentence: εἴ τῳ καὶ

---

[94] Cf. 330 (whatever we read there), 483f.

[95] μαραίνει τε καὶ φλέγει (codd., 714). The last three words, not found in Stobaeus and deleted by some editors, are defended by Knox, *HS* n. 128, de Romilly, *TGT* 100, and (more hesitantly) by Kamerbeek. I remain doubtful: the Chorus is thinking of the extinction of Ajax's blazing passion; there is no need for them to express the other half of the twofold process of 647 or much desirability that they should.

[96] Cf. Bowra 36; Whitman 70f.; and many others. If Ajax had refrained from suicide, what would the Greeks have done? The question so obviously will not arise that perhaps Sophocles did not mean us to consider it (Gellie 16). But cf. n. 84 above, on 731f.

[97] *PGT* 77. On this speech see also Perrotta 158f.; Dirlmeier 314ff.

λογίζεσθαι σχολή (816), 'if a man had leisure for reflection'. It is, as Jebb saw, the scornful apology of the man of action. But σχολή is a word of time. Ajax, to be saved, needed time – and reason. He has time, but will not give himself enough; when he reflects, it is upon essentially irrational considerations – that this sword is the ill-omened gift of Hector, that the very earth is hostile in which it is stuck.[98] Ajax may reflect thus, but it is clear that his act is determined by passion.

At the human level Ajax has made his preparations well: now he turns to the gods. And first he prays to Zeus, as he had prayed to him at 387ff. that he might kill Odysseus and the Atridae before he died – a prayer that was not answered. He asks for a help that he is entitled to receive (καὶ γὰρ εἰκός);[99] he asks for his rights, for a *geras* (and the word is characteristic). There is of course irony in the fact that he speaks of burial as 'no extensive privilege', when this is to be the issue of the whole second half of the play, and when it will be obtained for him not by Teucer but by Odysseus. This prayer, then, is answered, though not as he envisages.[100] From Olympian Zeus he moves to chthonian Hermes, link between the two worlds; from Hermes to the most awful, and most tragic, of chthonian powers – to the Erinyes, with a prayer for vengeance. He calls upon them to take note how he

[98] On the sword of Hector see Kitto, *FMD* 193–5; *Poiesis* 179–87; *YCS* 25 (1977) 325f. He demurs at the idea that this is mere primitive superstition; and indeed it is unlikely that Sophocles introduced the theme three times – twice from Ajax and once (at considerable length) from Teucer – merely to characterize the speakers as superstitious. Perhaps we should make a distinction. The speakers are looking for causes: failing to comprehend the true cause of Ajax's disaster, they have recourse to the ominous character of a certain action. So far as it has a rational aspect this lies perhaps in a feeling that it was a bad thing to mitigate hostility with an exchange of gifts. For Sophocles, however, there may be a deeper symbolism. As Kitto points out, this is not the only place in Sophocles which shows 'the dead reaching out to destroy the living'. Teucer speaks of the sword as forged by an Erinys (1034); and that is a name which Sophocles does not use lightly. See further, pp. 162, 210.

[99] What does he mean by καὶ γὰρ εἰκός? Is it because Zeus is his ancestor (cf. 387)? Or is there a suggestion that Ajax as greatest of men requires a service of the greatest of gods? Cf. Stanford ad loc., and Perrotta 158, who writes: 'Anche la sua preghiera estrema a Zeus non è molto pia.'

[100] It is often said that Ajax's prayer was answered by the arrival of Teucer, e.g. Adams 37: 'Zeus himself, then, looks with favour on the man.' But the 'swift rumour ὡς θεοῦ τινος' (998f.) came impartially to all the Greeks and, if Teucer arrived first, it was for some other reason.

is destroyed by the Atridae and to bring them to utter ruin like his.[101]
Was the prayer answered? Upon Agamemnon, but not upon Menelaus. Was it justified? Upon the assumptions of Ajax it was, since he
ascribed the Judgement of the Arms to the malice of his enemies.[102]
But justification on this score, if it was justified, becomes immaterial,
when Ajax, proceeding from unreason to greater unreason, urges the
Erinyes, swift and punitive, to drink unsparingly of the blood of the
whole Greek army (843f.). It is an amazing curse, which so many
critics, amazingly, have taken in their moral stride.[103]

From the dark world of the dead back to the daylight, from the
chthonians back to heaven (οὐρανόν) and the Sun-god that drives his
chariot up the steep slope of heaven. He, like the Erinyes, is a seeing
god, and it is because he sees that he can tell.[104] What he will now
have to tell the aged parents of Ajax is not merely his madness (ἄτας)
but his death (μόρον).[105] Ajax thinks for a moment of his mother and

[101] This must be the general sense. 841f. as they stand are full of difficulties and best
expunged with Bothe, cf. Fraenkel, *Sem.* 29.

[102] By the time that Teucer repeats and amplifies his brother's curse (1389–92) the
Atridae have put themselves firmly in the wrong. See also p. 210.

[103] Not so Perrotta, 159, who writes: 'A questo punto, lo sdegno e l'odio diventano
giganteschi: confondono insieme colpevoli e innocenti'; and if he finds something god-like in this, that is not altogether without reason! Cf. Fraenkel, *Sem.*
30. Contr. Adams 36: 'He is the victim of a base decision, and in all that host no
voice was raised against it.' But according to Agamemnon (1243) it was a
majority vote. All the evidence for a general hostility of the Greek army towards
Ajax (assembled by Davidson 167) postdates his attack on the flocks (and their
attendants). A similar passionate resentment evokes a similarly comprehensive
curse from Philoctetes (*Phil.* 1200), on which see p. 292 n. 39 below, Cf. also
Homer, *Il.* 16.97ff.
    Ajax calls the Erinyes 'swift', because that is what he wants them (vainly) to
be, not what they always were. For the adjective cf. 822, 833, 853. Ajax would
cut time short.

[104] Rosenmeyer, *MT* 186 and Vandvik 137 call attention to the quite extraordinary
request that Helios shall stay his chariot (847) and so interrupt the orderly
sequence of nature. For the sun as source of information, cf. *Trach.* 94ff., as
messenger, cf. *Odyssey* 8.270f. But is there any parallel for this? For Rosenmeyer
it is significant that 'on the threshold of his death . . . Ajax once more strains his
whole being to interfere with the stream of time'. This perhaps reads too much
into a characteristically self-centred and grandiose conception.

[105] Such a distinction is not important here, but looks back to the First Stasimon
(596ff.), on which see p. 37 above.
    Ajax thinks of his parents, and especially of his mother. Not a word of
Tecmessa or even of his son. It is because his mother belongs to his past and to his
breeding: she was his τροφός. The notion is picked up at 861, 863; it looks back to
the theme of nurture in the First Stasimon.

her lamentations, but cuts himself short: his business is with Thanatos. But immediately he returns to the sun and bids his farewell to the world of light, to the day, to this day.[106] He bids farewell to Salamis (where it all began), to Athens and the race that bred him; and then to the springs and rivers and plains of Troy that took over his nurture. Eriboea, Salamis, the Troad: what kind of a man was it that they bred? Every tone in this speech rings true when tried against the tones of Ajax in the earlier phases of the play. To what degree, and in what sense, is this still true, when we examine the speech – the famous, the controversial speech – which he makes, sword in hand, in the presence of Chorus and Tecmessa?

Ajax had gone into his hut, telling Tecmessa not to be a fool and think she could school his *ethos* at this late hour; and the Chorus then sang their song about his mental sickness and about time. At the end of that song he comes out carrying a sword and makes a speech which is taken by Tecmessa and the Chorus to mean that he has undergone a change of heart; he says he will submit and be reconciled to the Atridae, and implies that he has learnt to be *sophron*. There has been a great deal of debate about this speech.[107] Was it intended to deceive (a *Trugrede*)? Or has Ajax changed his mind, to change it yet again? The

---

[106] A case for deleting 854–8 is put by Fraenkel, *Sem.* 30.

[107] The spectrum of interpretation is vast and varied, and the controversy has been reviewed by Johansen in *Lustrum* and, recently, in *YCS* by Moore and Sicherl (2). I place here a brief and incomplete survey of opinion. Ajax has abandoned his intention to commit suicide, but reverts to it when alone (Webster, Bowra). He has abandoned an original intention to attack the Greeks in favour of suicide and has done this in the interest of Tecmessa and his son, but conceals his intention from her (Errandonea). Changing from a man of action to a man of thought, he finds a good instead of a bad reason for committing suicide (Simpson). He accepts the truth of what he says with his mind, but his *ethos* is too strong for him (Stanford). He has learnt *sophrosune,* but shows it by the very act of suicide (Schadewaldt, Sicherl). Thus his acceptance is sincere, his *sophrosune* new-learnt and admirable, but they lead paradoxically to the traditional suicide. By contrast: he accepts the truth of what he says, for others but not for himself (Torrance); he rejects a world in which these things are true (Knox); he leaves a world in which the Atridae are victorious as no place for him (von Fritz).

It will become clear that I am an adherent of this last view, of which Reinhardt is perhaps the protagonist. 'Dem Aias öffnen plötzlich sich die Augen, er erkennt die Welt, doch nicht, um als Erkennender sich in sie einzufügen, nicht um ihrer Ordnung sich zu beugen, nicht um dem γνῶθι σαυτόν zu folgen, sondern um in ihr das Fremde, Gegenteilige zu sehen, woran er nur teilhaben könnte, wenn er nicht mehr Aias wäre' (34). Cf. also Méautis 36–41.

audience knows that, unless Sophocles has taken an incredible liberty with the traditional story, Ajax will kill himself: but can they be certain – at least at the outset – whether he is sincere or insincere in what he says now? The speech is full of double meanings, of hints at his death,[108] but this does not settle the matter one way or the other, since there are two sorts of dramatic irony, one of which the speaker is conscious, one of which he is not. But when Ajax reappears obviously bent on suicide, then, in default of any indication (and such indications are strikingly absent from his final speech) that he has – once more – changed his mind, that he has found the line of *sophrosune* impossible to maintain, an audience must, it would seem, conclude (what it may already have divined) that his former speech was a deception. This is the conclusion drawn by Tecmessa (807f.), which, if there is nothing at all to contradict it, must surely be taken as correct.

The point need not be laboured, since most recent interpreters accept that Ajax all along intends to die and many that he intends to deceive.[109] But the establishment of this point does not mean that interpretation of the speech has become simple – a *Trugrede*, necessary to the dramatic structure and decked out in magnificent Sophoclean language. The speech indeed contains some of the noblest poetry even Sophocles ever wrote. It is not only magnificent in its language but, in its thought, it ranges wide and deep in its generalizations about human life, which it places against a background of natural process. It opens with the famous lines about time; and time is a theme which has dominated the preceding choral ode. Time and Ajax. When Ajax himself speaks about time and the effects of time, it is likely to be significant, it is likely to express an insight into the situation. The mind of Ajax is at work. But on what lines?

The mind of Ajax is at work. To say that he is oblivious of the

---

[108] Carefully examined by Sicherl (1) 23–8; (2) 77–85.

[109] 'Kann Aias lügen? Und wenn Aias lügt, weshalb?' (Reinhardt 33). These questions have been endlessly debated, not without some sophistry. The simple answer to the first is yes: 'er . . . nicht nur täuscht, sondern bewusst täuschen will'. So von Fritz 247, whose comment quoted above (n. 20) is as relevant to this deception as to his earlier action. The second question can also be given a simple answer on dramaturgical grounds, cf. e.g. Lattimore, *PGT* 68f., provided we realize that Sophocles' purpose is not merely 'to get Ajax alone with his sword, before our eyes, so that he can fall upon it': the Deception Speech itself is to be the supreme – ironic – revelation of the mind of Ajax through the expression of its reverse, as the Suicide Speech reveals when it comes.

presence of Tecmessa and the Chorus; that he is talking to himself;
that this is hardly less of a soliloquy, for most of its length, than his
final speech goes too far.[110] (Why should he waste so much irony on
himself, most of all when he speaks of going to the meadows by the
shore and burying his sword?) But it has a degree of important truth.
The Chorus had described Ajax as 'ranging in the solitude of his own
mind'; and this is still true, even when he issues from the hut. Real
human contact is limited to the staccato commands of his closing
lines. He is isolated and lacks precisely that rapport with his fellow-
men which, if the words of Calchas have been correctly interpreted,
might have saved him.

The speech begins with time, long and countless. Within the
process of time all things grow, come into the light of day, and then
pass to darkness. Anything can be expected to happen. The strongest
things are at the mercy of time: the awful oath is vanquished, and the
mind ($\phi\rho\acute{\epsilon}\nu\epsilon\varsigma$) like hardened steel. Anything can be expected to
happen, even what is most unexpected, as to the Chorus was a change
of mind in Ajax (716). And Ajax now implies that he has changed his
mind ($\kappa\grave{\alpha}\gamma\grave{\omega}\ \gamma\acute{\alpha}\rho$). His terrible endurance had been like tempered
steel, but now its edge is blunted – by a woman, so that he has become
womanish and feels pity for her in her widowhood and for his orphan
son. The words are ambiguous and need not mean that he will save
them from a pitiable fate. This in fact he will not do, and such pity as
he feels does not dictate his action. That would indeed be to play the
woman; that would indeed be *aelpton*; and it does not happen. 'The
falseness of the pretence', writes A. M. Dale,[111] 'should be so strikingly apparent as to warn us against believing the rest of the speech.'
Everything, then, is at the mercy of time – everything but the
determination of Ajax. Nothing is unexpected – nothing except that
Ajax should change his mind.

Ajax says that he will go to the sea-shore, purify his defilements,

---

[110] Knox, *HS* 12–14; Perrotta 136.
[111] *Collected papers* 223. $\dot{\epsilon}\theta\eta\lambda\acute{\upsilon}\nu\theta\eta\nu$ is the impossible word, cf. Dirlmeier 313f. $\sigma\tau\acute{o}\mu\alpha$
is carefully chosen to indicate that it is his words only which are softened, but
there is surely an ambiguity here, *pace* E. Fraenkel, *MH* 24 (1967) 80 n. 4.: $\sigma\tau\acute{o}\mu\alpha$
relates to both the notions in 584 ($\gamma\lambda\tilde{\omega}\sigma\sigma\acute{\alpha}\ \sigma o\upsilon\ \tau\epsilon\theta\eta\gamma\mu\acute{\epsilon}\nu\eta$). The contrast
$\phi\rho\acute{\epsilon}\nu\epsilon\varsigma\ /\ \sigma\tau\acute{o}\mu\alpha$ (cf. Perrotta 153 n. 1: 'ci aspetteremmo invece, $\dot{\epsilon}\theta\eta\lambda\acute{\upsilon}\nu\theta\eta\nu\ \phi\rho\acute{\epsilon}\nu\alpha$)
would be too obvious, were it not cloaked by the ambiguity? Cf. Knox, *HS* 15:
'We can see, in the words he uses, the heart harden afresh, the sword regain its
edge.'

and so escape the heavy wrath of the goddess. He says that he will hide this sword of his, digging a hole in the earth, and will place it in the safe-keeping of night and Hades; and he blames the sword for his misfortunes, since it was the gift of his great enemy Hector and, after he received it, he had no good of the Argives. Ajax may have believed that by a ritual purification he could be rid of Athena's wrath, the cause of which is not yet clear to the audience and will never be to him; to him her wrath had been shown by his delusion and the frustration of his vengeance – it was essentially connected with his attack upon the flocks, the blood of which he will now, so he says, wash off. He may have believed that the gift of Hector was somehow responsible for his troubles; and he affects to believe that, if he gets rid of it, his relations with the Greeks will improve. Ajax believes that his troubles were caused, not in any way by himself, but by the wrath of Athena and the malice of the Greeks; and the two actions which he announces – the purification and the hiding of the sword – aim, ostensibly, at restoring relations with his enemies divine and human. 'And so, for the future, I shall know to yield to the gods, I shall learn to reverence the Atridae' (666f.).[112]

Ajax speaks of yielding (εἴκειν) to the gods, reverencing (σέβειν) the kings. Surely he should have reversed the verbs.[113] He uses of the gods a word he might have used of men: though not in itself at all blasphemous, it suits the lack of deference that appears in all the utterances of Ajax to and about the gods. He uses of the Atridae a word appropriate to gods, which therefore admits an extreme claim to royal authority, which, if it is barely tolerable by normal Greek standards, was impossible for Teucer to admit and must be impossible for Ajax.[114] If there is anything in the speech which betrays its 'insincerity', it is this choice of words. He then reverts to the normal word: 'They are rulers (ἄρχοντες), so that one must yield (ὑπεικτέον)' (668).

[112] The force of τοιγάρ (666) can perhaps be seen, if we realize that the gods and the Atridae at 666f. balance the goddess and the Argives at 654–65. 'And so' – having put paid to the past by purification ceremonies (the gods) and by burying the sword of Hector (fatal to his relations with the Greeks) – 'for the future' . . . he will take up an attitude of submission to both gods and Atridae.

[113] Cf. e.g. Knox, HS n. 85; Kitto, FMD 189 (contr. Fraenkel, Sem. 21).

[114] For Teucer's reaction see esp. 1097ff., on which see p. 64 below. The word σέβειν is used twice by Creon in the Antigone, in a political context, in both cases (166, 744) of reverencing the office rather than the man. In the Oresteia σεβίζειν at Agam. 258 is insincere, not so at 785 (cf. σέβας at Cho. 54).

Ajax amplifies his reason for yielding. The horizons expand, and we return to the breadth of vision – the cosmic scale – of the opening lines of the speech, which spoke of time, of the growth and decay which takes place within it, of the breaking of what appeared most strong.[115] There we had time, now we have the regular successions of nature which are the measures of time. These are formidable things, the strongest things in the world, and yet they yield to dignities, to prerogatives, to τιμαί. Why then should not Ajax yield? (And we remember that his whole life had been based upon the emotions which surround τιμή; that he was bent on suicide because he felt himself *atimos*.) Winter gives place to summer, night to day, storm to calm, sleep to waking. 'How shall *we* not learn to be *sophrones*?' (677).

If the speech returns to the cosmic themes of the opening, there is a curious difference in the argument. Jebb refers, not unnaturally, to the famous speech of Ulysses in *Troilus and Cressida* about 'degree'; and the word τιμή might in itself suggest a hierarchy of kings and lesser princes and squires, each with his own defined status. And indeed it is the rational train of Ajax's words that he will now recognize the paramount authority of the Atridae. Yet what seems at first to be an argument for discipline in terms of hierarchy[116] turns out to move in a quite different range of ideas: the basic theme is not hierarchy but alternation. It is true that the elemental forces have their own privileged spheres of operation and do not encroach upon one another's, but this is in no way analogous to the relationship between Ajax and the Atridae. One must ask what reason Sophocles had for departing so radically from this analogy. It is not enough to say that the sole link is that of yielding, though it is of course significant and effective (and corresponds to the opening) that, whereas the great powers of nature yield, Ajax will not yield.[117]

Observe, then, that in each case cited from the realm of nature there is a change from 'bad' to 'good': from winter with its snows to the

---

[115] The two passages are linked: 669 (τὰ δεινὰ καὶ τὰ καρτερώτατα) recalls 650 (ὃς τὰ δείν᾽ ἐκαρτέρουν τότε).

[116] So taken by Rosenmeyer, *MT* 184: 'For without a hierarchy, without a chain of command, the world would collapse.'

[117] Nor is it enough to say – what may well be true – that Sophocles has deliberately used language which might recall to an Athenian audience the succession of magistrates in the Athenian constitutional system (cf. Knox, *HS* 23f.). Magistrates did indeed yield annually to their successors, but there is a gulf between this and the regular reciprocal alternations in nature of which Ajax is made to speak.

fruits of summer; from dreary night to the white horses of the day; from storm to calm; from the fetters of sleep to the freedom of waking life.[118] It is characteristic of summer and winter, day and night, sleep and waking, that they are in regular alternation. But the night of death is irreversible, the sleep of death is endless. Is Ajax then moving from storm to calm, from darkness to light? From the storm which has already been used as metaphor of his mental plight?[119] The Chorus will greet his supposed change of heart as the bright light of fair weather (708f.). But it had not taken place. Perhaps the question is not so much whether Ajax will yield to the Atridae as whether Ajax sick will yield to Ajax sound. 'How shall *we* not learn to be *sophrones*?' But he has not learnt; the storm intensifies, and he leaves the sunlight for the endless night of death (856ff.).

In the next six lines of the speech (678ff.) the notion of change – of alternation – is applied to human affairs, to friendship and enmity. Though those too are polar opposites, this might seem an abrupt descent from the cosmic level of the preceding passage; and it is abruptly introduced.[120] By returning to the cosmic themes of its opening the speech had seemed to be on the way to a close; and the final line of the passage appears definitive. Yet what follows is perhaps the most significant section of the whole speech. For it shows us not only that Ajax will die, but the spirit in which he will die: it implies

[118] Cf. Kitto, *Poiesis* 181; Lattimore, *PGT* 70 n. 22 (on 674f.); Gellie 12.

[119] 206f., 257f., 351–3. See Stanford's App. C, 275f., for the symbolism of storm, and of light and darkness. I cannot agree that when Ajax hails the light of the sun in his closing words (845ff.), 'Sophocles is making it clear that in the end Ajax has reached the light again' or that 'the ultimate triumph of Ajax's great-heartedness is reflected in his last great invocations to the light'. Such a conclusion seems quite at variance with the general tone of the speech and, in particular, with his invocation of the Erinyes. He is bidding farewell to the light he has rejected (or which has rejected him), and now he is 'for the dark'. H. Musurillo, *The light and the darkness* 10–11, calls attention to the symbolism. 'The light and the dark express the two sides of Ajax's nature', but it is going too far to say that 'in his saner moments, Ajax recognizes the two sides of his character' under this imagery (citing 394ff.).

[120] The word σωφρονεῖν at 677 is the meeting-point of two different, but not unrelated, meanings. It implies not only the acceptance of discipline (reverting in ring-composition, as Kamerbeek points out, to 666–8) but also the abandonment of his turbulent hatred and so leads into 678ff. On that passage cf. *BICS* 26 (1979) 2f., where the textual problem of 678 is discussed and it is suggested that the varying use of singular and plural for the first person may be a clue to its solution.

'his final reassertion of hatred, his passionate vindication of the old heroic code'.[121]

For to yield to the Atridae would be not only an unthinkable acceptance of inferiority and discipline but also the surrender of a view of friendship and enmity upon which he had based his life. In his code, which was the heroic code, friends and enemies – and the duty to love the one and hate the other – had an importance close to – and closely related to – the notion of honour (*timē*). How can he accept humiliation? How can he be reconciled to his 'false' friends? To the first question he had already given an answer which is no answer: he answers the second now. He has come to realize, he says, that friendship and enmity are not the absolutes he had supposed: enemies will become friends and friends enemies, and our actions must be governed by this prospect, so that neither friendship nor enmity must be pushed to an extreme. When Ajax appeared to be surrendering his ideal of personal honour, there was a note of exaggeration – in his talk of 'reverencing' the kings – which cast doubt on his sincerity. When he speaks of friendship and enmity, he runs from one extreme to another. He affects to see those attitudes which were once kingpins in a structure of values as a matter of mere alternation, like the phenomena of nature. This is a sort of *sophrosune*, and it can be mean.

There was a maxim attributed to Bias of Priene to the effect that men should 'love as if they would one day hate and hate as if they would one day love'. This maxim was susceptible to a prudential and to a cynical interpretation: it is quoted by Aristotle to illustrate that mistrust which experience has bred in the elderly.[122]. It is mean, if it detracts as much from friendship as from enmity; it is mean as Ajax expounds it, saying that services should be restricted by the knowledge that friends may turn enemies. Is this the *sophrosune* that Sophocles is supposed to have preached, that the gods love, and that Odysseus exemplifies? The exemplification by Odysseus, which must certainly have been in the mind of Sophocles at this point, is crucial. There is indeed irony in the fact that at the end of the play the arch-enemy of Ajax will act as a friend. But he did not act on a cynical calculation; he did not hedge his bets or cease to be the loyal and dependable friend of the Atridae (which alone made his support of

[121] This is well brought out by Knox, *HS* 28, from whom these words are quoted.
[122] *Rhet.* 2.13.4, cf. 2.21.13. On the Bias maxim see Jebb's Appendix p. 231; von Fritz 246; Knox, *HS* 10, 17; and *BICS* 26 (1979) 3.

Ajax effective). 'I hated', he says, 'when to hate was honourable (*kalon*)' (1347). He acted as a friend, at some risk to himself, because the Atridae pushed enmity too far, beyond the bounds of religion and humanity.[123] He still remained a friend to the Atridae, while becoming (within this context) the friend of Teucer. This is perhaps unheroic, perhaps politic: it is wise and humane.

A very different change of front was in the mind of Ajax. In his view, his Greek friends had turned enemies, at the Judgement of the Arms; and, as an enemy, he had gone out before the play opened to kill them. They have changed, and he has changed, but the notion that the attitudes of friendship and enmity should be modified by the possibility of such mutation is abhorrent to him. Beneath the surface of a cynical maxim rankles a regret that he should ever have served such false friends and burns a determination to press his hatred to the uttermost extreme.

Now at last he turns to Tecmessa and to his comrades and gives them his orders.[124] They are peremptory and expressed in language containing an extraordinary accumulation of dental consonants.[125] It seems that Sophocles may have used this phonetic device to indicate the suppressed passion of Ajax surging beneath the words of outward resignation. 'Do you do what I tell you, and perhaps you may hear that, though now I am in misfortune, I have been saved' (691f.). Saved in what sense? Saved by the salutary mind, by *sophrosune* (677)? Or kept safe below, like his sword (660), in the night of Hades? The word is picked up in the following scene (779).

Has Ajax changed? If so, it is not in his emotions – that is proved by his suicide-speech. But are we to say that he has come to a new

---

123 See p. 66 below.

124 His true friends, for he still believes in friendship, though the circle has narrowed. It may not be accidental that he is made to use ἑταῖροι (687) after ἑταιρείας (683): see Stanford ad loc.

125 Noted by Kirkwood, *SSD* 218, and Stanford. Attaching emotional significance to alliteration is a slippery and subjective business. It is generally held that, at *O.T.* 370f., the dental consonants are expressive of anger. In this play, apart from 684ff. (esp. 687f.), we have (both from Ajax) 105f., which could be an expression of cruel rage, and 527f. *Trach.* 445–7 may be worth noting, since there too we have a character suppressing emotion (in that case, it may be, striving desperately to believe that what she says is true). Sophocles had set himself a difficult task in writing a speech which should deceive Tecmessa and the Chorus, but should not deceive – or not wholly deceive – the audience. He may have hoped that the actor, with the aid of phonetics, could at this point provide the audience with more than an inkling of the truth.

understanding of the world? To a 'moment of unclouded vision', as Knox puts it?[126] To the realization of a mutable world, in human affairs as in nature, which he did not understand before and to which he must take up a position? That the mind of Ajax was simple before the series of emotional crises which began with the Judgement of the Arms, but that now he has pondered and reflected and knows the only action he can take?[127] We have seen him in his delusion, in his passionate response to humiliation and frustration, in his grim decision that he must kill himself in order to prove that he is *eugenēs*. Nowhere is there great philosophic depth, but no suggestion (as with Teucer[128]) of intellectual inadequacy. In the *Trugrede* we see something like a philosophic mind, with a power to generalize, but at the same time a narrow vision and a limited self-knowledge. Is it Ajax or Sophocles who is the philosopher?

Perhaps it does not matter greatly how we answer that question. What matters is that Ajax recognizes the principle of mutability in the world and will have none of it. It is no world for him, and he will take himself out of it: he will surrender his *Eintrittskarte*.[129] Then so much the worse for the world. This we might say of some tragic suicides: but do we say it of Ajax? What matters is that we should determine, if we can, the tone of his rejection, the tone of his farewell. Regret, that 'his pride has put it beyond his power to respond to Tecmessa's cry, even when he would'?[130] An actual *sophrosune*, as a yielding to the gods and the Atridae – the only form of yielding that is possible for him?[131] Apprehension, since he knows the power of time and is determined to forestall it?[132] Or is it simple pride?

---

[126] *HS* 10.

[127] von Fritz 251.

[128] See p. 61 below.

[129] Sicherl (1) 21f.; (2) 77 (citing Dostoevsky).

[130] Kitto, *FMD* 191.

[131] This view of the speech has been developed in detail by Sicherl (1) and (2), for whom Ajax tells the truth throughout, but a truth which his auditors are incapable of comprehending. It is only through death, however, that he can show his newly gained *sophrosune* and make his peace with the gods and with the Atridae; his death *is* for him summer, light and tranquillity. This view is incompatible with the tone and content of the Suicide Speech; and this appears most clearly in S.'s treatment of 679–82. 'He complies with this law [the Bias-maxim] by dying: for when he is dead, he will cease to hate his enemies, and they will cease to hate him.' Does the man who believes this invoke the Erinyes against those enemies?

[132] Biggs 227: 'He knows that time has the power to make him betray himself, and

Time changes everything, nothing is unexpected: everything except the resolve of Ajax, nothing except that Ajax should change his mind. An Ajax bent on death proclaims his exemption from proverbial truth. Let his action be determined by pity for Tecmessa? That would be womanish and unthinkable, and so pity and all sense of mutual obligation are thrust away. Yield to the gods? Who have shown their hostility and to whom he has disclaimed all indebtedness (589f.)? *Honour* the Atridae who have wronged him irreparably? Pass from storm and darkness to calm and light? No, he has been rejected by the world of light and longs passionately for the dark world to which he now belongs. Be *sophron*? Not in *their* sense. Abandon his enmity, in favour of a principle of mutability which he deliberately states in its meanest form? Never, he will go on to the end hating his friends turned enemies and will leave them with a curse.

Ajax dies in the spirit of that final speech, the same Ajax that he ever was; and it is the same spirit that allows itself to appear throughout his earlier speech of apparent submission. His courage we take for granted; that his pride rules out self-pity we can admire. He is a tremendous figure – tremendous and horrifying. He is horrifying as the obsessed are always horrifying, when they have soared or sunk out of contact with humanity. He leaves a world to which he has ceased to belong; and when he bids farewell to the light and to all the places of his greatness and his fall, we extend to him the pity for which he does not ask, and which he does not receive from the gods.

Our minds may return to the words of Athena, when she said that the gods love the *sophrones* but hate the base (*kakoi*). It was an extraordinary choice of words – much odder in Greek of the fifth century than it can sound in any English translation. The *kakos* is the bad, the base, the coward; and it is an astonishing word to apply (even by implication) to a supreme exemplification of heroic *arete*, to an ἀνὴρ ἄριστος.[133] It can only suggest that the *arete* of Ajax was

---

so he takes his decision before it is too late.' A not unattractive view, but I am not sure that Ajax knew this, though Sophocles did (cf. *O.C.* 437ff. and p. 43 above). Miss Biggs writes: 'The man who can live for even a few hours with his first humiliation has survived the worst.' But long brooding (cf. 193) had only intensified the resentment of Ajax at the Judgement of the Arms.

[133] Cf. Adkins, *MR* 172ff. The normal use of κακός is found in the words of Ajax at 456. Athena's use, in relation to Ajax, remains very striking, even if it can be paralleled. Adkins quotes two instances from *O.C.* (a late play), neither of which is quite parallel. On *O.C.* 270ff. he writes: 'Here again *kakon* is (implicitly)

frustrated, even nullified, by his utter lack of mental balance, of self-knowledge, of *sophrosune*. And that was his tragic fate.

opposed to *dikaios*.' But the point is actually more subtle: the contrast lies with παθὼν ἀντέδρων, and it is a mark of the *agathos* (and of the *dikaios*?) to retaliate a wrong: how then can he be regarded as κακὸς φύσιν? At *O.C.* 919f. it is a matter of *paideusis*: the injustice consists in seizing suppliants and not behaving properly as a *xenos*, both matters covered by the old code. Prior to Sophocles, we find κακοί characterized by lawlessness and injustice at Aesch. *Suppl.* 402ff. (cf. Adkins, *MV* 113).

CHAPTER THREE

The burial of Ajax

With the suicide of Ajax something has reached completion, not only an action but the revelation of a mind which accounts for that action. The play begins again, with a new Parodos. The Chorus re-enters in two groups, searching; and the scene has justly been compared with the searchings of Odysseus at the beginning of the play.[1] What was Odysseus looking for, and what did he find? He was looking, as ever – so Athena says – for some way to get at his enemies: what he found was an object-lesson in the frailty of human fortunes, he found Ajax in an aspect with which he had not reckoned. With the suicide this lesson is complete. The Chorus and Tecmessa lament. Something is over, but something is about to begin. Enter Teucer: a new character, a new tracker (997), brought by a new *phatis* (978), a new *baxis* (998); and his entry leads into a new issue. Ajax must be buried; and upon the burial of Ajax the whole of the remainder of the play turns.

It is an old problem. Does, or does not, interest go out of the play with the death of Ajax? Not, perhaps, if we use our eyes and see the corpse, with a child and a woman in attendance; not, perhaps, if we use our imaginations to enter into a Greek preoccupation (which we are, oddly, supposed not to share) with the disposal of a dead body. Sophocles was fully competent to maintain the interest and wrote scenes which are effective even upon the modern stage. It is sometimes said that the second part of the play is necessary in order to rehabilitate Ajax; and it is sometimes added that this is because he was a great Attic cult-hero, as though Athenian feeling would not have tolerated it, if he had been left humiliated and unburied.[2] The value of

---

[1] See Kamerbeek on 874. The first speech of Athena is full of words of seeing: then, at the end of the scene, 118 (ὁρᾷς), 125 (ὁρῶ). Cf. 876–8; 992–1004.

[2] Cf. e.g. Adams 23–6; Rosenmeyer, *MT* 187; contr. A. C. Pearson, *CQ* 16 (1922)

this point is not easy to estimate. One must, moreover, ask in what sense he is rehabilitated.[3] In the sense, certainly, that this proud man obtains a recognition of his services grudgingly conceded to the advocacy of his greatest enemy, which is ironical. It is the tribute of Odysseus which, if anything, might be said to constitute rehabilitation. Yet this tribute establishes nothing we did not know. Odysseus testifies to his *arete* (1357); it is a brave man's corpse (1319); after Achilles he was the best man (1339–41) that came to Troy. All which in itself implies nothing whatever except that his prowess as a fighting-man was outstanding. In this respect Odysseus places him next to Achilles, that is above himself. And here we return to an issue on which interpreters are deeply divided. Is this not an admission that the Judgement had been unjust?[4] Sophocles must have meant his

129; Kitto, *FMD* 182f. P. H. Burian, 'Supplication and hero cult in Sophocles' *Ajax*', *GRBS* 13 (1972) 151–6, points to the remarkable combination of motifs at 1168–84, where the child Eurysaces not only guards the corpse but also places himself as a suppliant under its protection; he suggests that this ceremony enacts, at least symbolically, the consecration of Ajax as a *heros*. If there is a hint of hero-status here, it would not seem to have much prominence. It is not so much that a burial in the Troad lacks relevance to Attica: locality could be important, as in the case of Oedipus, but the fact that the only known tomb of Ajax was far away did not prevent him from having cults in Salamis and Athens or from exercising powers of protection there. The point is rather that there is so little hint in the play of that posthumous power to help and to harm on which *Oedipus Coloneus* is as insistent as *Ajax* is reticent. 'We can read what Sophocles did say; are we to neglect that in favour of what he did *not* say?' So Kitto in *YCS* 25 (1977) 322 at the end of a pungent paragraph which seems to me adequately to dismiss that over-emphasis on the notions of 'rehabilitation' and 'consecration' found, for instance, in the same issue in Sicherl (2) 97f.

[3] Torrance 276: 'Though his heroism, his *arete* (1357), has won him a degree of vindication, that vindication is valid, and could exist, only in the eternal changelessness of death, for the terms on which it rests are incompatible with the flux which is life . . . What has happened to Ajax, his crime and his fall, has not been undone, and could not have happened otherwise.' He criticizes the exaggerated terms of Whitman 63, 68, 72. This is not to deny that the worse the Atridae behave the more the sympathies of an audience turn away from them and towards Ajax, which is a not uncommon dramaturgical effect. Compare the reaction in favour of Pentheus at the end of *Bacchae* (esp. 1308ff.); and something similar happens in *Agamemnon* (esp. 1489ff.). The mourning figures of Tecmessa and Eurysaces contribute to this movement, and so do the words of the Chorus at 1211ff.

[4] Cf. e.g. Adams 34, 36; Perrotta 137; Whitman 72; I. M. Linforth, 'Three scenes in Sophocles' *Ajax*', *U.Cal. Publ. in Class. Phil.* 15 (1954) 25; Ronnet 78f. The best statement of this case is by Knox, *HS* 23. Contr. Kirkwood, *SSD* 72. There are two separate issues: whether the Judgement was rigged, whether it was (by heroic standards) unjust.

audience to think of the Judgement at this point, because he twice uses
the word *atimazein*: Odysseus says not only that it would dishonour
Ajax, unjustly, to refuse him burial (1342) but also that he would not
dishonour him by denying that, after Achilles, he was best of the
Argives (1339). And it was precisely the *atimia* that drove Ajax to
attempt murder and to commit suicide. Yet Odysseus had accepted
the Arms, though we need not believe with the Ajax-party (and with
Pindar)[5] that he had intrigued for them. Nor perhaps was he called
upon, within the play, to say whether the Greeks were right or
wrong, nor, if he had said they were wrong, would he have advanced
his immediate cause. Nevertheless, Sophocles has used his words to
suggest, at this late stage, that the Judgement was unjust. It was unjust
on one assumption, which Ajax makes: that the contest was in point
of *aristeia* (443), that the sole criterion was *arete* in the narrow
traditional sense which Ajax exemplified. If the judges applied
another criterion, they were moving perceptibly out of the old heroic
world. And the play itself so moves.

That it moves into a fresh environment after the suicide of Ajax is
clear enough. The first part is played mainly within the inner circle of
Ajax and his friends[6] – entirely so, if it were not for the Prologos and
for the Messenger's speech. With these exceptions, our view of the
wider world of the Greek army as a whole comes to us through the
eyes of Ajax, Tecmessa and the Chorus. They think Odysseus is a
heartless villain, but we, from the Prologos, know that he is not. The
impression which we gain from the Messenger is ambiguous: the
attack made upon Teucer was an understandable reaction to Ajax's
own assault upon the Greeks, yet the tumult was composed by the
diplomacy of elders. Calchas was friendly, but he had separated
himself from the circle of the chieftains. Ajax thought that the Greeks
would kill him, and he may have been right. We do not know. He
thought that the Judgement was corrupt, rigged by the Atridae at the
instance of Odysseus, which is what he was bound to believe. We do
not know anything, except that Odysseus is wise and humane. What,
then, shall we learn when we are taken out of this Ajax-dominated
atmosphere into a larger world?

---

[5] Pindar, *Nem.* 8.25ff. In the *Nekuia* (*Od.* 11.543ff.), when Odysseus saw the shade
of Ajax, he wished that he had never won the Arms, but said nothing about the
justice of the award.

[6] See p. 24 above.

We shall learn nothing new about Ajax, but a great deal about Teucer, Menelaus, Agamemnon and Odysseus, when the unburied corpse of the hero (as that of Polynices in *Antigone*) provokes the behaviour of others for good or ill.[7] The interest moves, but perhaps we need not say that it moves to a disparate theme. In the first part of the play Sophocles had been extracting tragic implications from the old heroic code of honour. The political and social background was almost exclusively Homeric;[8] and against it we see an Ajax who embodies the old heroic *arete*, but carries it to a point that is more than Homeric, with a logic that has nothing to do with reason. No mitigations are accepted; and heroic self-sufficiency is shown in the process of destroying itself. For how can this ideal be reconciled with social life? A contradiction is revealed inherent in the code between its social and its individualistic aspects. The individual strives to be outstanding and to obtain the greatest possible prestige, but it is only within a community and in the eyes of his fellows that the prestige can be won.[9] If his claims are uncompromising – and not admitted, he can only cut himself off from the community; and this is what Ajax did, first by his attack upon the Greeks, and then by his suicide; and in the interval lived in a private world. In these circumstances, it will be noted, no appeal to *aidos* can have meaning. As Adkins writes: 'It must be such *aidos* which holds Homeric society together, in so far as it is

---

[7] On the burial-issue Letters 133ff. is answered by Kitto, *FMD* 181f. On *Ant.* see p. 120 below.

[8] Except, perhaps, that the reference to the position of the Atridae at 668 anticipates the later debates. See Stanford ad loc. and p. 283 n. 3, though I cannot follow him all the way. See also Knox, *HS* 23, but, if there is any hint here at Athenian magistracies, it cannot be a very strong one, for reasons given at p. 50 above.

[9] A. W. H. Adkins, *JHS* 89 (1969) 7–21, has some illuminating remarks on 'the psychological pressures of living in a shame- (or results-) culture' (p. 18) as reflected in Homeric vocabulary. 'Not good intentions, but results, are demanded of the Homeric ἀγαθός, in all his activities: he is constantly faced, or threatened, with a demand that he should succeed in doing what he cannot do; and a psychological response of frustration, distress and anger, all confused together, seems not inappropriate to his situation' (p. 15). M. Simpson, *Arethusa* 2 (1969) 88ff., has a good reference (p. 92) to 'the potential for chaos within the heroic world' and 'the contradiction inherent in heroic society'. I cannot follow him, however, when he suggests that Ajax's madness (in taking animals for men) is the product of conflict, the Atridae and Odysseus being at once both friends and enemies, creating an impasse, an unbearable contradiction, so that he opts out of reality. Ajax is too monomaniac for this, his sense of honour so hypertrophied that, after the Judgement, his attitude towards them switches, completely and at once, to an extreme of enmity.

held together, for a society of *agathoi* with no quiet virtues at all would simply destroy itself.' And, Sophocles would seem to add, an *agathos* without the quiet virtue of *sophrosune* is liable, like Ajax, to destroy himself.

It was pointed out in the last chapter[10] how strange is the terminology of Athena's motto-couplet (132f.), what an extraordinary word *kakos* is to be used in connection with a supreme embodiment of heroic *arete*, how strong is the suggestion that his *arete* is frustrated, even nullified, by his utter lack of mental balance, of *sophrosune*. For the couplet, though general in expression, must bear upon Ajax; and its significance, in terms of divine hostility, only becomes clear when Calchas tells of his arrogance towards the gods. His rejection of divine help is a denial of human status. And it is precisely by acknowledging human status that Odysseus shows his *sophrosune* and wins approval from the gods.

The role of Odysseus, then, at the end as at the beginning of the play, is in a pattern with that of Ajax. Teucer too is in the pattern, because he is an Ajax-substitute – and a poor one. His attitudes and preconceptions are those of Ajax, though he is not called upon to carry them to an extremity. If his loyalty and courage are appealing, his inadequacy is pathetic.[11] The real difficulty in the closing scenes is to understand the Atridae and what they stand for. Foils to Odysseus, they are also foils to Ajax; and this is not simply because they are lesser men, but because they belong to another world.[12] With them a

---

[10] See pp. 55f. above.

[11] Bowra 51 calls Teucer's answer to Menelaus 'intellectually inadequate', which it is, not so much because he fails to dispose of the latter's arguments, but because of the almost hysterical way in which he rejects the notion of discipline. Indeed one gets throughout his part an impression of pervasive intellectual inadequacy. Note the cheap sarcasm of 1093ff., the futile exercise of 1150ff. (on which see n. 21). And it is all part of a characterization which deserves careful study as an example of Sophocles' skill in conveying character by tone of voice as well as by what is said. Teucer is insecure and on the defensive, rendered so by his bastardy, his bowmanship, and by having lived under the shadow of Ajax now dead. Torrance 279 sums him up well: 'Yet Teucer, though our sympathies lie with him, is not a character to command deep admiration. He is too small, too rigid, too vitriolic; he lacks vision and stature.' Torrance also points out how heavily the emphasis of this last part of the play falls upon *words*. (To his references one might add 1096, 1107, 1110, 1116.)

[12] Kirkwood, *HSA* 56: 'There is not the slightest trace of Homeric quality in either one of the Atridae'; and he adds: 'Agamemnon . . . is an Athenian, not a Homeric, conception.'

Teucer can make no effective contact, but an Odysseus can. For Odysseus too – and this has been freely recognized by critics, though with differing emphasis – belongs to a world which has passed beyond the primitive heroism of an Ajax. A more modern world, we may say; and it could be a function of the second part of the play to relate ideas developed in its earlier phase to later Greek experience.[13] But what aspects of that – or any other experience – are represented by a Menelaus or an Agamemnon and developed in these two wrangles, both characterized by vulgarity?[14]

Menelaus begins his long speech with a statement of acknowledged facts, but one which omits, ungenerously, all the services which intervened between the coming of Ajax to Troy and his attack upon the Greeks. This attack, which he calls the *hubris* (1061) of Ajax, had been diverted upon the flocks by the action of a god. Missing the point of the divine intervention, he draws from the facts the wrong conclusion – that Ajax should not be buried. At the end of his speech, after a disquisition upon authority, he appears to shoot off at a tangent. 'These things', he says (1087f.), 'go by alternation (παραλλάξ). Formerly *he* was hot and outrageous (ὑβριστής), now it is my turn to have big thoughts.' Menelaus is looking at *hubris* as a reciprocal process;[15] and all the goddess has done is to put him in a position to be hubristic in his turn, to have great thoughts (as Ajax had had great thoughts). The Coryphaeus makes an incisive comment: Menelaus has laid down wise principles, but should not himself outrage (ὑβριστής) the dead (1091f.).

Principles he has indeed laid down in a passage which could well be the most significant element in his speech; and we should ask ourselves why Sophocles gave him an excursion into political theory which moves right out of the heroic context. Menelaus insists on the need for discipline in army and *polis,* and for this discipline to be based upon fear (δέος, σέβας) and respect (αἰδώς, αἰσχύνη). If he is himself paying lip-service to *aidos,* if by *aidos* he means respect for his own authority and by fear means fear of his own and his brother's power,

---

[13] The point is made by J. Kott, *The eating of the gods* (London 1974) 72.

[14] On the duplication see Gellie 23–6. On the vulgarity of Menelaus see Fraenkel, *Sem.* 34–6.

[15] Foreshadowed by the language of 1058–61 and re-emphasized by 1089f. Kamerbeek may be right to see a relationship between ἐνήλλαξεν (1060) and παραλλάξ (1087).

still the statement is in general terms. And it has naturally been compared with the similar argument advanced by Creon in *Antigone* (663ff.).[16] There Creon seems to be applying to the *polis* standards of discipline appropriate to an army; here Menelaus, where it is essentially a question of military discipline, is made to drag in the civil state: indeed his one reference to an army (1075) is enclosed between two references to a *polis* (1073, 1082).

Creon's speech in *Antigone* is not, however, the only – or the closest – parallel in Greek tragedy. When Menelaus stresses the role of fear, we ought not to forget – and Sophocles, whose thought never strayed far from Aeschylus, is likely to have had in mind – the song of the Erinyes, and the words of Athena, in *Eumenides*.[17] Erinyes and Athena, though they draw different conclusions, are at one that fear has a part to play in political life. Fear is well in its place, sing the Erinyes: it leads to *sophrosune* and respect for justice; the mean between anarchy and despotism is to be commended. Athena, constituting the Areopagus, rejecting both anarchy and despotism, advises her citizens not to cast all fear out of the city: τίς γὰρ δεδοικὼς μηδὲν ἔνδικος βροτῶν (*Eum.* 698f.). Justice depends on fear; the rightful fear of the Areopagus will be a bulwark of salvation to the city of Athens. If our present passage echoes the speech of Athena and the song of the Erinyes, the relevance must reside in the twinned rejections of anarchy and despotism in a context of the role of fear. There are two kinds of fear in the *Oresteia*.[18] There is the fear associated with the unreconciled Erinyes, with the retaliatory process that works through the resentments of individuals, which is endless and reciprocal. But there is also the salutary fear associated with the Areopagus and Athens. Menelaus may seem to be founding his argument on that second kind of fear, but by the end of his speech it has become clear that he is still actuated by the old vindictive principle; that the specious political theory is a mere façade; that the *sophrosune* (1075, cf. 1080) which he demands as a condition of political stability does not belong to him in his own person; that what he demands of right (1071f., δικαιοῦν) is absolute subordination to his own personal authority.

Just as Creon in *Antigone*, after his specious statement of principle,

---

[16] See p. 124 below.
[17] *Eum.* 516ff., 696ff. (cited by Jebb on 1076).
[18] Cf. de Romilly, *CA* passim.

is progressively revealed as a tyrant, so Menelaus – and after him his brother – are shown to be despotic. But is it fair to say that Teucer stands for anarchy? We turn to his reply for the answer, given in a characteristic Sophoclean accumulation of significant words. When this man of the Homeric world rejects the principle of supreme authority, not only is his tone almost hysterical, but in fourteen lines he uses fifteen words of rule (1097–110). Perhaps, then, it is a purpose of this episode to bring out a certain kinship between the old heroic anarchy and a post-heroic despotism (here masquerading as military and political discipline), both operating upon a similar emotional basis, productive of *hubris* and counter-*hubris*. Teucer's reply incites Menelaus to vulgarity, where before he had been ungenerous and hubristic: the old quarrel of the bowman and the hoplite is stagger-ingly irrelevant to the tragic issue.[19] But it serves to re-introduce the theme of boasting. 'Greatly would you boast, if you got a shield' (1122). 'When justice is with a man, he may have great thoughts.' Menelaus must answer this, and again we see that his notion of justice is essentially one of retaliation. The code demands retaliation upon an enemy,[20] and Menelaus assumes that this can – and should – be carried to the point of desecrating his dead body. The wrangle ends with an exchange of fables.[21]

The episode is self-contained and inconclusive: Menelaus is the lesser brother, and it is clear that the outcome of this confrontation will not be final. We wait for Agamemnon, whose entry is elaborately pre-pared. The child and the woman return to the stage after a long absence and are placed beside the corpse as suppliants, with locks of hair in their hands. A curse is pronounced upon the violator with the utmost formality of phrase and with a symbolic act of cutting. It is as

---

[19] But not irrelevant to the psychology of Teucer. Nor without a certain contem-porary interest, perhaps, cf. Bowra 53f.; N. O. Brown, *TAPA* 82 (1951) n. 23, though it is rash to use the evidence (his n. 17) for dating the play. See too Adkins, *MV* 65 7.

[20] Editors comment on Menelaus' use of the word πολέμιος at 1132 and his reply to Teucer's rejoinder: 'if he was not πολέμιος to me, at least he was ἐχθρός' (Jebb). Ajax did in fact conduct a sort of hostilities against the Greeks. Menelaus gives the wrong answer, not for the only time: he should have pleaded the hostilities of Ajax, but instead he speaks in terms of mutual private enmity.

[21] On this popular form, see E. Fraenkel (ed.), *Aeschylus' Agamemnon* (Oxford 1950) p. 774. Teucer's attempt to use it is characteristically incompetent: he merely describes the actual situation, substituting the third person for the first and second.

though the old world was mustering its religious forces to defend the hero's body. There is a long pause, Teucer absent, a tableau in the eye of the audience, the Chorus singing their nostalgic ode. We wait for Agamemnon – and for Odyssseus.

It is sometimes said that Agamemnon is a more impressive figure than his brother, with more authority, more dignity. More authority, certainly; more dignity, if it is more dignified to call your opponent a bastard than a bowman. One wonders, however, whether the entry of Agamemnon may not be a calculated disappointment, because he is so like his brother, the tone of the two scenes so similar. Vulgarity is still pervasive. But perhaps the most striking feature of Agamemnon's first speech is his complete disregard of the burial-issue as such. He is preoccupied with the issue of insubordination, which he affects to see in terms of a half-barbarian bastard, who is Teucer, defending an Ajax who, being dead, is nothing and who, alive, was deserving of no particular respect. Teucer replies with a courageous and just defence of Ajax against the gross under-valuation of Agamemnon but also, in defending himself against the stigma of bastardy, rakes up scandals of the house of Atreus. Again, a controversy quite irrelevant to the tragic situation. There is an impasse, and Odysseus must enter, since it is time the accents of nobility were heard. We are often told that Sophocles, by the great urbanity of his style, makes his heroes talk like gentlemen, which is true when a Philoctetes speaks with a Neoptolemus, an Oedipus with a Theseus. He can also, short of colloquialism, make them wrangle like stall-holders in the agora.

In his long speech, Agamemnon had written off Ajax as a *megas bous,* commending those of sound mind (οἱ φρονοῦντες εὖ, 1252). He could well be thinking of Odysseus. He goes on to warn Teucer that he will taste the same medicine, unless he acquires some sense (εἰ μὴ νοῦν κατακτήσῃ τινά). He is defending a dead man: ἀνδρὸς οὐκέτ' ὄντος ἀλλ' ἤδη σκιᾶς. But what man is more than a shadow? This is something that Odysseus knows (125f.) and which will lead him – the free man who comes to plead the case for Teucer (1260f.) – to defend the dead from outrage, which will be the supreme testimony to his own *sophrosune.* When Agamemnon speaks of *hubris* (1258) and *sophrosune* (1259), he has no perception that he commits the one and lacks the other, but the Coryphaeus sees it, when, listening to the final preposterous insult, he commends *sophrosune* to both participants (1264f.).

Odysseus enters to meet a certain situation, to achieve a certain purpose, towards which he must speak what the situation allows and the purpose demands. An Athenian audience, so sensitive to the arts of persuasion, will have observed the skill of this famous practitioner as he persuades Agamemnon to allow the burial of Ajax. To what world does *he* belong? Certainly to a world which reasons and argues.

His first utterance sets the tone. The corpse of Ajax is *alkimos nekros*; and it is the basic contention of Odysseus that the warlike services of Ajax should not be forgotten in his death. Since, however, the Atridae regard those services as nullified by his final acts, if indeed they are not seizing upon those acts as an occasion to disparage him, Odysseus must do more than restate the Ajax-tradition. After a preliminary dialogue which moves entirely within the heroic world,[22] he begins an argument of many strands. And his first point is that the refusal of burial is cruel, insensitive (1332f.).[23] It is an act of violence. Whereas Menelaus thought it shameful (1159f.) for those who had power not to use it, Odysseus implies that *bia* is something to be resisted (μηδὲ ... νικησάτω), as though a temptation to which holders of power are prone.[24] Superior force enables a man to carry personal hatred (ἐχθρός, 1355) a long way, but there is a point beyond which it should not be carried (which was not admitted by Menelaus). That point is delimited by justice (δίκη). But what does justice mean? Teucer and Menelaus saw it in different lights (1125f.), and Odysseus must amplify his argument: essentially he takes the side of Teucer. Since the Judgement of the Arms, Ajax had been most hating and most hated and therefore to be harmed, but not contrary to *dike*, which – the new world joining hands with the old?[25] – is presented in terms of *time*. To withold burial is to deprive a great hero (1340f.) of his due honour, and this Agamemnon cannot justly (ἐνδίκως) do: Ajax has done his duty (cf. 1282) and should have his rights.

Nothing so far about the gods, who are now introduced into the argument with an apparent lack of logic which must be deliberate. It is not *just* to dishonour Ajax (1342); it is not *just* to harm a good man,

---

[22] 1320–5. For retaliation in word as well as action, cf. pp. 222f. below (on *Electra*).
[23] ἀναλγήτως (1333, cf. 946) is reinforced by μὴ τλῆς.
[24] *Bia* implies a contrast with *peitho* and leads ultimately to the Aeschylean (and no doubt proverbial) paradox of 1353: yield to the persuasions of friends and you are still the master. Cf. Aesch. *Agam.* 943 (with Fraenkel's note).
[25] Cf. Rosenmeyer, *MT* 196.

when he is dead, however much you hate him (1344f.). In between
come the words: 'For it is not he, but the laws of gods, you would be
destroying' (οὐ γάρ τι τοῦτον, ἀλλὰ τοὺς θεῶν νόμους φθείροις ἄν). It is
not, however, *because* non-burial infringes divine law rather than
harms the dead man that it is *unjust* to dishonour him. At least not
obviously. Perhaps Odysseus sees a weakness in his case. Agamemnon
might answer: yes, he was a great hero, but his subsequent conduct
has wiped this out, so that it is now *just* to dishonour him. So
Odysseus slips in a reference to divine law which demands that the
dead be buried. The issue of justice is then re-stated, with the addition
of εἰ θάνοι. It is unjust to withold burial, because Ajax was *esthlos* (a
man of *arete*), because he is dead; and the concept of *dike* now
embraces the divine laws, which it is *right* to obey. The decree first
stigmatized as cruel is now seen as impious.

Odysseus thus opposes it, because it is cruel and an abuse of power,
because it is unjust in terms of *timē,* and because it is impious. But
Agamemnon is only interested in two points which touch him
personally:[26] the issue of authority (1350) and, above all, the issue of
personal enmity. (After all, Ajax had tried to kill Agamemnon.)
Friends and enemies: the theme is, as we shall discover, recurrent in
the plays of Sophocles. Sophoclean heroes – an Ajax, an Antigone, an
Electra, a Philoctetes, the Colonean Oedipus – live in a world polar-
ized between friends and enemies; and when some person passes, or
seems or seeks to pass, from one camp to the other, the experience is
traumatic and fraught with powerful emotions. Such a passage is
reciprocal. Ajax finds enemies in his old friends, and he becomes their
enemy.[27] Where does Odysseus stand?

'Do you fight for him against me?' asks Agamemnon. 'Yes, but I
hated him, when to hate was *kalon*' (1346f.). *Kalon* is a broad term of
praise for whatever is socially acceptable.[28] Agamemnon does not
see, any more than his brother, that trampling on the dead should be
excluded. So Odysseus repeats the word and tells him not to take
pleasure in 'gains that are not honourable' (κέρδεσιν τοῖς μὴ καλοῖς).
Such a revenge is the gratification of a passion and so a *kerdos,*[29] but it

---

26 As often in Sophocles, the use of emphatic or contrasted personal pronouns is
   worth noting: cf. 1346 and 1370–3. See Stanford on 1346ff.
27 See pp. 52f. above.
28 So commonly in tragedy, but Adkins, *MR* 43–5, points out that the use is not
   Homeric.
29 For the notion that revenge is a *kerdos,* cf. Aesch. *Sept.* 697, where there can be

is not *kalon*. In a closely similar context at *Ant.* 1056, Creon, who had taken a similar revenge, is rebuked by Teiresias, using the word *aischrokerdeia*, which he says is characteristic of the tyrant.[30] It is often alleged that, when Agamemnon replies that 'it is not easy for a tyrant to be pious (εὐσεβεῖν)', he is pleading *raison d'état*.[31] But this is wrong. Unlike his brother, Agamemnon does not indulge in political theory. Rather, it is a half-confession that the temptations of power are too much for him and a half-admission that there is an argument of *eusebeia* against him. In the end, however, it is not considerations of piety or justice, still less humanity, that weigh with him, but a calculation of the value of Odysseus' friendship.

Before he yields, he makes one more effort, reminding Odysseus of the kind of man to whom he is doing a service (1354); and the passage, rightly taken, is not without interest. Odysseus replies: 'The man is an enemy, but once was noble (γενναῖος).' 'What are you going to do? Are you respecting the body of an *enemy* so?' 'Yes, for *arete* weighs far more with me than enmity.'[32] 'Yet men like that are utterly capricious (ἔμπληκτοι) . . . Do you commend the acquisition of such friends?' It is surprising that the adjective ἔμπληκτος has so often been taken as referring to Odysseus,[33] whose friendship for the Atridae and its value are fixed points never called in question. Agamemnon is saying in effect: granted the one-time *arete* of Ajax, what value has it in point of friendship, when it can change in a moment to murderous

little doubt that the 'gain' in question is the killing of Polynices. Cf. *YCS* 25 (1977) 24–8.

30 See p. 126.

31 e.g. 'As a king, he must uphold the common weal, and punish treason' (Jebb); 'his position as commander-in-chief compels him to be inexorable' (Stanford). But cf. 1334f., as discussed above.

32 The sense of 1357 emerges from a corrupt text (cf. Dawe, *STS* 172). It is clear that ἀρετή looks back to 1355 (γενναῖός ποτ' ἦν), ἐχθρός to 1356 (ἐχθρόν); and the words are generally, and perhaps rightly, taken to refer to the ἀρετή and ἔχθρα of Ajax. Perhaps, however, they are so generalized as to apply equally to Odysseus, who feels it incumbent upon one *agathos* to recognize the merits of another. Teucer (1381ff.), addressing Odysseus as ἄριστος, praises him precisely for having defended Ajax against outrage, although he (Odysseus) was his greatest enemy.

33 Contr. Kitto, *FMD* 194, who without comment takes it, rightly, of Ajax. The point is argued in *BICS* 26 (1979) 3f. As to 1359, it has no more profundity in relation to the Ajax-situation than the hero's own words at 678ff., which it recalls (on which see pp. 52f. above). Greeks of this generation had doubtless been struck by the mutability of friendship and enmity between states (cf. also *O.C.* 610–15 and P.A. Brunt, *CQ* 19, 1969, 245). But what real bearing has this commonplace upon the megalomaniac reactions of a heroic Ajax?

attack? Are not such friends capricious and unreliable? The point is not without validity as a criticism of the unstable emotionalism of Ajax; and Odysseus cannot answer it, except with a trite generalization inviting a rejoinder which in its turn does not lack force. 'Do you commend the making of *such* friends?' Odysseus cannot answer this: he can only bring a charge of obstinacy against Agamemnon. For Agamemnon is stubborn in his way, like Ajax, but he has the sense to yield, as a favour to his valued friend (χάριν, 1371), though he yields with a bad grace and without responding to the humanity and piety of Odysseus.[34]

To examine the ideas, the standards, the mental processes, presented in the second half of the drama may not have been without value. In contrast to the cumulative revelation of the mind of Ajax which builds to a climax in the suicide, we have a variety of scenes and people and a more fluid play of thought: a Menelaus who propounds political theory, an Agamemnon who asserts authority tyrannically, an Odysseus who deploys every argument in favour of a generous cause; and, in the background of it all, the issue of vengeance, of retaliation, and how far it should be pressed. The range of ideas and values is partly Homeric – revenge, prestige, the polar opposition of friendship and enmity, the reciprocity of *charis*. It has been felt, however, that the second half of the play moves, to some extent, out of the Homeric context, though it is hard, for several reasons, to estimate this extent precisely. Not least, because there survived in the more sophisticated world of fifth-century Athens standards and emotional attitudes (including those listed above) which were inherited from an earlier age. When a late fifth-century Greek can accept the old definition of *arete* – doing good to your friends and harm to your enemies – as a definition of justice, it might seem that little has changed. Yet it *is* now a definition of justice, and justice has become problematic; and justice (δικαιοσύνη), along with *sophrosune*, is on the way to become a virtue (an *arete*).[35]

---

[34] Odysseus' 1365 (καὶ γὰρ αὐτὸς ἐνθάδ' ἵξομαι) of course recalls 124, the sentiment of which Stanford well describes as 'the enlightened egoism of classical humanism'. And I think that, in his notes on 1365–6 and 1367, Stanford is right that, for tactical reasons, Odysseus accepts the cynical interpretation placed by Agamemnon on his words, which actually implied the moral of 125f.

[35] It is defended as a defnition of justice by Polemarchus at Plato, *Rep.* 332d, 334b; it survives as a (partial) definition of *arete* at *Meno* 71e. For other references see

Justice is problematic – and fundamental – for Aeschylus. The ideal of *sophrosune* had come into being as an antidote to that abuse of power with which the emulous Greeks were only too familiar and had gathered force during the archaic period, with encouragement from Delphi. The fifth-century Athenians gave thought to these things. They also considered the problem of the state and the basis of its authority, distinguishing the arbitrary rule of the tyrant from the rule of law in oligarchy and democracy, yet conscious of the wide differences between these two latter forms, conscious too of the widely different climates of Sparta and Athens, as they gradually moved into a position of mutual hostility. All these things were discussed and debated both before and after the coming of the sophists; and we catch echoes of these debates in great literature – in Herodotus, naturally, and in the speeches of Thucydides, but also in the *Eumenides* of Aeschylus, the *Antigone* of Sophocles. It could be that the *Ajax* is an important document for a transitional period of Greek thought.

But it is not an easy matter to draw conclusions, because the body of evidence is so slight, and because of the nature of drama. What did Sophocles himself think about state-authority and the role of fear? He does not tell us, either here or in *Antigone*. Indeed, he has as it were short-circuited the issue in both plays, since the advocates of political discipline turn out to be tyrannically minded and the fine principles which they express go for nothing. In *Ajax,* in the scenes with Menelaus and Agamemnon, perhaps the most striking feature is the way in which the Atridae, despite some 'modern' language, prove to be actuated by the most traditional of motives. Sophocles might be thinking of the Greek tyrants, of whom there was a stereotyped picture; and yet tyranny, though a lively memory and a fear, was a remote issue in mid-fifth-century Athens. May it not be that he was not only conscious of the strong survival in his contemporary world

Knox, *HS* n. 12 on p. 29. When did *sophrosune* and *dikaiosune* become *aretai*? It is clear from Plato's dialogues that, in certain intellectual circles, they were so regarded in the latter part of the fifth century. E. A. Havelock, '*Dikaiosune*: An essay in Greek intellectual history', *Phoenix* 23 (1969) 49–70, calls attention to the rarity of pre-Platonic examples of the word; he suggests that the Herodotean instances, occurring in more or less dialectical contexts, derive from the debates of intellectuals, to whom we should ascribe the coinage of the term. (Theognis 147 cannot be dated.) The coinage, if it is one, though on normal lines, could, I suppose, have been made on the analogy of *sophrosune* at a time when the standing of both qualities was much under discussion.

of heroic values and attitudes, but also, as a tragic poet, aware of the disastrous consequences to which they might lead, not least when they masqueraded behind specious talk of justice and moderation? Thucydides knew this: so why not Sophocles?

There are Menelaus and Agamemnon; there is also Odysseus. The first half of the play begins with a searching Odysseus and discovers the nature of Ajax; the second half begins with the people of Ajax searching and ends with the discovery, to their astonishment, of an Odysseus who is emancipated from a self-destructive heroism without falling victim to an equally self-destructive despotism. If he belongs to a world which reasons and argues, it is not the world of *Realpolitik*, regardless of everything but power, regardless of religion and humanity, but a world which, because it acknowledges human status, possesses the virtue of *sophrosune*, a world which could look at friendship and enmity without the cynicism of a Bias or the frenzied emotionalism of an Ajax or a Teucer. Did Sophocles believe in the existence or the possibility of such a world? The question is unanswerable. But perhaps for Sophocles the most admirable thing about this Odysseus he put upon the stage was that, like Tecmessa, and no doubt like many ordinary Athenians, if few men in power,[36] he was capable of pity. That human pity wins a victory, that persuasion wins a victory over violence at the end of the play, is not the least striking feature of this Sophoclean tragedy. Such victories seem to have been a feature of the later trilogies of Aeschylus, but in the other extant plays of Sophocles it is rarely, if ever, that persuasion prevails for good.[37]

At the beginning of the preceding chapter, we considered the form of the play: the way in which the Ajax-tragedy is framed between two appearances of Odysseus, the theme of *sophrosune* being also prominent, through Calchas, in the centre of the play – a form which carries a dangerous temptation to over-simplify the interpretation in terms of a hubristic Ajax justly punished and, by contrast, an Odysseus who has the fine role. There is also a danger, not avoided by all critics, of playing-down the latter. He is, by comparison with the protagonist, unheroic, which is enough to damn him in the eyes of some. Yet he is admirable; he is humane and redeems a brutal

---

[36] I have in mind the Mytilenaean affair, when, as Thucydides tells us, the Athenians began to reflect that their decree was cruel and excessive; Cleon attempted to stifle their impulse towards mercy and Diodotus thought it unwise to answer him except upon his own ground (cf. *BICS* 12 (1965) 70–82).

[37] Cf. e.g. p. 274 below.

situation by his persuasions. And he is socially significant, if humanity
and reasonable persuasion have a part to play in society and politics.
When there are so few plays remaining (and dates are so uncertain),
one must hesitate to draw conclusions concerning any views which
Sophocles may have held at the time of writing this play about the
development of Greek, or specifically Athenian, society.[38] One cannot, however, help wondering whether, shown in the role of Odysseus, there was a hope – a trace of Aeschylean 'optimism' – which was
to be extinguished by the harsh experiences through which Sophocles
would live.

But the play is *Ajax* and rightly ends with Ajax – with the old
world, with burial-ritual and the inner circle of Ajax's friends, with a
curse and an Erinys. Teucer acknowledges that Odysseus is *esthlos*
(1300), a man of *arete*, astonished that the worst of enemies should
alone be ready to help, and should refrain from *hubris* towards his
dead enemy (1382ff.). But he cannot accept him to take part in the
burial. If this strikes the modern reader as ungenerous, it might not
have struck the average Greek spectator so.[39] In any case it is right
that Odysseus should leave the scene before the final procession,
should leave the dead Ajax alone with Teucer and the Chorus, with
his woman and his child. Odysseus does not belong.

---

[38] Various attempts have been made to relate the play to contemporary politics. N.
O. Brown, 'Pindar, Sophocles and the Thirty Years' Peace', *TAPA* 82 (1951)
1–28, argues that *Ajax* is Sophocles' answer to Pindar's interpretation of the
Ajax-myth. I find it hard to believe, however, that the Sophoclean Ajax stands for
the ideal of aristocratic *arete* practised in the first half of the fifth century by such as
Cimon. Brown's views are critically examined by V. Ehrenberg, 178–82 (App. C,
'A new historical interpretation of the *Ajax*'). See also J. H. Finley, 'Politics and
early Attic tragedy', *HSCP* 71 (1966) 1–13.
[39] Cf. W. K. Lacey, *The family in classical Greece* (London 1968) 148.

CHAPTER FOUR

Trachiniae

Only a minority of the extant plays of Sophocles can be firmly dated, which is tiresome. *Ajax*, with which we have opened, may well be, but is not certainly, the earliest; *Antigone* must have preceded 440 B.C. by a year or two. *Trachiniae*, though it cannot be placed in relation to either of those plays, probably belongs, more or less, to the same creative period;[1] and there is a convenience in taking it next. It shares with *Antigone* an important Sophoclean interest, often neglected, upon which *Trachiniae* throws a light which helps the interpretation of the other play. It shares with *Ajax* the phenomenon of a formidable male hero. If Ajax stood alone in the theatre of Sophocles, one might hesitate to find such repellent aspects in him. If, however, he is – apart from Theseus – the greatest of heroes with Athenian connections, there was a pan-Hellenic hero who might seem the very paradigm of heroism; and if we find some degree of kinship between Ajax and Heracles – a similar combination of great and repellent qualities – it may serve to confirm the view which has been taken of Ajax in preceding chapters.

Throughout in Sophocles the heroes, their nature and their fates, stand in a problematic relationship to the gods, with whom Ajax put himself in the wrong from the start. If it is true that the gods love the 'moderate', they cannot love Ajax and he is bound to destroy himself by his excesses. Heracles was the son of Zeus; and early in *Trachiniae* the Chorus of innocent girls, to console Deianira, had sung: 'Who has seen Zeus so careless for his children?' Towards the end of the play Hyllus, with a formal and emphatic antithesis,[2] calls upon his attend-

---

[1] On the dating of *Trach.* see App. G p. 341

[2] Made all the more arresting by the length and parallel formation of the contrasted words and also by the rarity of συγγνωμοσύνη, which is only found here.

ants to grant him *suggnomosune* (which means not just 'forgiveness', but entering sympathetically into his feelings) and to recognize at the same time the great *agnomosune* (or insensibility) of the gods. That Hyllus who has lost both mother and father in appalling ways should be bitter, that the son should find evidence of the heartlessness of the gods in Zeus's apparent disregard of paternal obligations,[3] need not surprise us. That Sophocles, if he was really so pious, so acceptant, so uninterested in theodicy as we have sometimes been told, should have permitted so loud a note of protest to be heard towards the end of his play is perhaps more surprising; and some scholars have therefore pointed to the actual closing words as though they modified or even contradicted the bitter complaint of Hyllus.[4] 'And there is none of these things that is not Zeus' (κοὐδὲν τούτων ὅ τι μὴ Ζεύς, 1278). But in themselves the words, whoever spoke them, are completely neutral. The destruction of Heracles, however we judge it, is attributable to Zeus.

The destruction of Heracles – and no less the destruction of that most appealing of Sophoclean women, so ill equipped (it might seem) for the role of tragic heroine, so lacking the strength of an Antigone or an Electra.[5] But should Deianira be called a heroine? The formal problem of the play has been much discussed: it is one of division, not unlike similar problems in *Ajax* and *Antigone,* but more acute.[6] *Ajax* falls into two parts but is united at least by the continuous presence of the hero, alive or dead. If Antigone drops out of her play two-thirds of the way through, Creon plays a central role throughout. In *Trachiniae* the entry of Heracles is postponed until the story of Deianira's suicide has been told, but he then dominates the last three hundred lines of the play. There is, thus, a problem of form, and it cannot be solved by calling Deianira a minor character.[7] There is, as

---

[3] αἰσχρά (1272) is not a general moral judgement but refers specifically to the shame brought on a parent who has failed his son; for a similar notion (in reverse) cf. *Ajax* 506ff.

[4] E.g. Bowra 158. The words are probably addressed by the Coryphaeus to the Chorus: that they are addressed to Iole, brought back as a silent witness of the final scene, is virtually unthinkable, cf. Kamerbeek on 1275; Gellie 286 n. 33. M. Vuorenjuuri, *Arctos* n.s. 6 (1970) 157f. is non-committal.

[5] Kirkwood, *SSD* 115 n. 17.

[6] Bowra 116; Gellie 53f.

[7] 'It is essentially a minor role that she plays in the *Trachiniae*' (Adams 109f.). Contr. Ronnet 45 (who reviews opinions in n. 2): 'Déjanire est incontestablement l'héroïne tragique.' Both wrong, cf. Gellie 285 n. 1; Perrotta 474f.

we shall see, a sense in which her tragedy is derivative from that of Heracles, but to call her a minor character disregards dramatic reality. Physically present upon the stage for so long, she is the focus of attention; her situation and personality are gradually and subtly revealed; she is led to a disastrous decision, being the only person who takes such a decision within the play, and to a suicide which is described at length. This is not the dramatic treatment of a minor character. She has her tragedy; it is expounded, developed and carried to completion before Heracles appears. The Nurse's comment at 943ff., with its proverbial pessimism, recalls the proverbial wisdom with which Deianira herself opens the play (1–3) and so rounds off that whole section which is primarily concerned with her tragedy.[8] The Nurse's words ring like the end of a play, but they are not the end of this play, which Sophocles has so written that it is not a sensible question to ask whether Deianira or Heracles is 'the central character'. It is a play – and the same is true of *Antigone* and *Philoctetes* – about two personages involved in a single situation; and the only question worth asking is how he has imposed unity upon a play with two central characters who never meet. The answer is a simple one: this is a tragedy of sex.

One must begin with Deianira who presents the easier aspect of the problem, for we only find ourselves in difficulty when we approach that nice apportionment of blame to which critics are so much more prone than dramatists. She is a prey to fear and capable of pity. Sophocles sometimes uses key-words or themes in the Aeschylean manner; and that is how he uses the notion of fear – and words of fear (ὄκνος, φόβος, ταρβεῖν, δεδοικέναι, and others) – in this play.[9] One might say that the rhythm of the first half of the play is the rhythm of Deianira's fears. The Prologos tells the story of a life of fears. First, fear of marriage to the monstrous river-god (7, 24). From this she was saved by Heracles, by the dispensation of Zeus Agonios, who brought the struggle to a good end. If it was truly good. For marriage to Heracles only caused her fear after fear (28), as he came and went on his labours. These labours are now surmounted, and her fears should be over. But they are not. 'Now when he has risen above those trials – now it is that my fears are strongest' (36f.); and she tells of his long and

---

[8] Whitman 107.
[9] Observed by Torrance 302.

sinister absence. This latest fear, set against a background of a whole
life of fears,[10] is also the theme of her long speech to the Chorus after
the Parodos, which ends with an emphatic twofold expression
(φόβῳ . . . ταρβοῦσαν, 176). Enter a citizen. 'Queen Deianira, first of
messengers I shall free you from fear' (ὄκνου σε λύσω, 180f.). Heracles
lives and is victorious. Another fear has proved illusory; now at least
everything will surely be well, and the first movement of the play
ends with a hymn of joy from the Chorus.[11] Enter Lichas, followed
by captive maidens; he tells his story. Note, then, how Deianira
responds. How should she not rejoice? And yet . . . 'for those who
take right views there is room to fear (ταρβεῖν) that he who prospers
may still come to grief' (296f.). Is there no satisfying this woman? Is
the habit of fear so engrained in her? And yet of course she was never
so right to fear as now – to fear not for Heracles but for herself; and
the evidence to justify her fears is actually before her eyes, though she
does not yet understand it. The ground she gives for her fear is Greek
proverbial wisdom – the instability of human fortune, which she
illustrates by reference to the fate of the captives. Ironically, the
instance of the general truth is also the particular danger that threatens
her. It is the sight of Iole and her companions that makes her afraid
(306). Her fear is mediated by pity (298).

When Deianira first saw the captives, she asked who they were: 'for
they are pitiable (οἰκτραί), unless their plight deceives me' (243). Now
she says: 'a strange pity comes upon me as I see them' (οἶκτος δεινός)
(298). Iole she pities above all, 'as she alone shows a due feeling for her
plight' (312f., ὅσωπερ καὶ φρονεῖν οἶδεν μόνη). Jebb's translation and
note seem to be on the right lines:[12] without knowing it, Deianira is
pitying Iole for possessing the same fine sensibility that she herself
possesses. She is pitying, moreover, one whose fate is parallel to her
own.[13] When the truth comes out, as it soon does, she still pities Iole,
'because her beauty has destroyed her life' (463ff.); and that was true,

---

[10] The Chorus refers to her fear at 108, where τρέφουσαν recalls 28 (ἀεί τιν᾿ ἐκ φόβου
      φόβον τρέφω) and suggests a constant fear, almost a quality of life. On τρέφειν in
      Sophocles see p. 37 n. 82 above. For the Parodos see App. A.

[11] On the song of joy cf. Beck 17, and on the theme of joy App. A.

[12] Contr. Kamberbeek, and Mazon's translation. But why should self-control on
      Iole's part cause Deianira to pity her more than the others? And why should
      Lichas' description of her demeanour during the journey be false? Least of all
      should this interpretation be supported by a reminder that Iole 'is entering
      Heracles' house as his mistress'.

[13] Easterling, *BICS* 63.

in a sense, of Deianira also. It is this human sympathy in her – and not
the tough methods of the Messenger[14] – that wrings the truth from
Lichas. His opening words (at 472ff.) should be carefully noted: 'Dear
mistress, since I see that you, a mortal, have mortal thoughts and are
not without pity . . .' (θνητὴν φρονοῦσαν θνητὰ κοὐκ ἀγνώμονα).[15]
They should be noted, because, if we are to believe some statements of
the thought of Sophocles, such a condition of mind ought to be an
effective prescription for the avoidance of tragic disaster. That a state
of mind which was the merit of Odysseus in *Ajax* did not save
Deianira is a feature of irony in this most ironical play. So far from
saving her, it precipitated, if it did not cause, her disaster.

And so the second movement of the play ends with the justified
fears of Deianira. 'What am I to do, ladies?' she had asked (385). By
the time of her reappearance she has thought what she can do: she can
use the 'love-charm' given her by the dying Nessus. I assume that to
do this was not in her mind at the close of the preceding scene.[16]
Apart from a common tendency in Greek tragedy for changes of
attitude to take place 'between the acts', it is essential to the irony of
that scene that she shall not yet have made her plan, particularly when
she reads Lichas a lecture on honesty (453–5). Sustained dissimulation
is at variance with the basic simplicity of her character; it would also
be discordant with the pity, the human sympathy, which is the
keynote of her role at that point. Deianira is still trying to make
herself believe that the situation is after all tolerable for the woman she
thinks herself to be.[17] But, while the Chorus sing of the power of

---

[14] Cf. Perrotta 498ff. Justice has been done to this fine speech by H. A. Mason, *Arion*
2 (1963) 113ff. ('a speech of power without violence'), cf. Whitman 117; Perrotta
479.

[15] With ἀγνώμονα here cf. 1266. It is uncertain – and not very important – whether
we should take the word as neuter plural or feminine singular.

[16] The case is well argued by T. B. L. Webster in *Greek poetry and life* (ed. Cyril
Bailey *et al.*, Oxford 1936) 171f.: cf. Bowra 124f., Whitman 117f., Perrotta 501,
Gellie 61. Contr. Reinhardt 34, 54ff., whose argument must be taken very
seriously by all who believe that Ajax spoke to deceive. For Reinhardt both Ajax
and Deianira pretend to accept 'das Gesetz des Wechsels' (she in relation to love)
with no intention of acting accordingly. It is true that Sophocles has a way of
repeating effects from play to play, but there is a fundamental difference between
the two situations which may have dictated a different treatment. What is out of
character for Ajax is the submission he feigns; what is out of character for Deianira
(see p. 78 below) is the action she finally takes. Cf. Kamerbeek, *Introduction* 15f.

[17] 'She is speaking with a wisdom beyond her strength' (Webster (op. cit., n. 16));
'For the moment Deianira thinks that she can handle it all' (Gellie 61). But she is

Kypris, she comes to realize that it is intolerable. 'This, then, is my fear
(φοβοῦμαι), lest Heracles be called my husband but be the younger
woman's man' (550f.). And so we return to the theme, and to words,
of fear.

It is sometimes said that the action of Deianira is, dramatically
speaking, unprepared. I would say rather that it is as carefully prepared as any action in Greek tragedy, only the preparation is ironic
and oblique. We are shown the last woman from whom, on a
superficial consideration, such an action could be expected: a woman
so lacking in initiative[18] that she has to be prompted by the Nurse to
send in search of her husband, so diffident that she defers to the
opinions of a chorus of young girls; a woman whom many fears and
grim experiences, including the episode of Nessus itself, have made
distrustful of life, and yet this one action she does not mistrust. We are
shown a modest wife of conventional virtue who performs a daring
deed. She acts out of character; deserting her own line of country for
one in which she has no guiding marks, she makes the inevitable
disastrous mistake.[19] But this does not mean that consistency of
character has gone by the board or that the effect lacks its cause. The
less characteristic the act, then the greater is the evidence of her
desperation – and of the power of Kypris, about which the Chorus
has been singing. Kypris is in the centre of the theme of the play.[20] To
Kypris – and to this choral ode – we shall return.

We can blame Deianeira, if we will, and as she blamed herself,
though Sophocles may have been more concerned to show what
happened, how and why it happened, than to determine the degree of
her guilt. The crucial passage is 582–97. Deianira has taken the sinister
ointment out of the cupboard where it has lain in the dark all those
years; she has anointed the robe but not yet made her final decision to
send it. Her conscience is not clear.[21] 'Acts of wicked daring may I

under strain. And it could be that Sophocles has indicated this by the accumulated
dental consonants of 445–7 (noted by Kamerbeek): cf. p. 53 n.125 on *Ajax* 684ff.

[18] Cf. Gellie 55; Easterling, *G & R* 24 (1977) 123, demurs at this.

[19] Cf. *Phil.* 902f.

[20] This is clearly recognized by (among others) Linforth (1952) 260f., 267; see
especially Easterling, *BICS* 15 (1968) 58–69, who takes a view of the theme of the
play closely similar to my own. My chapter is based on a paper written and read
many years ago, but I have reshaped it to take account of her excellent observations.

[21] Cf. Gellie 65f. The point is controversial and involves two questions: (i) What
kind of judgement was to be expected upon a woman who resorted to this kind of

neither know nor learn to know; women who commit them I detest. But if by love-spells I can prevail against this child – by charms aimed at Heracles, the means to the deed are ready.' She knows that what she is proposing may be regarded as an act of *tolma*, but weighed against this in the balance is the chance that she may regain the love of her husband. She adds: 'Unless I am thought to be acting wickedly (μάταιον). If so, I will stop at once.' And so she would undoubtedly have done. Here Sophocles has given a twist to the screw of irony. We can imagine what the Nurse with her peasant shrewdness would have said, but at this moment of crisis Deianira's advisers are a set of inexperienced girls; and she is as innocent and guileless as they.[22] It is not unfair to paraphrase her exchange with the Coryphaeus on these lines: 'If you have reason to believe it will work, we think your plan is a good one.' Deianira is honest: 'I *think* it will work, but I have never put it to the proof.' 'It is only by trying that you can tell.' Deianira has leaned upon a reed which breaks. Lichas approaches, and she must ask the Chorus for their secrecy: 'Act in darkness, and, though your deeds are shameful, you will never be brought to shame' (596f.).[23] This is a

magic? (ii) What did Deianira have in mind, when she spoke of κακαὶ τόλμαι? On (i) we have extreme views from Bowra 127 (strongly condemnatory) and from Whitman 114 ('Sophocles did not wish the use of this love potion to be considered criminal'). On (ii) Ronnet 101f. suggests that killing Iole or spoiling her beauty were the criminal acts which D. had in mind. More probably we should look, with the scholiast, to the murder of a husband: Perrotta 504f. translates by 'le audacie omicide', and Reinhardt 42 n. 2 (p. 251) compares the return of Heracles (with Iole) to the return of Agamemnon (with Cassandra). The Greek attitude towards the use of such magic was probably ambivalent: so too, as I see it, was that of D., who draws a distinction between κακαὶ τόλμαι (with a shade of emphasis on the epithet?) and the use of φίλτρα (thrown out emphatically and then re-inforced by θέλκτροισι τοῖς ἐφ᾽ Ἡρακλεῖ). At least she hopes that such a distinction *can* be drawn. But her conscience is not clear, and at 587 she *does* say μάταιον (which means more than 'futile'). And is μεμηχάνηται altogether a happy word?

22 For the youth of the Chorus, deliberately stressed, cf. 141ff.; also 821 and 1275 (with n. 4 above). For the Nurse as a wise counsellor, cf. 52 f. No doubt Kitto's Chorus of Solicitors would have been even better!

23 596f. are taken otherwise by Whitman 115; Kamerbeek ad loc.; Ronnet 102. All take πράσσειν in the sense of 'suffer' or 'fare', which of course it can well bear with a neuter adjective (Whitman cites Eur. *Or.* 538, among other passages). Ronnet argues that πράσσειν accompanied by an adverbial accusative always has the sense of 'aboutir à tel résultat, être dans telle situation'. But why need this accusative be regarded as adverbial (any more than that at *Or.* 535)? As I see it, there is no essential difference here between αἰσχρὰ πράσσῃς (597) and τι . . . πράσσειν μάταιον (586f.). Deianira fears that the attempt itself, and not merely its failure, will entail an adverse judgement, if it becomes known. Cf. Kirkwood, *SSD* 114 n. 16.

sad tumble after the lecture she had read to Lichas.

Her tragedy works to its inevitable conclusion, and little more need be said about it. The theme of fear is re-introduced at the end of the scene (630ff.), perhaps to remind us that Deianira, who had been urged by the Chorus in the Parodos to fear less and hope more, now hopes too much and fears too little. The next scene opens with the last, the worst, and the most certain, of her fears. 'Ladies, how I fear (δέδοικα) that I may have gone too far in all that I have just been doing' (663f.). The flock of wool she had used to anoint the robe had crumbled and foamed away in the sun's warmth. Now she thinks, too late, of all the good reasons for mistrusting the Centaur. She says she will die rather than live dishonoured. Honest again, she rejects the half-hearted consolations of the Coryphaeus. Hyllus arrives to confirm her fears; and she must listen to her own son saying he wishes she were dead or not his mother. She leaves the stage in silence. The Nurse tells of her suicide in a speech which balances the prologue speech of Deianira. That told how she became the wife of Heracles; this describes the end of a woman for whom it was the whole of life to be his wife, the mother of his children, but above all his bedfellow. She kills herself in his bedroom and upon his bed.[24]

Some commentators have been reluctant to admit that this middle-aged woman, this Greek wife and mother, felt – and acted under – the power of Kypris, 'She feels herself', writes one, 'threatened in her position of housewife'; and another speaks of her as 'thrust into a corner in her own house'.[25] It is not the house, but the bed which she is asked to share. 'And now there are two of us waiting under a single blanket to be embraced' (539f.).[26] This is one of the most striking expressions in the play; and, if it is coarse (which it is), that is not because Sophocles wished to display coarse fibres in the gentle soul of Deianira, but that, being a Greek and writing of a Greek, he could tell the truth. A little later, in lines already quoted (550f.), she puts the matter squarely: 'What I fear is this, that Heracles be called my husband but be the younger woman's man.' When, at the beginning of an earlier speech, she says (444f.): 'Eros rules the gods as he will – yes,

---

[24] See n. 28 below.

[25] Cf. also Ronnet 101. 'The commentators seem anxious to make Deianira respectable' (Easterling, *BICS* 65). But cf. Bowra 120; Whitman 112, 116; Perrotta 476.

[26] On ὑπαγκάλισμα see Easterling, *BICS* 63; Long 119f., 145 n. 108. On μία χλαῖνα Kamerbeek ad loc. remarks that it is 'as it were, the symbol for a pair of lovers': cf. B. Gentili, *Quaderni Urbinati* 21 (1976) 17ff.

and me also', this is no distant recollection of youth, but a statement of present fact. (She even seems to assume that Iole, having slept with Heracles, must be in love with him.)²⁷ When she stabs herself upon the bed, Sophocles, with a characteristic verbal technique, accumulates words – four of them within three lines – expressive of the sexual relationship.²⁸ Could he have made her feelings clearer?

While the tragedy of Deianira unfolds, there is a simultaneous, though less immediate, revelation of Heracles. We see him first through the eyes of his loving wife. He is introduced as 'the glorious son of Zeus and Alcmena' (19), who came to save Deianira from marriage to the monstrous river-god. This was an *agon* (20, 26), involving *ponoi* (21); and by tradition Heracles was essentially a man of contests and toils and great ordeals (*athloi*, 36). Indeed it was

27 This is controversial. Two passages are involved. Who is the subject of ἐντακείη at 463? It is so natural to understand Iole (as Jebb and others do) that one must have a strong reason for not doing so. Of course D. knows that Iole was not a free agent, but that does not settle the question, given the nature of sexual jealousy. 'It is pathetically natural that D. should assume I.'s passion as a matter of course' (Jebb). Natural, if she was herself in love and unable to believe that a woman could sleep with H. and not be in love with him. The other passage is 444f. After the words quoted in the text, D. continues: 'And why not another woman such as I?' It is impossible to hear the genitive ἑτέρας and *not* think of Iole. Was D. thinking of her? That she was may be indicated by the particle τε at 445. 'Both Heracles and . . .'. H. was caught with the disease, the madness of love; the force of ληφθέντι need not carry on into 447, but is not excluded from it. In such a matter one must tread gingerly as on the verge of a minefield. Beck 16 is no doubt broadly right: Iole has no '*Wesen*', no active role, no '*Persona*'. One might say that her reaction to slavery is inside the drama, her reaction to Heracles is not. Nevertheless, what D. believed her reaction to be might be relevant. (A similar view is taken by Stinton 135f., who defends 444 against the assaults of Wunder and M. D. Reeve, *GRBS* 14 (1973) 167.)

28 The construction is deliberate: in 920 λέχη looks back to δεμνίοις τοῖς Ἡρακλείοις in 915f., νυμφεῖα to τὸν Ἡράκλειον θάλαμον in 913. Cf. *BICS* 16 (1969) 46 and n. 18; Easterling, *BICS* 66. Mrs Easterling has pointed out to me that εὐνατήριον and εὐνατρία are rare (and thus arresting?). Cf. Musurillo 74. The suicide of Deianira has been discussed at length by G. Devereux (*Tragédie et poésie grecques*, (Paris 1975) ch. v), who has transformed a non-problem into a most diverting mare's nest. Why did a woman, instead of hanging herself (as any decent conventional woman would), commit hara-kiri? Because Sophocles was, inadvertently, revealing his homosexuality? No, the answer is simple, and should attract a Freudian! For a woman to hang herself is not sexually suggestive; for a woman to strip herself half-naked on the marriage-bed – as she had often stripped herself for Heracles – and stab herself in the belly is very suggestive indeed. D. Wender, *Ramus* 3 (1974) 1–17, raises the same point about the mode of suicide, but gives, like Devereux, a wrong answer, though a different one.

because of this that marriage to Heracles brought Deianira nothing
but fear upon fear, as he came and went upon his labours. There is a
hint of his servitude to Eurystheus (35, λατρεύοντά τῳ). There is
mention of the killing of a certain Iphitus, which has led to the exile of
Deianira and to the disappearance of Heracles. Next we learn, from
Hyllus, that, incredible as it may sound, he has been in servitude to a
'Lydian woman'.[29] We learn that he is now attacking the city of
Eurytus in Euboea, but we do not know why. This too is called an
athlos (80), which brings it into relation with the traditional series of
his labours, but also with the winning of Deianira. Which does it most
resemble?

The answer awaits the arrival of Lichas, whose first narrative
contains one great lie, but much truth – and truth that throws light on
Heracles.[30] The drunken quarrel with Eurytus must be true and, for a
reason which will appear, touches an aspect of the traditional Heracles
that, at first sight, is more proper to comedy. The treacherous murder
of Iphitus must be true, for it brought as its punishment the servitude
to Omphale. The lie is about the motive of Heracles. The attack on
Eurytus and the enslavement of Oechalia were not, as might be
thought, a straightforward act of retaliation within the heroic frame.
The beautiful Iole – and she alone – was the cause of the war, the
reason for the *athlos,* for the last 'labour' of Heracles. As the first
movement of the play ended with the news of his triumph, the second
ends with the revelation of his defeat; and the words of Lichas are of
cardinal importance: 'In all else champion by his might, he has been
utterly overcome by his passion for this girl' (488f., ὡς τἄλλ' ἐκεῖνος
πάντ' ἀριστεύων χεροῖν | τοῦ τῆσδ' ἔρωτος εἰς ἅπανθ' ἥσσων ἔφυ). The
Chorus sings of the power of Kypris.

There is defeat as well as victory. In war he wins the *aristeia*,
appropriate to the man whom Deianira described as 'the best of all
men' (πάντων ἀρίστου φωτός, 177). Her passionate love for Heracles
remains unshaken, but at 541 the word *agathos* returns with a note of
sarcasm: what was the reward that this husband whom she had called
faithful and good (ὁ πιστὸς ἡμῖν κἀγαθὸς καλούμενος) had sent in
return for her long home-keeping?[31] It was Iole to share the mar-

[29] λάτριν (70) picks up λατρεύοντα (35).
[30] On Lichas' narrative see App. B.
[31] Perhaps the issue is whether Heracles' conception of *arete* includes a sense of
obligation towards his wife. A similar issue arises in *Ajax*, where Tecmessa appeals
in vain by the mutual *charis* of their relationship to a partner who subordinates

riage-bed. In the following ode, the Chorus sings of Heracles hastening home 'with the spoils of all prowess' (πάσας ἀρετᾶς λάφυρ' ἔχων, 645f.). Firstfruit of the spoils was Iole, the symbol of his defeat. In Euripides this would be ironical: can we be sure there is no irony intended here by Sophocles? What kind of a man was Heracles? And in what did his *arete* consist?

The shirt of Nessus is dispatched, received and donned – by Heracles in a good mood (763, ἵλεῳ φρενί), as he is making lavish sacrifice to the god his father. The altar-flame kindles, and the poison begins to work. From now onwards Heracles is in torment; and we do not judge a tormented man by ordinary standards. Yet, while we remind ourselves of this, we are bound to ask whether something of the true character of Heracles is not revealed under torture. The man who seized Lichas by the foot and hurled him over the cliff had hurled Iphitus to his death, on which occasion, if he departed from his norm, it was in respect of treachery but not in respect of violent retaliation. The man who wished to take Deianira and spoil her beauty as his strength had been spoiled (1068f.) was the normal Heracles, determined in death as in life to retaliate upon the 'bad' (καὶ ζῶν κακούς γε καὶ θανὼν ἐτεισάμην, 1111). It might be admitted that he is one of the most unpleasant characters in Greek tragedy.[32] And that is interesting. For why should Sophocles have chosen to present so great a hero in such a guise? There is a horrific and repellent quality in him, but also, if we are right, in Ajax. Ajax and Heracles share at least one characteristic in common, which is a complete absorption in themselves; and recent critics have rightly stressed the self-centredness of Heracles.[33] When the poison has begun to work and he sees Hyllus in

everything to his traditional *arete* conceived in the narrowest traditional terms. Cf. *Ajax* 520–4 and p. 30 above.

[32] Cf. the strong words of J. H. Kells in *CR* n.s. 3 (1962) 185 n. 2. Ronnet 94 reviews opinions and cites for a more favourable view of H. (which she does not share) e.g. Méautis, Maddalena, Adams. To find H. repellent does not mean that we should withhold from him the pity he demands. The pathos of 1089ff. is indeed extraordinary. One is reminded of the tears shed by Anatol Kuragin (in *War and Peace*) over his amputated leg and the pity which they won even from Andrei Bolkonsky.

[33] V. L. Ehrenberg, *Aspects of the ancient world* (Oxford 1946) 144–66, in an illuminating comparison between *Trach.* and Euripides' *Heracles*, finds that the Sophoclean Heracles is drawn, to some extent, as a fifth-century individualist, the moral being that concentration upon self is the wrong path for human-beings to follow. On the isolation and alienation of H., cf. *BICS* 16 (1969) 45f.; Biggs, 228f.

the crowd, he does not just say, as any normal man might do, 'Come and help me': he says 'Come to me, my son, do not shun my trouble, not even if you must share my death' (797f.).[34] The closing scene is governed by this attitude towards his son, of whom he makes a series of outrageous demands. It is not perhaps simply that he holds an extreme view of *patria potestas*, but rather that he can regard Hyllus in no other light than as an extension of his own individuality,[35] his own *phusis*, which explains, among other things, his insistence that he and no other shall go to bed with Iole.[36] This attitude is characteristic and might be described as a lack of *suggnomosune*, of that power to enter into the feelings of another that Deianira had shown. Heracles is self-centred and ruthless in every relation – towards his enemies, but also towards his servant Lichas, towards his son and towards his wife. Without pity as he has been without fear, he is the complete antithesis of Deianira. Heracles feels pity only for himself and only in the extreme of agony and weakness, when he seeks from others the pity he has never shown (801, 1070f., 1080).

We are made to see Heracles in a repellent light. But that is not how Deianira saw him, nor Hyllus, nor the Chorus. They see him as a very great man. They see him, we may say, in his traditional role (or one of his traditional roles) as καλλίνικος, ἀλεξίκακος, ἀγαθός, a supreme embodiment of *arete*. If there is a clash here, it is not used, as it might be by Euripides, for satirical effect, but is inherent in the facts of the situation. Heracles is a great man who has done great things, carried through a whole series of ordeals (*athloi*), and rid the world of destructive monsters. This he had been able to do only because he was supremely strong and supremely hard. In dealing with monsters he had matched crude violence with greater violence.[37] This was the life he had led, and this was the man he was. His *arete* was indeed supreme: it was physical strength, endurance and courage carried to their highest conceivable point.

With great strength of body go great physical appetites. This too was part of the traditional role of Heracles – the great eater and drinker, the great lover: an aspect, naturally, developed in satyr-plays and comedies, as for instance in the *Frogs*. The drunkenness of

[34] Kitto, *Poiesis* 169f.; Ronnet 97.
[35] Is the attitude of Ajax towards his son so different? See ch. 2, p. 31.
[36] See n. 39 below.
[37] See p. 89 below.

Heracles in *Alcestis* is the one clear 'pro-satyric' element in the play. Heracles gets drunk – once – in the *Trachiniae*. Why? Perhaps to remind us of this other side of the tradition. The drunken Heracles is also the amorous Heracles.[38] And Sophocles has in this play done a bold – and perhaps original – thing. He has taken the amorous Heracles and made him the theme of tragedy. Along with the physical strength of Heracles go over-mastering sexual desires which he gratifies ruthlessly and, as Deianira tells us (459f.), promiscuously. But the light is focused upon two women, both won by violence, and upon the havoc he worked in both their lives (25, 465). Women he needed to have and, if need be, took by violence and did not regard as of the first importance. That is, surely, a legitimate inference, for, when he bids Hyllus take Iole to his bed, he twice makes the point that it is a *small* favour (1217, 1229). A small favour, but one which bulks large in the closing scene. It has been said, by Bowra (142) for instance, that this demand was motivated by a tender consideration for Iole, but that would be quite out of character. It is pointed out, by Jebb and others, that from the union of Hyllus and Iole sprang a glorious progeny of Spartan kings. Of this fact Sophocles was well aware, but it cannot account for the language he uses to express the reaction of Hyllus, which is that of disease or mental sickness. The demand is outrageous and offensive: what caused Heracles to make it was not a mind unbalanced by physical suffering so much as his erotic passion for Iole, still alive in him, which could not bear to think of any other male body in contact with hers – 1225f. is quite explicit – except that of his other self, his son.[39]

It is the irony of the fate of Heracles that he is destroyed by a woman – or rather by the conjunction of two women. He is not only destroyed, but reduced to crying like a girl (1071f.), he is reduced to woman's status (1075). The irony of this catastrophe he can see: what he does not see, though Lichas saw it (488f.), is that, through his lust, he was the slave of women at the moment he thought he was most

---

[38] The two motifs are combined in the story of the rape of Auge. For this – and certain speculations about the narrative of Lichas – see App. B.

[39] On Hyllus and Iole, cf. Kitto, *Poesis* 170–2; Segal, *YCS* 151–3. I discuss 1230f. and 1235f. – and the *nosos*-theme in general – in *BICS* 26 (1979) 4f., where I point out the relationship of 1230f. to 543ff. and suggest that ὧδε δρᾶν (Groddeck and Wunder) should be read for ὧδ' ὁρᾶν at 1231. See also ch. 9, p. 214 below. Whether Heracles intended marriage or concubinage (cf. J. K. MacKinnon, *CQ* 21 (1971) 33–41) is not relevant to the present argument.

triumphant. When Deianira heard that Heracles had been in servitude to a woman, she could hardly believe her ears (69–71). But we can now perhaps see a relevance and a symbolic truth in the punishment of Heracles by being made the slave of Omphale. We can also see that his last labour no less than its predecessors was imposed upon him by a servitude, that he was the slave of Iole as truly as he had been the servant of Eurystheus.[40]

The tragedies of Deianira and Heracles are both tragedies of sex, since both are destroyed by a Kypris to whom alone belongs the power and the victory, but the same power works upon them in different ways. The asymmetry is obvious. Heracles wins a woman for whom he fought with a monster; the fight, so graphically described in a choral ode (497ff.), was brutal and animal, and the stronger brute won, while Deianira waited in fear for the outcome. One writer[41] who has written admirably about the ode speaks of the sequel as 'the animal seizure of the wretched prize'. This, surely, is off the mark. For Deianira Heracles' victory over Achelous was liberation from a ghastly fear, a good dispensation of Zeus Agonios. She was glad to be the bride of Heracles and, being a woman of normal sexuality, loved him. Her fears were for his absences, while his manifold sexual conquests were a matter of relative indifference to her, until, when her own youth was fading, he sent back to her home a young woman of great beauty to supplant her in his bed. She found she could not tolerate this and took action, enlisting, without her knowledge, the aid of a brute whose sexuality matched, but whose brute force could not match, that of her husband. Convinced that it is hopeless to fight against the gods, she tries to force their will with magic, not knowing that the 'magic' she uses is the product of a sexual conflict, the shrewdly calculated revenge of a lustful monster. The very antithesis of Heracles, timorous and sensitive, under the power of the same force of sex, she brings about his destruction; the least brutal of human beings, she brings about what the brutes could not, unaided by her, achieve.

Deianira is a normal woman; Heracles is a phenomenon. And he is the son of Zeus. It is the character and career and tragedy of Heracles,

[40] Mrs Easterling has pointed out to me that the rather frigid contrasts between free and slave at 52f. and 62f. may be leading towards this theme.

[41] Gellie 63f.

dramatically anterior to the tragedy of Deianira, which raise a question of theology and theodicy. The power and the victory belong to Kypris; 'there is none of these things which is not Zeus'. The Chorus sings the one, the Coryphaeus says the other.[42] What does it mean? It may be worth looking at a set of correspondences in the play, of a kind which we associate particularly with the dramatic techniques of Aeschylus, but which Sophocles also sometimes employs to make a dramatic point.

When, in the Prologos, Deianira tells of the fight between Heracles and Achelous, she says that it was Zeus Agonios who brought it to a good end. When the Chorus sing of that same fight, a different god presides: 'Kypris, goddess of fair brides, was there with them, sole umpire between them' (μόνα δ' εὔλεκτρος ἐν μέσῳ Κύπρις ῥαβδονόμει ξυνοῦσα, 515f.). A small point, it might seem, and one that raises no problem. The responsibility of Zeus follows appropriately upon the introduction of Heracles as his son (19); that, not for the last time, he conferred agonistic success upon that son is part of a pattern of events which misleads the Chorus into supposing he must continue to do so (139f.). To have introduced Kypris at this stage would have forestalled the point which Sophocles wished to make by gradual revelation. When, however, the power of lust over Heracles has been revealed (488f.), Kypris is appropriately seen to preside over that earlier conflict between two lustful males for a woman's beauty. We remind ourselves that an umpire – a *rabdonomos* or *brabeutes* – while regulating the contest and pronouncing a verdict, does not otherwise determine its outcome.[43] Which is true, but misses a striking feature of the ode. Strongly epinician in tone,[44] it celebrates the victory not of Heracles, but of the goddess herself, umpire but, in the upshot, herself sole victor. What, then, in terms of power and authority, is the relationship between Kypris and Zeus?

The question recurs with even greater force in the matter of Iole. For the ode which celebrates the power of Kypris, reverting to the incident described in the Prologos, does not thereby desert the imme-

---

[42] 497: μέγα τι σθένος ἁ Κύπρις ἐκφέρεται νίκας ἀεί. This line, which I do not venture to translate, raises difficult problems of interpretation, but it is clear that both strength and victory are attributed to Kypris. For a careful examination see Stinton 136–8, who revives Wakefield's proposal to punctuate after Κύπρις: 'mighty strength is Kypris; she ever bears away victories'.

[43] Cf. Kamerbeek ad loc.

[44] For the epinician character of the ode see Easterling (in her forthcoming edition).

diate dramatic situation[45] but rather focuses upon an essential aspect
of it: by evoking the youthful beauty of Deianira, it reminds us that
her youth is past and that the Heracles who fought for her has now
fought a ruthless war for the girl who possesses youthful beauty in her
turn. In Lichas' story only one god is mentioned, and it is Zeus; he is
mentioned several times, and responsibility is attributed to him. Of
the servitude to Omphale Lichas could speak, he says, without offence,
since Zeus had brought it about; the alleged circumstances
are set out at 274ff., with two mentions of Zeus (275, 279). And they
are alleged truly. Where Lichas lies is in representing the sack of
Oechalia as due directly to the humiliating punishment which Zeus
had inflicted. The story told to the people of Trachis had been
different: 'It was Eros alone of the gods under whose spell Heracles
wrought these deeds of arms' (354f.). There is still a later passage
which should be taken into consideration. At 860f., immediately
before the news of Deianira's suicide, the Chorus, singing how the
spear of Heracles won a bride from Oechalia, uses these words: 'And
Kypris, ministering in silence, has been plainly shown the doer of
these deeds.' For the second time the invisible presence of the goddess
is expressed in an image: then she was umpire in a sexual struggle,
now she is the attendant of a bride, silent and subordinate, yet
manifestly in both cases the cause of all that happens. The words that
are used here (φανερὰ τῶνδ' ἐφάνη πράκτωρ, 860–2) can hardly fail to
recall the words which Lichas used of Zeus (Ζεὺς ὅτου πράκτωρ φανῇ,
251).[46]

This set of passages not only brings out the correspondence
between the two struggles, but also raises in either case the question of
divine responsibility. It is wrong to suppose that Sophocles saw two
powers at odds with one another[47] or the role of Kypris in the action
as diminishing the authority of Zeus: if so, he could hardly have ended
the play as he did. Perhaps the average Greek did not worry too much
about departmental conflicts within the divine world, but Sophocles
had learnt from Aeschylus to seek a tragic unity amid diversity. One
thing is clear: that, if we would form a conception of the government
of Zeus, we cannot disregard, but must include within our view, the

[45] Cf. Perrotta 502f. ('un nesso sottile stringe il passato al presente'); Easterling, *BICS*
63.
[46] Cf. Easterling, *BICS* 65.
[47] Contr. Musurillo 79.

devastating power of Kypris which, whatever the degree of the responsibility of the human agents, has destroyed both Heracles and Deianira. There is one world, and it is Zeus's world.

And it is a tragic world. Heracles is the son of Zeus. It is thanks to Zeus's favour that he has surmounted a whole series of ordeals which would have overwhelmed a lesser man; and since thereby the earth was cleansed of destructive monsters, his career could be seen – and was seen – as part of a beneficent purpose. But monstrous violence could only be put down by an answering excess of violence[48] and by a man of peculiar and astounding quality for whom nothing counted except the cultivation and exercise of his abnormal strength and courage, of his narrow traditional *arete*. Yet it is the very qualities in virtue of which he can perform his function that bring about his undoing. Nothing else counted, least of all those relations with women which his great physical strength demanded. Twice within the play we see him at grips with a lustful monster, himself actuated no less by the force of sexual desire. We see him wrestling with the monstrous river-god; we see him shooting down the Centaur who tried to rape his wife. The Centaur has his revenge, as he knew he would, but only Heracles could give it to him, by his callous disregard of anything that stood between him and his desires.

It is a tragic world: is it also a just one? Zeus was supposed to concern himself with justice; and it would be possible, though no one inside the play looks at it in that light, to see the destruction of Heracles as the justice of Zeus. Justice is not a theme, or *dike* and *dikaios* words, which receive much prominence in the play.[49] Nevertheless, when the Chorus learns that Deianira has taken her own life, they sing that 'the new bride has borne a child to the house – a great Erinys' (893f.). Erinyes are ministers of divine justice and, by Aeschylean tradition, closely associated with the justice of Zeus. There are three direct references to an Erinys or Erinyes in the second half of the play; and if we are fully to understand how the divine world enters

---

48 Both Biggs 228f. and Easterling, *BICS* 65 have good observations on the relationship of Heracles to the monsters against whom he has warred. Easterling, calling attention to certain correspondences, writes: 'I believe that the effect of these echoes is to give us the impression that the bestial victims of Heracles, linked together in a sinister way, are rising up and punishing him with their own weapons, in dramatic terms the poison from one of his victims which he used to subdue another, and on another level the wild-beastlike violence of passion.'

49 See ch. 9 n. 26.

into it, those references should be investigated. They may throw light upon the motivation of Zeus, but also upon that of Heracles; they may raise the question whether he was the son of Zeus for nothing. But this must wait for a later chapter.[50]

Meantime let us move on to another play. In moving from *Ajax* to *Trachiniae* we encountered a striking contrast of theme and setting. The two harsh warlike heroes proved indeed to have much in common and war enters into both plays, but at a different level of immediacy. The setting of *Ajax* is an armed camp, whereas that of *Trachiniae* is a home to which the victor returns. In both cases there is a loving woman. Tecmessa ennobles her play, but exists to suffer; Deianira acts, disastrously, causing the death of her man – and sharing the play with him. The fatal issue in *Ajax* is a matter of martial *arete*, but what brings about the deaths of Heracles (himself supreme in that *arete*) and of Deianira is the power of sex. The goddess in the play is Aphrodite, not Athena. When we move from *Trachiniae* to *Antigone* (again I stress that we do not know the temporal order of the three plays), what do we find? The aftermath of a war, raising great issues of politics and religion, focused upon the conflict between a man and a woman, both of whom (again) have claims to be the 'central' character. They clash on the great issues, but their polar opposition is complicated by a lover and by the theme of passion, which is more prominent in the latter phases of the play than has always been allowed. No more than *Trachiniae* can *Antigone* be adequately interpreted, unless justice is done to this theme, the importance of which is more than peripheral. To it a chapter shall now be devoted; and it is devoted in the main to an examination of three choruses.

[50] See ch. 9 n. 33.

CHAPTER FIVE

Sophocles and the irrational: three odes in *Antigone*

In *Trachiniae*, at a critical point in the action, Sophocles has placed an ode (497ff.) which celebrates the invincible power of love, or lust. It is prompted by Lichas' revelation (488f.) that Heracles, champion in all else by the might of his hands, has been utterly worsted by his love for Iole. It is also prepared by the words of Deianira, that it is ill fighting against the gods (492), which is what in effect, with a fatal weapon, she will try to do. In the event both she and Heracles are defeated and destroyed, leaving Kypris sole victor on the field. There is a more famous ode upon this subject in another play. If Deianira uses the verb *dusmachein,* the Chorus of *Antigone* calls Aphrodite *amachos;* if the women of Trachis sing that Kypris ever wins the victory, the Theban elders address Eros as unconquered, or unconquerable, in battle.

Aphrodite, or Kypris, as a goddess fit for tragedy we know well from Euripides' *Hippolytus;* Sophocles' *Phaedra* which preceded it was a famous play. Curiously enough, however, in general discussions of the divine world of Sophocles and its impact upon his heroes, we read little about this goddess. Consult the indexes of standard works, and you will find few entries under Aphrodite, Kypris, Eros, love, lust, or sex. It may be that this theme did not fit some preconceived notion of what ought to have interested Sophocles. It may be, partly, that some of the more important evidence takes the form of choral odes, greatly admired as poetry, recognized as relevant to the dramatic situations in which they are placed, but not always given their due weight in the total interpretation of the plays. The present chapter will be concerned, largely, with three odes in *Antigone;* and the reader is warned that an element of speculation will enter, progressively, into the interpretations offered.

1. *Antigone 781–800*

The scene between Creon and Haemon has ended in a violent quarrel; Haemon rushes off, and the Chorus sings an ode, brief but striking (781ff.). He is in love, and it is the unconquerable power of love which has caused his unfilial behaviour. But – and scholars sometimes notice the obvious – the debate between father and son is not about love at all: it is about politics, and about wisdom as manifested in the political field. Perhaps, then, the Chorus is wrong to see the power of Eros at work. This view has been put forward by an eminent scholar and has won some acceptance.[1] Indeed a Chorus need not be right. In what way, if at all, is this Chorus wrong? A distinction needs to be made. (i) Insofar as the Chorus brush aside everything else in the preceding scene and choose to regard Haemon's behaviour as a wrong reaction determined simply by the power of love, we can indeed say, if we will, that they are making a 'wrong diagnosis'. 'The just themselves have their minds warped by thee to wrong for their ruin',[2] (σὺ δὲ καὶ δικαίων ἀδίκους φρένας παρασπᾶς ἐπὶ λώβᾳ). This would certainly seem to imply that, if Haemon had not been under the influence of Eros, he would have accepted his father's will and that this would have been right (δίκαιον), which of course by-passes the whole issue of the rightness of Creon's decision seen as a political and moral act. (ii) But does this mean that Haemon was *not* influenced by this power? Did he threaten, and then commit, suicide because he thought his father was behaving as a bad king?[3] If he does not expatiate upon his passion for Antigone, this was forbidden, though not so much by the conventions of Greek tragedy[4] as by the requirements of the situation, by the fact that Haemon must speak words that will serve and not frustrate his cause, as it would surely have been frustrated by a

---

[1] K. von Fritz, 'Haimons Liebe zu Antigone', *Philologus* 89 (1934) 19–33, reprinted in *Antike und moderne Tragödie* (Berlin 1962) 227–40. Müller (2) 171f., while admitting that the ode looks forward ironically to Haemon's suicide under the power of Eros, accepts von Fritz's view that, where it stands, it presents an incorrect explanation of his mental state.

[2] 791 (Jebb's translation).

[3] For various views see Linforth (1961) 219 n. 3; H. Lloyd-Jones, *Gnomon* 34 (1962) 739f.; Gellie 43f.; Ronnet 84 and 153 (Haemon's world is broken by the scene, indignation at his father's cruelty and insulting words count for more than 'une blessure pour l'amoureux').

[4] Hippodameia – a woman, and a woman in Sophocles, not one of the infamous *pornai* of Euripides – speaks very frankly of her passion for Pelops (fr. 474 P).

passionate rhapsody or an emotional appeal; forbidden equally by the fact that the political theme, and the revelation of Creon's mind in the political context, are important themes which must be developed here. There were limits upon what Sophocles could do. Within those limits, it is hard to see how he could have given more emphasis to the theme of passion.

It is prepared in dialogue between Creon and Ismene, by the vulgarity of Creon at 569[5] and the striking reply of Ismene (οὐχ ὧς γ' ἐκείνῳ τῇδέ τ' ἦν ἡρμοσμένα),suggestive of a close union of hearts between two lovers;[6] by the outburst of 572, whether spoken by Ismene or Antigone.[7] It was, however, at the entrance and exit of Haemon that Sophocles was free to make his point – and then to reinforce it in the most obvious and traditional way by means of a choral ode.[8] The entry of Haemon is remarked by the Coryphaeus: 'Here comes Haemon, last of your sons. Has he come grieving for the fate of his promised bride,[9] in bitter sorrow for the bed of which he is cheated?' (628–30). It is a question; and a question also when Creon addresses him: 'Surely it cannot be that, hearing of the irrevocable condemnation of your future bride, you have come in mad rage against your father?' (632f.). The question seems to receive a negative answer,[10] when Haemon speaks with studied (if ambiguous) moder-

---

[5] Cf. Segal, *Arion* 59.

[6] The tone of 570 is not easy to seize or the language easy to parallel. Jebb cites Pindar and Herodotus for ἁρμόζειν in the sense of 'betroth', but that does not settle the question of tone. I find it hard to believe Ismene meant as little as that, from a social point of view, the match was eminently suitable.

[7] The question is vexed. Kitto (*FMD*) 162f. and Linforth (1961) 209f. argue, respectively (and persuasively), for Antigone and Ismene. The dialogue falls, as often in stichomythia, into two-speaker groups: 536–60 Ismene and Antigone; 561–71 Ismene and Creon; 574ff. Creon and the Coryphaeus, but it is not out of the question that, for a special effect, Sophocles should have made Antigone exclaim and be addressed by Creon. But is his rejoinder appropriate to her? 'An impossibly mild exclamation for Creon to use if he were addressing Antigone' (Linforth). What may be decisive is the fact that it is Ismene and not Antigone who has raised the issue of a marriage. τὸ σὸν λέχος: 'the marriage you speak of' (cf. *El.* 1110; *Phil.* 1251). The weight of argument inclines strongly towards Ismene. (Contr. R. D. Dawe, *Studies on the text of Sophocles* III 106.)

[8] Cf. Gellie 44.

[9] At 628f. τῆς μελλογάμου should be retained.

[10] On ἆρα μή see Denniston, *Greek particles*² (Oxford 1953) 47f. Such questions hope for, but are liable not to receive, the negative answer (whereas *num* is to be answered with a confident no). Unthinkable, but true, cf. Denniston's comment on *El.* 446.

ation.[11] But we must wait for the end of the scene. Haemon's
self-control cannot stand the strain. Already at 751 he is thinking of
suicide, but it is the coarse brutality of Creon's threat, that Antigone
shall be executed before the eyes of her bridegroom, which evokes his
final outburst (762–4), determined, not by the rejection of his good
advice, but by the strength of his passion. The Coryphaeus (766f.)
refers to his anger (ἐξ ὀργῆς) and his grief (ἀλγήσας), echoing the
language with which they greeted his entry (627ff.). But it is Creon's
comment which is most significant: φρονείτω μεῖζον ἢ κατ' ἄνδρ' ἰών
(768). Not easily translatable, it means, as Jebb rightly says: 'Let his
passion overpass the human limit.' And so it will, for a more than
human force is in control of his mind, the force of invincible Eros,
though this will not become clear until the scene at the cave (1231ff.),
when he glares at his father with wild eyes, spits in his face, and draws
a sword on him[12] – the sword which he then plunges into his own
side and so attains a union with his bride in death.

   Haemon is in love, but we are not meant to see him as a romantic
hero in the modern style. However much we may sympathize with
him, his passion is displayed not as a sympathetic or admirable trait,
but as a tragic fact – and the power of Eros as a dangerous and
potentially tragic element in human life. That is how the Greeks saw
sexual passion, as a madness sent by a god; and that is what the Chorus
sings – 'He who has you is mad' (ὁ δ' ἔχων μέμηνεν). Do we also say
that the man who resists the god is mad? Deianira thought so (*Trach.*
446, 490–2). If Creon feared that his son was approaching in a state of
frenzy (λυσσαίνων, 633), Haemon left him with an accusation of
madness (μαίνῃ, 765). This is a matter to which we must return. We
are not yet done with the Eros-ode.
   As so often, the lyric style of an ode presents us with difficulties.
The Chorus goes on, in the second stanza, to sing something which, as
the text stands, is very puzzling, but which, in one way or another,
raises the question of the status of sexual passion in the moral governance of the world. About sexual attraction in its most seductive

---

[11] Haemon takes advantage, as many a hard-pressed Greek must have done, of the
    ambiguity of his participles (635, 638), which could be circumstantial or condi-
    tional. Cf. C. Knapp, *AJPh* 37 (1916) 307.

[12] 1235: αὐτῷ χολωθείς. 'His frantic impulse is instantly followed by violent
    remorse' (Jebb), cf. Gellie 51 (and for the popular morality which might prompt
    such remorse Dover, *GPM* 273f.). But is it not equally likely that he was angry
    because of his failure to retaliate upon the author of Antigone's death?

aspect they sing not only that it wins a victory but also, if the text is sound, that it sits as assessor alongside the 'great laws' (μεγάλοι θεσμοί) in their 'magistracies'. These laws must include – and in this context must denote especially – the duty of a son towards his father; and it is therefore puzzling that, after singing that Love warps the minds of the just towards injustice, the Chorus should go on to imply that sexual desire has an honourable place beside the laws. Naturally the text has been suspected,[13] but no convincing emendation is yet proposed. Perhaps there is deliberate paradox, a sign of puzzlement on the part of an often puzzled Chorus. But whether *himeros* sits with the *thesmoi* or perverts the minds of just men to act against them or (paradoxically) both, the fact remains that Sophocles has raised the question; the fact remains that Aphrodite is a goddess and is *amachos,* just as Eros is *anikatos;* mother and son, and the desire which they manifest, are alike invincible. That is how the Chorus sees it, thinking of Haemon.

'Sexual attraction in its most seductive aspect': βλεφάρων ἵμερος εὐλέκτρου νύμφας. A distinguished translator[14] has written that 'ἵμερος must refer to the bride as well as to her admirer or the passage

---

[13] The problem is in the context, not in the Greek, which is unexceptionable, nor in the metre, the responsion of πάρεδρος ἐν to φύξιμος being unwelcome rather than fatal. τῶν μεγάλων . . . θεσμῶν is vouched for by the words of the Coryphaeus (801), who feels that his tears are a breach of political duty akin to Haemon's breach of filial piety. As to πάρεδρος, in Pindar Rhadamanthys and Themis, in different contexts, are πάρεδροι to Zeus. The term was used in Athenian public life of the assessors who sat with various magistrates; and this makes πάρεδρος ἐν ἀρχαῖς ring true, not least in a play so 'political' as *Antigone*, not least after the scene between Creon and Haemon. The word occurs in Sophocles only here, but at *O.C.* 1382 Dike is said by Oedipus to be ξύνεδρος Ζηνὸς ἀρχαίοις νόμοις, which provides some kind of a parallel to the phrase under consideration. The word suggests, if less than supreme authority, at least some power or influence; and it suggests collaboration. Therein lies the difficulty. G. Müller would read ἀργός for πάρεδρος, but strong objections are brought against this suggestion by B. M. W. Knox, *Gnomon* 40 (1968) 758f., who adds: 'This surely is a case for the obelus.' He may be right.

[14] Lattimore, *SPGT* 75f. in n. 34. That the eyes of the beloved are a source of sexual desire is virtually a commonplace of Greek poetry. It is examined by A. C. Pearson in *CR* 23 (1910) 256f. See also W. S. Barrett on Eur. *Hipp.* 525–6 and 530–4 (for βέλος as 'amorous or love-provoking glance'); Müller (1) 410f., and (2) 178. The eyes of the beloved are a source of ἵμερος: so much is clear. But is this due to an objective quality residing in them? (*Liebreiz* and *Liebesverlangen* being covered by the same word ἵμερος: so Müller.) Or does the glance provoke desire by revealing it? Different answers may apply in different cases. In Soph. fr. 474, 2f., there is desire in both parties, and the same may be implied at Aesch. *Suppl.* 1004f.

is untranslatable'. The point is arguable but had better not be argued here. Was Antigone herself in love? What is certain is that the bride, the *numpha*, of whom the Chorus has sung immediately appears and herself sings about marriage. The ode is immediately followed by a reference to the 'chamber where all are laid to rest' (τὸν παγκοίταν . . . θάλαμον), which combines a familiar commonplace about death with the notion of Antigone finding her bridal-chamber in death. The epithet *pankoitas* is picked up from the Chorus by Antigone and followed by a threefold reference to wedlock (ὑμεναίων, ἐπὶ νυμφείοις, νυμφεύσω) which in a careful writer like Sophocles must be deliberate.[15] The theme is then dropped until 862ff., when the fatal marriages of the Labdakidai (there are four words of marriage in that stanza) lead back to Antigone as ἄγαμος and ἀνυμέναιος (867, 876) and so to her famous: 'Oh tomb, oh bridal-chamber' at 891. Was Antigone also in love? The matter is difficult and not without importance for the understanding of Antigone:[16] its importance for the Eros-ode is limited, and for the following reason.

To regard sexual passion merely as a factor in the characterization and motivation of Haemon and (possibly) of Antigone is to miss an element of structural importance in the play. The play opens with Antigone determined to bury her brother in defiance of Creon's edict; it continues up to the discovery that she has indeed done so and to her confrontation with Creon, and all without a word about her betrothal to Creon's son, until 568, when Ismene bursts out: 'Will you kill the bride of your own child?' To which Creon makes a coarse reply. A new motif of significance has been introduced into the play, but not all critics have appreciated how persistent it is from then onwards.

Let us return to the Eros-ode. It begins with Eros unconquerable in battle (ἀνίκατε μάχαν) and, with victorious *himeros* intervening, ends with an Aphrodite who is ἄμαχος – with whom one cannot or should not engage in battle, because she plays with (ἐμπαίζει) her opponents. The Chorus is thinking of the power of Eros and Aphrodite over Haemon; and the strength of their power does indeed show itself in the subsequent action, with a devastating effect upon Creon. Rightly,

[15] At 810 Blaydes' πάγκοινος is plausible but quite unnecessary. For bridal in death, cf. 653f., 816, 891, 1240f. At 814 it is immaterial to the argument whether we read ἐπὶ νυμφείοις or (with Dindorf and Jebb) ἐπινύμφειος.

[16] See p. 143 below.

for it is he that has provoked the manifestation of the power. Now it is characteristic of the odes of this play that they tend, ironically, to carry a secondary reference to Creon which cannot be in the minds of the singers.[17] Thus, in the present ode, if they are thinking of Haemon, the poet invites his audience to think of the unequal battle which Creon has joined with a great cosmic force. This was seen by Méautis, but Kitto alone,[18] so far as I am aware, has given due weight to the issue in interpreting the play, by pointing out that Creon sets himself not only against family affection and the tie of kinship but also against the power of sexual passion. Jointly they take their revenge upon him, when Haemon commits suicide for the loss of his beloved and Eurydice for the loss of her son. Now at last, surely, we can see the full scope of the relevance of this central ode to the themes of the play. Inadequate perhaps as a choral comment on the preceding scene, it is a vital foreshadowing of the scene at the cave. But it was not only to throw light on Haemon that Sophocles wrote it and placed it here. It is Creon who fights the power of Eros and Aphrodite; it is Creon who is mocked.

If the power of Eros is one of the central themes of the play, an understanding of this fact may help to solve an ancient riddle; an understanding of the Third Stasimon may throw light upon the Fourth. Our earlier examination has shown how the theme of marriage persists in the farewell *kommos* of Antigone and how the effects of sexual passion show themselves in the Messenger-speech. Between the exit of Antigone and the entrance of the Messenger we have the scene with Teiresias, concerned (primarily but not exclusively)[19] with the issue of burial, but also two choral odes, the Fourth and Fifth Stasima. Is the theme of passion, then, silent during this long stretch of the play? In the Third Stasimon it is sung of Eros that 'he who has him is mad' (ὁ δ' ἔχων μέμηνεν). Creon had feared that Haemon might be mad (λυσσαίνων) at the loss of his love, but hoped that he was not: that his hope was vain was shown at the cave. But Haemon left the scene

<hr>

17 The choral use of dramatic irony is recognized and expounded by G. Müller in his edition and, previously, in Müller (1) 398–422, esp. 409, 406 n. 1, 415 n. 1.

18 Méautis 209 (of the Chorus in this ode): 'Il sait que l'amour gouverne le monde. Il sait que l'amour est un pouvoir primordial, un de ceux qui sort à la racine même du monde, là aussi, sans le vouloir, il prophétise: Créon en ne tenant pas compte de cette force invincible, court à l'abîme.' Kitto FMD 163, 167, 176f.

19 Cf. 1068ff., where the non-burial of Polynices and the burial alive of Antigone are represented as parallel acts of impiety.

attributing madness to Creon (765). The next we hear of madness is in
the Fourth Stasimon.

II. *Antigone 944–987*

The problem of the Fourth·Stasimon of *Antigone* is familiar, and can
be stated briefly. Antigone has been led away to her rocky tomb.
How does the Chorus react? By singing of Danae, of Lycurgus, of the
Phineidae and Cleopatra. These must be cited as, in some way,
parallel cases; and in the case of Danae the parallel is clear and clearly
brought out. The difficulty lies in understanding why Sophocles
should have moved from Danae to Lycurgus, from Lycurgus to the
Phineidae and Cleopatra. It is not that formal links are absent, but that
the links are so formal. One looks for some coherent intelligible
structure or, failing that, for a significant set of aesthetic relationships.

The case of Danae is parallel indeed, since she, as Antigone will do,
exchanged the light of heaven for a dark tomb-like chamber: οὐράνιον
φῶς ἀλλάξαι . . . ἐν χαλκοδέτοις αὐλαῖς; she too was a princess, but not
immune from the power of destiny. We move from Danae to
Lycurgus. The first word of the antistrophe picks up the κατεζεύχθη
of the strophe: ζεύχθη . . . πετρώδει κατάφαρκτος ἐν δεσμῷ. So
Lycurgus too was shut up – and, like Antigone, in a rocky prison. But
what else have Lycurgus and Antigone in common, except perhaps
royalty and misfortune? Unless it be that the imprisonment of
Lycurgus, unlike that of Danae, was a punishment? From Lycurgus
we pass to the Phineidae, and the link is in the first instance purely
local: we pass from one Thracian myth to another. What other link
can be found? The theme of the second strophe would seem to be the
blinding of the sons of Phineus by their stepmother and nothing else.
We do indeed learn from the scholiast, though not (oddly) from the
text, that the blinded sons were shut up in a tomb.[20] According to
Jebb, 'the fate of the sons is made so prominent only because nothing
else could give us so strong a sense of the savage hatred which pursued
the mother'. This, if true (which may be doubted), absolves us from
the necessity of finding a link (other than the dubious imprisonment)
between the Phineidae and Antigone. To quote Jebb again: 'It is the
fate of Cleopatra herself which Sophocles means to compare with

---

[20] κατατακόμενοι (977) is consistent with imprisonment, but does not in itself imply
it: cf. *El.* 123, 187, 283, 835.

Antigone's.' That there is such a comparison is clear from the closing words of the ode: 'yet upon her also bore the long-lived Fates, my child' (ἀλλὰ κἀπ᾿ ἐκείνᾳ Μοῖραι μακραίωνες ἔσχον, ὦ παῖ, 986f.). But in what does the link consist? In a distinguished ancestry for one thing: Antigone, like Danae, was γενεᾷ τίμιος; Cleopatra was more, she was θεῶν παῖς; and yet the Moirai bear upon her, just as Danae – and Antigone – were subject to the power of fate. This is a twofold link. Is there another? Was Cleopatra also imprisoned? Yes, according to one authority, but this fact (again oddly) is not mentioned by Sophocles in this passage. There is a reference to caves, but caves in which this child of Boreas was reared to the freedom of the winds.

Is there an intelligible scheme? Is there an aesthetic pattern? It would take too long to review the various attempts of interpreters to wrestle with this problem. The most whole-hearted efforts to find – or to impose – a clear intellectual structure have been made by Bowra and Errandonea,[21] but both schemes are open to serious objections. It is more usual, and doubtless more prudent, to accept the surface links as truly superficial, while seeing beneath them a play of subtle suggestion irreducible to any kind of pattern. Linforth,[22] for instance, writes: 'The ode is like a formally constructed musical composition with three variations on the principal theme – the reversal of fortune for distinguished persons – but snatches of subordinate themes – imprisonment, guilt, fate – also appear and are left undeveloped.'[23]

This could be the right approach: the poetry is subtle and elusive, and he would be a rash scholar who claimed to provide clear and lucid solutions to all the problems of this ode. It may be possible, however, to carry the matter a little further towards a solution, to establish at least the relationship between the Danae and Lycurgus stanzas in a way which is consistent with the dramatic themes of the play. The problems of the second half of the ode are more intractable, and I shall confine myself to making a few suggestions and speculations.

But first for some brief prolegomena. One need not deny that the idea of fate is a unifying theme. It enters specifically into the first and last stanzas; and in the third, when the singers refer to a curse and to

[21] Bowra 104f., criticized by Waldock 116ff., Goheen 66f. Errandonea: *Mnem.* 51 (1923) 180–201; *Phil. Woch.* 1930, 1375–5; *Emerita* 20 (1952) 108–21 (German version in *SO* 30 (1953) 16–26); *Sofokles* (1958) 95–108.
[22] Linforth (1961) 231–3. See also G. M. Kirkwood, *Phoenix* 8 (1954) 18.
[23] Cf. Kitto *FMD* 172f.

avengers, it may be suggested that Sophocles is using a cluster of inherited notions including the curse, the Erinys it evokes, and the implacable fate of which the Erinys is an agent. It may indeed be doubted whether the theme of fate has always been given its due weight in the interpretation of the play.[24] Certainly this theme in this place should be related to the first two stanzas of the Second Stasimon (on the fate of the house of Labdacus) and to the second half of the *kommos,* where Antigone sees her fate as determined by a curse (868). It is, moreover, an apt preparation for the entry of Teiresias, prophet and spokesman of the divine powers. But of course this theme, important though it may be, can in itself provide no explanation of the poet's choice of cases by which to illustrate it.

Next, it should be noted that the ode has its symmetry. Themes from the first stanza are repeated in the last, in the familiar ring-composition;[25] Danae is balanced by Cleopatra, both female victims of fate and so related to Antigone. In the interior stanzas we have a male offender punished and male victims, and a puzzling lack of relevance to Antigone (apart from the theme of imprisonment, which is certain in one case and possible in the other). The question has been raised – and rightly raised – whether there is not relevance to Creon.[26] And this brings us to another point. It seems certain that Creon is present during the singing of this ode (as also during the Second Stasimon and perhaps the Third).[27] This raises questions about the attitudes and the handling of the Chorus in this play which cannot be dealt with here,[28] except to say that since the presence of Creon must exercise an inhibiting effect upon the Chorus, it is rash (with Bowra) to interpret the ode in terms of the attitudes of the Chorus rather than the themes of the tragedy; that, if the words of this and other odes in the play have a secondary reference to Creon which may be more significant than their primary reference to Antigone, this does not imply that the Chorus are in their own character making a covert criticism of Creon;[29] and that his mere presence may invite the

[24] On fate in Sophocles see ch. 7 below.
[25] Cf. T. B. L. Webster, *IS* 188 (Note S). It is only in these two stanzas that Antigone is addressed (948, 987), cf. the twofold reference to fate (951, 987).
[26] On the shift from Antigone to Creon, cf. Goheen 68.
[27] See ch. 6 below, p. 136 n. 58.
[28] But see pp. 137f. below.
[29] As Errandonea, *SO* 21, seems to imply. The effect is rather one of tragic irony. Cf. n. 17 above.

audience to find in the words sung a relevance to him and to his actions.[30] But what has Creon in common with Lycurgus?

First, however, for Danae. There is an overt parallel between Danae and Antigone, since both were imprisoned in the dark; and the parallel goes beyond the mere fact of imprisonment. Antigone's tomb is also a bridal-chamber: ὦ τύμβος, ὦ νυμφεῖον (891) still rings in our ears.[31] It is a bridal-chamber to which, despite Creon, the bridegroom will come, though too late, and in which bride and bridegroom will lie together in death (1240f.). The chamber of Danae is like a tomb (τυμβήρης), but a θάλαμος, to which will come the golden seed of Zeus. The story was well known.[32] To Danae's father Acrisius it had been foretold that he would die at the hands of her son; in his fear, he shut up his daughter; in seeking to evade his fate, he set himself to obstruct the power of sex. But this was futile, since it was the *moira* of Danae to be Zeus's bride, of Acrisius to be killed by her child. It was futile, in this case, because the lover was Zeus, who could impregnate Danae miraculously. Creon also sought to obstruct the power of sexual passion, by taking Antigone from Haemon, by shutting her up to die. With a mortal lover he could succeed, but his success was bought at a price. If it was the *moira* of Antigone to die, it was the *moira* of Creon to lose his son and his wife (1337f.).

To those who have read the preceding discussion, if they have been at all convinced of the fundamental importance of the sexual theme in the *Trachiniae* and in our present play, this way of looking at the Danae-stanza will not, I trust, appear far-fetched; and we can turn to the antistrophe with a well-founded belief that the strophe bears on Creon (through the act of Acrisius) as well as on Antigone (through the sufferings of Danae). That it implies the fate of Acrisius is of course no new suggestion: after all, it was he, not Danae, that disposed of those resources of wealth and military force (953ff.) which are helpless to evade the terrible power of fate.[33]

Between strophe and antistrophe the verbal linkage may be all the more emphatic for the apparent tenuity of the parallel between Lycurgus and Antigone. Lycurgus too was shut up in a rocky prison. The imprisonment was in both cases a punishment (a fact we may

---

[30] The point is made by Kitto. Cf. Müller (1) 406, 416f.
[31] Cf. n. 15 above.
[32] And may already have been treated by Sophocles; cf. Webster, *IS* 173.
[33] Cf. Müller (1) 416.

suppose to have been in the minds of the singers). It is over the nature of the offence that the parallel breaks down. Antigone was imprisoned for disobeying a civil power which has become more and more clearly seen as a tyranny, Lycurgus for opposing divine powers (while Antigone claimed to be obeying such powers). A further point of discrepancy might seem to be that, whereas Antigone's is a death-sentence, Lycurgus, if imprisonment were all, would be mildly punished for such an offence. But was imprisonment the full extent of his punishment?[34] In Homer (*Il.* 6.130) he was blinded by Zeus and did not last long. How he was punished in Aeschylus we do not know, but the manner must have been terrible. In Apollodorus (3.511) his imprisonment on Mount Pangion was followed by his death, torn to pieces by horses at the command of Dionysus. More significantly, it was preceded by his madness, itself a punishment for rejecting the god and his worshippers; and in his madness he killed his own son Dryas.[35] There are vase-paintings which show him killing his son and his wife. Hence it has been suggested[36] that he stands here in a relation to Creon who caused the deaths of his son and his wife, the death of his son being at this point particularly relevant, after Haemon's threat of suicide. Still, the relevance might seem a little remote, the point to be taken rather obscure, depending upon an unmentioned fact[37] in a

---

[34] As Bowra, 105, rather strangely, seems to assume. Naturally the imprisonment is stressed, because it is the point of contact with Danae – and with Antigone; and naturally, if there *is* a relationship between Lycurgus and Creon, the death of Lycurgus will not be stated, since Creon will not die.

[35] How much in Apollodorus is Aeschylean? The abuse of the god and the persecution of his followers, certainly. The madness of Lycurgus and the killing of Dryas? A return to sanity, when (like Agave) he realized what he had done? Apollodorus says ἐσωφρόνησε; in the Sophocles chorus we find ἀποστάζει and ἐπέγνω.

[36] By Errandonea.

[37] It may be observed that Lycurgus is not called by his own name, but 'son of Dryas', and the grandfather may suggest the grandson.

   Can there be any reference at this stage of the play to the death of Eurydice? Unless (which we have no reason to suppose) the death of Creon's wife was a staple feature, such a reference could not have been seized by an audience at the time; and one is reluctant to suppose that Sophocles made points the effect of which depended on a remote and improbable retrospection. This affects Errandonea's interpretation of the third story in the ode. Cleopatra and her two sons are equated with Eurydice in the loss of both Haemon and Megareus. It is not so certain that an audience might not have assumed the death of Megareus, the references to which (1303, 1312f.) are so elliptical that Sophocles would seem to be taking some familiar story for granted. Creon had in some way been responsible for the death of Megareus; and one naturally thinks of Menoiceus in the *Phoenissae*. There Creon tries to save his son, which looks like a characteristic

myth well-known perhaps, but not obviously connected with the dramatic situation. To make this explanation really plausible, one must show Creon connected not merely with the punishment of Lycurgus which may be implied but also with his offence which is explicitly and emphatically given.

We are told, in this stanza, two things about Lycurgus: that he was angry and that he was mad. He was quick to wrath (ὀξύχολος, κερτομίοις ὀργαῖς) and expressed himself in abusive language (ἐν κερτομίοις γλώσσαις). The wrathfulness and the abusiveness of Creon need no illustration: they are felt in every scene, and particularly in his scene with Haemon. Towards the end of that scene Haemon, still striving to keep his temper, says (755): 'If you were not my father, I should have said you were not in your right mind (οὐκ εὖ φρονεῖν).' Ten lines later, the time for tact being over, he leaves the stage with a reference to such friends of Creon as are willing to put up with his mad company (ὡς τοῖς θέλουσι τῶν φίλων μαίνῃ ξυνών). If Creon is mad, in what does his madness consist? In what did the madness of Lycurgus consist?

The word μανία occurs twice in the stanza. It may have been – and I think was – intended to remind the audience of the well-known fact that, when mad, he killed his son. But, as it is put, the madness is associated rather with his opposition to the god whom he abused; it lies in his crude opposition to the god. Not only in his abuse (of which echoes reach us from the *Edoni* of Aeschylus), but in his whole policy (964): παύεσκε μὲν γὰρ ἐνθέους γυναῖκας εὔιόν τε πῦρ.[38] He tried to

Euripidean variant on a standard version in which he sacrifices him to the good of the state (as our Creon on his principles would do). It has been suggested that Teiresias' remark at 994 refers to this incident. Cf. 627 (νέατον γέννημα).

[38] Continuing: φιλαύλους τ' ἠρέθιζε Μούσας. One would dearly like to know whether the Muses had been brought into this affair before. Oddly, in the affair of Orpheus and the Bassarids, the Muses seem to have been on the other side (cf. fr. 83a Mette). Dionysus has a title Μελπόμενος (Farnell, *Cults of the Greek states* v (Oxford 1909) 307); he is associated in art with the aulos, the barbiton and the krotala. One would expect him to be associated with the Muses in the same kind of context that associates him with Aphrodite (see text below). Cf. Eur. *Bacch.* 409f. At *O.C.* 691f. the Muses and Aphrodite balance Dionysus at 678ff.: there may well be a reference to the dramatic choruses at Athens (cf. Knox, *HT* 154). It was in the theatre above all that the Muses were φίλαυλοι (though cf. Homeric Hymn to Hermes 540–2 and some fifth-century art). Did they also take their revenge? If so, it was through tragic poetry.

Edoni: cf. Dodds, *Bacchae* xxviii, who cites fr. 61 'and probably 59, 60, 62' (Mette 72, 73, 75, 74). The scene was the model for the first scene between Dionysus and Pentheus in the *Bacchae*.

stop women who were inspired by the god. These women were Maenades, and their god a god of madness; it was madness to oppose him. Madness on the one side, madness on the other. Now let us turn back to Creon and Haemon. Haemon tells us that Creon is mad; then, twenty-five lines later, the Chorus sings that the lover is mad: ὁ δ' ἔχων μέμηνεν. Again, madness on both sides.[39]

This surely reveals the pattern and the point of the first two stanzas of the Fourth Stasimon – and the reason for the introduction in the second stanza of a myth, at first sight not too apt, about Dionysus.[40] The close associations of Aphrodite and Dionysus in Greek art and literature need no demonstration.[41] Normally they are associated in contexts of relaxation and joy, but each has a double aspect. They are both powers of overmastering emotion, both productive of *mania*, with a potentiality of tragic disaster. Creon set himself against the power of Aphrodite, as Lycurgus set himself against Dionysus. In both cases it was an act of madness to oppose a god of madness and brought its own punishment. Creon was punished through the madness of Haemon's love which drove him to suicide. Dryas did not contribute to his own death, and this may be one reason why that death is not expressly mentioned, though it seems likely that Sophocles counted on his audience's knowing what Lycurgus did. However that may be, it is the parallel between the offences of Creon and Lycurgus that stands in the foreground; and in fact it is the offence of Lycurgus that takes up the greater part of the stanza. In the end Lycurgus came to recognize the god (ἐπέγνω) and that he was mad to assail him. So too Creon learns too late through the fruits of his unwisdom (1261ff., esp. 1272).[42]

I have tried to demonstrate a thematic relationship between the Danae- and Lycurgus-stanzas, and between both and the dramatic situation of the play. The issues and the facts are relatively clear. When we turn (as we must) to the remainder of the stasimon, we begin to labour under great difficulties, and what follows is said with

[39] Cf. 754f. and pp. 97f. above.
[40] There was a story that Acrisius too resisted Dionysus. It is known to us only from Ovid, *Met.* 3.559f., 4.606ff. We cannot say if it was known to Sophocles and have no reason to suppose that it was in his mind here.
[41] Cf. Dodds on *Bacch.* 402–16, who cites Anacreon fr. 2 Diehl, Eur. *Cycl.* 69ff. and vase-paintings; cults at Argos and in Achaea.
[42] The point is made by Errandonea, *SO* 22.

reserve. In considering the structure and relevance of the ode as a whole, it may be a matter of arguing towards the Cleopatra-story rather than from it.

The main difficulty is in the allusive lyric style of these two stanzas. It may not differ greatly from the style of the Danae and Lycurgus stanzas, but there we know, broadly and subject to one or two details, what Sophocles expected his audience to have in mind. It is not that we lack information about Cleopatra and the sons of Phineus: from play fragments, from scholia, from historians and mythographers we have almost too much. We know that Cleopatra was the daughter of Boreas and Oreithyia and that she married the Thracian king Phineus by whom she had two sons variously named. After her death, or while she was still alive, Phineus married Idaea or Eidothea,[43] and, for one reason or another, the sons of Cleopatra were blinded by their stepmother, by their father, or by their own mother. Phineus, for one reason or another, was blinded, and persecuted by the Harpies. The sons of Cleopatra died or had their sight restored, by Boreas or by Asclepius. In one version at any rate Cleopatra lived to triumph over her enemies. At some stage she or her sons or both may have suffered imprisonment. To sort all this out would take much space, but Jenssen has done it for us in Roscher, and there is a characteristically lucid account in Pearson, *Sophocles fragments* II 311ff.

It is clear that Sophocles expected his audience to recognize one version in particular, probably from a play, and very likely from a play of his own. Sophocles wrote two plays about Phineus, one of which may or may not be identical with the *Tympanistae*. One of the Phineus plays probably dealt with the release of Phineus from the

---

[43] Schol. Ap. Rhod. 2.178 ascribes to Sophocles (fr. 704 P) the story that Phineus was blinded because he himself blinded the sons of Cleopatra πεισθεὶς διαβολαῖς Ἰδαίας τῆς αὐτῶν μητρυίας. This is clearly not the version followed in the *Antigone* chorus. Schol. *Ant.* 981 states that after the death of Cleopatra Phineus married Ἰδαίαν τὴν Δαρδάνου, κατὰ δέ τινας Εἰδοθέαν τὴν Κάδμου ἀδελφήν, ἧς καὶ αὐτὸς Σοφοκλῆς μνημονεύει ἐν Τυμπανισταῖς· ἥτις ἐξ ἐπιβουλῆς τυφλώσασα κτλ. What follows *may* be the version envisaged in the chorus, i.e. Sophocles was cross-referring to his own *Tympanistae* (see below). Does this mean that the stepmother's name was Eidothea? Not necessarily, since κατὰ δέ τινας . . . ἀδελφήν may be parenthetic, referring back to Ἰδαίαν. We know so little of Eidothea that it is hard to say whether her link with the royal family of Thebes could have had any significance here. To some it has seemed that a princess from Asia Minor (as Idaea was) might well have been attended by τυμπανισταί in the service of the Great Mother. The whole matter remains most doubtful.

Harpies (and is likely to be irrelevant to our purposes), the other may have ended with the rescue of the Phineidae and the execution of their vengeance. This is Pearson's tentative conclusion, and a plausible one. Without possession of the play which lies behind the *Antigone* stanzas it is doubtful if we can ever solve the problem of their relevance; and the sensible motto is perhaps: *quod uides perisse perditum ducas.* I shall confine myself to making three or four suggestions or speculations.

(i) One thing is clear; that the children were blinded by their stepmother. But was their own mother alive or dead? If alive, was she in prison? We cannot even settle these questions. The evidence of the scholiast[44] strongly suggests that she was dead, but she cannot have died a natural death, by reason of the phrase with which she is first introduced (980). Her blinded sons weep for their piteous sufferings: ματρὸς ἔχοντες ἀνύμφευτον γονάν. The phrase is rightly translated and explained by Jebb: 'those sons of a mother hapless in her marriage'. What made her marriage hapless? Not premature death; murder perhaps, though there is no such murder in the tradition. But if she was set aside to make room for a rival the phrase bears its full weight of meaning.[45] The external evidence for her imprisonment is weak,[46] but Jebb was probably right to assume it, and for two reasons. First, though it is wrong to interpret the ode entirely in terms of the thought-processes of the Chorus, still the singers must be allowed a thread of thought. The thread which joins Lycurgus to Danae in their minds is the stout cable of imprisonment. When they pass through the feeble link of Thracian locality to the Cleopatra-story, they should not be supposed to have lost all sense of relevance, particularly as they revert to Antigone at the end. After all, what set their minds working was the departure of Antigone for the tomb. My second argument is aesthetic, and perhaps therefore suspect. The salient feature of the last stanza[47] is the picture of this daughter of Boreas 'reared in far-distant

---

[44] Quoted by Pearson II 267. This evidence is admittedly very strong, since it comes from comment on the passage and is the only other testimony which makes the stepmother herself do the blinding. Two phrases invite comment. μετὰ τὸν Κλεοπάτρας θάνατον: this is naturally, but not necessarily, taken of 'natural' death. ἐν τάφῳ καθεῖρξεν (of the sons): 'in a tomb'. Whose tomb? Cleopatra's?

[45] Μοῖραι in the antistrophe is of course consistent both with death and with grievous trials which (like Danae) she survived.

[46] It could hardly be weaker, consisting in the statement of Diodorus (4.44.3) that Heracles, after killing Phineus, brought Cleopatra out of prison (ἐκ τῆς φυλακῆς προαγαγεῖν) and restored the Phineidae.

[47] Much clarified by H. Lloyd-Jones, *CQ* 51 (1957) 24f.

caves with the Storm-winds of her father, riding the air with them over the steep mountain-range'. A pretty picture for its own sake, perhaps. But can we not entertain the notion that, whereas Danae lost the light of heaven, this daughter of the gods lost the freedom to ride winged through heaven itself?[48] The point is not to be pressed, but, if the description of the Boread maiden implies her subsequent imprisonment, it may also imply her release and restitution by Boreas or the Boreads – and the punishment of her persecutors (like the punishment of Acrisius).

(ii) It is the strophe, not the antistrophe, that raises real difficulties about relevance. We can say with Jebb that the sufferings of the Phineidae are merely ancillary to the fate of Cleopatra, but that does not seem quite how Sophocles has written it. Cleopatra does not enter until the second line of the antistrophe; then there is the link with Athens (self-justified in any Attic tragedy) and a working back through the picture of the untrammelled Boread towards a relevance to Antigone. The strophe, after the initial topographic link, is concentrated upon a brutal act and its pathetic consequences; and this theme is carried on into the first lines of the antistrophe. One might add that it implies the punishment of this act. When we look at the compressed and striking language of the stanza, we must observe that the wound is ἀρατόν; the orbs of the eyes struck with the shuttle are ἀλαστόροισιν – they call down vengeance.[49] Now, generally speaking, in Greek tragedy a curse implies its fulfilment (which is a reason among others for supposing that the version here is one in which the Phineidae and their mother were avenged). An avenged crime might have its relevance to Creon. Is the crime also relevant, as we have seen the crime of Lycurgus to be? Here we are at a loss in our ignorance, and particularly because we do not know the part played by Phineus (who may have been innocent or associated with the guilt of his new wife). In view of the relationship which I have sought to establish between the Danae and Lycurgus stories, one would like to see in this case also some futile opposition to the forces of emotion, but this is not easily found, though it might be suggested that the poet now turns to the other sin of Creon – not the sin against ἔρως, but the sin against φιλία? This was a crime within the family, against the family (particularly if Phineus connived at it), and so appropriate to the curse and the

[48] Lloyd-Jones uses the phrase ἐν οὐρανῷ ἱππεύουσα (cf. Eur. Phoen. 212).
[49] On the language of this passage see Goheen 71f.

Fury. The next scene in the play will deal with the issue of burial – the non-burial of Polynices, the burial alive of Antigone; and Creon will be told by Teiresias (1074ff.) that Erinyes are lying in wait for him. That there *is* a relevance to the offence of Creon must be highly probable, but we cannot be much more precise.[50]

(iii) What, finally, of the role of divine powers in the economy of the ode? It has long been recognized that the power of fate may be a unifying theme, and something has been said about this already. But, if there is the power of Fate, there are also specific gods at work. Aphrodite is not mentioned in the Danae-stanza, but after the Third Stasimon her agency can perhaps be taken for granted; Dionysus controls the action against Lycurgus quite specifically. One expects the third episode also to have its significant presiding deity. One expects it, and one finds it. Ares stands in the forefront, his name coming immediately after the geographical introduction of the scene and before the statement of the action: ἵν' ἀγχίπολις Ἄρης | δισσοῖσι Φινείδαις εἶδεν ἀρατὸν ἕλκος. Ares is appropriate, because he is a Thracian god, and because the action is cruel (though one might say that a blinding for private motives is not obviously appropriate to Ares). 'He saw the wound dealt', writes Jebb, 'i.e. it was a deed such as he loves to see.' But Jebb also says that, when Ares is given the epithet ἀγχίπολις, there may be a special reference to some local shrine. One would certainly like to suppose that the connection of Ares with the action was rather closer than Jebb's quoted comment assumes. Herkenrath,[51] among many unprofitable speculations about the *Tympanistae* (which he believed to lie behind the *Antigone* passage), suggested that the shrine of Ares may actually have been the scene of the atrocity. The suggestion is attractive, but cannot be proved. Ares I believe to be a clue, but a clue which we may never be in a position to follow up.

[50] In lyrics such as these there may be many suggestions which appear and disappear like will-o'-the-wisps deluding the critic. Take the theme of blindness, for instance. At the end of the ode there enters a blind prophet. Phineus was, traditionally, a blind prophet. Then Phineus was, in this version of the story, punished with blindness? This could hardly be asserted! Oedipus blinded himself, in a context of curses. References to the self-blinding are, however, absent from the play, apart from 49–52. Are we meant to think of him, putting ἀραχθέντων (975) alongside ἀράξας (52)? It is more than doubtful. If Idaea, instead of killing her stepsons, blinded them and left them to die, this could have been a futile precaution against blood-guilt, like Creon's (775f.).

[51] E. Herkenrath, *Berl. Phil.-Woch.* 1930, 331.

This is because we have lost the vital play, and because we know so little about the Thracian Ares. Sophocles doubtless knew more. What little we know is summarized by the sober Farnell:[52] 'a war-god, who sometimes assumed the form of a wolf, who gave oracles, who delighted in human sacrifices, and who at times died and was buried; and *such a god might have been a double of Dionysus*' (my italics). Jane Harrison (*Proleg.* 375ff.) has more to say about the relationship between Ares and Dionysus, whom she sees as Thracian rivals. Herodotus[53] tells us that the gods principally worshipped in Thrace were Ares, Dionysus, and Artemis. The Thracian Artemis is likely to have resembled the Great Mother rather than the virgin goddess, and there is a prima facie likelihood that all these Thracian cults were orgiastic. The interest of this for our investigation lies in the possibility that in the background of the Phineus story lay an orgiastic cult. I cannot refrain from referring once again to the *Tympanistae* of Sophocles, which certainly seems to have dealt with the story of Phineus and Cleopatra, and which had as its chorus players on the tambourine. But in whose cult they played we do not know.

This is all very vague and tantalizing. I merely insist that we should not overlook the role of Ares as the presiding deity of the third episode of this choral ode. Aphrodite, Dionysus, Ares. Aphrodite the companion of Dionysus in joy and madness; Ares the lover of Aphrodite; Dionysus and Ares rival or brother gods in Thrace. Yet all three having links with Thebes. Antigone, as she leaves the stage, calls to witness the city of her fathers and the princes of Thebes who form the Chorus, but also (rather oddly) 'the gods our forebears' (θεοὶ προγενεῖς, 938). 'She thinks esp.', I quote from Jebb (and I am glad these are his suggestions, not mine), 'of Ares and Aphrodite, the parents of Harmonia, wife of Cadmus . . . Dionysus, the son of "Cadmean" Semele (1115), is another of the deities meant.' If we are looking for intelligible structure in the ode which immediately follows, it is worth considering whether it was not, for one thing, built around these three great gods who played a role in the story of the Theban royal house – gods whose nature was not irrelevant to the disastrous action of our play. There is still, perhaps, something to be said about Dionysus, though it is said with considerable reserve.

[52] *Cults of the Greek states* v 400.
[53] v. 7.

III. *Antigone 1115–52*

We have been considering the Fourth Stasimon of *Antigone*. That Ares enters into this ode, along with Aphrodite and Dionysus, as one of a trio of deities, a third power of irrational emotion within the human soul, is a speculation which has its attraction but can hardly be substantiated upon the evidence available to us. The argument which relates the first two stanzas in terms of the respective powers of Aphrodite and Dionysus, the folly of those who set themselves up in unreasoned opposition to them, seems to rest upon a more solid foundation; and, if there is anything in the argument, it should not be without significance for the attitude of Sophocles towards the gods. It is a commonplace that his world was full of gods and that he interpreted human life in relation to divine powers; and in the discussions of modern scholars we read much about a Zeus who exercises stern justice, an Athena who commends *sophrosune,* and about the god of Delphi. About the gods of unrestrained emotion little or nothing is said.[54] To Euripides (and no doubt also to Aeschylus) they were very real, very dangerous, very much a part, if a problematic part, of the divine universe. If this were not true of Sophocles, no doubt our ingenuity could find reasons for it: but, in the light of *Trachiniae* and *Antigone,* can we be so sure that it is not true?

Yet, when modern scholars write on Sophocles, we read little about Aphrodite – and less about Dionysus. And for that there is more excuse. Reinhardt[55] points out that, unlike Aeschylus and Euripides, Sophocles does not represent *enthusiasmos* on the stage; and indeed he appears never to have written a *Bassarids,* a *Pentheus,* a *Bacchae.* Dionysus will have come into some of his satyr-plays (*Dionysiscus,* for instance). The *Hydrophori* may have dealt with the birth of the god from Semele. There is reason to suppose that the wife of Athamas, in the play of that name, had joined the Maenads in their worship.[56] Granted that there was no chorus of devotees (not even in

---

[54] But cf. Segal, *Arion* 3 (1964) 2.58, who, writing of *Antigone,* speaks of 'the increasing prominence of Eros and Dionysus, the mythical embodiments of the least rational or "controllable" elements in human experience, in the odes of the second half of the play'.

[55] *Sophokles* 86.

[56] Cf. Pearson 1 3.

Tympanistae?), it may be rash to draw the obvious conclusion that Sophocles was not interested, rash to forget that he, no less than Euripides, was familiar with the two Dionysiac trilogies of Aeschylus (and it may well be the *Lycurgeia* that in part lies behind the second stanza of the Fourth Stasimon). Dionysus may have meant more to Sophocles than has generally been supposed.

Dionysus enters into *Antigone* three times, as he has every right to enter into a Theban play. At the end of the Parodos (147ff.), the Chorus, in the joy of victory and in a desire to forget war (which Creon will not let them do), sing that they will visit all the temples of the gods with night-long dances, and they ask that Bakchios, the shaker of Thebes, may be their leader. That is his first entry. His last is when Creon has yielded to Teiresias and appears to be on the way to undoing his harmful acts. Then, as the Fifth Stasimon, the Chorus sing and dance a hymn to Dionysus which Jebb describes as a 'strain full of gladness, invoking the healing presence of the bright and joyous god who protects Thebes'; and he refers, rightly, to other plays in which Sophocles has employed a similar ironical device – a song of gladness immediately preceding a catastrophe. Between these two passages comes the Fourth Stasimon and the story of Lycurgus which shows Dionysus in a very different role. The double aspect of this god, developed with such explicit emphasis in the *Bacchae,* must have been familiar long before Euripides and may well have been emphasized in the Dionysiac trilogies of Aeschylus.

Now the simple supposition is that in *Antigone* Sophocles has taken the two aspects of Dionysus and used them as each was appropriate and without relation to one another. But, for my part, I cannot help wondering whether the irony of this hymn of joy (if it is rightly so described) may not lie a little deeper than in the mere fact that it is joyful; whether the audience is meant to forget the story of Lycurgus (and its bearing on Creon and Haemon) which precedes the Teiresias-scene, when it hears the hymn to Dionysus which follows it and precedes the entry of the Messenger. It depends of course on how close one thinks the texture of a Sophoclean play to be; it depends also upon the tone and content of the song. The hymn ends, in the convention of such kletic hymns, with the appeal for a manifestation (προφάνηθ' ὦναξ, 1149); they pray that the god may appear, along with the Thyiads who are his companions – the Thyiads who in madness (μαινόμεναι) dance all night long the dance of Iakchos the

Dispenser (τὸν ταμίαν).[57] Are we so sure that the events of which we are now to hear are not dispensed by the god and a manifestation of his divinity? The last time we heard of Maenads was in the Lycurgus-stanza of the Fourth Stasimon; and the last time we heard of madness it was the madness of Lycurgus who set himself against the Mad Women. It has been suggested that the opposition of Lycurgus to the cult of Dionysus stood in close relation to Creon's opposition to the mad forces of emotion roused in Haemon's breast by that other patron deity of passion, the invincible goddess Aphrodite. The madness of Haemon has punished the madness of Creon, and this is about to become known. It might seem therefore that a lyrical appeal to Dionysus to manifest himself with his Maenads could be a not inappropriate introduction of the Messenger.

To the Messenger himself the downfall of Creon seems to be a matter of tuche (four times in 1158f.), just as another ordinary man of little insight – the Watchman – thought it was a matter of tuche whether the criminal was caught or not (328) and expressed himself in very similar terms. And they both mean blind chance. The Messenger (who need not have been present during the Teiresias-scene) adds that no one can prophesy (μάντις οὐδείς) to men about things which are 'firmly settled', but Teiresias[58] had already foretold the end of Creon's prosperity; and when he told him that he stood 'upon the razor-edge of fortune' (ἐπὶ ξυροῦ τύχης, 996), he meant by tuche something different – he meant θεῶν τύχη, the fortune that the gods dispense. Now whether chance played any part in these events,[59] and if so whether such 'chances' were merely fortuitous or part of a divine plan are questions not easy to answer. But one thing is fairly certain: after the Teiresias-scene, after the appeal to Dionysus to manifest himself and his description as tamias, and before the Messenger's news, the stress on tuche at 1158f. cannot be itself fortuitous.

Interpretation must depend, however, upon the tone and content of the song; and the tone of lyric poetry, and particularly of Sopho-

---

[57] The word is common of men and of gods, and among gods especially of Zeus (cf. fr. 590 P). One would like to think it was associated with Iakchos at Eleusis, but I know of no evidence for this.

[58] Cf. Kitto, FMD 175.

[59] Cf. Linforth (1961) 247. Was it chance that Creon came first to the body of Polynices and wasted time (note the elaborate operations of 1203f.)? Was it chance that Eurydice heard the news (1182, 1186) before the return of Creon who might have prevented her suicide?

clean lyric, is hard to judge, not least when he is writing a hymn and using the themes and language proper to a hymn.[60] Nevertheless the attempt must be made. It is, says Jebb, 'a strain full of gladness', akin to other songs of joy in *Oedipus Tyrannus, Ajax,* and *Trachiniae*. But Sophocles who often seems to be repeating from play to play devices which he has found effective is always found on examination to be making subtle variations. How joyful in fact does this song turn out to be, when we examine it? And first it must be observed that Dionysus is not (as in the Parodos) summoned to preside over a joyful celebration but to come 'with purifying foot', to come as healer. To this expression we shall return, for it is crucial.

The first stanza opens with the vocative πολυώνυμε: Dionysus is a god of many names, of many cults, of many aspects. Thebes, naturally, comes first and last, but there is mention of Italy (or Ikaria?)[61] and of Eleusis, which links him with Athens – but also with the realm of the dead. In this stanza there is no light or colour or time of day; there is no movement – Dionysus is here, is there, he dwells in Thebes, mother-city of Bacchanals. In the second stanza movement begins. The Corycian nymphs of Bacchus move in their dance. The god is seen in Delphi; it is night, and there could be something sinister in the murky light of the torches (στέροψ λιγνύς).[62] Then the god himself is on the move, from the hills of Nysa with their ivy and vines; he is on the way to Thebes, and we sense his approach, which could be frightening. But he honours Thebes above all cities – he and his mother whom the lightning slew. So the Chorus pray him to come 'with purifying foot', over the height of Parnassus or the Groaning Strait. If he is coming from the East, from Nysa, he is nearer now, at the Euripus: he is very near. With the fourth stanza, the appeal reaches its climax. He is hailed as leader of the dance of the stars, of the stars which breathe fire (ἰὼ πῦρ πνειόντων χοράγ' ἄστρων). The editors have no difficulty in illustrating the association of Dionysus with the dance of the stars, perhaps a feature of Eleusinian ritual. But what an

[60] Cf. A. E. Harvey, *CQ* n.s. 7 (1957) 215 n. 2.
[61] See the editions of Jebb and Müller. The former has a well-balanced discussion of this difficult issue, on which I express no opinion.
[62] Cf. Müller's edition p. 246. His analysis (244–50) of the thought and diction of the Fifth Stasimon has much in common with my own, but I cannot follow him when he finds a relevance to Antigone first in the fate of Semele and then in the Maenads of 1150. He is probably right, however, to stress the chthonian associations of Dionysus as a feature of the ode.

extraordinary epithet the stars are given! In how many passages in Greek literature is πῦρ πνεῖν or πύρπνοος used without a suggestion of hostility?[63] Have we here a vague hint, in lyrical terms, of hostility in the heavenly world of night? The lights flashing in the darkness may belong to the order of the lightning that blasted Semele.[64] Fire is dangerous. It was the fire of Dionysus that Lycurgus tried to stop (964) and that Pentheus in the *Bacchae* tried to put out.[65] Dionysus is leader of the dance of the stars, he is master of voices in the night, his companions dance all night long – and they are mad. The Dispenser is near at hand.

From these vague suggestive phrases let us turn to something more solid. The Chorus appeal to Dionysus to come and purify, which is to cure, because the city and all its people are held by a violent plague (βιαίας . . . ἐπὶ νόσου).[66] To purify is indeed a function sometimes, though not often, attributed to him, perhaps mainly through his paradoxical association with the god of Delphi (whence he may now be on his way to Thebes). The Chorus may be thinking particularly of the words of Teiresias: 'it is from your mind that the city is thus sick' (καὶ ταῦτα τῆς σῆς ἐκ φρενὸς νοσεῖ πόλις, 1015); thinking of the pollution arising from the non-burial of Polynices; counting on Dionysus to sanction and support the efforts which Creon so conscientiously makes to rectify his error. But may it not be in connection with the other crime of Creon – the burial alive of Antigone – that Dionysus will manifest himself?

---

[63] Cf. Hoey, *Arion* 9 (1970) 344, with references in n. 11, where Pindar, *Ol.* 7.71, is cited as the sole exception, the notion there being 'vigorous, if not violent, effort', but with no implication of destructive violence.

[64] Müller (2) 247: 'Schon daraus [the epithet 'fire-breathing'] wird deutlich, dass wir die göttliche Majestät des Feuers als schrecklich verstehen sollen, im gleichen Sinne, wie es der Blitzstrahl des Zeus für Semele war (1139).' Genealogy is a staple feature of hymns, and that of Dionysus was bound to imply the violent death of Semele (which was also her glory). One cannot be too confident, therefore, in attaching significance to the bold κεραυνίᾳ at 1139 (cf. 1116), while noting that it is immediately followed by a reference to violence and then by an apparently menacing fire. The savage snake of 1124 is another abhorrent ingredient in this remarkable lyric.

[65] Eur. *Bacch.* 622ff.

[66] 'Die Krankheit der Stadt heisst ja auch βιαία nicht nur, weil sie selbst gewalttätig ist, sondern auch, weil sie durch einer Gewalttat entstand' (Müller (2) 247). If there is deliberate ambiguity here, as I incline to think, it may be rather wider: 'a violent plague', 'a plague of violence' (which Dionysus will intensify rather than cure).

Goheen,[67] who studies the metaphor of disease throughout the play, remarks on this passage that 'the actual "cure" takes place through the more terrible and real process of tragic retribution and tragic waste rather than at the hands of a *deus ex machina*'. Müller sees that the Chorus jump to conclusions too soon, believing that the problem is solved and the moment for joy arrived, not knowing that the god is bringing something which, if terrible *(das Schreckliche)*, he sees as good and wholesome for the city and for Creon, a *katharsis*. This is not quite in focus. It is true that the city needs purification, but even Creon through the formal act of burial can bring this about. It is true that the breaking of Creon's own life, when he is given over to remorse, could be seen as a kind of atonement.[68] But perhaps it is the irony of the Chorus' prayer which is most salient. What takes place, what the Messenger relates, is an outbreak of pathological violence which it would be vain to hope that Dionysus would cure, since it springs from mad emotion.[69] That is the epiphany, that is the dispensation.

Let us return briefly to the Parodos,[70] at the end of which Dionysus is prayed to lead a joyful celebration of peace (150–4). It has been pointed out[71] that this, as a preparation for Creon, is parallel to the preparation of the Messenger's entry by the prayer to Dionysus in the Fifth Stasimon – both ironical, since Creon will ensure that war is not forgotten and the Messenger will reveal something very different from the hopes which the Chorus place in Dionysus. I have suggested that the Stasimon embodies some sinister hints of the destructive aspect of the god which is so prominent in the Fourth Stasimon. Of this the close of the Parodos might seem quite innocent. But the specific naming of the Bacchic god (154) is not the first reference to Bacchic worship in the song. There is the metaphor which, at the beginning of the second strophe (135f.), describes the assault of Capaneus 'the fire-carrier' *(πυρφόρος)*, who is said to 'revel with mad

---

[67] 43.

[68] Cf. 1284, with Jebb's note on δυσκάθαρτος λιμήν.

[69] This is irony of the same order as when, in the *Tyrannus*, Jocasta comes out of the palace, makes sacrifice to Apollo and prays him to provide 'a pure solution' (*O. T.* 921). Cf. p. 182 below.

[70] There comes a point at which the speculative interpreter is wise to hold back, if he is not to destroy his own credit! Any reader who feels that this point has been reached (or passed) should perhaps refrain from reading the remainder of this chapter.

[71] Müller (2) 247.

impulse' (μαινομένᾳ ξὺν ὁρμᾷ βακχεύων); and this is the first, but by
no means the last, reference to madness in the play. If this were a
common metaphor in Sophocles, we should make nothing of it, but
Jebb writes that 'this is the only place where Sophocles connects *evil*
frenzy with the name of a god whom this same Ode invokes (154)'.
The statement is correct, except insofar as it may ignore some of the
implications of 955ff. It may not be too rash, then, to suggest that he
may have used the metaphor with deliberation and in the knowledge
of all that would be said and shown about Dionysus in the remainder
of the play and, above all, as a qualification of the aspect in which the
god is seen at the end of the Parodos. The two references are in strong
contrast, one in a context of war, the other of peaceful celebration,
but they stand close to one another and between them embrace the
last strophe and antistrophe. If, as may well be possible in lyric poetry,
the first reference sheds an influence on the second, the innocence of
'the shaker' may be contaminated with the violence of Ares (139) and
the whole phrase (Θήβας ἐλελίχθων Βάκχιος ἄρχοι) take on a sinister
import. An ode which began with the rays of the sun, the bright light
of victory, ends in the darkness of night. If it ends with war forgotten
and the victory celebrated in joy, the sequel, thanks to Creon, will be
far different. It could be that the closing words of the Parodos are a
more appropriate preparation than one had supposed for the entry of
a Creon whose emotionalism precipitates new disaster.

CHAPTER SIX

Creon and Antigone

To take the *eros*-theme, as we have done, and examine it more or less in isolation from the rest of *Antigone*, gives a distorted impression of the play as a whole. It is only one figure in the pattern, though perhaps a more important one than has generally been recognized. But where does its importance lie? Haemon was in love and acted tragically under the influence of Aphrodite's power, but he is a minor character; if Antigone was in love, her tragic action was otherwise determined. I have argued above that the theme bears most significantly upon a Creon who set himself to fight against that unconquerable force who is *amachos*. And the persistence of this theme in the second half of the play might lead us to regard Creon as the central character. Creon or Antigone? This is one of the issues upon which interpreters have been divided.

Antigone is a singularly difficult play to understand. Which is strange, since it makes a universal appeal and has probably been acted in modern times more frequently and more successfully than any other Greek tragedy. Some might say that we make the difficulties for ourselves by seeking more in the play than Sophocles was minded to put into it, though I doubt if this is true. Certainly the divergence of critical opinion has been extreme,[1] with the currents surging this way and that. There is of course an easy way of interpreting *Antigone*, as there is of interpreting *Ajax*. We can interpret them both as essentially Aeschylean tragedies of the punishment of *hubris* – in *Antigone* the *hubris* of Creon.[2] That there is no validity in such interpretations I

[1] Brought out, with a very full bibliography, by D. A. Hester, *Mnem*. s. iv 24 (1971) 11–59.
[2] Torrance 299f.: 'Seen as the tragedy of Creon the play is a perfectly rational dramatization of the familiar *hybris–ate* formula'.

117

would not seek to maintain. Yet, in the comparisons which have been made between the two plays, it is Antigone who finds herself compared to Ajax, while Creon finds his counterpart in the Atridae.[3] Let us look first at Creon's claims to be the major character.

These claims are prima facie strong. There is the sheer length of his part, far longer than Antigone's. Antigone opens the play with Ismene,[4] but after the Parodos until the end of the play Creon is seldom 'off the stage'. This is more than a cliché, for – and this is unusual – he is certainly present during two of the choral odes, and perhaps during a third,[5] which means that he is visible to the audience for a longer continuous period and for a greater total length of time than could be paralleled of one who is not central to his play. Moreover – and this is not unconnected with his presence on the stage – it is characteristic of choral odes in *Antigone* that, by a variety of tragic irony, they have a relevance to him which is not in the minds of the singers.[6] The closing scene is his, and the closing comment of the chorus-leader is evoked by his fate and derives its truth from his character and actions. (This comment at least, whatever may be true of some, is not a set of trivial commonplaces uttered while the audience relax and rustle.)

'Wisdom (τὸ φρονεῖν) is by far the first foundation of happiness (εὐδαιμονίας). Yes, and it is essential never to lack piety towards the gods. Great words of over-proud men, paying the penalty of great blows, teach wisdom in old age.' Creon has spoken proud words; Creon has suffered great blows; Creon has learnt, too late, that he lacked wisdom. The theme is Aeschylean: *pathei mathos*. Unlike many Aeschylean figures, Creon learns in his own person, for he remains alive, coming on stage like Xerxes at the end of the play a broken man. There is much in the language and tone of the Exodos to remind us of the *Persae*: the remorse of the hero, the recriminations of the Chorus. And if Creon seems to have learnt more than Xerxes, there are limits to what he has come to understand.[7] That *Antigone* is full of

---

[3] Torrance 297f.

[4] In the four plays which have one obviously central character *(Ajax, O.T., El., O.C.)* that character is introduced before the Parodos. In *Trach.* Deianira shares the interest with Heracles, in *Phil.* Neoptolemus with Philoctetes. But we have too few plays to generalize about Sophoclean practice.

[5] See p. 136 n. 58 below.

[6] On choral irony see Müller (1) passim; Bowra 114f.; Coleman 5.

[7] See p. 164 below.

Aeschylean echoes has long been recognized. When the Coryphaeus, at the end of the play, spoke of great and boastful words, Sophocles may have meant to recall an earlier choral comment: 'Zeus strongly hates the boasts of a great tongue' (128, Ζεὺς γὰρ μεγάλης γλώσσης κόμπους ὑπερεχθαίρει); and, when that was followed by a specific reference to the fate of Capaneus (134ff.), members of the audience may have recalled the 'Redepaare' in the Septem, the arrogance of those who were attacking Thebes, the sobriety of its defenders.[8] It could well be that the background of the history of the Labdacid house assumed by Sophocles owed more to the Aeschylean trilogy than we can discern in the absence of its two earlier plays; and in particular that we should assume for Antigone a father more Aeschylean than the Oedipus whom Sophocles had not yet created. As it is, for an Aeschylean treatment of a doomed house we must go to the Oresteia; and it is in the light of the Oresteia that we must view the Second Stasimon of Antigone, the roles played in it by Zeus and an Erinys, and certain features of the kommos between Antigone and the Chorus.

So we are back with Antigone, which is what tends to happen in the study of this play. It is Antigone who belongs to the doomed house, to which Creon is connected only by marriage[9] (and by the prospective marriage of his son). Antigone dies, joining all the dead of her family who lie in Hades. How Aeschylean is the fate of Antigone? To this also we must return, first noting that the Aeschylean hero collaborates in his own downfall. And who could have collaborated more whole-heartedly than Antigone in bringing about her death? She collaborates with her enemy; the typical Aeschylean hero collaborates with the gods by his own wrongdoing. Did Antigone do wrong?

So we come back to the old questions. Was Antigone right (or wholly right)? Was Creon wrong (or wholly wrong)? It is not certain that these are the most interesting questions to be asked about the play, at least when put, flatly, in this way. Or rather Sophocles could have made them more interesting – and more difficult – but chose not to do so. There was a conflict – a Hegelian conflict – between the

[8] Adams 46 finds a reminiscence in Creon's use of the 'ship of state' metaphor at 162f. and 178. This metaphor has indeed structural importance in Septem, but it is relatively common in tragedy, which makes one hesitate.

[9] Coleman 13.

claims of the family and the claims of the city.[10] And at first it seems as though Sophocles is going to develop his play upon the lines of this conflict, when Antigone is shown in the Prologos narrowly concentrated upon the family and utterly indifferent to the city, when Creon, in his speech after the Parodos (a position of great importance in a Greek play), is given his case as spokesman of the *polis,* saying things, for instance about the subordination of personal attachments to the public interest, to which an Athenian audience might well respond favourably.

Aeschylus had written a trilogy on the Theban legend, of which we possess *Septem* only. It must have been in the mind of Sophocles and, for him and many of his audience, may have had the character of a standard version of the story. In the trilogy the fates of *genos* and *polis* were dangerously intertwined and the salvation of the *polis* depended on the destruction of the *genos.*[11] In *Antigone* Sophocles dramatizes the final – and non-Aeschylean – phase of the destruction of the *genos,* in which a member of the *genos* sets herself up against the *polis* – and is destroyed. Does she endanger it, and does her destruction save it? So Creon thinks, or purports to think. And he is proved wrong. As we shall see, Sophocles progressively undercuts the moral stance of Creon, showing him up not only as a tyrant but, despite all his gnomic utterance, as an emotional creature compounded of fear and ambition; deserted by Haemon, condemned by Teiresias, he is ultimately punished through his family. His case is whittled away and with it the play that Sophocles might have written but preferred not to write.

The issue on which the action turns is burial and the refusal of burial. Not to bury is ugly; it is decreed, as in *Ajax,* by a man who turns out to be tyrannically minded. Therefore Antigone was right. But this oversimplifies the issue as presented in the course of the play. One critic writes:[12] 'It is not . . . evidently repugnant to leave the corpse of a *polemios* unburied: what is at issue in *Ajax* and *Antigone* is the status of the dead man.' To reply that an action described as Sophocles has described it is inherently repugnant does not settle the

---

[10] On this cf. (most recently) Vickers 544.

[11] Cf. *YCS* 25 (1977) 1–45.

[12] O. Taplin, in a review of Gellie, *CR* 26 (1976) 119. Cf. W. R. Connor, *The new politicians of fifth-century Athens* (Princeton, N.J. 1971) 51: 'It would be perfectly all right to leave an enemy unburied, but kin, Polynices, must not be treated in this horrible way.'

matter, since it might be regarded as one of those things, like warfare itself, repugnant but justifiable on political grounds, which is, broadly, Creon's position, though perhaps he shows some sign of relishing the act. Nor can we settle the matter by searching the mind of Antigone. It is true that, when forced to argue by Ismene, she accuses her sister of 'dishonouring what the gods' – and she means the nether gods – 'hold in honour' (76f.), but there was doubtless no clear distinction in her mind between the duty of burial which those gods imposed upon the kin and the right of the dead as such to be buried.[13] Haemon twice refers (745, 749) to the claims of the nether gods, but, to make the distinction clear Sophocles needed Teiresias, who plays a similar role in this play to Calchas in *Ajax*, clarifying late in the play a religious issue which (despite earlier hints) has been left unclear. About the authenticity of 1080–3 there is doubt.[14] If the lines are genuine, *polemioi* have been left unburied, with deplorable results in prospect for the city, but even from those lines which are concerned with Polynices (1064ff., cf. 1016–18) it is clear enough that Creon's offence was not that he had obstructed the burial of a kinsman but rather that, just as he has sent a living soul to a tomb, he has kept a dead man from the realm to which he belongs. For this he will be punished by 'the Erinyes of Hades and the gods' (1075). Erinyes punish breaches of divine justice; Antigone had spoken of a Justice which dwells with the nether gods (451). However much or little she understood, Antigone was right.[15]

The conclusion is inescapable, but not in itself sufficient to sustain the weight of this great play without the strength and depth of the characters involved. What sort of a man was Creon and how did he come to act as he did? What sort of a woman was Antigone and how did she come by her formidable heroism? As has often been remarked, the issue from beginning to end of the play is a matter of *phrenes*, of states of mind, which may be good or bad, wise or foolish, salutary or destructive, which determine decisions for good or ill. That is the issue between Antigone and Ismene in the Prologos, between Creon and Antigone, between Creon and Haemon; it is the

---

[13] In which, as such, she was not interested? Her remark at 517 need not perhaps be taken too seriously (she is not a good arguer) or matched too closely against 519; on 10 see n. 55.

[14] Defended by Jebb and retained by Pearson, the lines were deleted by Wunder, who is followed by Müller (v. ad loc.).

[15] Right for the wrong reason? Cf. Knox *HT* 116.

gist of Teiresias' criticism of Creon and a theme which dominates the
closing scene and the final choral comment. πολλῷ τὸ φρονεῖν
εὐδαιμονίας πρῶτον ὑπάρχει (1347f.). *To phronein:* what is it?[16] The
semantic range is wide. 'Wisdom' is often a serviceable translation;
and we then say, with some truth, that it illustrates a Greek tendency
to intellectualize the expression of ethical matters. 'Wisdom' or
'sense', 'good sense' – or indeed 'sanity'; and the difference between
sanity and madness is not simply intellectual. The term – or
terms – clearly are not limited to what we should call intellectual
processes but include emotional factors: they refer to 'states of mind'
in the widest sense. Now there are fields to which the state of a man's
mind is of particular significance – the field of religion above all; and
it is such a field that the Coryphaeus contemplates at the end of the
play. But every aspect of the drama reflects in some degree the states
of mind of the participants. Just as in *Ajax* the state of the *phren* or
phrenes of the hero (regarded in terms of sanity and madness) is a
cardinal issue, no less is it true of *Antigone* that the state of the *phrenes*
of Antigone and Creon (and Ismene and Haemon) is crucial. 'It is
impossible', says Creon (175–7), 'to learn of any man his *psuche* and
phronema and *gnome* until he has been put visibly to the test in office
and in law.'[17] Perhaps we can discover the states of mind of Creon
without too much difficulty.

It is as general (8) that he first makes his proclamation:[18] he enters,
from the battlefield, as king (155) – as a *new* king. He has summoned a
council of elders, to whom, now in the civil sphere, he promulgates
his decree. But first a disquisition, a statement of principles. The elders
have been chosen for their loyalty to the throne: of Laius, of Oedipus,
of their sons. Very discreet here, about Laius and Oedipus, until he

---

[16] The language is carefully examined by C. Knapp, 'A point in the interpretation of
the Antigone of Sophocles', *AJP* 37 (1916) 300–16.

[17] Long, 53, speaks of 'an unnecessarily detailed inventory' of psychological qualities
and remarks that 'an interest in precise definitions, uncharacteristic of Sophocles,
is shown throughout this play'. Dodds, *GI* 139, says that 'Sophocles is arranging
the elements of character on a scale that runs from the emotional *(psyche)* to the
intellectual *(gnome)* through a middle term *(phronema),* which by usage involves
both.' It may not be accidental that it is the broadest term, inclusive of emotion,
which is picked up at 207. In any case, the use of three terms puts great emphasis
upon the mentality of Creon.

[18] The use of this word has been much discussed, cf. e.g. Kells, *BICS* 62 n. 3; Ronnet
87. *Pace* Ehrenberg, there need be no reference to Pericles.

comes to the sons. (Very different from the impassioned outburst of Antigone at 1ff., the anguished recital of Ismene at 49ff.) It is perfectly natural, and it brings out a relationship of this Chorus to the 'establishment'. But if it also makes us ask where Creon was during these events, the answer is that he was in the corridors but not at the centre of power (for there is no question here of an earlier regency). Late in life he has come to a throne which he may or may not have desired. Late in life he is put to the test; and, as he says, it is not until a man has been tested by rule that his true character is revealed. Creon is becoming interesting.

In the principles he lays down there is much that would sound most acceptable to a fifth-century Athenian who knew that his own well-being was bound up with that of the *polis,* who knew the difference between a patriot and a traitor.[19] The refusal to allow a traitor to be buried in Attic soil was not unknown to him, though no doubt reactions to such a refusal will have differed: the reaction of the Chorus is studiously non-committal.[20] On the whole, however, and on the surface, Creon does not come too badly out of his first appearance. The real interest of the speech is in discerning what warning signals Sophocles has given, even at this stage.[21] Does Creon dwell with a certain relish on his new-found power (173) and the *sebas* which attends it (166)? Is the first person singular pronoun too insistent (173, 178, 184, 207)?[22] At the same time, is he afraid (180) of not showing strength (and we know he will be challenged by a woman)? There are after all many other reasons for bad decisions. Is this perhaps the *only* temptation of which he is aware – and fatally aware? His view of the situation seems strangely exaggerated.[23] Does he really believe that to bury Polynices, to treat him as a *philos,* will bring *ate* upon the citizens (185)? (The irony here is obvious.) Note that for Creon *philoi* are made (188, 190), not born. Natural *philia* is, or seems to be, nothing to him (yet he will be punished by the loss of his own son). Funeral rites are nothing to him except as a reward to be

---

[19] Cf. Knox, *Gnomon* 40 (1968) 749, reviewing Müller. On the conflict between obligation to friends and obligation to the city, cf. Connor (op. cit. n. 12) 47–53; Dover, *GPM* 304f.

[20] On the attitudes of this Chorus see pp. 137f. below.

[21] Bowra 69: 'Sophocles surely intended us to be a little wary.'

[22] The use of emphatic personal pronouns in Sophocles might be worth studying, cf. Select Index.

[23] Linforth (1961) 189f.

conferred upon the patriot (196f.).[24] A philosophy antithetical to that
of Antigone, but it all sounds well enough – or fairly well – until we
come to 205f.: 'to leave his body unburied and to be eaten and
mangled by birds and dogs, visibly'. The word of seeing comes
unexpectedly at the end, making it vivid and hideous.[25] Does Creon
relish it? At any rate, it is immediately followed by τοιόνδ' ἐμὸν
φρόνημα, recalling 176. This is what his notions of honour for the
patriot involve; this is the kind of mind he shows in office.

Warning signals; and I have expressed them largely as questions.
The whole of Creon's first speech is shot through with hints and
ambiguities which qualify the surface impression of political wisdom.
To examine the whole of his part in similar detail might be tedious.
Some modern critics, reacting against a generally hostile view, have
put the case for Creon more sympathetically.[26] But it is Sophocles
who has loaded the dice against him, ensuring that wherever his case
sounds strong and his words wise he shall immediately betray the true
quality of his mind. He presents himself to the public view as the man
in authority, by virtue of which, and in the interests of the state, he
demands absolute obedience. He preaches order and discipline, to the
exclusion of all else. Discipline in the city, in the army, in the
household: all the same thing, and anarchy equally fatal to all. This is
the message of his little sermon to Haemon (however we take the
order of lines);[27] and, in modern terms, we might see a bluff soldier
who applies the standards of military discipline to his own family and
would apply them to politics – a narrow and dangerous man, but not
ignoble, a man of principle. But note how Sophocles has embraced
this disquisition (655–80) between two references to the woman: first
the woman who has disobeyed (655f.), then, with all possible
emphasis in the three closing lines,[28] the resentment of Creon that his
authority has been challenged by a woman. Does not the highly
personal reaction deprive the gnomic statements of some of their

[24] Cf. 207f. For *timē* from Antigone, cf. 22, 25, 77 (of the gods), and Knox, HT 92f.
[25] Goheen 134 n. 24. The effect of 207 after 205f. is similar to that of 31 after the hideous 29f. Cf. Vickers 528.
[26] Opinions of Creon are reviewed by Ronnet 86 n. 1. For a recent more favourable view see J. C. Hogan, *Arethusa* 5 (1972) 93–100, but Vickers 527–41 is to be preferred.
[27] Seidler's transposition of 663–7 after 671 is adopted by Pearson and defended by Müller (on 668–78), rejected by Jebb (on 661–71) and by Fraenkel on *Agam.* 883 (II 397 n. 1).
[28] Note the emphatic ABA arrangement of 678–80.

effect? It is almost crude, for Sophocles (though the dramatic effect is obvious), the way he constantly brings Creon back to this point at the climaxes of his rhetoric. When Antigone has made her big speech about Zeus and the unwritten *nomima,* we may think of good answers Creon could have made, but we listen to the bad answer he makes. He speaks like the Atridae in *Ajax,* he speaks of slaves and of their *hubris.* And we then see why: it is because his authority *(krate)* has been challenged by a woman (484f.). The complexities of the stichomythic dialogue between him and Antigone (508–25) are important for an understanding of Antigone: for Creon they culminate in six words of Greek – 'While I am alive, no woman shall rule *me*' ἐμοῦ δὲ ζῶντος οὐκ ἄρξει γυνή (525).[29]

Creon speaks, mostly, of his office, but thinks of himself. His demands are absolute, his attitudes those of a tyrant. The point does not need to be laboured, since it has been fully recognized and documented by successive writers.[30] It is in his scene with Haemon that his tyrannical attitude emerges most clearly; and Haemon makes the just comment that Creon would do well as sole ruler in a city void of men (739). But this is the man who has already spoken of Antigone as his 'slave' (479); who saw his subjects as animals beneath the yoke (291f.). That last passage is indeed of great interest and significance (289–314). Creon has heard the Watchman's first story of the 'burial'.[31] To the Coryphaeus, who sees the hand of a god in this mysterious event, he reacts with suspicious violence, as always to

---

[29] There is perhaps a further nuance. Let Antigone find her friends among the dead: Creon is alive. 'But *I* am alive, and (while I live) no woman shall rule *me*.'

[30] E.g. Podlecki, *TAPA* passim. On the implications of 666f. see P. Siewart, *JHS* 97 (1977) 105–7.

[31] On the 'double burial' see A. T. von S. Bradshaw, *CQ* 12 (1962) 200–11; H. Lloyd-Jones, *CQ* 22 (1972) 220 (on Tycho Wilamowitz's handling of the subject); and the sensible remarks of Gellie 38f., who calls attention to the dramatic advantages Sophocles obtained by this means – a far more important matter than Antigone's reasons for returning to the body. For she did return. Marsh McCall, *YCS* 22 (1972) 103–17, has recently championed the old view of Adams that the first burial was miraculous and carried out by the gods. He argues the case with some skill but (among other things) cannot get over the difficulty of 423–7. 'She cursed those who did the deed, i.e. who uncovered the body.' But how did she know it had been uncovered, unless either she had 'buried' it herself or had arrived in time to see the buried body being uncovered? Which assumption was an audience more likely to make? And which better suits the intensity of her emotion? The gods are at work? Yes, as Kitto saw (*FMD* 138–58), through Antigone – in both burials.

anything that suggests he might be wrong. In any case this is a world which means nothing to him, for whom gods are the gods of the city and nothing else; the visible is all.[32] He immediately finds a political explanation of a kind that he can understand (not knowing the deed was done by a woman who cared nothing for the city). Men restive against his rule have bribed the guards. It has often been observed that Creon imputes corrupt motives (here and to Teiresias), because this was a level of motivation within his comprehension. Here the point is developed at great length, in terms of *misthos* and *kerdos,* and reaches an emphatic and gnomic conclusion. 'Base gains, one can see, bring most men ruin rather than salvation' (313f.). The language is inflated; the big notion of *ate* returns (from 185). Whose *ate*? That of the conspirators and the guards? But *ate* is waiting for Creon. Whose base gain, then? What is Creon after?

To find a reference here to Creon's motivation might appear extremely far-fetched, but for one thing. Allegations of bribery return with Teiresias:[33] it was a stock charge against prophets, no doubt often well merited. There is an angry exchange. Creon asserts that the whole tribe of prophets are money-lovers (1055); Teiresias rejoins that the tribe of tyrants loves 'base gain' ($αἰσχροκέρδειαν$). Again, we should not make too much of this, were it not that in another play another spokesman of wisdom accuses another tyrant (much like Creon) of rejoicing 'in gains that are not honourable' (*Ajax* 1349, $κέρδεσιν τοῖς μὴ καλοῖς$). In Agamemnon's case the gains in question were the assertion of authority, the gratification of pride, the ultimate triumph over a dead adversary. Is this not what Teiresias saw in Creon also? Dishonourable gratifications, for the sake of which, in Creon's own words (1045–7), a man will give shameful words a colour of honour and lay up for himself a shameful fall. Teiresias knew where Creon's true advantage stood (1062). It stood in yielding. And Creon does yield, but too late.

Creon is a tyrant – or well on his way to be a tyrant. But he is not the mere stereotype of a tyrant. He is a recognizable human-being, of coarse fibre, commonplace mind, and narrow sympathies. He is a politician without the capacity to be a statesman, because he cannot resist the temptations of power. He is a 'realist', for whom only the

[32] Goheen 84–6. On Creon's religon cf. Bowra 76; Knox, *HT* 82; Ronnet 91.
[33] Goheen 14 (and, on 'the money sequence' in the play, 14–19). Did Teiresias set Creon off by his unfortunate choice of word at 1032?

visible is real. The range of motives he can understand is limited, including lust for power and greed for money. The fact of death he must accept, but the invisible realm of the dead means nothing to him.[34] He believes in the efficacy of the threat of death: that someone should choose death not in defence of the state but in opposition to the state, not for money but for an emotion and a principle – that is something quite outside his experience and his comprehension. His coarseness of fibre is shown in his disregard of other people's feelings, and notably in his attitude towards Haemon's marriage, since for him one woman is much the same as another – or ought to be; he under-estimates the daemonic power of Haemon's feelings and so loses his son. What does that mean to him? To judge by what he says at 641–7, it was the loss of a utility, of an ally in the battle of friends and enemies. But Creon can never be judged by the straight meaning of what he says, least of all when his words, as so often, are gnomic.[35] Sophocles has an ironic reversal in store for us. When Creon is turned inside out, he is found to be empty (709)[36] – empty of all the principles he has proclaimed. The strong man, who in his obstinacy and self-will had seemed a worthy antagonist to Antigone, collapses. The political man, full of wise saws, who seemed to subordinate all personal relationships to politics, is utterly broken by the loss of a son and a wife. The pasteboard tyrant becomes the most ordinary, if the most unhappy, of men.

The Messenger on his entrance makes this point for Sophocles, who did not waste the seventeen lines of that opening speech (1155–71). As we have already seen,[37] the Messenger's standpoint is that of the average man. When he assumes that chance governs all, he is as wrong as when he denies the possibility of prophecy. Perhaps he may be nearer the mark in his last seven lines, when he reflects upon the downfall of Creon, which he does in terms of pleasure and joy. The theme is insistent (1165, 1170f.). Wealth and power (which had seemed to be the aim of Creon's ambition) he will retain, but joy will be lost, because he has lost his son and, though the Messenger does not know it, will lose his wife. Creon, the political man, in his lust for power, has destroyed his real sources of happiness, which reside in

[34] Knox, *HT* 100.
[35] Podlecki, *TAPA* 362.
[36] The point is well made by Knox, *HT* 75, 103, 110.
[37] See p. 112 above.

philoi. He, not Antigone, ends the play as a 'living corpse' (1167), longing for death but forced to remain in the visible world of life (1332).

From Creon we return to Antigone. That Sophocles has worked out his play in terms of contrasted pairs, that the roles of Creon and Antigone are antithetically disposed for irreconcilable conflict, would be generally accepted by interpreters of the play. This does not mean that Antigone is easy to understand. There is a fundamental sense in which Antigone is right as Creon is wrong. But among the antitheses of the play a simple contrast between villainy on the one hand, sweetness and light on the other, finds no place. Knox says that Antigone is 'more like Ajax than any of the other Sophoclean heroes'.[38] Perrotta, for whom she is 'questa terribile eroina', speaks of an 'Antigone inzuccherata *ad usum scholarum*'.[39] How well we know her, and how well we are rid of her! Choruses are not always right, and the Chorus of *Antigone* is more likely to be wrong than many: but when the Coryphaeus describes her as the harsh daughter of a harsh father, he must be saying something which conveys an aspect of truth.[40]

At the outset, she rides into the play on a torrent of negatives, to meet the balanced statements of Ismene's reply.[41] We have two sisters, alike in heredity and in experience, confronted with the same situation, but the awful past (1ff., 49ff.) which dictates submission to Ismene only strengthens the obstinate resolve of Antigone. Two sisters, two brothers (to whom we must return), and the state, the *polis*. The issue, as seen by Antigone, is put strikingly at the end of her first speech. The general has made a decree to the city in arms: does not Ismene see that 'against friends are coming the ills of foes' (10)?[42] Friends and enemies: it is the standing antithesis upon which so much of Greek morals and politics is based. Antigone takes her stand upon *philia*, in the sense of kinship, and the duty to bury which it imposes.

---

[38] *HT* 65.

[39] Perrotta 113f.; cf. Whitman 85.

[40] 471f.: δηλοῖ τὸ γέννημ' ὠμὸν ἐξ ὠμοῦ πατρὸς | τῆς παιδός. ὠμός is an Ajax-word (*Aj.* 205, 548, 930); and it is worth noting, with Kells, *BICS* 61, that the *omos*-character in this play is on the 'right' side. See, however, Diller, *WS* 69 (1956) 76 n. 17, but it is hard to agree that the word in Sophocles is 'wertmässig neutral'.

[41] A supreme example of characterization through style.

[42] On the interpretation of this line see n. 55 below.

But the city too has friends and enemies? The *polis* means nothing to her, nor does Creon – the 'good' Creon as she sarcastically calls him.[43] There are *philoi* and *echthroi*, in relation to the family, and this is a polar opposition which admits of no intermediate degrees; and Ismene, when she withholds her support, passes immediately and automatically into the opposite camp (45f., 69ff., 86f., 93f.).

Friends and enemies. The antithesis figures prominently in several of the extant plays of Sophocles. In *Ajax* it is a fairly straightforward matter within a military context; in *Antigone* the poet exploits ambiguities inherent in the Greek usage of *philos*. The Homeric usage is at first sight puzzling, but can be explained[44] in the light of early heroic society: this is a word which can be applied to whatever the hero can rely upon in a hostile world, whether it be his family, his friends, his dependants, or his own stout heart. Many later reactions stem from this, including the ubiquitous maxim that one should 'do good to one's friends and harm to one's enemies'. A special – and specially close – set of *philoi* are kinsmen; and the word often denotes precisely that, not least in tragedy (and so in Aristotle's *Poetics*). Whether because the family – and in a lesser degree any bond of loyalty and mutual dependence – generates affection, or for whatever reason, *philos* the adjective commonly – and *philein* the verb virtually always – connote some degree of love (or liking); the words are common of lovers and *philon* comes to be used of anything of which you are fond. In *Antigone*, it would seem, two ambiguities come into play: there is *philia* as kinship, and there is *philia* as a socio-political relationship; there is *philia* as kinship, and *philia* as affection. Both are involved in the question of burial.

Of the brothers one is the 'friend' and one the 'enemy' of the state, whereas, in relation to one another, they are simultaneously *philoi* and *echthroi* – a fact to which, as we shall see, Creon forces Antigone to pay attention.[45] For Creon himself, just as burial is a civic matter – a reward given to those who deserve it, so *philoi* are made not born – and a son is a utility (though that is not how he feels when he loses Haemon). He says he will execute Antigone for her disobedience

---

[43] Linforth (1961) 191. The sarcasm is not quite as it might appear to us: she is asking what right Creon has to be considered *agathos* when he treats a member of the family thus. But see also n. 25 above.

[44] Cf. A. W. H. Adkins, *CQ* 13 (1963) 30ff.

[45] See p. 131 below.

'whether she is a sister's child or nearer in blood than the whole circle of Zeus Herkeios' (486f.). Only those who serve the *polis* will he recognize as *philoi*. Equally straightforward is the distinction which Antigone draws within the family context. 'Friends' promote, 'enemies' attack, the interests of the family, which include the right of due burial for its members at the hands of their kin. When Ismene refuses to participate, thereby she acquires the status of an *echthros*. Forced by her to argue for a case beyond argument, Antigone maintains that to bury her brother – and so to die – is not only *kalon* (72), not only in accordance with a social standard, but holy, because she will be honouring what is held in honour by the gods (76f.). And she means the gods of the nether world who demand this tribute. For her it is all one complex emotion which hardly distinguishes as occupants of the nether world between her family dead and the gods in whose protection they lie and she herself will lie.

It is a strong emotion, and the words of 'hatred' which she addresses to Ismene are strongly emotional. And indeed what makes a martyr die for a cause and a principle is no cool calculation. But before we see Antigone in this light, there is something which makes us wonder, the note of a personal passion. Polynices was her brother (21, 45), her kin – and so a *philos*. The word can, but need not, connote deep affection; the superlative *philtatos* must surely do so. And Polynices, for whom she will heap a tomb (80f.), is her dearest brother. It can be no accident that, when she speaks of her state in death (73), she is made to use language – 'I shall lie with him, dear one with dear one' (φίλη μετ' αὐτοῦ κείσομαι, φίλου μέτα) – appropriate to lovers. Who can lay his hand on his heart and assert with confidence that Sophocles did – or did not – wish to suggest a special relationship of deep affection between Antigone and Polynices? (In the end she lies in death with Haemon.)

If Antigone is difficult, ideas are easier. The complexities of *philia* and *echthra* are exposed in the Prologos, to be taken up again and examined in a vitally important dialogue later in the play. Antigone re-enters in charge of the Guard. Before she speaks, we see and hear her through his eyes and ears, wailing shrilly at the sight of the bare corpse, calling down terrible curses upon those who had done the deed (423–8). The sequence which follows is complex. The Guard tells his story and goes, leaving Antigone and Creon in confrontation. They make their long speeches. Creon sends for Ismene. Before she is brought in, there is a close-packed stichomythia between accuser and accused which could be one of the most significant passages in the play.

Faced with Creon's brutal questions (441–9), Antigone must once again argue; and she makes a famous speech (450–70). In the Prologos she had only once referred directly to the gods, when she claimed to be honouring what the gods honour. This time she begins with the gods, and she begins with Zeus: 'It was not Zeus that made this proclamation' (οὐ γάρ τί μοι Ζεὺς ἦν ὁ κηρύξας τάδε 450). She begins with Zeus, but goes on to speak of a Justice that dwells with the gods below; and the unwritten laws which she contrasts with Creon's edict are those which demand the burial of the dead and impose this ritual duty on the kin – a duty in which she dares not fail, for which she will face death.[46] More, she will welcome an early death, which will come as a gain to one who, like her, lives in the midst of many evils. Death will be no grief to her: what would grieve her would be to leave unburied her own mother's son.[47] So from the sublime generalizations with which she began her speech she works back to the theme of *philia* and to the brother unburied. And she has given us a picture of one preoccupied with death and perhaps determined to die. Why? Because her life was in the family, and her family – all but Ismene – now belong in the realm of the dead. Her last words revert to the sharpness, the near-insolence, of her first replies to Creon (443, 448) and evoke from the Coryphaeus that comment on the harshness she has inherited from a harsh father (471f.).

Ismene is fetched, and, while we wait for her, there is dialogue between Antigone and Creon. When she claims the support of public opinion (502ff.), she could be right or wrong: Haemon will have something to add. Creon brushes aside her claim to *kleos* and forces her, once more, to argue with what might seem a debating-point but is something more. She had two brothers: by honouring the one is she not dishonouring the other (512–15)? Antigone replies that the dead Eteocles will not so testify. We must go back.

[46] Knox *HT* 95ff. At 452 the text is uncertain. Dain–Mazon put a strong case for Vollgraf's emendation of οἵ to οὐ: 'rien n'est plus frappant que le ton de ces dénégations énergiques'. We might compare the piling-up of negatives in 4ff.

[47] The repetitions here (noted by Levy 141) characterize Antigone's passionate rhetoric: κέρδος (462, 464); ἄλγος, ἤλγουν, ἀλγύνομαι (466–8, with ABA arrangement); μῶρα, μώρῳ, μωρίαν (469f.). Cf. the preceding note.

Antigone's appeal to Ismene was based upon the solidarity of the family; her first word was *koinon* (1), and it is the breaking of *koinonia* which was Ismene's great offence. One recalls, almost with amazement, that the sufferings to which Antigone refers in 4–6, the shame and the loss of *timē,* had come about through the actions of members of the family towards one another; that this was the very archetype of a divided family; that, if the parricide of Oedipus had been unwitting, his sons had offended him, he had cursed them and they had quarrelled fatally. This was the cause of the situation and the background to her emotions. She knows this, but does not say it: she knows that, if Eteocles and Polynices were on an equality as members of the family and in their claims to burial, they were equally hostile to one another. It is Ismene, the realist, who speaks of the mutual fratricide, first at 14 and then, in her one long speech, at 55–7.

The brothers were *philoi,* but also *echthroi;* at variance in life, they had only their death in common (57).[48] Creon, naturally, makes a point of the hostility of the brothers and does so, naturally, from the political angle. Antigone, in mere faith, denies that they are enemies after death (515, 521). This was not an article of Greek belief: indeed, a Greek, particularly if he remembered his Nekuia and the turning-away of Ajax,[49] might have been more inclined to agree with Creon, when he says (522) that an *echthros* is never a *philos,* not even when he has died. Nor is it the comforting revelation of a truth about the divine world – that there is love after death (*heroes* still hate and harm from their graves). It is, rather, the heroic fiat of Antigone who is determined to cancel the hatreds of her house, who declares peace, ratifies it by the act of burial, and looks forward to reunion with a loving family in the world below (897ff.).[50] Not because it is courageous, but as a supreme effort to impose heroic will upon a recalcitrant world, it could be regarded as the most 'heroic' act in Sophocles. But what alone has made it possible is the fact of death. It is only in death that the honour lost in the living world can be restored; it is

---

[48]　This sharing in death, no less than their hostility in life (cf. *Sept.* 674f.), is much emphasized in the Aeschylean play, which may well have been the starting-point for the dramatic thought of Sophocles – no less than the ambiguous role of Eteocles, at once defender of the city and accursed son of Oedipus. Cf. my article cited in n. 11.

[49]　Cf. *Ajax* 1394f. (Teucer to Odysseus).

[50]　Somewhat fancifully, one might say that, thanks to her *autognotos orga,* she will cancel the terrible *autos*-acts which have preceded (51ff.).

only in the context of death that Antigone's heroic nature can fulfil itself.

When Creon insists that enmity continues even in death, Antigone replies that it is not her nature to join in hatred but in love (οὔτοι συνέχθειν ἀλλὰ συμφιλεῖν ἔφυν, 523), which is perhaps the most famous line in this famous play – and much has been built upon it. Its primary meaning is beyond doubt; it arises in the context set out in the preceding paragraphs. Creon has faced Antigone with an apparent dilemma: if the brothers were kinsmen *(philoi)*, they were also bitter enemies who had killed one another. She says, then, that she will not participate in their enmity (now terminated by death) but in their *philia,* their blood-relationship (which makes equal demands upon her). But *philia* is not simply a matter of status – not in this play. If *philos* need not imply a deep personal emotion, the verb *sumphilein* can hardly fail to do so. Moreover, Antigone says *ephun;* and, if *phunai* can often be little more than a synonym for *einai,* it is hardly to be believed that here she is not making a statement about what is – or what she thinks to be – her nature, her *phusis.* She claims, it would seem, to be a 'loving' and not a 'hating' character. Are we back with that Antigone *inzuccherata* so justly deplored by Perrotta? It will be best to return to this issue when we have looked at Ismene.

Creon sends for Ismene. We did not expect to see her again, or perhaps to hear of her, least of all an Ismene so different from that embodiment of *sophrosune* we met in the Prologos; and now we learn that she is raving and out of her senses (λυσσῶσαν . . . οὐδ' ἐπήβολον φρενῶν, 492). There are few things more irritating in the criticism of Greek tragedy than the prim disparagement of Ismene we sometimes read – as though we were all heroes. But we must understand her rightly in this scene. It would still be touching, if she came before us full of remorse for a missed chance, longing to retrieve her moral position, but showing a pathetic incompetence in the pursuit of martyrdom. But that is not, I think, how Sophocles presents her. Ismene never wished – and does not now wish – to be a hero. She never approved – and does not now approve – Antigone's choice to die. When Antigone says (555): 'You chose to live, I to die', she replies: 'But not at least without my words being spoken.' Those words – her recognition at once of the duty to bury (99) and of the impossibility of carrying it out (79, 92) – she does not now take back. By her transparent subterfuge (536f.), she does not seek death for the

sake of the dead, but of the living now condemned to die. Of the dead
she speaks three words at the end of a sentence (545), but the whole
stress of the dialogue is upon Antigone and the desire to share her fate:
she loves her sister and cannot bear to live without her (548, 566).
Selfish Ismene! Unheroic, ignoble Ismene!

The theme of sharing is important.[51] *koinon* is the first full word
heard in the play, as Antigone addresses Ismene with the barely
translatable ὦ κοινὸν αὐτάδελφον ᾽Ισμήνης κάρα (1), but, when her
sister refuses to support her, she regards their *koinonia* as at an end. The
notion, not unnaturally, returns in the present scene. 'You were not
willing, and I did not make you my partner' (539); no more shall she
share her death (546). This is her answer to Ismene's repeated preposi-
tion (three times in nine lines – ξυμμετίσχω, ξύμπλουν, ξὺν σοί); and
Ismene replies by asking what life is hers, if she is bereft of Antigone.[52] The contrast between the two sisters, though bound up with
the concept of heroism, does not reduce to a crude antithesis. Ismene
does not share Antigone's obsession with death and the world of the
dead, her feeling that that is where she already belongs and where the
family feuds can be resolved. She will not face death for this, but seeks
it, when she finds life is not worth living without the sister she loves.
This kind of love – and this kind of death – Antigone rejects: coming
at the wrong time and in the wrong way, they do not arise out of the
complex of emotions by which she has herself been actuated – her
feelings about the family, about burial, about death.

It is sometimes said that, when Antigone treats Ismene so harshly in
this scene, she is trying to save her from Creon.[53] But this is clearly
wrong. In the Prologos, Ismene declines to help, declines (we may
say) to collaborate in the imposition of *philia* upon a divided family;
whereupon Antigone excludes her from the ranks of *philoi;* she does
not merely withhold her love or speak in tones of cold contempt, but
uses words of enmity, of hating (86, 93f.). Ismene is in Creon's camp,
and there, for Antigone, she remains. 'Ask Creon; for you are on his

---

[51] W. Jäkel, 'Die Exposition in der Antigone des Sophokles', *Gymn.* 68 (1961)
34–55, provides a useful study of personal pronouns in the Prologos (pp. 37–40).
He points out (p. 40) that, by contrast with Antigone's *koinon,* Ismene's first word
is the stressed *emoi;* and that her first dual is at 50 (in a context of deterrence).

[52] On the text of 550f. see *BICS* 26 (1979) 6f., where I suggest that two lines have
fallen out between 550 and 551.

[53] But see Perrotta 102, Kells, *BICS* 55, as against Adams 51 and (sadly) Knox, *HT*
65.

side.'[54] The line (549) is vicious and sincere. What, then, do we make of Antigone's claim which immediately preceded the entry of Ismene – the claim that it was in her nature to share in love but not in hatred?

That, in the immediate context, an Antigone who acts out of deep affection has the moral advantage over a Creon who pursues enmity beyond the grave is a fact that need not be questioned. Can we be so sure, however, that there is no irony in her claim? It is not an accident, surely, that this claim is immediately followed by a scene in which, with hostile language, she rejects the offer of a loving Ismene to share her death – no accident that this scene mirrors the Prologos in which she excluded her sister from the family, assuming the hostility of Polynices towards her and sharing it (93f.).[55] Is this not *sunechthein?* If there is irony here, it is far from superficial: it is tragic, and bound up with the whole tragedy of Sophoclean heroism. Antigone follows the old traditional code, with its polarity of friendship and enmity, an opposition which cannot be bridged, for where there is friendship there will be enmity also, and the stronger the *philia* the stronger the *echthra.* Antigone may believe that it is her nature to share in love, but she is caught up in a code which equally demands hatred. We think of Ajax, of Philoctetes, of the Colonean Oedipus equally strong in love and in hate. It is only non-heroic characters who are free from this tragic antithesis.

It is Ismene who is all affection. Observe, then, the extraordinary

---

[54] On κηδεμών see Knox, *HT* 176 n. 7: 'The word in Antigone's taunt suggests that Ismene devotes to Creon the "care" she should have shown for Polynices.'

[55] At this point I should like to return to line 10 (πρὸς τοὺς φίλους στείχοντα τῶν ἐχθρῶν κακά), which admits of more than one interpretation. It is discussed at length by Jebb, Knox, and Kells, all of whom take the view that τῶν ἐχθρῶν κακά, means 'ills appropriate to foes', i.e. public enemies. This could be right, but I feel increasingly doubtful about it. (i) Admittedly, the prose-distinction between ἐχθροί and πολέμιοι is not always maintained in tragedy, and ἐχθροί is in fact used by Creon in this play of public enemies. (ii) It can also be admitted that Antigone may have been indifferent to the non-burial of non-kinsmen. And this yields a dramatic – and ironic – point. (iii) Nevertheless, it is just because Antigone *is* kinship-oriented that one doubts whether she spared a moment's thought for the enemies of the state. It is because of the basic structural importance of ring-composition in Sophocles that one is reluctant to separate the *philos/echthros* antithesis in 10 from the three words of enmity directed against Ismene at the end of the scene (86, 93f.). Ismene is now in Creon's camp; Creon is the enemy; the ills are coming from the *echthroi* of the family. No other 'enemies' enter into the vision of Antigone. I incline therefore to return to L. Campbell's view, cf. *Paral.* 3.

word that Creon used (492) to describe her state of mind: she was in frenzy (λυσσῶσαν) and not in control of her *phrenes*. To this state she was reduced by the love of sister for sister.[56] The same word (slightly varied) recurs at the entry of Haemon. Can it be that he is in frenzy (λυσσαίνων, 633) against his father? And in the end we find him acting as the mad lover of whom the Chorus sang (790). The theme of sexual love has been treated in an earlier chapter, and we shall have to return to it before long. It is introduced by Ismene. Now, perhaps, we can see why she has been brought back into the play. It is not only, by contrast, to resume her function of exploring the nature of her sister's heroism, but it is wholly appropriate that she, whose life is wrecked by that heroism, standing as she does in a relationship of deep personal affection towards Antigone, should be the one to tell us of the relationship of Haemon to Antigone. The next scene is Haemon's scene. The next shows us an Antigone who has rejected Ismene's love going to her death left, by Sophocles, in ignorance that he has championed her cause and quarrelled with his father.

Antigone is led away in bonds. Creon's comment as she goes is that 'even the bold seek to fly when they see Death already closing on their life' (580f.). What Creon says – for he utterly fails to understand Antigone – may or may not be true of her. We must wait to see – wait till she returns under guard on her way to be buried alive. For Creon changes his mind:[57] she shall not be stoned to death but walled up in a rocky cave with a meagre provision of food. Antigone returns and engages in a long *kommos* with the Chorus. Then Creon (if he was absent)[58] comes back and speaks. Antigone makes a final

---

56 With the importance of her role goes a degree of characterization which is missed not only (naturally) by Tycho Wilamowitz but also by E. Fraenkel who quotes with approval the former's judgement that Ismene is 'gar nicht was wir einen Charakter nennen' (see H. Lloyd-Jones, *CQ* 22 (1972) 215 n. 2). 491f. alone should guard us against under-estimating the individuality of Ismene.

57 On the motivation of Creon's change of mind see Bowra 103; Letters 173; Kitto, *FMD* 166; Knox, *HT* 72.

58 Creon is not present during the First Stasimon, but at that time the Chorus does not know that Antigone is the offender. Clearly, he is present during the Second and Fourth. Is he also present during the Third? In which case he is also present during the ensuing *kommos*. Kitto *FMD* 167ff. says yes. The matter is not easily decided. His entry, unheralded, at 883 to cut short lamentations seems adequately paralleled by *O.C.* 1751 (cf. E. Fraenkel, *Zu den Phoenissen des Euripides* (Munich 1963) 75). One might prefer that Antigone should have her *kommos* alone with the

speech. There are exchanges in anapaests before she leaves the stage
for the last time. Whereupon the Chorus sing their Fourth Stasimon.
There are difficulties of many kinds, not least that we seem to be
seeing a new Antigone. Was Creon right about the effect of the
approach of death even upon the bold?

The relative shortness of Antigone's part has been remarked. She
appears in three scenes. There is the Prologos which, though important, is not very long. There is the long scene we have just been
examining in which we see her with Creon and then with Ismene.
The *kommos* and its sequel (801–943) contain a very substantial
portion of the total role of Antigone. It may not be very likely, then,
that Sophocles has abandoned his portrayal of the heroine in order to
play a brilliant variation upon a conventional theme and situation – the virgin bride of Death.[59] The scene must be studied with
some care. There are difficulties, not least in understanding the
reactions of the Chorus, about whom a few words must now be said.

Choruses in Sophocles are characterized, within appropriate limits
(which vary from play to play), and the characterization is in general
consistent. Choral odes have such structural and thematic importance
that the connections between the song and the character of the singers
may become rather tenuous, if it never completely disappears, but the
attitudes and sympathies of a Chorus tend to be straightforward and
readily explicable by their role. In *Antigone,* the attitude of the Chorus
towards Creon veers from ostensible, if not unreserved,[60] support to
a degree of censure which might seem to qualify them as the least
helpful Chorus in Greek tragedy. We can say, if we like, that they
only wait for the moral support of Teiresias to voice misgivings that
they have long felt (and of which indeed there have been pale hints). It
is, however, in relation to Antigone that it becomes important – and

Chorus, but this is a rather subjective point. On the other hand, if (as has been
argued above, pp. 96f.) the ode, though directed towards Haemon, bears on
Creon, his presence while it is sung would help to bring this out, just as his
presence during the other two stasima directs the attention of the audience to the
irony inherent in the words of the Chorus.

[59] Which is what worried Perrotta 115ff.

[60] At 211ff. they could hardly be more non-committal. Cf. Linforth (1961) 190; B.
Alexanderson, 'Die Stellung des Chors in der Antigone', *Eranos* 64 (1966) 88.
Alexanderson's general conclusion (op. cit. 103) is, however, too sweeping: 'Der
Chor hat tatsächlich zwei Gesichter. Bis auf Teiresias' Erscheinen ist der Chor eine
Person im Drama. Nach Teiresias wird der Chor von der Handlung losgelöst und
wird ein Sprachrohr des Dichters.'

difficult – to determine the nature and degree of their sympathies. At
504ff. Antigone claims that the Chorus – for they must be included in
her sweeping statement (τούτοις . . . πᾶσιν) would openly favour her,
if they were not afraid of a tyrant. She could be right or wrong: she is
quite capable of assuming what she wishes to believe. But, when
Haemon (at 692ff.) states that the city laments her and regards her
actions as 'most praiseworthy' (εὐκλεεστάτων), he must be right,
Now, normally, a Chorus of Elders might be expected to voice the
reactions of the *polis*. But reactions favourable to Antigone cannot be
expressed in the hearing of Creon, who is present almost throughout.
Do we then say that the Chorus *really* have far more sympathy for her
than they dare express? This is a simplistic view which disregards a
factor of some dramatic importance. The isolation of Antigone is an
essential requirement. To this end Sophocles has given her, unlike
most heroines (if she is the 'heroine') in Greek tragedy, a male Chorus
and (to make matters doubly sure) has put them in a situation which
forbids them to speak freely. But that is not enough: the audience as
well as Antigone must *feel* a lack or limitation of sympathy.[61] We
may say, then, that this Chorus is not only male (and so naturally
disapproving of a woman's boldness) but, being nobles (843, 940), a
council and close to the throne (160f.), have more regard to the
maintenance of authority than the commonalty of whom Haemon
speaks (700).[62]

The attitude of the Chorus towards Antigone during the *kommos*
(801–82) has been much debated. When they see her appearing on her
way to death, they cannot restrain their tears, for which they apolo-
gize, finding an analogy between Haemon's emotion and their own,
both in breach of law, of *thesmoi*. This could be a tribute to Creon (if
he is still present) or to their principles (if he is not). The sequence of
emotions in Antigone is closely bound up with the interventions of
the Chorus.

Antigone had chosen death (555), counted herself already a dead
soul (559f.), told Ismene that death was *kalon* (72) and Creon that it
was *kerdos* (462, 464). She had seemed already to belong, emotionally,
more to the nether than the upper world. Now she is going to her

---

[61] Perrotta 83f.; Ronnet 147, Vickers 534.
[62] We may even feel – though this is the last way a critic should get out of his
difficulties – that, in the handling of this Chorus, Sophocles had set himself a
problem which did not admit of a completely successful solution.

death and she laments. She calls her hearers to witness; she sings that this is her last journey, her last sight of the sunlight; she deplores that she will die unwedded, that she will be the bride of Acheron. Poignant though the words may be, the themes are conventional for one in her situation. Has Sophocles forgotten his Antigone in the desire to write a pathetic scene? Or are we to remember the words of Creon that even the bold flee from the close approach of death? Is Antigone's nerve broken? Does Perrotta's 'terrible heroine' turn out to be a vulnerable girl? Certainly to deny her the right to quail before death is to press consistency with a more than Aristotelian insensibility. But Sophocles had a finer art than simply to show the martyr shrinking from the flames. One thing has changed since Antigone left the scene: now she knows the manner of her death. The first half of the *kommos* – Antigone's first three stanzas and the intervening anapaests of the Chorus – is dominated by the theme of living death.

The thought of being buried alive has always had a peculiar horror for the human mind. I am not, however, suggesting that it is simply this natural revulsion which accounts for Antigone's change of mood. Let us see how it works out. In her first stanza, along with other themes, she sings that Hades is dragging her 'alive' (ζῶσαν) to the shore of Acheron. The tone of the Chorus' reply has been much debated. But, so soon after the tears of 803, it can hardly be hostile or sarcastic (however much they disapprove).[63] It seems as though they have beaten around for some consolation to offer and hit upon the exceptional mode of her death as a source of fame: alone of mortals she will go down alive (ζῶσα) to Hades. It is the living death that turns the thoughts of Antigone towards Niobe.[64] Hers was a dreadful way

[63] In a long note Knox, *HT* 176f., sets out the problem well. He suggests reading οὔκουν at 817: she is *not* κλεινή, she has *no* ἔπαινος (or funeral eulogy) as she would have had if she had died of disease or in war. This is ingenious, but it will hardly do, since it gets the feeling of the οὔτε ... οὔτε passage quite wrong (especially in view of φθινάσιν). 'If only you had died of a wasting disease ...' Can that be the implication? Surely οὔτε ... οὔτε must indicate aspects advantageous to Antigone. Interpreters have in general underestimated the sheer embarrassment of the Chorus during this *kommos*.

[64] At 823ff. I see no trace of the notion of Niobe as a great sinner (contr. Müller (2) 186) – neither there nor in the response of the Chorus. This lyric stanza is of great subtlety. Jebb argues effectively for Musgrave's change of ὄμβρῳ to ὄμβροι. It goes something like this: 'What takes the place for her of tears, as a wasting expression of her grief, is never-failing rain and snow; what is wetted by her tears is not a human body, but rocks'. The whole comparison is embraced between ὄμβροι and δειράδας: rain for tears, rock for body.

to perish (λυγροτάταν ὅλεσθαι): yet why most like to Antigone's (ᾷ με δαίμων ὁμοιοτάταν κατευνάζει)? Because Antigone is obsessed with the rocky cave to which she is condemned. There among rocks, as a rock, abides Niobe, rain for tears and stone for body: no hint of a passage to the nether world. There among rocks stays the imagination of Antigone, half-way between life and death. The Chorus, still trying ineffectively to console, hardly know what to say: if their first words are, as one writer puts it, a rebuke for 'presumption', they go on, sympathetically, to 'excuse her exaggeration'.[65] Still, they say, it is a great thing to be said of a woman that has died that she has shared the lot of immortals 'in life and then in death' (ζῶσαν καὶ ἔπειτα θανοῦσαν). Perhaps it is the mention of life and death that stings her, makes her feel that she is being mocked and insulted. She calls her fellow-citizens to witness. To what? That she is passing – by what an ordinance! – to a tomb-prison blocked with rocks, to a tomb of a new kind (ποταινίου) where she will have community neither with the living nor the dead.[66] This is the climax and conclusion of the first half of the kommos.

Of the polar opposites in the play none is more insistent than that of life and death. Two separate realms, and Antigone has chosen the realm of death to which her dear ones belong. She had expected stoning to death (36), a sudden dramatic transition from one world to the other: she is confronted with a continuance of life in a tomb, cut off alike from the living and the dead, utterly alone. For the moment she can see no further.

She is addressing the living, herself alive and visible (842); and it is perhaps the embarrassed glibness with which the Chorus speak of her

---

[65] Knox, HT 66.
[66] Fortunately, the corruption of the text (reconstruction is uncertain) does not obscure the general sense. From 806 onwards words of life and death are insistent: it is only at this point (a dividing point in the kommos) that the basis of Antigone's emotion is made specifically clear. At 810ff. she sings that Hades is dragging her 'alive' to the shore of Acheron, and this is already suggestive, since in the normal case a human-being is dead when he leaves the world of the living and during the transit to Acheron. The suggestion of 821f. is similar, though for the Chorus the stress may be on autonomos. But to Antigone it suggests comparison with Niobe, still in the world of the living, yet turned to stone, yet still weeping. At 838, the very phrase of the Chorus, with its temporal distinction between life and death (ζῶσαν καὶ ἔπειτα θανοῦσαν), may remind Antigone that this distinction will be obliterated in her living tomb, and this may contribute to the bitterness of her rejoinder.

living death that she takes (wrongly) for malice. She addresses the Chorus: in the dramatic case there is no one else for her to address. The way in which she addresses them is surely rather striking. They are citizens of her native-land (806). They are the *polis*, embodied in its wealthy land-owners (843f., ὦ πόλις, ὦ πόλεως πολυκτήμονες ἄνδρες). It is striking, for Antigone had seemed to care nothing for the *polis*. (So Creon had seemed to care nothing for kinship, but is broken by the loss of his kin.) In her last hour she calls upon the *polis* to bear witness, but the way in which she is made to address the Elders who represent it is not the most obvious: she calls them 'men of the city, men rich in possessions'. Which could be a sign to the audience that these are 'establishment' figures – later she will call them 'princes of Thebes' (940). But how does Antigone think of them? They are the wealthy, the heads of great aristocratic families (like her own), who should be sensitive to the claims of *philoi*, to the traditional rites of burial, to the immemorial *nomoi*. To them she looks, but looks, as she feels, in vain.

The Chorus has been called to witness. What can they say? What can they be thinking – these religious old men with their traditional background – of the *potainios taphos* and, for that matter, of the non-burial of Polynices? On these matters they cannot speak frankly. Now in song[67] they try to give an explanation, which might also be regarded as a justification, of what is happening to Antigone. The thought and language are Aeschylean. Antigone had called them to witness under what sort of *nomoi* she was suffering: they offer an explanation in terms of traditional religion. It falls into two parts.

Taking a word from Creon (580, 752), they sing of her *thrasos*, her extremity of *thrasos*; and that in her criminal boldness she has run up against the lofty altar of Justice (Δίκας).[68] Therefore, it is implied,

---

[67] The change from anapaests to lyrics marks a transition. Hitherto the Chorus have been responding, within their emotional limits, to the predicament of Antigone; now they attempt a 'theological' interpretation and an Aeschylean mode of thought, to which, since syncopated iambics are so frequent in the 'theological' choruses of *Oresteia*, their metre is perhaps appropriate.

[68] 853ff. The question here is whether Antigone is to be conceived as suppliant at the altar of Justice or as offending against it (for which the salient parallel is Aesch. *Agam.* 383). For the former view see Lesky, *Hermes* 80 (1952) 92 and *TD* 115 n. 3; Goheen 73f. But what, in the text, can the Chorus have in mind? Antigone's words at 451f.? But, as Linforth (1961) 223 points out, the idea of supplication is quite inappropriate to her attitude there. And would the minds of the Chorus revert to 451, disregarding 839ff. which make no reference at all to *dike*? It is far

punishment is her due reward. They are making that same equation of justice with the laws of the state (the decrees of a Creon?) which they have made before (cf. 368f.), but they use a metaphorical expression which invites personification: Justice is a goddess with an altar and so, surely, the audience is reminded that the *thrasos* of Antigone had been in the service of that Justice that dwells with the nether gods (451). Sophocles is moving towards that relationship or lack of relationship between Antigone and the gods which is to dominate her exit.

The second part of this four-line system consists in a single line. Stern though their theme is, there can be no hostility towards the girl they address as *teknon* (855). But a child has a father, and *teknon* leads into the last line: 'But in this ordeal you are paying perhaps for a father' (πατρῷον δ' ἐκτίνεις τιν' ἆθλον). Their movement of mind may be something like this: How did it come about that this young girl, to their sorrow, had advanced to such an extremity of rashness and brought this fate upon herself? It must be – and this they feel as a kind of mitigation – the work of an evil inheritance. The theme is new to this scene, but not new to the play.[69]

The effect upon Antigone is striking. It is like the breaking of a barrier to release a new flood of emotion. In the first part of the *kommos* her imagination could not pass beyond the living death of the rock-tomb to the true realm of the dead. Now once more she can speak of herself as going to dwell with (*metoikos*) her dead.[70] The horror is no longer the isolation of the tomb, but herself as caught in a dreadful chain of doom, with father, mother, and brother. The whole emotional background of her situation and action comes flooding out (in words which are like a commentary upon her first speech in the play), as we hear of her grief, her repeated lamentations for the *atai* which had brought her to birth.[71] She feels herself under a curse

more likely that these staunch upholders of authority think, in Aeschylean terms, of Antigone as having run up against *dike* (which they equate with the ordinances of the state) through her *thrasos*. For the 'Aeschylean' interpretation see also Knox *HT* 178 n. 12 and Lloyd-Jones, *JZ* 195 n. 63 (who defends the emendation ποδὶ at 855).

[69] It is in fact resumed from the Second Stasimon (583ff.). Cf. Dain–Mazon 104 n. 4.
[70] Contr. 868 with 852. This is no careless slip.
[71] 857ff. There are difficulties in the text which do not, however, affect the general tenour. At 862 R. D. Dawe, *HSCP* 72 (1967) 112 makes a strong case for reading πατρῷαι, contr. Müller ad loc.

(*araios*); product of an incestuous union, she is herself dying unwedded (*agamos*). There are four words of marriage in the stanza; *agamos* (867) is then picked up by *anumenaios* (876); a few lines later (891) she will apostrophize the tomb which is a marriage-chamber. 'We can make far too much', says one critic,[72] 'of Antigone's laments that she will never know the married state. They are in large part conventional for one in her situation. Compare Macaria.' But for Macaria, and one supposes for most dying virgins, the husband whose loss they deplore is hypothetical: not so for Antigone who was betrothed to Haemon in what Ismene seems to have regarded as a close union;[73] and Haemon has just played a scene upon the stage and his love for her has been asserted by the Chorus with all the power of Sophoclean lyric; and the language of wedlock was heard, insistently, at the opening of the *kommos*. Was Antigone in love? Sophocles has ensured that we shall ask the question, but has not provided the answer. (We are in fact led to ask a kind of question, essentially unanswerable, which is generally thought inappropriate to the criticism of a Greek play.) Whatever feeling Antigone had for Haemon she has sacrificed to the love and duty she had for her family and for Polynices. And it is with Polynices that the stanza ends.[74]

'In your death', sings Antigone (871), 'you destroyed my life.' And the Chorus knows how it was. In a cryptic embarrassed phrase (σέβειν μὲν εὐσέβειά τις)[75] they pay a half-reluctant tribute to her piety. Yes, that is one sort of *eusebeia*. But what if it comes up against a rival claim

---

[72] Waldock 109 n. 2. Lattimore, *SPGT* 75ff. demurs.

[73] See p. 93 n. 6 above.

[74] There is a difficulty at 870. 'His marriage with Argeia, daughter of the Argive king Adrastus, was the seal of the armed alliance against Thebes, and thus the prime cause of Antigone's death' (Jebb). In a tense recital of horrors a mention of this diplomatic union might seem to strike a jarring note; and it is not surprising that some scholars, against all probability, have assumed a corruption of τάφων into γάμων (cf. Müller ad loc.). A difficulty remains, which is to some extent bound up with 872ff. (see the following note). If γάμων is genuine, one can only suggest that Sophocles made Antigone refer to her brother in this of all ways because he wanted to continue with the theme of marriage.

[75] The expression is really rather extraordinary, and one can see why some editors, e.g. Müller, wish to supply an object to σέβειν by reading μιν. But this upsets the balance of the sentence: we need μέν. However, σέβειν by itself remains very difficult, since Antigone has not raised the point herself or (unless we read τάφων) referred specifically to the burial. Perhaps the Chorus are themselves reluctant to be too specific, mutely supplying the idea that she acted out of piety. σέβειν μέν – then, as it were with a shrug of the shoulders: 'well, that is one sort of piety'.

to *sebas*?[76] A claim backed by power? The Chorus has abandoned the religious standpoint, harsh but lofty, of their last short song to take their stand on the stark fact of power, Creon's power (ὅτῳ κράτος μέλει). The theme of hereditary guilt which they had raised and Antigone had taken up from them they do not overtly pursue, but, when they sing of the 'self-willed temper' (αὐτόγνωτος . . . ὀργά) which has destroyed her, they may well be thinking, as we are bound to think, of her inheritance from Oedipus (471f.).

The *kommos* is rounded off by a short stanza in which Antigone again bids her farewell to the world of light, again laments that she is unwept (cf. 847), unfriended (for Ismene no longer counts), unwed (for there is no Haemon). It is her fate to die with no friend to weep for her.[77] She is completely isolated. Creon now speaks, and it is on her isolation that he insists, but her isolation in the living tomb. When he says (887ff.) that she shall be deprived of community (*metoikia*) with the upper world, we are bound to remember that once she saw burial alive as deprivation of community with both worlds, but also that she had sung of going to dwell with (*metoikos*) her father and mother among the dead.[78] With the thought of her dead she can now see the tomb as a passage towards them in the realm of Persephone; with her long speech in trimeters come echoes of the Prologos. If she dies untimely, she still nurtures a strong hope that, when she comes, she will be dear to her father, dear to her mother, dear to her brother Polynices[79] by tending whose corpse she has reaped this reward.

---

[76] Cf. 166, 730f., 744f.

[77] The tears of the Chorus (803), if Antigone ever regarded them – she is thinking of closer *philoi* than them – have been long lost in the sands of religion and politics.

[78] Knox, *HT* 114.

[79] To take κασίγνητον κάρα at 899 as referring to Eteocles, as is commonly done (contr. D.B. Gregor, *CR* n.s. 9 (1959) 12), is a gross intrusion of logic upon poetry. The objection is not that the bodies of both brothers were presumably together upon the battlefield, since Sophocles might well have intended us to forget that Antigone had no opportunity to take part in the funeral of Eteocles (or its preliminaries). But is it conceivable that, after 870–2 and all the concentration of Antigone on Polynices, and without the naming of the other brother, an audience would understand this as referring to Eteocles? Who is only mentioned by her at 21–5 and (prompted by Creon) at 512–15, and in whom (whether because he has been duly buried or for whatever reason) she is made to show little interest? Is it not most probable that ὑμᾶς in 900 refers only to father and mother, passing over the mention of Polynices, only to return (with νῦν δέ) to him and the special circumstances of his case? Is it not enough to turn back to 857–71: father, mother, Polynices?

At this point an ogre stands across the critic's path. As the text is read in the MSS, Antigone now argues that what she did she would have done for a brother alone, and she argues upon the same lines as the wife of Intaphernes (Herodotus 3.119), who chose that her brother rather than her husband or one of her children should be spared. 'This famous passage', writes Jebb, 'affords one of the most interesting exercises for criticism which can be found in ancient literature.' Interesting, but maddening. The passage was in Aristotle's text. The issue, then, is whether there is enough which is abhorrent in the content and style of 904–20 (for the lines stand or fall together) to outweigh the improbability that Aristotle had an interpolated text. Scholarly opinion has been about equally divided, with great names upon both sides, but with a recent tendency to defend the passage.[80] Weak-minded persons like the present writer have changed their view again and again. I will only say that I now believe the passage to be spurious, and for the most subjective of reasons. The first thirteen lines of Antigone's final speech (891–903) could stand for an example of Sophoclean eloquence at its highest point of virtuosity, deeply moving, seemingly effortless. The last eight lines in their different way are not inferior. Can this be said of the intervening passage with its contorted argument and awkward locutions? If not, can this be accounted for by the supposed movements of Antigone's mind? I doubt it.

[80] For the balance of opinion, see Hester (op. cit. n. 1) 55–80. Jebb, in his Appendix 258–63, gives a characteristically fair and lucid statement of the problem; and Müller, who rejects the passage, rehearses the arguments on both sides at (2) 198ff. and 206ff. Knox, *HT* 104ff., defends its authenticity upon lines on which it must be defended, if at all. 'In the almost hysterical hyperbole of her claim that she would not have run such a risk for that husband and those children she will now never live to see, she is telling Polynices that no other love, not even that she might have had for the child of her own body, could surpass her love for him.' My own rejection is based, essentially (and hazardously), on *Stilgefühl*. It may be noted, however, that in the *kommos* Antigone makes no reference to children, though this in a hypothetical case would be a standing feature of the *topos*. It is omitted to stress the loss of the *real* Haemon, but an interpolator is bound by the Herodotean source to mention children. Note too that the 'interpolator' makes Antigone refer to Creon by name, which otherwise she does not do between 806 and 943, using instead the impressive plurals of 927f. and 942. Finally, I observe (for what it is worth) that at 920 κατασκαφή in the sense of 'grave' is uncommon, but paralleled by Aesch. *Sept.* 1008, 1037, themselves under suspicion of interpolation! (See now A. L. Brown, *CQ* 26 (1976) 215.) For a recent voice in favour of authenticity, cf. H. J. Blumenthal, *CR* 24 (1974) 174f., who points to a possible reminiscence of the Sophoclean passage at Eur. *Alc.* 282ff., produced some three years later.

Antigone is dying miserably (895). She looks to the love with which she will be greeted in the world below. To what else can she look?[81] Not to the gods, who will not fight for her. For what justice of theirs has she transgressed? She has been pious, and all she has gained is the fate of *dussebeia*. If those are the standards of the gods, she will learn her mistake by suffering; if the mistake is *theirs* (she means her adversaries'), may they suffer no worse misery than they, unjustly, inflict on her!

The Chorus recognize her tone, better perhaps than some modern interpreters. 'Still the same winds, the same storm-blasts of the soul are in control of her' (929f.). She is still the same Antigone who faced the threats of Creon; her spirit is still unbroken; indignant rather than perplexed, in her ultimate and total isolation she confronts the gods with boldness and justifies her action in the teeth of fate.[82] She is the Antigone who, still *autognotos*, will cut short her agony by suicide and join her dead. Her last words are spoken as a princess of her father's house. She calls on the land of Thebes as her father's city, on the gods her ancestors, on the Chorus as princes of Thebes. They are to witness what she suffers, and from what kind of men, τὴν εὐσεβίαν σεβίσασα.[83]

The procession leaves; Antigone leaves the play. The Chorus sings its enigmatic song, the interest of which is divided between her and her adversary. For the parallels which they cite are relevant not only to her approaching end but also – in part and perhaps in whole – to the offences of Creon. There follow Teiresias, the vain repentance and the punishment of Creon, whose tragedy is brought to its completion. With this we may return to the old question: who is the 'hero', the central character of the play?

On the face of it a bad question, it may admit of an interesting answer. It is a bad question insofar as it implies that we *must* find one

---

[81] If 904–20 are excised, there is nothing offensive in the transition from 903 to 921, except that it may seem a trifle abrupt. But of course, if there has been an interpolation, something may have been lost.

[82] But see Waldock 139, Levy 144; and, for a different interpretation of τῶν ἀνέμων ῥιπαί, Schadewaldt 86 n. 2. Does Antigone speak 933f. (as in the tradition)? It is not out of the question that she does. More probably, however, ταύτῃ (936) refers to her and the preceding lines should therefore be attributed to the Chorus.

[83] Hardly translatable. 'Because I feared to cast away the fear of heaven' (Jebb). Mazon's French version is preferable: 'Pour avoir rendu hommage, pieuse, à la piété.'

central character. The purpose of the foregoing review has been, partly, to show the depth and solidity of the characterization in this play. The confrontation between Creon and Antigone is a confrontation of persons and owes its dramatic effect largely to this fact. The balance is well held. If this is also a play of great issues – burial and non-burial, family and state, friends and enemies, they are brought out through the antithetical attitudes of the persons, both of whom are essential to their deployment. There are structural polarities, but we cannot answer our question simply in terms of these, or by observing who is right and who wrong, who lives and who dies. There are two tragedies unfolding simultaneously: the tragedy of Creon and the tragedy of Antigone. Why have so many scholars insisted upon the primacy of Antigone? There is a simple, sufficient, significant – if, as now put, rather crude – answer, which is that the tragedy of Creon is 'Aeschylean', whereas it is the tragedy of Antigone which raises the great Sophoclean issues.[84]

On the Aeschylean aspect of Creon's tragedy enough has already been said.[85] He offends and is punished; he is proud and brought low; he is infatuated and brings disaster upon himself. Which is not to say, of course, that he is handled in the Aeschylean style, for in the relation of character to action and suffering there are complexities which we should not expect to find in Aeschylus. And that is no less true of his relation to the gods. Creon believes in them and yet is convicted as *theomachos*. If the play has been rightly interpreted, he is doubly found in opposition to the gods. He opposes the powers and rights of the dead (though a Zeus who cannot be confined to either world is in the background), and for this he is condemned, overtly, by Teiresias and the Chorus. But he also opposes the force of a great power of the living world – the power of sexual passion. And it is characteristic that in each case he outrages human feeling and personal relationships:

[84] This is the justification of those who, like Diller (*WS* 69 (1956) 70ff.), insist that Antigone is the central character. Similarly, Heracles and Philoctetes are the 'Sophoclean' heroes in their plays (though I would not admit that the tragedy of Deianira is not Sophoclean). It is important, however, to recognize that Sophocles was prepared, in all three plays, to maintain a balance of interest between two characters, one of whom is not 'heroic'.

I say 'crude' – and put 'Aeschylean' in inverted commas – because the tragedy of Creon is closer to *Persae* than to the more complex theodicy of *Oresteia*. 'Traditional' might be a better word. See, further, on the Second Stasimon, in the following chapter.

[85] Cf. Letters 169.

the feeling of a family for its dead, the feeling of a lover for the
beloved. He believes in gods, but identifies them with the interest of
the state and, in the last analysis, the state with himself, his ambition
and his power. We see character and action in that perfect balance
which is typical of Sophocles. It is a fine dramatic theme effectively
developed.

No one, however, discussing the distinctive features of a Sophoclean hero is likely to spend much time on Creon. For, as Knox has
observed,[86] he turns out to lack the ultimate heroic obstinacy; in the
end he gives way, as other heroes do not and Antigone does not. It is
Antigone who stands along with Ajax and Electra and Philoctetes,
like them in their very different ways raising questions about the
nature of heroism, the possibility of its survival in a recalcitrant
world, and its relationship to divine governance. It is she whose
attitudes towards the great issues are truly significant, whereas those
of Creon are trite and deliberately diminished by the dramatist. She
upholds the ancient sanctities of the family and proves herself the
better citizen thereby.[87] She takes her stand on *philia,* with a supreme
heroic purpose which (it has been argued) goes far beyond the
courageous defiance of authority, yet she cannot evade the conflicts
inherent in her code.[88] And she raises a question of theodicy more
acute than any other in Sophocles. She raises it in her last words.

The closing comment of the play is not directed towards Antigone
or evoked by her fate. It is irrelevant to her, unless, when the
Coryphaeus speaks of 'lacking not piety towards the gods', we
remember that she went to her death with the proud claim that she
had served the cause of piety. It is a claim which must not be denied.
What just ordinance of the gods had she offended (921)? None. Yet, if
the gods avenge her, they do not save her. That a woman who, so far
from breaking divine law, had carried out a religious duty should die
shamefully and under the imputation of impiety, if it justifies her

---

[86] Knox, *HT* 72ff. It is striking that, at 1099, Creon – like Deianira – asks the
Chorus what he should do.

[87] On the evidence of Teiresias. Which is ironical in view of her disregard of
state-authority, but Sophocles may well have believed that the family was the
custodian of values which the state could only threaten at its peril, of decencies and
religious observances were were – and ought to remain – among the established
nomoi.

[88] See pp. 132f. above.

indignant protest, might well cause poet and audience to reflect upon the kind of world in which such things happen.[89]

There is one further point of contrast between Creon and Antigone remaining to be mentioned; and it involves a theme – and an important choral ode – not yet discussed. Antigone comes, nobly, to her disaster; Creon, in his ignoble fashion, comes to his. Why did these things happen? The strands of causation are manifold in point of circumstance and character. It was the fate of Creon to be confronted with an Antigone, of Antigone to be confronted with a Creon, in a situation which provoked a fatal clash. The antecedents of Creon are hardly relevant:[90] he is given, dramatically, as we find him. Not so with Antigone, whose heredity is stressed. She is what she is, in part at least, because she is the daughter of her father, having inherited a strain which the Chorus sees as 'harshness' from an Oedipus unknown to us. She is not only the daughter of Oedipus but member of a doom-laden family; and to this theme Sophocles has devoted the Second Stasimon of the play. It deals with Zeus and an Erinys and the traditional notion of *ate*. When Antigone has left the stage to be buried alive, the Chorus, in the Fourth Stasimon, sing of the Moirai and kindred themes. Our next subject must be Fate in Sophocles, and it will lead up towards *Oedipus Tyrannus*.

[89] It may not be enough to say, with Kitto (*FMD* 170), that 'a bad man can kill a good one' and that 'in no adult religion do the gods intervene to stop him from doing it; it remains only for the bad man to take what consequences there may be'. Certainly Antigone did not see it in quite that light. It was a common Greek belief that the credit of the gods was involved in the justice which was seen or not seen to be done upon this earth.

[90] Neither his heredity nor his past experiences (apart from some elusive hints in his first speech, on which see p. 123 above).

CHAPTER SEVEN

Fate in Sophocles

We shall all die, at a moment unknown and in circumstances no one can foresee: this is the ultimate dispensation. The Greeks, at some early stage in their thinking about the world, came to conceive of powers which they called Moirai. If these were spirits who presided over birth as well as determining death, it is not hard to see why. The individual comes to birth with an apportionment (a *moira*) of life, and nothing is more striking in the lot of human beings than the difference in their life-spans and the unpredictability of their deaths. There must be some power or powers which determine these things: not only birth and death but the events of life, particularly perhaps those which are dramatic and disastrous and lead towards death.[1] The history of such beliefs and feelings is notoriously complex and debated. There is much evidence in Homer and Hesiod, but behind the poets a long tradition will have led back into the early history of the race and related races.[2] When did cults of the Moirai originate? When did the singular *moira* acquire a degree of personification and approach the notion of a generalized power of destiny? These and many other questions are not very important for our study, since it is clear that the dramatists had inherited a whole cluster of conceptions which were available to their use, including the plural Moirai, a singular Moira with personification and an unpersonified *moira* (a fate). What they have in common is the suggestion of something inevitable, something that 'has to be', that is 'bound to happen'. There is a whole vocabulary of the inevitable. *Aisa* as well as *moira* and the related *heimarmenē* (sc. *moira*); not only *peprotai*, *pepromenos* (with *hē pepromenē*, sc. *moira*), but also the verbs *chrēnai* and *mellein* and various

---

[1] On the social aspect of *moira*, which may also have come in early, see p. 155 below.
[2] Cf. R. B. Onians, *The origins of European thought* (Cambridge 1951) passim.

nouns. There is *potmos* which, if it means 'what befalls', is akin to
tuche, though with a stronger suggestion of destiny. There is *aion,*
which came to have a strong temporal sense of 'life' (always human
life) or life-span, but retained some notion of a determined quality of
life.[3] There is *daimon*; and this word confronts us with a fundamental
problem.

If the Greeks spoke of a *moira* in connection with an individual's lot,
they also spoke of his *daimon.* This word (which may or may not
mean 'apportioner') has a stronger suggestion of personal agency but
is conceived in this association vaguely, as a divine power co-existent
with a man and determining the course of his life: when it determines
for good, he is *eudaimon,* but *dusdaimon* when it determines for ill.[4]
But the same word is also used of divine powers more specifically
conceived: not only of minor deities, many of them in the chthonian
realm – so that we can without being obviously misleading call them
'demons', but also of gods in general, when it is virtually a synonym
of *theos* – and the abstract *to daimonion* virtually a synonym of *to theion.*
We approach anthropomorphic gods, and the problem takes on a
new aspect.

The world of the Greek was full of gods, and they were gods of
power. At every point he was conscious of superhuman influences
which were the subject of his hopes and fears, the object of his prayers
and sacrifices. Often he might speak of *a* god or *a* daimon (for how
could he be sure what power was at work?), but the gods who had
cult he knew, whether it was in his own home or at a cave of the
Nymphs or in a prouder temple dedicated to one of the Olympian
gods. And he knew legends of the gods and their dealings with men.
A strong concrete imagination, reinforced by the work of poets (not
least of Homer) and later of the sculptors, had imposed clarity of form
upon the gods (or many of them), had given them quasi-human shape
and emotions and family relationships, so that we call them anthropomorphic. It was no task for the ordinary man to reconcile his belief in
the operative power of such beings with his vaguer feelings about
destiny: it was no task for the early poets either. We seek vainly in

---

[3] Cf. Onians, (op. cit. n. 2) 405f., where he suggests that in certain passages 'αἰών
appears to mean something like δαίμων' (cf. 405 n. 8). On *ananke* see p. 154 below.
B. C. Dietrich, *Death, fate and the gods* (London 1965) 249–83, has a useful review
of the Homeric vocabulary of fate.

[4] δυσδαίμων is not found before Empedocles and the tragedians.

Homer for a consistent theology, with a strict logical relationship between fate and the gods.[5] The gods – and particularly Zeus who is supreme among the gods – are so powerful that the decrees of fate are naturally regarded as decrees of the gods; and yet there are times when a feeling comes to the surface that even the gods cannot – or must not – abrogate the decrees of fate, particularly where the death of a man is concerned.

These issues are not clearly thought out, yet they affect the answer given to the question Why. Which is a question human beings are bound to ask, particularly when evil befalls. Why does a man suffer? Why does he fall from the height of prosperity into the pit of disaster? One does not perhaps ask these questions of a vaguely conceived *moira* or even of one's *daimon*, though one may sense hostility and express resentment. We ask such questions of gods. There are two differences indeed between a vague destiny and an operative god. In the first place, destiny is inexorable, whereas gods, it is hoped, can be moved by prayer and sacrifice. Secondly, gods are likely to have intelligible motives. Thus the greater the clarity with which divine powers are envisaged the more insistent enquiry becomes; the more human the gods the more their motivation is called in question. Being anthropomorphic, they are thought likely to respond to situations in ways similar to their human counterparts – to powerful men. They have their friends whom it is a point of divine honour to support; they have their prerogatives and resent any infringement of them, any derogation from their *timē*. Collectively, it may be thought, they have the prerogative of greatness and untroubled prosperity and so tend to resent too much prosperity in mortals and bring it down. The common notion of the *phthonos* of the gods ranges from sheer malignancy to a grudging jealousy. But if, among men, the *agathoi* were jealous of their prerogatives, the common people looked to them – and according to Hesiod looked too often in vain – for justice. They looked beyond them: the forces of greed and aggression being so strong, a divine sanction was sought. Perhaps the gods, above all Zeus, like good rulers cared to maintain justice; perhaps the disasters which befall men are in the nature of punishments sent by the gods.[6]

[5] Cf. Dodds, *GI* 21 n. 43 (with bibliography): the problem 'cannot be solved in logical terms'. See also M. P. Nilsson, *A history of Greek religion* (Oxford 1925) 171.

[6] 'Man projects into the cosmos his own nascent demand for social justice; and

In human experience there was evidence one way and the other. The jealousy and the justice of heaven fought a battle in the Greek mind.

There was evidence one way and the other. Great offenders were seen to come to a bad end, but others lived out their lives in peace. There were two ways of solving this problem of theodicy. There was post-mortem punishment, in which the Greeks, particularly perhaps in their old age, tended to believe, without its ever playing a dominant role in their morality.[7] There was the collective responsibility of the family: if the offender escaped punishment in this life, then doubtless his descendants would pay in due course. Not only is it a common fact of human experience that children suffer for the sins of their parents, but the Greek feeling for the solidarity of the family was so strong that they were able to take this perplexing notion in their moral stride as part of the process of divine justice. For it *is* perplexing in relation to individual responsibility and human freedom. If a man suffers for his own acts, that is one thing; if he suffers as a member of a doomed family, that is another. At least that is how we tend to see it. Tragedy was much concerned with such cases. In Aeschylus' *Agamemnon* two trains of causation lead to Agamemnon's death. There is the sacrifice of Iphigenia and, inextricably bound up with it, the blood shed in the Trojan war, so that he suffers for his own acts; but there is also the Thyestean banquet, the Furies haunting the house, so that he suffers for the act of his father.

Agamemnon suffers for his own acts: but were these free acts? No question has been more ardently debated than this. It shall not be debated here. But it must be pointed out that the notion of fatality, whether it is vaguely conceived under the name of Moira or a *moira* or more specifically regarded as the will of gods, of a god, of Zeus, does raise a problem of human freedom.

Free-will versus determinism is (so put) a philosophical issue, but the conflict implied is also a fact of life. There have been times and places, in human history, at which the feeling of inexorable fate has been so strong as to sap vitality: if what is bound to be will be, then all human striving is futile. The Greeks of the classical period were not

when from the outer spaces the magnified echo of his own voice returns to him, promising punishment for the guilty, he draws from it courage and reassurance' (Dodds, *GI* 32).

[7] Cf. S. G. F. Brandon, *The judgment of the dead* (London 1967) 76–97; Dover, *GPM* 261–8; Adkins, *MR* 140–8.

like that at all: vigorous, self-assertive, emulous, ambitious, they
pursued their aims in some confidence that they could attain them.[8]
And freedom, as individuals and as communities, they valued above
most other things. The terms of the philosophical debate about
free-will and determinism are modern. It is however a great mistake
to suppose that the real issues of this debate were not present to the
minds of Greeks and could not be expressed in their language.
Slave-owners and farmers, they were provided with insistent paradigms of the deprivation of liberty.[9] The free man acts without
compulsion, but the slave does what his master tells him, the yoked
animal goes where his master makes him go. The metaphor of the
yoke is common, particularly in poetry, particularly in tragedy. It is
often used of slavery, but also of any situation in which men lose the
liberty of choice. Another word commonly heard in this connection
is *ananke,* which (whatever its etymology) carries the notions of
constraint, compulsion and rigidity: it is indeed a not unimportant
member of the vocabulary of the inevitable. The free man delights to
be free, not under the yoke, not subject to *ananke.* And yet, when he
looks at the circumstances of human life, when he reflects upon the
power of the gods or of destiny, he must wonder, in view of the
constraints which are put upon him, how much freer the free man
actually is than the slave or the ox. That is what much Greek tragedy
is about.

It has seemed desirable to preface a discussion of fate in Sophocles
with an examination, however brief and inadequate, of some of the
issues and notions which are involved in the treatment, by the
dramatists, of the role played in human fortunes by divine power.
The elements of the problem are destiny, the gods, justice and human
freedom. That there are limitations upon human freedom is obvious.
That justice can be sought, if not found, in the operation of gods
conceived in the likeness of men is understandable. That there is
justice in the decrees of fate is another matter. Aeschylus was much
concerned with such questions. Before, however, we consider, as we

---

[8] They had misgivings of course from time to time, feeling (as we all do) that fate or
 fortune was against them. It was, however, the aggressive vigour of the Greeks
 which evoked the cautionary side of their popular morality, which was not so
 much associated with the notion of ineluctable fate as with punishing gods.
[9] Onians' study (op. cit. n. 2: passim) of the early terminology suggests that the
 contrast between bonds and freedom is fundamental to traditional notions of fate.

must do, how Moira and the Moirai enter into his drama, there is a gap to be filled.

In Homer, in addition to the notion of individual fate, the thread spun at birth, we find another association of *moira*. It is associated with the idea of order, regularity, propriety. Some scholars have indeed thought that *moira* was in origin a social conception, its application to individual fate, and especially to death, being secondary and derivative. This is hardly the impression we gain from Homer, where the notion of *moira* as 'order' is mostly found in a limited range of phrases. There is, nevertheless, a strong likelihood that this way of looking at *moira* was an ancient feature of popular thought, together with the notion of Erinyes as punishing breaches of *moira*. When we turn to Hesiod's *Theogony*, we find a double parentage for the Moirai.[10] In one passage they are, with the Keres, daughters of Night; in another they are daughters of Zeus and Themis, like the Horai (whose names are Eunomia, Dike and Eirene). This double parentage seems to reflect two aspects of *moira* both valid for popular thought; and there is an apparent breach between the spun thread (and its spinners) and a principle of order and regularity. It should be noted, however, that already in the earlier passage they are linked. The list of Night's progeny begins with Moros and black Ker: as West rightly remarks,[11] 'Moros is a man's appointed death, Moirai are the goddesses who appoint it.' Yet, when six lines later we come to the Moirai, they are associated with Keres, who are no longer simple fates of death, but qualified as *neleopoinoi*, 'pitiless punishers', and said to attend to the transgressions of men and gods. But are all fated deaths – and for that matter ill fates in life – in the nature of penalties, that is to say, related to justice? The exploration of justice, human and divine, was a primary purpose of Aeschylus. Let us turn first to *Persae* and then to *Oresteia*.

Xerxes, defeated and humiliated, returns to his kingdom; and his first words are these. 'Wretched I who have met with this hateful fate (μοίρας) most baffling. With what cruel intent has a *daimon* assaulted the race of Persians' (909ff.). He complains that the *daimon*, cruel, fickle and incomprehensible, has turned against him (942f.). His words echo similar language used earlier in the play by Atossa and the

---

[10] 217ff., 904ff., on which see M. L. West (ed.), *Hesiod Theogony* (Oxford 1966), ad locc.; also F. Solmsen, *Hesiod and Aeschylus* (Ithaca, N.Y. 1949) 36ff.

[11] On 217.

Chorus of Persian elders. But Darius had meanwhile propounded a very different way of looking at events. Disasters are the stern chastisements of Zeus and *ate* the fruit of *hubris* (821–8). If Xerxes had suffered a sickness of the mind (νόσος φρενῶν), if a great *daimon* had come upon him so that his mind was not good (ὥστε μὴ φρονεῖν καλῶς), it was that the god had joined forces with a man already set upon his course.[12]

Morally, *Persae* is a study in black and white; theologically, justice displaces jealousy, the arbitrary becomes intelligible. We find much the same doctrine in a famous chorus of *Agamemnon* (750ff.). *Oresteia* is, however, a more complex essay in theodicy (if that is the right term), and in it Moira and Moirai play a more debatable part. On the face of it, this is the story of a doomed family which from generation to generation seems predestined to crime: 'Who can cast out from the house the seed of curse? The race is glued to disaster' (*Agam.* 1565f.). When the story is brought to an end with the acquittal of Orestes and the 'conversion' of the Erinyes, the escorting Chorus sings – and it is the last statement about the divine world in the trilogy – that 'all-seeing Zeus and Moira have come together' (*Eum.* 1045f.). The words, if they do not necessarily imply a reconciliation of divergent interests, certainly imply a convergence, and certainly distinguish between Zeus and Moira as powers.[13] In what sense, and in what contexts, are these powers distinguished in *Oresteia*?

Clearly, they are both associated with justice.[14] In the impressive anapaests which introduce the great *kommos* of *Choephori*, the Coryphaeus prays (306ff.) the Moirai to accomplish the course of what is just (*to dikaion*) – to accomplish it *Diothen,* as emanating from Zeus, and then goes on to a clear statement of the *lex talionis* put into the mouth of a personified Dike. Word for word, blow for blow, the doer must suffer: it is an ancient saying. But this principle had already

---

[12] *Pers.* 725, 742, 750. On the interpretation of *Persae* see *JHS* 93 (1973) 210–19.

[13] *Eum.* 1044 is unfortunately corrupt.

[14] In *Agam.*, personified Moira occurs rarely, the Moirai not at all. In the Parodos, where the notion of fatality is found at 68 and 157, Moira (130) is the agent of death, lavish and violent, at the sack of Troy; and there seems little doubt (cf. H. Lloyd-Jones, *RhM* 103 (1960) 76f.; *CQ* 12 (1962) 189) that, when the prophet speaks of flocks, the poet means us to think of the common man, whose sufferings in the course of divine justice are much stressed in the play. At 1535 the text is doubtful, but it is probably Moira who sharpens the sword for a new deed of justice (cf. Fraenkel ad loc.). Cf. also 910–13 (σὺν θεοῖς εἱμαρμένα, after Δίκη).

been formulated in similar terms by the Chorus of *Agamemnon* (1563f.) as a law which will abide while Zeus abides upon his throne. The law is reformulated later in the *kommos* (400ff.) and associated with an Erinys. Zeus and Dike, Moirai and Erinys: all concerned with the law of retaliation.[15]

Indeed the most striking feature, theologically speaking, of the *kommos* – and of the play as a whole – is the convergence of divine powers.[16] To Zeus and the Erinyes, already implicated in *Agamemnon*, are added Moirai, Earth and the power of the dead, and (though not in the *kommos*) Apollo, who has sent Orestes, and Hermes, who aids him. All these powers converge to compel him towards matricide, driving him towards the dilemma which is expressed at 924 f. It is expressed in terms of hounds, who are Erinyes, but it has been preceded by a striking reference to Moira, itself in the form of a dilemma. For, when Clytemnestra pleads that Moira was part-cause of what she did (910), Orestes replies that her own death is being brought about by Moira.

At the end of *Choephori* a conflict begins to take shape between Apollo the defender and the Erinyes, now the persecutors, of Orestes; and the third play of the trilogy, in strong contrast to the second, is characterized by a divergence of divine powers, the Erinyes at odds with Apollo, the old gods at odds with the younger, with Apollo and (after the verdict) with Athena. Where do Moira and Moirai stand?

15   ἀλλ' ὦ μεγάλαι Μοῖραι, Διόθεν
         τῇδε τελευτᾶν,
         ᾗ τὸ δίκαιον μεταβαίνει.
         ἀντὶ μὲν ἐχθρᾶς γλώσσης ἐχθρὰ
         γλῶσσα τελείσθω· τοὐφειλόμενον
         πράσσουσα Δίκη μέγ' ἀυτεῖ·
         ἀντὶ δὲ πληγῆς φονίας φονίαν
         πληγὴν τινέτω. δράσαντα παθεῖν,
         τριγέρων μῦθος τάδε φωνεῖ.   (*Cho.* 306–14).

     μίμνει δὲ μίμνοντος ἐν θρόνῳ Διὸς
         παθεῖν τὸν ἔρξαντα· θέσμιον γάρ.   (*Agam.* 1563f.)

     ἀλλὰ νόμος μὲν φονίας σταγόνας
         χυμένας ἐς πέδον ἄλλο προσαιτεῖν
         αἷμα· βοᾷ γὰρ λοιγὸς Ἐρινὺν
         παρὰ τῶν πρότερον φθιμένων ἄτην
         ἑτέραν ἐπάγουσαν ἐπ' ἄτῃ.   (*Cho.* 400–4)

16 On the divine responsibilities in this play, see (from a rather different point of view) K. Reinhardt, *Aischylos als Regisseur und Theologe* (Bern 1949) 125ff.

The Moirai and the Erinyes are sisters, both daughters of Night.[17]
The Erinyes claim that the pursuit of homicides was a function
conferred on them at birth by Moira (or a *moira*, 333ff.) – an
ordinance ratified by *moira*, though granted by the gods (391ff.),
whose benefactors they are by freeing them of a loathsome task. Of
Zeus they speak only to say that he rejects their company (365f.) and,
unlike Apollo and Athena, Zeus's children, they never claim to speak
with his authority.

The conflict is of course resolved by the persuasions of Athena,
whereupon it is said that Zeus and Moira have come together. But
what does it mean? This separation of Zeus from the Erinyes with
whom he has been so closely implicated in the earlier phases of the
trilogy?[18] This apparent distinction of Zeus and Moira/Moirai as
authorities? It may be suggested that what has taken place is a
deliberate sorting-out of elements which have been problematically
fused, but in preparation for the establishment of an ultimate har-
mony. *Talio* is a mode of justice, with divine backing. But, whether at
the divine or human level, it involves violence, cruelty and indiscriminate suffering, of which the Erinyes are symbols. Moira, then,
and the Moirai are used to stand for the primitive, the rigid, the
intractable, the violent, the blind, the dark, aspect of divine operation.
It is not for nothing that the Moirai and the Erinyes are daughters of
Night; it is not for nothing that Persuasion has eyes (*Eum.* 970) and the
Zeus who joins forces with Moira is all-seeing (1046). For it is the
power of rational and benevolent persuasion that has now been added
to the mode of force.[19]

---

[17] Erinyes: 321, 745, 791f., 844, 1034. Moirai: 961.

[18] 'One is tempted to say, with some slight exaggeration, that, in the *Agamemnon*,
every reference to Erinyes is associated, textually, with Zeus, every reference to
Zeus with Erinyes, express or implied' (*JHS* 74 (1954) 20). At the outset 56ff.;
subsequently cf. e.g. 469 after 462, 990ff. after 973, 1485ff. after 1481, 1565 after
1563.

[19] I have based my account of Aeschylus on the sure ground of *Persae* and *Oresteia*,
where all the evidence is before us. One has only to consider how our view of
moira in the trilogy would be affected if one or two of the plays were missing to
realize how we are hampered in dealing with e.g. *Septem*, where in the absence of
the lost plays the relationship of divine power to human responsibility remains
problematical. Cf. *YCS* 25 (1977) 1–45, esp. 44f. As in *Cho.*, we find a multipli-
city of divine powers all converging to bring about the same result, but the
specific problem of *Eum.* seems not to be raised and its solution is therefore absent.
Besides the incompleteness of the evidence, there is a further reason for omitting

We shall return in later chapters[20] to the Aeschylean conception of the Erinyes and to the role of persuasion, to consider how they may have affected the tragic thought of Sophocles. What is immediately relevant is to observe that there are two traditional ways in which the notion of an ineluctable Moira can be conceived and used to account for what happens to men. It can be seen as a pre-existent decree which may well appear arbitrary and unintelligible. This is how it was seen by Xerxes and his Persian friends, but that is not the most characteristic Aeschylean view. When Orestes rejoins that Moira has brought about his mother's death, it is not meant that a mysterious dispensation has singled her out of all people to meet this of all fates but rather that she is involved in a process which leads inevitably to the matricide. At the same time it is ironically true of Orestes himself, not that he has been chosen by a malign fate to murder his mother (as Oedipus to lie with his), but that the course on which he is set will inevitably result in his pursuit by Erinyes. The process is inevitable, but far from unintelligible, being part of the divine justice, problematic though that may for long appear. It is the inevitability that is seen in the light of destiny.

It is relevant to consider how either or both these ways of regarding fate show themselves in Sophoclean tragedy. Sophocles has often been seen as a tragedian whose dramas turn upon remorseless destiny.[21] If some critics have played down this notion, it is presumably because it seems to detract from the freedom of the human agents and turn men into puppets of fate; and to see the masterful Oedipus, for instance, as a mere puppet seemed – and in some degree is – absurd. The fact remains that, however masterful an Oedipus, an Ajax, a

any consideration of *Prometheus Vinctus* from my text, since I no longer have any confidence in its Aeschylean authorship. It does, however, stand in a close relation to Aeschylean thought and contains a passage (511–20) closely relevant to the themes discussed above. See App. c.

20 Chapters 9–11.

21 This view, whether right or wrong, owes much to *Oedipus Tyrannus* and to the fact that, in that play and in some others, prominence is given to oracles which, sometimes in unexpected and ironical ways, find their fulfilment; and an oracle which is bound to prove true appears to imply a destiny which is bound to be accomplished. The Nun's Priest in Chaucer, familiar with the theological problem raised by divine foreknowledge in relation to human freedom, refused to commit himself; and we can follow his example. The Greeks (like ourselves?) possessed simultaneously a sense of destiny and a sense of freedom, but the poetic and dramatic impact of the oracles must have been as stated. On oracles in Sophocles see further p. 181 n. 4.

Heracles, may appear, they are all in one way or another, in one
degree or another, constrained and brought down by superhuman
power, whether this is seen as a specific deity (or deities) or a vaguer
daimon or *moira*. Why?

When we examine the texts of the plays, what we find in the first
instance is, of course, the answers given by the participants themselves
when, confronted with some disaster, they ask this question. For it is
asked in plays as in life. Why is this happening to me, to my friend?
The answer of Greeks is likely to be in terms of gods or of 'fate'.
Answers are given by characters and by choruses. Indeed choruses,
especially perhaps choruses of elders, are great explainers. They think
they know: sometimes they are right, but equally they can be wrong,
or partly wrong. The Chorus of *Antigone* are partly wrong, though
essentially right, when they diagnose the mind of Haemon.[22] Faced
with the approaching fate of Antigone, is that same Chorus right to
see it as the outcome of mental folly? If so, whose folly is it? Is the
Chorus in *Oedipus Tyrannus*, beginning to fear for Oedipus, right to
relate ill-fate to the offences of a hubristic man?

To those odes we shall return. There are other choral explainers,
whose proclivity is less theological. Not elders, but, as in *Trachiniae*, a
chorus of young girls, capable of illuminating the action in terms of
Kypris, rather at sea perhaps with Zeus.[23] Not elders, but, as in *Ajax*,
simple sailors who in their puzzlement can tell us many things that the

---

[22] Cf. ch. 5 p. 92.

[23] As much as any play, divine power presides over the action of *Trach.* (cf. Bowra
149; Reinhardt passim), but it is mainly associated with specific deities: with Zeus,
whose son Heracles is; with Kypris, to whose power both Heracles and Deianira
fall victims; and (as I shall argue), since the notion of retaliation bulks large in the
closing stages of the play, with the Erinyes. How Heracles, being what he was,
and Deianira, being what she was, under the influence of these divine powers
worked out their tragic destinies is clearly shown. Each had an *aion* (2, 34, cf. 81),
but the question – the antecedent question – why the *aion* of each was such and
such, the question of *moira* and *daimon* is hardly raised. But, in the case of Heracles,
there are those riddling oracles, the meaning of which is revealed only after the
event, bound to be fulfilled (cf. n. 21); and it is mainly in connection with the
oracles that the language of fatality is employed: e.g. 79–81 (μέλλει); 169f.
(εἱμαρμένα). The most interesting passage is perhaps 849f., where 'the coming
fate' (μοῖρα) is said to bring to light 'a great and guileful disaster' (ἄταν). This is
immediately proclaimed as the manifest work of Kypris (860f.). A little later in
the scene, the new bride is said to have given birth to a great Erinys. See pp. 212ff.

It will be argued in later chapters (9–11) that the operations of the divine world
in *El.* and *O.C.* are conceived in close relation to the Aeschylean concept of the
Erinyes. See, on fate specifically, p. 321. On fate in *Phil.* see ch. 12 p. 300.

dramatist wishes us to know, but, with the exception of one passage,[24] do not explain in metaphysical terms. Perhaps one should look
at them as being, collectively, only one member of a group, the inner
circle of the hero's friends, linked to him by dependence, loyalty, and
affection, all alike shattered by the catastrophe, all seeking to account
to themselves for a hardly explicable disaster. Ajax himself leads the
way, followed by the Chorus, Tecmessa and (finally) Teucer. It may
be worth returning, briefly, to the play.

The hero suffers a series of disasters culminating in his suicide. He
loses the Judgement of the Arms; his vengeance is frustrated by a
crude delusion; when he returns to a kind of sanity, he is in a state of
mind which can only lead to self-destruction. His disasters are described, by himself and others, with the word *ate*[25] which, in tragedy,
covers both objective disaster and subjective infatuation: the origin of
the disaster or infatuation, its relationship to divine power and to
human culpability, can seldom be inferred from any isolated use, but
the word tends always to have a strong flavour of theology. We hear
the word first from Odysseus (123), who sees in the delusion of Ajax
an instance of mortal insecurity; when he says that Ajax has been
yoked to an evil *ate,* he is no doubt thinking of the overriding power
of a goddess. His words are immediately followed by her motto-
couplet which relates divine pleasure or disfavour to the *sophrosune* or
'badness' of a man. Gradually, as the play progresses, the role of
Athena falls into perspective. We come to see that Ajax is being
punished for his boastful pride, but we see also this pride as a disease
with a long history, coming to a crisis and culminating in the final

---

[24] See n. 31 below.

[25] On the notion of *ate* cf. R. D. Dawe, 'Some reflections on ate and hamartia',
HSCP 72 (1967) 89–123, who is doubtless right to maintain that the sense of
objective damage or harm is prior to that of mental blindness (p. 86). The word
occurs some forty times in Sophocles, nearly always in the former sense. Nearly
half the cases come from *Ajax* and *Antigone*; and it is in these two plays alone that
we can sometimes discern the further meaning of infatuation. (Dawe maintains
that the word was on its way out, 'its last efflorescence coming in the famous third
stasimon of *Antigone*'.) Whether the notion of a god-sent blindness is present or
not, the disaster tends to be thought of as god-sent, though this is not always the
case. Dawe has explored the links between this concept and that of *hamartia* and
suggests that links also exist 'between Ate, Blabe, Erinys, Moira (and Moirai), and
some of the less common sinister figures that haunt Greek poetry, like Aisa'. This
is a fundamental study, even if one cannot always accept his conclusions. (For
some hostile criticism see Vickers 159, n. 21.) Recently, on *ate,* see G. Vlastos,
Plato's universe (Oxford 1975) 13–17.

disaster. It is the pride of Ajax which explains the wrath of Athena, to which it is antecedent (whereas the power of Aphrodite is antecedent to the lust of Heracles which it explains). A symbol of divine hostility to human pride, she explains not what Ajax is but what, being such, he must suffer.[26]

For Ajax, to whom it never occurs that he might himself be in any way to blame, she is half the explanation of everything. Both in the *kommos* and in his first long speech he blames, jointly, divine and human enmity.[27] Seeing the world as always in terms of friends and enemies, he sees Athena as the divine enemy, ally and protectress of his principal human foe, mocking and insulting as enemies do. So, in the deception-speech, he lets it be supposed that he will be reconciled to the gods and to the Atridae.[28] But here there is an interesting variation, when he ascribes the enmity of the Greeks to his possession of the sword of Hector; alone with the sword, he reverts to the same notion; and, when Teucer sees the sword, he too finds in it a kind of explanation. Clearly, Sophocles did not duplicate and re-duplicate this theme without significance, and we must return to it.[29]

For it is not only Ajax but all his friends who must find their reasons. And it is not surprising that, in the main, they see things in the same light as the hero. At 891 Tecmessa discovers the body, and there is an epirrhematic scene of lamentation between her and the Chorus. We hear again of Odysseus and the Atridae, of insult and mockery, of the favouritism of Pallas. It is Tecmessa, herself the victim of a *daimon* (504), who attributes all responsibility to the gods and forbids her human enemies the right to triumph (950ff., 970). For her, looking at events in the light of her own tragic fate, the divine responsibility outweighs the human. How does Teucer see them?

He too must seek a reason, and one is presented to him by the sight of the familiar sword, to which he refers with an agent noun and a personal construction, seeing now that it was a murderer (ὑφ᾽ οὗ φονέως ἄρ᾽ ἐξέπνευσας, 1025f.). He addresses the dead man: 'Do you see how Hector was bound in time, though dead, to destroy you?' Unknowingly he echoes a phrase (χρόνῳ ἔμελλε) of the Chorus;[30]

---

[26] On the role of Athena see further p. 318.
[27] 379ff. 401ff., 445ff.
[28] 654–67, on which see ch. 2, p. 49.
[29] See pp. 210.
[30] On which see n. 31.

unknowingly he has picked up his brother's theme, which he carries further, reasoning it out with a *men* and a *de* till he reaches a conclusion. Ajax and Hector had exchanged gifts; in the event Hector had been dragged by the belt of Ajax, Ajax had fallen upon the sword of Hector. What first appears an ironical 'happening' (1028) is then seen as something devised by the gods to the detriment of men (1036f.). With this conclusion he is satisfied (1038f.).

Like Ajax, his friends blame the gods: Tecmessa thinking of the malice of Athena, Teucer believing that in the exchange of gifts, as in all things, they were devising evil for men; he speaks of an Erinys forging the sword of Hector. The Chorus uses the language of fate. 'So you were bound in time' (ἔμελλες χρόνῳ) – the phrase echoed by Teucer – 'unhappy man, hard-minded that you were, to accomplish an evil *moira* of immeasurable troubles' (925ff.).[31] But we have also heard a god and a spokesman of the gods. From Athena and Calchas, jointly, we learned that her wrath was the penalty of pride. She did not send the pride but punished it. From our earliest knowledge of him he was inordinately proud and, being also stubborn and inflexible (*stereophron* and *omophron*), nurtured his pride as a disease. To be so was his destiny – and to be placed in precisely those circumstances which caused his disease to erupt into disaster. He was born with his stubborn pride into a world of ruthless conflict. When Teucer said that the sword had been forged by an Erinys, it was less a primitive superstition than a primitive truth, that violence breeds violence,

---

[31] The notion and vocabulary of fate enter into their short stanza at 925–36, the structure of which is interesting. It could be paraphrased as follows: 'We ought to have known (ἄρα) that, being στερεόφρων, you were bound (ἔμελλες) to bring about a *moira* of immeasurable troubles. Such were the bitter complainings which, as we heard, you, being ὠμόφρων, uttered day and night against the Atridae. We can now see (ἄρα) that that time was a potent source of woes when the contest for the arms was set up.' The word χρόνος, so important in the play, enters twice. On the second occasion, the singers have in mind that span of time, brief but powerful in its effect (so μέγας, cf. 714), which embraced the Judgement of the Arms. They see it, like others within the play and many modern scholars, as the beginning of woes. When, however, at the beginning of the stanza they sing: ἔμελλες χρόνῳ ἐξανύσσειν μοῖραν they are, surely, using language more appropriate to the fulfilment over a long span of time of a pre-destined fate. The second half (with its repetition of χρόνος) merely shows how unduly narrow their time-scale is by comparison with the far-receding perspective offered by Calchas – and the poet (cf. pp. 40f. above). Ajax was indeed in the long course of time fulfilling a destiny inherent in his nature, which was to be στερεόφρων and ὠμόφρων.

even after death.[32] Tecmessa at 485ff., addressing Ajax as her master
and speaking of her condition as a slave, says she has been subject to
anankaia tuche in the loss of liberty (for so it seemed good to the gods
and to his powerful hand); she tells him what her plight will be, if he
dies. For her, she says, it will be another stroke of a (her) *daimon* (κἀμὲ
μὲν δαίμων ἐλᾷ 504),[33] but for him it will be shame. A passive victim,
she thinks of him as the hero, the free agent, the man of power. But
does not Ajax also have his *daimon*? Is he not also subject to *ananke*, the
prisoner of his past and, it may be, of his own predestined character?

Divine power broods over the action. Ask the question Why?, and
there is always a divine component, though not necessarily the sole
component, in the answer. When we ask the same question of *Oedipus
Tyrannus*, what shall we find? Or of *Antigone*?

Why did these events fall out as they did? Why for Antigone? Why
for Creon? To the latter question there might seem a simple answer in
the closing anapaests: he is punished for his arrogance and impiety.
His final entry is greeted with the choral comment that his disaster
was the fruit of his own error (οὐκ ἀλλοτρίαν ἄτην ἀλλ' αὐτὸς
ἁμαρτών, 1259f.); and Creon accepts from the Chorus – and from
Teiresias (1023ff.) – that he has erred, that his wits were astray and his
counsels wrong. It has been shown[34] that *ate* and *hamartia* are closely
linked in traditional (and tragic) thought, but the genesis of the
infatuation which leads to the fatal mistake need not always be seen in
the same light. Creon attributes his error to the antecedent influence
of a god (1271ff.); and both he and the Chorus regard the disastrous
outcome as his destiny. Twice he uses the word *potmos*; and, when the
Coryphaeus hears him wish for death, he says that 'mortals have no
escape from a destined disaster' (πεπρωμένης . . . συμφορᾶς, 1337f.).
We may be reminded of Xerxes ascribing to the incomprehensible
cruelty of a *daimon* what Darius had revealed as the chastisement of
Zeus. What kind of *moira* is this? What kind of *ate*? We need not
expect much enlightenment from Creon, but the Chorus have pre-
tensions to theology and have sung a song about *ate* to which we shall
shortly return.

---

[32] See also p. 44 n. 98.
[33] δαίμων at 504 balances τῆς ἀναγκαίας τύχης at 485, rounding off the first half of
her speech in a kind of ring-composition.
[34] Cf. n. 25.

Antigone is more important – Antigone and her fate. The word
moira does not occur in the closing scene (though *potmos* does): indeed
it occurs only twice in the play, but once in an interesting context,
where it is associated with the adjective *moiridia*. This is in the Fourth
Stasimon.[35] Antigone has left the stage for a living tomb, and the
Chorus call to mind other figures of legend whose fates were in some
way similar. The figures who stand closest to her are Danae, in the
first stanza, and Cleopatra, in the fourth – both women, both innocent victims. In the first case we hear of the terrible power of fate
(951f.); in the second we are told how the long-lived Moirai bore
upon Cleopatra also – on Cleopatra as well as upon the child Antigone. The Chorus are confronted with a ghastly event for which they
find it hard to account (they have tried out their theology in the
kommos): the notion of fate comes into their minds.

Indeed Antigone has already sung of her *daimon* (833) and her
potmos (881), but also of the *potmos* which she shares with the whole
ill-famed family of the Labdacids (857ff.). If the antecedents of Creon
are dramatically unimportant, it is otherwise with the heroine;[36] and
this is not only because she has inherited from her father that 'harshness' and 'self-willed temper' which enabled her to do what she did.[37]
She acts and suffers as a member of a doomed family. This is brought
out in the Prologos, in the opening speech of Antigone and Ismene's
recital (49–57) of the terrible events they both have known. And if, as
is understandable, for them the horror begins with Oedipus and they
speak only of the small immediate group of *philoi* that constituted
their world, Creon takes matters back to Laius whose reign was
within his experience and that of the Chorus.[38] The doom of the
Labdacids is the theme of the Second Stasimon. The ode comes near
the half-way mark of the play: it is long and elaborate and, in much of
its language and thought, highly traditional if not Aeschylean. The
name of Zeus is central to it – the Zeus that Antigone saw (2f.) as
accomplishing evils upon her and Ismene, the Zeus from whom she
will claim an authority for her act of rebellion. Close to Zeus come
the nether gods and an Erinys. The ode begins with *ate* and ends with

---

[35] For an interpretation of this ode, see ch. 5 pp. 98ff.
[36] See ch. 6 p. 149.
[37] See ch. 6 ibid.
[38] See ch. 6 p. 123.

ate. For the theological interpretation of events it is likely to have crucial importance.[39]

Str. α´ (582–92). The Chorus contemplates the approaching deaths of Antigone and (as they think) Ismene, the sole remaining members of the house of Oedipus; and it is in terms of an ill-fated house that they seek to account for what is going to happen. The first word of their song is *eudaimones* (582): 'well-fated are those whose life (*aion*) has no taste of evils'.[40] A trite generalization applicable to all individual fates? But they go on immediately to sing of a *domos* in which, when it is once shaken from the gods (*theothen*), generation after generation no sort of disaster (*atas*) fails to come about (583–5).[41] They illustrate with a simile, elaborate and sustained somewhat in the Aeschylean manner: the storm-winds drive the surge over the darkness of the waters below the surface, and black sand is rolled up from the depths; the headlands groan and roar under the blows of the wind (586–92). It is a picture of darkness visible (*erebos, kelainan*), with a suggestion that the order of nature is reversed, that what should be below has been brought up into the higher world. The contrast of light and darkness, of upper and nether, is a striking feature of the ode.[42]

Ant. α´ (593–603). The generalizations of the first stanza are applied in the second to the Labdacids. Woe after woe, death after death – all going back, as they see, to an ancient origin (*archaia*). This word, together with the name of the house, takes the story back behind Oedipus, back to Laius, back perhaps to the curse of Pelops, though Sophocles is not specific.[43] Generation after generation, and the race

---

[39] Mrs P. E. Easterling's admirable examination of the ode did not appear until my own discussion had reached an advanced stage of preparation. I have, however, been able to add references in the footnotes and have modified my text at one point.

[40] 'εὐδαίμων sollte hier schon im ersten Wort thematisch den δαίμων hörbar werden lassen' (Müller (2) 140). On αἰών see p. 151 above.

[41] σεισθῇ (aorist) of the initial stroke, however motivated. 'Likened to a storm, or earthquake, that shakes a building' (Jebb). Imprecise in itself, the metaphor leads into the great simile that follows. Cf. Easterling, *Ant*. 143.

[42] Cf. Goheen 56ff.; T. F. Hoey, 'Inversion in the *Antigone*: a note', *Arion* 6 (1970) 340f. For a not dissimilar fusion, or confusion, of the two worlds, cf. *Ant*. 415–21, on which see ch. 9, n. 21 (with *BICS* 26 (1979) 5f.).

[43] Back, one might say, to whatever constituted the initial disaster – the πρώταρχος ἄτη – in the Aeschylean trilogy. See Lloyd-Jones, *JZ* 120, who makes the valid point that, if Laius spoke the prologue of the first play (as we have reason to suppose), he must have had something to say and may have told the Chrysippus-

has no deliverance from the stroke of a god. They see this clearly now, for only Antigone and Ismene are left, who are to die. They sing of a light spread in the house of Oedipus and of its last root, but these in their turn are to perish. They sing of the nether gods and an *erinys*; they sing of folly.

My mention of themes may seem strangely selective. The unfortunate fact is that the text and interpretation of this crucial passage are highly – and rightly – controversial. Something must be said, however reluctantly, about this controversy. What is it that destroys the root (or the light, or the root which *is* the light of hope)?[44] In the received text are three nominatives, and the first is *konis*: 'the bloody dust of the nether gods' (φοινία θεῶν τῶν νερτέρων . . . κόνις). And Antigone is about to suffer for casting dust over her brother's mangled body to meet the requirements of the nether gods. This is splendid,[45] but the verb is *kataman*, which means to mow or cut down. Dust may quench a light: but can it be said to cut a root? It is not surprising that Jortin thought of *kopis* or 'chopper' (though that cannot quench a light). *konis* or *kopis*: scholars will continue to take sides in this controversy, they must do so with full cognizance of the difficulties of the ensuing line, which appears to provide us with two more nominatives: *anoia* and *erinus*. Since three separate subjects seem a bit much, it is likely that, if the text is sound, the second and third nominatives are in apposition to the first, that (difficult though it may be) the 'dust' or 'chopper' is described as, or equated with, 'folly of

story. *Why* was he not to have a son? As against this, *Sept.* 720–91 has so much the character of a resumé that one hesitates to assume any antecedent that is not stated or implied in the course of that ode. One must, I fear, confess ignorance. Cf. *YCS* 25 (1977) 29ff. On the difficulties of 594f. see Easterling, *Ant.* 145.

[44] The text is uncertain. I hesitate between ὑπέρ (which Easterling defends) and Hermann's ὅπερ, with which ρίζας becomes a defining genitive, the 'light' or hope of salvation consisting in the last survivors of the stock. This is, however, only the first of the textual problems that bedevil this passage, on which see H. Lloyd-Jones, *CQ* 7 (1957) 17–19 and Easterling, *Ant.* 146–9.

[45] Dust, as a word of darkness, would pick up the language of the great simile in the *strophe* and, equally, contrast with the brilliant light in which, as we shall hear, Zeus lives. Cf. Goheen 60. The essence of this singularly intractable problem is that the poet, having spoken in the first part of the sentence of 'light' and 'root', then (if the text is sound) combines a noun appropriate to the former with a verb appropriate to the latter in a mixed metaphor which would raise an eyebrow in Aeschylus. If Easterling's objections to κοπίς (see below) are cogent, I still feel that her defence of the received text – and the triple subject – is a little optimistic. For further doubts see the following note.

speech' and what (if it is a tolerable locution at all)[46] can only mean 'madness of mind'. The word translated 'madness' is *erinus*.

In this unsatisfactory text the fixed points would seem to be that the nether gods are operative and that the notion of an Erinys is associated with a distracted mind. Within these limits we must try and follow the mental process of a chorus of traditional theologians as they contemplate the approaching end of Antigone in the light of the family history. The history was one of recurrent *ate*. When they used the word in the first stanza (584), they meant disaster as objective as the evils (κακῶν) of 582, the woes (πήματα) of 595. Disaster is sent by the gods (584, 596f.) and, until near the end of the second stanza, there is no direct reference to the human factor. It was, however, a traditional notion that the gods bring about the downfall of those whom, for whatever reason, they wish to destroy by inspiring them with an infatuate folly which leads to a fatal act. And now we hear of *anoia*. And it must be the *anoia* of Antigone: it can be no other.[47] And the *anoia* of Antigone consisted in her disobedience. And the Chorus know, as we know, in what that disobedience itself consisted. The paradox is extraordinary. The nether gods destroy her for an act of piety towards them, which is an act of infatuated folly; an Erinys works within her to her detriment, causing her to perform an action the non-performance of which would, if we may believe Teiresias (1074f.), be punishable by Erinyes. Like us, the Chorus has heard her speak of Zeus: of Zeus they now sing.

Str. β' (604–14). Their thought moves from the dark chthonian realm to the radiance of Olympus, to ask what contravention of men can hold in check the power of Zeus. And we are immediately

---

[46] φρενῶν ᾽Ερινύς as a locution and concept in Sophocles has been readily accepted by all interpreters, perhaps too readily. My doubts are expressed in *BICS* 26 (1979) 7f. The objection to this expression is that it waters down, if not abolishes, the personification which is strongly present in such non-literal references to Erinyes as *Trach.* 895 and *Aj.* 1034. It is an abstraction, balancing ἄνοια; and I find it hard to believe that Sophocles, in this ode of Aeschylean tone, following a reference to the nether gods, introduced, in close proximity to the name of Zeus, something which is unparalleled in his extant work, namely a dilute psychological Euripidean fury.

[47] At her entrance the Coryphaeus had spoken of her as caught ἐν ἀφροσύνῃ (383); and Creon has recently (561f.) described both Antigone and Ismene as ἄνους. But why stress 'folly of word' (603), when, to the knowledge of the Chorus, she had spoken no word of folly before her fatal action? They have indeed heard her obstinate defiance of Creon on the stage. Like so much in this ode, however, the true significance relates to Creon himself (see below).

confronted with a second and corresponsive paradox. Can we hear of a contravention, a transgression, without reflecting that she had 'transgressed' a man-made law which, so she claimed, could not prevail over the unwritten laws of the gods? It was not Zeus that made the proclamation, nor was it the Justice that dwells with the nether gods (450f.). Strong as is the contrast between light and darkness, between the upper and nether gods, we find them in this ode both working towards the punishment of the offender; and it was in Antigone's great speech that we first found them in association.[48] If the Chorus has forgotten that speech, the language of their song ensures that we shall not forget it, and not only by that reference to 'transgression'.

Of the unwritten laws Antigone had said that their life was 'not of today or yesterday but from all time' (456f.). Now we hear of the power of Zeus as unsleeping, ageless and unaffected by time. There is indeed a closer parallel in a passage which Sophocles had, presumably, not yet written, where, in the Second Stasimon of *Oedipus Tyrannus*, the chorus of that play sings of laws that were fathered by Olympus, that are not put to sleep by forgetfulness but have in them a god who grows not old.[49] The parallel is striking, for the laws in both passages relate to kinship. So, when our chorus goes on to sing of a law which will hold good in the future as it has in the past, we could almost expect that, contrary to all logic, they will sing of the duty to bury a blood-relation!

The law they state is different. Their train of thought has moved away from Antigone, away from the Labdacids,[50] to a wider application; and it is as though they are seeking a general formula which will cover all cases of *ate*. The 'law' (*nomos*) is not a command given to men, but a principle governing human life. 'To no mortal comes a life of great abundance without disaster' (ἐκτὸς ἄτας, 613f.)[51] Is this

---

[48] See ch. 9 p. 211 n. 21.
[49] See ch. 8 p. 187.
[50] Cf. Easterling, *Ant.* 142ff.
[51] I translate an emended text. The MS tradition (and scholia) give us πάμπολις, which is nonsense. The popular solution is Heath's πάμπολύ γ' 'nothing that is vast enters into the life of mortals without a curse'. So Jebb, who explains πάμπολυ in his commentary as meaning 'too much power, or wealth, or prosperity – anything so great as to be μὴ κατ' ἄνθρωπον'. Slightly cryptic, but perhaps not impossibly so. Lloyd-Jones (op. cit. n. 44) 19f., may have hit upon a better solution, reading βίοτος πάμπολυς, with a preference for οὐδὲν over οὐδέν'. Contr. Easterling, *Ant.* pp. 151f.

surprising? One thing is clear: they are using the traditional association of disaster with excessive wealth and prosperity, familiar from Herodotus, familiar from Aeschylus, in whose work it is well exemplified in *Persae*, but above all perhaps in a famous passage of *Agamemnon* (750ff.) where, if wealth is rejected as the sole and sufficient cause of disaster, its dangers and temptations are clearly recognized. So strong is this association that we find cases in tragedy in which it seems to be introduced without much relevance.[52] Is this such a case?

Before we write it down as such, we should reflect that in *Antigone* Sophocles seems often to have had in mind the Aeschylean trilogy of which *Septem* was the final play; and there are strong indications that wealth was an important theme in that trilology, a cause of conflict and of woe.[53] In our play it was no part of Antigone's 'folly' to lust after wealth. Turn, however, to the words of the Messenger who brought news from the cave. On Creon's fall from good to bad fortune he comments in conventional terms which might at first seem otiose.[54] Monarchical power Creon still has, but has lost all pleasure in life. 'Heap up riches in thy house, if thou wilt; live in kingly state; yet, if there be no gladness therewith, I would not give the shadow of a vapour for all the rest, compared with joy' (Jebb, 1168–71). Creon, if we have seen him aright, was ambitious for power; wealth is the base of power; wealth, power and kingship, form a traditional complex of ideas.[55] Perhaps we can now see that, in making his Chorus move away from the Labdacids, away from the family towards the individual offender, Sophocles is himself moving away from Antigone in the direction of Creon, whom we shall find without much difficulty in the final stanza of the present ode. It is the notion of wealth which leads into that stanza.

Ant. β' (615–25). They continue: 'For wide-wandering Hope is an advantage to many men, but to many it is deception by light-witted lusts' (615ff.). *Elpis*, here half-personified, is hope, perhaps ambition; and it works two ways. If it can be advantageous as a spur to effort,

---

[52] 'Irrelevant' cases: *Ajax* 130, 488; *Trach.* 133. On wealth in *Persae*, cf. *JHS* 93 (1973) 214, 216. On wealth in our play, cf. Goheen 14–19.

[53] Cf. *Sept.* 733, 771, 950, and *YCS* 25 (1977) 33f.

[54] Cf. ch. 6 p. 127.

[55] In *O.T.* we find the hero speaking of wealth and tyranny in one breath (380), the Chorus singing of the hubristic king whose *hubris* is caused by a satiety of many things (873ff.). See ch. 8 p. 189.

enabling men to improve their condition,[56] it may get out of hand, when *elpis* becomes *apate,* when men are deceived by their lust for wealth or power pursued in the false belief that these are exclusively desirable objects. It is a failure of judgement, and the man understands nothing until he burns his foot in the fire (618f.). The singers quote a proverb, a well-known expression of traditional wisdom (σοφία). 'When a god is leading a man's wits towards *ate,* the bad seems to him to be good; and he fares but a very short time free of *ate*' (620ff.).[57]

It is a general formula; and we have heard something like it before, men faring well and ill, and their ill-faring due to false standards (τὸ μὴ καλόν) and recklessness (τόλμα). This was in the First Stasimon, which hymns the achievements of human cleverness, but goes on to say that, despite man's art and contrivance, successful beyond all expectation (ὑπὲρ ἐλπίδα), he fares now towards evil and now to good. It has been well observed that the *elpis* of the Second Stasimon is not essentially different from the *deinotes* of the First, both the ground of optimism.[58] If the First Stasimon approaches very close to the contemporary world of Sophocles, the Second remains within the heroic context, or appears to do so, since it lacks the political theme of

---

56 Perhaps we find a similar notion in *P.V.* Why does the gift of hope (250) precede the gift of fire? Because without it men would lack the spirit to make use of fire and develop the arts.

57 At 625 the reading of the MSS is ὀλιγοστόν, which is untenable, and most editors adopt Bergk's ὀλίγιστον. Lloyd-Jones (op. cit. n. 44) 20–3, suggests dividing ὀλιγὸς τὸν and takes the resulting text as follows: 'but the small man, the poor man throughout his time fares outside of Ate'. This is ingenious (and *Sept.* 766ff. might provide a parallel), but I am not sure that he has disposed of the linguistic difficulties which he discusses (cf. Easterling, *Ant.* p. 154).

58 Müller (2) 139. One should observe the movement of thought which leads into the First Stasimon. Creon believed that his edict might have been transgressed from motives of profit: 'gain', he says, 'has often ruined men through their hopes' (ὑπ' ἐλπίδων, 221). Enter the Guard to be accused of having taken a bribe (322, 326). The Chorus then goes on to sing that men are amazing (332ff.); and the first instance they give is the risks that merchants take upon the sea. The unexpressed connection is this: it is amazing what men will do, how they will risk their lives, for the sake of money, of livelihood. The thought then moves on from trade to agriculture and to human achievement in general, returning at the end to point a traditional moral.

There are indications, apparently trivial, that Sophocles had the one ode in mind when he wrote the other (we cannot of course say which he wrote first). The epithet κουφόνοος occurs in both (342, 617). There is no thematic connection between the two occurrences, but the word may well have come into his mind when writing the one ode because he had been thinking about the other. The same might be true of the word ἕρπειν (367, 585, 613, 617).

the First, in which ill-faring is associated with a neglect of law and justice. But this is an illusion. The missing political factor is at once supplied by the scene between Creon and his son. Haemon is about to enter and reveal the full extent of his father's infatuation and, ultimately, to bring about his ruin. General as the statements may be, they apply to Creon—and they do not apply to Antigone.

The trains of thought are not too difficult to follow. The succession of disasters which dog the house; the operation of nether powers, and then of Zeus; a law that relates disaster to excessive prosperity and to the temptations which it offers men so that their judgement fails and disaster ensues. If the motivation of the divine powers remains imperfectly defined, human culpability is strongly indicated. And the culprit is Creon. His is the folly of word and action; it is he who will be pursued by a conjunction of divine powers for a breach of divine law; it is he who takes bad for good. It has been well observed how the notions of this ode are picked up in the closing scene, with its stress on error and false judgement.[59] But the singers are not thinking of Creon. If the ode is echoed in the closing scene, itself it echoes that earlier song sung of the person still unknown who had committed the crime, who had defied the edict and buried Polynices. And that person was Antigone. And it was the approaching end of Antigone which prompted this ode and the Chorus' desire to explain. Hence the twofold paradox: that she is at once meeting the demands of the nether gods and victim of an Erinys, that she is obeying a law of Zeus and destroyed by him. She knows it, and in her last words speaks of what she suffers *ten eusebian sebisasa*. According to the doctrine of this ode, Antigone should have been destroyed through her own infatuated error, transgressing the authority of Zeus in a desire for harmful things. The pattern has gone wrong; the explanation does not work out. If this is a world in which a Creon gets his deserts, it is also one in which an Antigone is destroyed for doing Zeus's bidding. We shall find a similar false explanation of disaster in a similar ode in *Oedipus Tyrannus*. There too it is the Second Stasimon and central to the play. It is extremely complex; its interpretation has been much debated, and it will be examined in the following chapter. Since it is much concerned with the fate of Oedipus, we must, however, first consider

[59] This is well brought out by Dawe (op. cit. n. 25) 112f.

how the notion – and the vocabulary – of fate enter into that play.[60]

Oedipus Tyrannus has always held a special place in the surviving work of Sophocles. The most powerful of his tragedies, it distils the essence of one aspect of his thought. I refer to the breach between the divine and human modes of existence, the frailty of man and his exposure to the power of gods. This thought receives its classic statement in the first stanza of the ode which the Chorus sings, when Oedipus leaves the stage having learnt the truth about his life. 'What man wins more of happiness (*eudaimonia*) than just a semblance and, after the semblance, a decline? I call no mortal blessed (*makarizo*), for I have before me the example of your *daimon* – wretched Oedipus' (1189–95).[61] What do they mean – what did Sophocles mean – by the *daimon* of Oedipus? And by *eudaimonia?* 'A third type of daemon', writes Dodds,[62] 'who makes his first appearance in the Archaic Age, is attached to a particular individual, usually from birth, and determines, wholly or in part, his individual destiny . . . He represents the individual *moira* or "portion" of which Homer speaks, but in the personal form which appealed to the imagination of the time.' The fate of Oedipus, then, is ascribed to a malign superhuman power which had attended him from birth.

The idea of malignity does not indeed occur in this stanza or in the following stanzas which speak of his greatness and his downfall. But go back a little in the play. To set the fears of Oedipus at rest, Jocasta has told him about the oracle given to Laius and, to all appearance, not fulfilled. But her mention of the place where three highways met rouses a dreadful apprehension in the king's mind, and at last he tells her the story of his encounter at just such a place. If there is any connection (as he puts it, euphemistically) between the old stranger he killed and Laius, then who could be more wretched, of a more hostile

---

[60] Much of what follows is repeated from Anderson (ed.) 32–8.

[61]
τίς γάρ, τίς ἀνὴρ πλέον
τᾶς εὐδαιμονίας φέρει
ἢ τοσοῦτον ὅσον δοκεῖν
καὶ δόξαντ'ἀποκλῖναι;
τὸν σόν τοι παράδειγμ' ἔχων,
τὸν σὸν δαίμονα, τὸν σόν, ὦ
τλᾶμον Οἰδιπόδα, βροτῶν
οὐδὲν μακαρίζω·   (O.T. 1189–95).

[62] GI 42. For a discussion of *daimon* in the play and of this particular scene see also Gould (1) 378–84.

daimon (τίς ἐχθροδαίμων μᾶλλον; 816), than he now is? For he is liable to his own ban pronounced upon the killer of Laius, and he is sleeping with the wife of the man he killed. Not only so, but he is (so he thinks) in exile from his native land for fear of wedding his mother and killing his father. 'Would not a man be right to judge of me that these things come from a cruel *daimon*' (ἀπ' ὠμοῦ ... δαίμονος, 828)? Oedipus, then, attributes to a cruel and hostile superhuman power the destiny which is so much worse than he yet knows. When it becomes known, when Oedipus, knowing it, has entered the palace, the Chorus argues the nothingness of man from the *daimon* of Oedipus.

Later in the ode they sing (1213f.): 'All-seeing time has found you out ἄκοντα; it brings to justice the monstrous marriage in which the begotten has long been the begetter.' This inadequate translation of the untranslatable omits to translate one word: ἄκοντα. 'Unwilling' or 'unwitting' as epithet of Oedipus. The conscious criminal seeks to evade detection which comes upon him against his will. But this does not apply. What, then, was contrary to the will or knowledge of Oedipus?[63] There is perhaps at this point a deliberate ambiguity which is cleared up, when, a few lines later, a servant comes out of the palace, now polluted (as he says) with new evils which will soon come to light – 'evils wrought consciously and not unwittingly' (ἑκόντα κοὐκ ἄκοντα, 1230). A distinction could not more clearly and emphatically be made between the unwilled and the willed deeds of Oedipus; and it is reinforced by the Messenger's general comment, that 'those griefs sting most that are seen to be self-chosen' (αὐθαίρετοι, 1231). The distinction is clearly made, and we expect it to be clearly maintained. When he killed his father and wedded his mother, Oedipus was a victim of the gods, but, when he blinded himself, he was a free agent. How attractive to look at matters in this way, and how limited the truth of it may be! But we have not heard the last about fate, about the *daimon* of Oedipus.

The Messenger tells his story of the suicide of Jocasta and the self-blinding of her son and husband. The doors open again, and the blinded Oedipus comes out. The reactions of the Chorus are governed, as those of any audience must be, by this sight, the most dreadful they have ever seen. 'What madness came upon you? Who

---

[63] 'He had not foreseen the disclosure which was to result from his inquiry into the murder of Laius' (Jebb). More significantly, surely, he had not known that his actions were crimes. Cf. *O.C.* 977, 987.

was the *daimon* that leapt, with a bound exceeding the extreme, upon . . .?' Upon what? The whole expression is, once more, essentially untranslatable,[64] and I can only conclude with a free expansion: '. . . upon that *moira* of yours that was already a *daimon*'s evil work'. The evil destiny of Oedipus had seemed to have reached an extreme point and to have provided the perfect paradigm of ill-starred humanity, but there was still a further point of misery to be reached, and that too is ascribed to the assault of a *daimon*. Later, groping in his sightlessness, hearing his voice (as Jebb well puts it) 'borne from him on the air in a direction over which he has no control', Oedipus exclaims: 'Oh *daimon*, that you should have sprung so far!' (*ἰὼ δαῖμον, ἵν᾽ ἐξήλου*, 1311). It is clear from his preceding words and from the response of the Coryphaeus that he is thinking of his blindness. Later again, the Coryphaeus asks: 'How could you bring yourself so to destroy your sight? What *daimon* moved you to it?' (*τίς σ᾽ ἐπῆρε δαιμόνων;* 1328). Oedipus might have said – and critics sometimes write as though he had said:[65] 'As for my other sufferings, they were the work of Apollo, but, when I struck my eyes, the responsibility was mine alone (and you are wrong to ask what *daimon* moved me).'[66] Actually he replies: 'It was Apollo, my friends, it was Apollo that was bringing these sufferings of mine to completion. But it was none other's hand that struck the blow: it was I.' The reiterated name of Apollo *must* be answering the question: 'What *daimon*?'; the expression 'these sufferings of mine' cannot exclude and may primarily denote the visible suffering which dominates the scene. It would be tidy to suppose that, whereas Apollo was, through his oracle, responsible for the earlier sufferings of Oedipus, the unprophesied self-

---

64
        ὦ δεινότατον πάντων ὅσ᾽ ἐγὼ
        προσέκυρσ᾽ ἤδη. τίς σ᾽, ὦ τλῆμον,
        προσέβη μανία; τίς ὁ πηδήσας
        μείζονα δαίμων τῶν μακίστων
        πρὸς σῇ δυσδαίμονι μοίρᾳ;   (*O. T.* 1299–1302)
Here Jebb's translation seems to miss the point through failure to relate the passage to the preceding choral ode.
65 So, apparently, Gould (1) 379; (2) 588.
66
        Ἀπόλλων τάδ᾽ ἦν, Ἀπόλλων, φίλοι,
        ὁ κακὰ κακὰ τελῶν ἐμὰ τάδ᾽ ἐμὰ πάθεα.
        ἔπαισε δ᾽ αὐτόχειρ νιν οὔ-
        τις, ἀλλ᾽ ἐγὼ τλάμων.   (*O. T.* 1329–32)
Sophocles might have written something like *τὰ μὲν ἄλλα . . .*, but he did not.

blinding was an act of independent will unmotivated by divine power. But that is not how it is seen by either Oedipus or the Chorus.

Two questions arise; and one of them, which is with what truth Oedipus ascribes his sufferings to Apollo, may be left for a later consideration. The other question is perhaps more fundamental. What does it mean that not only the unwitting crimes but also the deliberate self-blinding of Oedipus are seen as the work of a daemonic power? The answer can be sought in two directions. The self-blinding was, as Socrates might have called it, a mistake;[67] as the Chorus sees it, the result of an onset of madness (1299f.). They ask what *daimon* brought him to it, and the word they use (*epairein*) is appropriate to a transport of emotion. It is true that Oedipus, like a Greek, gives a reason: 'What needed I to see?' But we cannot suppose that he struck his eyes on a purely rational consideration.[68] And the argument progressively breaks down, as it becomes clear that all he has done is to lock himself in a dark prison with the memories of the past.[69] Now to see in an emotional impulse the work of a god or *daimon* is Homeric; it is Aeschylean; it is a commonplace of Greek thought. But we cannot leave the matter there, for this ascription of the self-blinding to a *daimon* is also part of the whole fabric of the play.

Much has been said – and well said – about the significance of this action. The long process of discovery has run its brilliant course towards the awful revelation of truth: nothing would seem to remain but the traditional horror. It was a challenge to the art of Sophocles to

---

[67] οὐδεὶς ἑκὼν ἁμαρτάνει. If the play was written in the early or middle 420s (which is as good a guess as any), the Socratic doctrine may already have been known. According to B. Snell (*Philologus* 97 (1948) 125ff.) Euripides was in controversy against this doctrine when he wrote *Hippolytus* in 428. This may or may not be true, but it is likely that the nature and origins of passion, and its relation to human responsibility, were a living issue about the time that *O.T.* was written. Most critics would now agree that Sophocles was well aware of contemporary intellectual movements, whatever he thought of them.

[68] R. W. Livingstone, in *Greek poetry and life* (ed. C. Bailey *et al.*, Oxford 1936)160f. and Knox, *OTh* 195ff., exaggerate the rationality of the act. 1271ff. express an instinctive revulsion rather than a train of thought; 1369ff. are a rationalization which is soon shown to be illusory (see n. 69.). This criticism does not of course affect the value of Knox's illuminating remarks about 'the recovery of Oedipus' (*OTh* 185). Cf. Gellie 102.

[69] The illusion of 1389f. (τὸ γὰρ | τὴν φροντίδ᾽ ἔξω τῶν κακῶν οἰκεῖν γλυκύ) is immediately dispelled as Oedipus reviews his life and, above all, by the vivid picture of 1398f. Cf. 1401 (ἆρά μου μέμνησθ᾽ ἔτι . . .), but it is Oedipus himself who must live with this memory (cf. 1318). Contr. 1386ff. with 1472ff.

make it other than a sensational anticlimax: he has made it the true climax of the play,[70] when this man of high intelligence and worldly insight, who has been at every point mistaken about himself and those who surround him, at last sees the truth in his mind and joins the blind prophet in physical darkness. The blinding was a given fact, and this is what Sophocles has made of it. It was a given fact, and maybe we should not pry too far into the psychology of the action.[71] Oedipus gives his reasons, which are bad reasons, rationally considered, but it was not a rational action. What we can say is that it was in the nature of Oedipus to act, and to act at once; that it was a necessity for him to give immediate expression to his revulsion not in words but in action. It was a characteristic act, and to act so was a part of his destiny: it was the culmination of that destiny. It is in this way that we can understand his ascription of this deliberate act as well as of his unwitting 'crimes' to divine influence. It has been pointed out[72] that the divinely appointed destiny of Oedipus comes about – and comes to light – largely through actions on his part which spring directly from his character: it was *like* Oedipus that he must leave Corinth to discover the truth about his birth;[73] it was *like* Oedipus to pursue his judicial enquiries with such energy; and so on. ἦθος ἀνθρώπῳ δαίμων: character is destiny. Yet, when, still acting characteristically, he blinds himself, the action is attributed to the influence of a *daimon* – and Heraclitus is turned inside out.[74] It needed the unwitting characteristic actions of Oedipus to bring about his fated destiny; it needed the influence of a *daimon* to explain his deliberate act. Here is that interpenetration of the divine and human worlds – Homeric, archaic, and Aeschylean – which we can describe, though not elucidate, with the blessed word 'over-determination'. It is something more than that: it is a recognition that there is a given factor in human character which is no less a part of man's destiny than those events which character may (or may not) help to mould. Ajax did not decide to be

[70] This is well brought out by Alister Cameron 97ff.

[71] Cf. Gellie 100f.

[72] Cf. Kitto *GT* 136f.

[73] On the meaning of ὑφεῖρπε at *O.T.* 786 see *BICS* 26 (1979) 8f.

[74] Heraclitus fr. 119 (ἦθος ἀνθρώπῳ δαίμων) is presumably directed against those who would shuffle off all human responsibility upon a *daimon* (cf. G. S. Kirk & J. E. Raven, *The presocratic philosophers* (Cambridge 1957) 214; W. K. C. Guthrie, *A history of Greek philosophy* I (Cambridge 1962) 482). One problem it does not solve, which is where the *ethos* comes from. Perhaps it makes as good sense the other way round?

omophron: he was *omophron*. Antigone did not choose to be the daughter of Oedipus or to inherit the hardness which was both her death and her glory.

But why Apollo?[75] Why does Oedipus attribute the accomplishment of his evils, including (if the passage has been rightly interpreted) his own act of self-blinding, to Apollo? Apollo is divine foreknowledge of what is destined to happen. Is he also an agent? Or is Oedipus under an illusion? If so, it is an illusion under which generations of readers have suffered. It is, surely, impossible to read the play without feeling that, in some more or less incomprehensible way, Apollo is at work; that the god who knows what is destined to happen is securing that it does happen and, having happened, is known to have happened. But Apollo is involved at a deeper level. If he is interested in the truth of his oracles, the god on whose temple was inscribed the motto *gnothi sauton* was concerned with human self-knowledge.[76] It is about himself that Oedipus is most ignorant and learns the most terrible truth. It is human knowledge and intelligence in which he has full confidence and must learn how limited is the one and how fragile the other. As the truth comes out and the oracles are revealed as true, it is with a sure insight that Oedipus sees Apollo at work. He goes on to put out those eyes which have given him that fallible knowledge of the external world.

One question remains. It was the fate of Oedipus to do dreadful things, to be discovered as having done them, and to inflict upon himself a dreadful penalty. Apollo presides over the process. The process at all points involves the character of Oedipus. Does it also involve his culpability? Is this *moira* a principle of order in accordance with which we suffer the inevitable consequences of our deliberate actions? Is there any justice, as human beings understand justice, in what happened to Oedipus? It would seem that Sophocles envisaged this issue quite clearly and dealt with it, not explicitly but in the full subtlety of his lyric technique, in a choral ode which stands, like the Second Stasimon of *Antigone*, central to its play. The following chapter will examine the Second Stasimon of the *Oedipus Tyrannus*.

[75] I return to this, briefly, in ch. 13 p. 319. For a good discussion see Gellie 102–5.
[76] Cf. Cameron 15ff.

CHAPTER EIGHT

The fall of Oedipus

The Second Stasimon holds a central position in *Oedipus Tyrannus*. It follows the elaborate preparatory scenes and immediately precedes the rapid march of the action towards its catastrophe. The ode is difficult to understand and has been variously interpreted.[1]

We expect a Sophoclean Chorus to react to the preceding episode; and the themes of this ode are indeed related to the long scene that has just been played. Interpreters are not agreed, however, on the precise character of this relationship, except in one particular. It is abundantly clear that the fourth stanza (898–910) relates to the scepticism on the subject of oracles and prophecy which was expressed by Jocasta at the end of the preceding scene. The concern of the Chorus arises, however, not so much from the fact that she expresses a sceptical view which might be thought shocking as from the grounds on which her view was based. On the face of it, and on the facts as stated, an oracle given by Loxias at Delphi has failed, once and for all, to be fulfilled.

---

[1] This study of the Second Stasimon of *Oedipus Tyrannus* is a slightly modified version of *JHS* 91 (1971) 119–35. In that article I carried forward a brief discussion of the Stasimon contained in Anderson 39–41, in which I suggested that Sophocles used the song of the Chorus to put forward – and by implication to reject – a religious interpretation of the fate of Oedipus which might be described as Aeschylean. A similar view was later advanced independently by G. Müller, 'Das zweite Stasimon des König Ödipus', *Hermes* 95 (1967) 269–91. There is a similar choice of readings in some crucial passages, and there are two fundamental issues on which we are agreed: (i) that, as e.g. in *Antigone,* the words of the Chorus are used ironically to convey an underlying sense at variance with the conscious mental processes of the singers; and (ii) that Sophocles is reacting to an Aeschylean interpretation or at least to an interpretation of a traditional kind for which the parallels are in Aeschylus (and Solon). I cannot follow Müller in imputing to the Chorus the *hubris* which they impute to Oedipus – nor indeed in the view that they are, flatly, accusing Oedipus (and Jocasta) of *hubris*.

They feel that, unless facts and prophecy are shown to be in full agreement, this will be the end of oracular authority and the end of religion (if that is how we should translate τὰ θεῖα); and they pray to Zeus the supreme king to give the matter his attention. It is the facts – the apparent facts – that cause their concern. But, when in the first stanza they sing about reverent purity of word as well as of deed, it is commonly – and I think rightly – held that they have in mind, among other things, the impious words of Jocasta. It may be a useful preliminary to the examination of the ode as a whole, if we first examine the 'impiety' (if that is the correct term) of Jocasta, endorsed, as it appears to be, by Oedipus.

Jocasta has not on the whole received very sympathetic treatment from critics, always more censorious than authors or audiences.[2] In order to set the mind of Oedipus at rest, she must disparage the authority of Teiresias (705ff.), and so she tells her husband of something that has long been in her own mind. She tells him of the oracle which foretold to Laius that he was fated to die at the hands of his son, whereas Laius, according to report, was killed by foreign robbers and the child had been exposed upon the mountain. She expresses herself with deliberate caution: 'I will not say the oracle came from Phoebus himself, but from his servants' (711f.). This carries scepticism no farther than the chorus carried it, when they sang in the First Stasimon (497ff.): 'Zeus and Apollo have knowledge of mortal things, but there is no judging whether a human prophet has knowledge more than mine.'[3] The purpose of Jocasta, as of the loyal Chorus, is to disparage Teiresias; and that is the point of her conclusion: 'Such was the clear pronouncement of prophetic voices: to which do you pay no attention. (τοιαῦτα φῆμαὶ μαντικαὶ διώρισαν, | ὧν ἐντρέπου σὺ μηδέν, 723f.). But are the cases quite similar? The words of an angry prophet in Thebes, the oracle from Delphi? Greeks in the fifth century were not disposed to accept anything and everything in all circumstances from prophets, whose fallibility, not to mention their venality, was common knowledge or common suspicion. That an oracle emanating from Delphi or some other oracular shrine was spurious or misconceived – this too, however, was a notion all too familiar in the

---

[2] Contr. Reinhardt 128f.; Lloyd-Jones, *JZ* 106.
[3] Clearly recalled by 708f.: μάθ' οὕνεκ' ἐστί σοι | βρότειον οὐδὲν μαντικῆς ἔχον τέχνης.

late fifth century. But Sophocles does not wish to leave things at that level.[4] When, at 720, Jocasta mentions the name of Apollo and says he did not bring it about that the child killed his father and the father died at the hands of his child, she might simply mean: 'as he would have done, if the oracle had emanated from him'.[5] But she may be slipping into a form of expression which reveals her true thought. Certainly at the end of the scene (853f.) she speaks of Loxias: 'who Loxias said clearly was to die at my son's hand'. And now she has more Delphic oracles to think upon than the oracle given to Laius, when she draws her conclusion that henceforth, so far as prophecy goes, she will look neither this way nor that (857f.). We need not excogitate subtleties to save the credit of Jocasta.[6] This, surely, is what she really thinks – and what it was natural to think. And it is what the chorus are afraid to think, when they sing the last stanza of the Stasimon (898ff.). They are not now interested in hypothetical distinctions between Apollo and his ministers. It is the credit of all oracular shrines, and particularly Apollo's, which is at stake; and this involves τὰ θεῖα and should be matter of concern to Zeus. The theme must, however, be pursued into the following scene.

The Chorus sings that Apollo is 'nowhere manifest in his honours'.

[4] When we are told that Sophocles wished to counteract that scepticism about prophecy which (together with credulity) became prevalent during the Peloponnesian War, we are entitled to ask what prophecies and what oracles current during this period he thought it desirable that his compatriots should believe, remembering that he was not a recluse who only emerged from his study to feed a Holy Snake but a man of the world who had held high office in the state. He must have known as well as anybody that most of the prophecies in circulation were fraudulent and that people were wise to be sceptical of them. He must have known that the warring parties desired to control oracular shrines (cf. Thuc. 1.112.5) not only for the sake of their treasures (Thuc. 1.121.3; 143.1) but for the propaganda value of their oracles; and, if he heard that Delphi had promised support to the Spartans (Thuc. 1.118.3), he will have drawn that same distinction between Apollo and his ministers that Jocasta makes and that even Spartans, used as they were to pro-Spartan oracles, were prepared on occasion to make (cf. Thuc. 5.16.2 and Gomme ad loc.). The more reverence he had for Delphi the more he will have regretted the necessity of making this distinction, but he could not mend matters by encouraging the Athenians to accept whatever emanated from this source. For us there is a danger that such a line of interpretation will obscure the prime function of oracles in Sophocles, which is to serve as supreme symbols of divine knowledge and thus of human ignorance. (These matters are well discussed by Gould (1) 604–8.)

[5] Cf. 724f.

[6] Cf. Jebb (on 711): 'in 853 . . . the name of the god merely stands for that of his Delphian priesthood'; Müller, OT 271. Contr. Knox, OTh 172; O'Brien 10.

Then, ironically, the sceptical Jocasta comes out and prays to Apollo. It is an idea which has 'occurred to her' (δόξα μοι παρεστάθη, 911) and only after admonition (παραινοῦσα, 918) has failed, and when she cannot persuade her husband 'to judge the new', as a rational man (ἀνὴρ ἔννους) would do, 'by the old'. She prays Apollo to provide 'a solution of purity' (λύσιν τιν' . . . εὐαγῆ), which, ironically, is just what he cannot and will not in fact do. Then, ironically, the prayer seems to be answered – and in the most paradoxical way, by the destruction of Apollo's credit. Not only the oracle given to Laius, but one half of the oracle given to Oedipus appears not to have been fulfilled. The messenger from Corinth enters at the close of Jocasta's prayer and reveals that the reputed father of Oedipus has died a natural death. And Jocasta reacts as we might expect. 'You oracles of the gods, see where you stand now!' (946f.). By oracles *of the gods* she means what she says,[7] here and when she addresses Oedipus (who now enters): 'Listen and take note to what have come the worshipful oracles of the gods' (952f.). The oracles, the prophecies, are now (sarcastically) σεμνά – a word which recalls the language of the preceding ode (864, 886, 899). Oedipus, whose assent at 859 had been perfunctory (his mind was on other things),[8] is now convinced, 'Why then should one look to the hearth of the Pythian seer or birds that scream above our heads?'[9] Yet he half-recoils; and this recoil is described by one critic as 'sincere and pious and characteristic of the hero'.[10] Sincere and pious it may be, but, in trying to rescue the credit of the oracle, he reduces it to complete triviality (969f.). Still, half the oracle stands unrefuted; still, since his 'mother' remains alive, Oedipus cannot be completely reassured. In the attempt to reassure

[7] This is denied by Jebb (on 946) and by Müller.

[8] Jebb ('he assents, almost mechanically') is right as against Knox, *OTh* 174, who speaks of 'firmly expressed approval'. The words (καλῶς νομίζεις) commit Oedipus to little; he is preoccupied with the thought that he may be the killer of Laius and sends for the eye-witness. Cf. Müller, *OT* 272.

[9] It was to Pytho that he had himself sent Creon (70f.). Bird-omens played no part at Delphi: the reason they are mentioned here is to remind *us* of Teiresias, who is not in fact much in the mind of Oedipus at this point. It is natural that the non-fulfilment of a prophecy relating to himself should make more impression on him than that of a prophecy given to Laius. So much so that he now seems to forget what he remembered then: the circumstantial evidence pointing to him as the killer of Laius. This now recedes into the background, but the hint of Teiresias (and his bird-watching) reminds the audience.

[10] J. T. Sheppard in his edition on 969 (εἴ τι μὴ τὠμῷ πόθῳ κτλ.). The triviality is such that Oedipus can go on to say that the θεσπίσματα are ἄξι' οὐδενός.

him, Jocasta for her part reduces the oracle to the level of a dream – and a particular dream which in the nature of things is virtually never fulfilled (981f.).[11] The messenger sets the fears of Oedipus at rest, and so the truth comes out.

How culpable, then, was the scepticism of Jocasta and, in its degree, of Oedipus? Sophocles may have been more disposed to bring out the irony of the situation than to impute blame to his characters. Nevertheless, what they say is impious and is proved false.

There is a further difference between the scepticism of the Chorus and that of Jocasta: the Chorus had only their feelings, Jocasta had evidence.[12] She argues from apparent facts. The oracle said that Laius would die at the hands of his son. But the child died in infancy and Laius was killed by strangers (perhaps, it seems, by the stranger Oedipus, which is bad enough). Therefore the oracle was not fulfilled. How then should she have argued, if she had had a firm religious faith in oracles?[13] She should have said: the son of Laius cannot have died, the killer of Laius, whoever he was, must have been that son – and, if Oedipus killed him, Oedipus was that son. Similarly, after the messenger has brought the news from Corinth (and before he has spoken of the parentage of Oedipus), Jocasta and Oedipus should have argued: Oedipus is prophesied to kill his father; Polybus has died a natural death; therefore, Polybus was not his father.[14] But this is not at all the way in which human beings could be expected to argue, least of all perhaps Greeks. Jocasta and Oedipus reason, as in the circumstances of human life people must reason, in a plausible way on the basis of apparent facts. Now there is a certain rashness always in trusting to appearances; and it is a hundred times rash for a character in Greek tragedy and in a tragedy by Sophocles. We can say, if we like, that Jocasta is intellectually superficial and Oedipus intellectually arrogant; and there is some truth, perhaps an important truth, in this. Oedipus trusts his intellect too much and must learn how fallible it is. Jocasta is governed by her affections and will use any means, whether

---

11 πολλοὶ γὰρ ἤδη κἀν ὀνείρασιν βροτῶν | μητρὶ ξυνηυνάσθησαν. Cf. Kitto, *Poiesis* 230. This reference to a 'Freudian' dream, in a context of triviality, is a clear indication that Freudian notions, relevant as they may be to the myth, are not so to the Sophoclean play.

12 She has σημεῖα (710). Cf. Gellie 88f.

13 The question seems hardly ever to have been asked, at least not so crudely!

14 And Oedipus ought perhaps to have remembered the drunken diner and the doubts that sent him to Delphi.

it is denial of Apollo or prayer to Apollo, if she can calm the disturbed
mind of her husband.[15] Here too we meet the Sophoclean irony. It is
the affectionate Jocasta who presses the argument to its logical conclusion; it is the rational Oedipus who is (for once) unreasonable in his
fears and is (for once) right to be so afraid, though not in the way he
thinks. One may add that, if Jocasta and Oedipus had clung to piety
rather than to reason, they would presumably have been led, not into
grasping the improbable truth (with a premature ending of the
tragedy), but into that state of bafflement in which we find the
Chorus, so appropriate to them, so unsuitable for major tragic characters; and that, if Jocasta would have been different, Oedipus would
have been abolished.

By normal standards of human behaviour Jocasta and Oedipus are
hardly to be blamed, though they were dreadfully wrong. Yet what
they said, with every reasonable ground for saying it, was impious
(ἀσεβές). We turn to the Second Stasimon and find the Chorus
praying for a *moira* which involves 'pious purity in all words and
deeds' (εὔσεπτον ἀγνείαν λόγων | ἔργων τε πάντων, 864f.). It was the
moira of Oedipus (and no less of Jocasta) to be impure (823) in deed,
though by human standards he was not to blame for this. It was also
their *moira*, in word, to fail in piety, in *eusebeia*; and it would seem that
they were hardly to blame for that either. We must now examine the
Stasimon in more detail.

The discussion has so far dealt with one obvious point of contact
between the ode and the preceding scene: the scepticism of Jocasta
which carries a taint of impiety and so threatens the religious world.
This apart, it is not so much the lack of relevance which has exercised
critics as the difficulty of seeing precisely how the development of
relevant themes relates. The whole Stasimon is, as one might expect, a
reaction to the preceding Episode, which fell into two parts. First,
there was the scene between Oedipus and Creon, with Jocasta intervening and the Chorus too playing a role. The scene is 'political' and
full of political language.[16] It was also disquieting to the Chorus. So
too had been the scene with Teiresias, but their loyalty to Oedipus,
firmly based on gratitude, there remained unshaken (483–511): they
had rather doubt the skill of the prophet than the wisdom of Oedipus,

---

[15] Gellie 95.
[16] From ἄνδρες πολῖται (513) onward.

at least until clear evidence was shown. In the Creon-scene, still loyal and grateful, they are disturbed at the apparent injustice of their king and plead with him – and it is to be noted that they plead success-fully.[17] In the ode they sing of *hubris* and tyranny; and these themes are, in all probability, suggested to their minds by the recent beha-viour of Oedipus, though they can hardly yet be regarding him as, in act, a hubristic ruler.[18] Certainly, however, the second stanza is 'political', in that it begins with 'tyranny' and ends with a reference to τὸ καλῶς ἔχον πόλει πάλαισμα (whatever exactly that may mean).

The second half of the episode was between Oedipus and Jocasta, and it revealed two things. It revealed a strong presumption that Oedipus was impure (ἄναγνος): actually impure, if he was the killer of Laius, now sleeping with the wife of the man he had killed (821f.), subject to the curse he had himself pronounced; potentially impure, if the oracle given to him should be fulfilled. He feels that on either score he is the victim of a *daimon*, hostile and cruel (816, 828). But is it certain that the oracle will be fulfilled? Jocasta had shown reason to suppose that another oracle had not been fulfilled and was led into words of scepticism. To the impurity of Oedipus, which in fact was shared by Jocasta, is added the impiety of Jocasta, which was to be endorsed by Oedipus. These are the themes which lead into the first stanza.

Strophe α΄, 863–72

'May it be my abiding *moira* to possess pious purity in all those words and deeds the laws of which, walking on high, are set before us, begotten in the heavenly aether; their father is Olympus alone, no mortal nature gave them birth, and oblivion will never lay them to sleep; a god is great in them and grows not old.'[19]

The Chorus prays for pious purity in word and deed, in accordance with laws (νόμοι) which are of divine origin, not subject to oblivion and decay. These are laws governing human conduct in various fields thought to be particularly a concern of the gods: relations, for instance, with the gods themselves, relations with parents. The singers

[17] 649–70.
[18] See below, p. 201.
[19] Here, and in the other stanzas, I am translating a text which is defended in the subsequent discussions. My sole aim is to get as close as possible to the sense of the Greek in an English which is at least barely tolerable.

couple words and deeds, as the Greeks so often do. Purity (ἁγνεία) is especially a matter of deeds, of acts (which, irrespective of motive, can automatically render a man impure); it is impossible not to recall the word 'impure' (ἄναγνος, 823), which Oedipus applied to himself. Piety (εὐσέβεια) can be a matter of deed or word. Here εὔσεπτος ('well-reverencing') will remind us of the 'impiety' of Jocasta towards oracles; and the stem is picked up twice (886, 898f.) in the closing stanza. The combination of εὔσεπτος ἁγνεία, moreover, echoes the apostrophe of Oedipus to 'pure and awful gods' (ὦ θεῶν ἁγνὸν σέβας, 830). The gods are themselves pure (ἁγνοί), and they demand reverence (σέβας). And now the words of Oedipus and Jocasta have diffused an atmosphere of impurity and impiety, vague and hard to seize. The Chorus is disquieted and prays for pious purity.

It is tantamount to a prayer, but expressed in a rather unusual way. They do not, being Greeks, pray for grace (in the Christian sense) or strength of purpose. They express a wish for a *moira*, the implication being that what they desire is something divinely apportioned. They ask that *moira*, or a *moira*, may be with them as they bear, or have, that reverent purity which seems to them to be so necessary. It has been suggested[20] that we ought to take it as follows: 'Would that destiny were with me so long as I maintain this state.' But that can hardly be right. Destiny (*moira*) is not to be thought of as a helpful power which may leave you in the lurch if you behave badly. This would not be a normal Greek way of looking at it and, as will be seen, is unthinkable in this of all places. Your *moira* is with you, for good or ill, inescapably, throughout your life: it is what in fact happens or is going to happen to you, which may be good or bad, which may be now good, now bad. The Chorus are now pure and pious and they long to remain so, but recognize that whether they remain so or not is a matter of their *moira*. So they express the wish that a *moira*, their *moira*, may stay with them being in that condition in which they now are, of possessing reverent purity.[21]

---

[20] J. C. Kamerbeek in his edition ad loc. and previously in 'Comments on the Second Stasimon of the Oedipus Tyrannus' in *WS* 79 (1966) 83f.

[21] φέροντι need mean no more than 'possess', here and at 1190 (cf. *Ant.* 1090). On the force of the participle see Jebb's note. The force of the article τάν? Does it mark an abstraction? Or look forward to the definition (865ff.), despite the fact that the antecedent of ὦν is λόγων ἔργων τε? Or could it have a possessive force: that purity which they now enjoy?

A *moira* that stays with you, associates with you, is not unlike a *daimon*. The two words can mean much the same, though *daimon* is often (but not always) more strongly personified than *moira*.[22] Both words are important in the play, important for the story of Oedipus. It was the *moira* of Oedipus to fall at the hands of Apollo (376),[23] of Laius to be killed by his own son (713); Oedipus will speak of his *moira* at 1458. But the crucial passage linking *moira* and *daimon* comes later (1300ff.), when the Coryphaeus speaks in one breath of Oedipus' *daimon* and of his *moira* as *dusdaimon,* saying that, with the self-blinding, a *daimon* had leaped with a mighty leap upon a *moira* that was already the work of an evil *daimon*.[24] Here, since the notions of *moira* and *daimon* are so closely linked, it is not possible to separate *moira* (863, and for that matter at 887) from what Oedipus has just said about his *daimon*: that, as the apparent killer of Laius, lying under his own curse, his *daimon* was hostile (816), and that, as the man to whom it was prophesied that he would kill his father and marry his mother, it was cruel (828f.). There was a time, then, when the *moira* of Oedipus included purity (and when Jocasta was pious), but that time, it seems, is no longer. The Chorus ask for themselves a continuance of 'pious purity'.

It seems that Oedipus is, or may be, in breach of the laws which demand purity (though, as we know, unwittingly in breach of them). If so, he must suffer: this is not stated, but implied. He is, or may be, in breach of the laws which govern relationship to parents; and to remind us of this (and indeed to make us think of Oedipus and his situation throughout the stanza) Sophocles accumulates, in his characteristic fashion, words of parentage as metaphors in the description of the divine laws: *begotten* (τεκνωθέντες)[25] in the heavenly ether, whose *father* (πατήρ) is Olympus alone, nor did the mortal *nature* (φύσις) of men *bring them to birth* (ἔτικτεν). That is their origin; and that is where

---

22 Cf. Dodds, *GI* 42 (and n. 79).

23 Despite Knox's argument (*OTh* 7f.), I still feel that Brunck's emendation is necessary. There is no question of a fall of Teiresias due to Apollo or otherwise nor of a *moira* of Teiresias, whereas the fall and *moira* of Oedipus are crucial. It is after πρός γ' ἐμοῦ that Oedipus thinks of Creon (so J. T. Sheppard ad loc.), a man who is not blind (contr. 374f.).

24 See previous chapter p. 175.

25 The sense of the strophe is unaffected by doubts about the text. I am happy to see that Housman's brilliant solution, adopted by Pearson, is now commended on metrical grounds by L. P. E. Parker, *CQ* 18 (1968) 253.

they dwell. They are ὑψίποδες,[26] (which is the first thing we are told of them): their feet move on high, which is their natural place, since they are not of 'mortal nature' like all the children of men – and like Oedipus. There is a great god in them (μέγας ἐν τούτοις θεός) – or great is a god in them – that grows not old and so secures them from oblivion. Greatness, perhaps, belongs only to the gods. In the last stanza, in their prayer to Zeus, the Chorus will return to the theme of divine power, but it may not be irrelevant to the stanza they are now about to sing.

Antistrophe a', 873–82

'Hubris is bred of kingship. Hubris, once wantonly sated with many things that are not timely or beneficial, having mounted to the battlements, plunges into sheer constraint where the foot loses its proper use. But the emulation that benefits the city I pray the god never to terminate. Never will I cease to hold the god as my protector.'

It is in the second stanza that we encounter the real difficulties of the stasimon. The stanza opens with hubris and 'tyranny'; and the connection of thought with the preceding strophe is not clear. The word hubris is picked up and becomes the subject of the following sentence, which constitutes the core of the stanza. It is hubris personified, standing for the hubristic man. Despite some uncertainties in the text,[27] the idea is straightforward and in tune with traditional thought. Hubris, glutted, after reaching the heights, falls headlong and helpless to the depths. Once it has begun to fall, the process is inevitable – a matter of ananke: no move can save it.[28] It has always

---

[26] I am inclined to agree with Knox (O Th. 182–4) that there is a play, here and in the antistrophe (878) and elsewhere, on the name Οἰδίπους. See, more recently, J.-P. Vernant, 'Ambiguïté et renversement: sur la structure énigmatique d'Oedipe-roi', in J.-P. Vernant and P. Vidal-Naquet, Mythe et tragédie en Grèce ancienne (Paris 1973) 113f.

[27] The problems of strophe (see n. 25) and antistrophe are interdependent. Wolff's ἀκρότατα γεῖσ' (for which see Jebb's references) is called 'very tempting' by Kamerbeek and 'most seductive' by Lattimore (PGT 97 n. 37), who, however, adds that it 'ought to be resisted'. Why? The text of 876–7 (and 892–4) has been discussed at length by N. Van der Ben, Mnem. 21 (1968) 7–21.

[28] A falling man cannot use his feet to counter, as we would say, the force of gravity. Lattimore (PGT 48 n. 25), in a different context, has an interesting note on ἀνάγκη, in which he justifies himself for translating it 'nature' and 'natural force' at Aesch. PV 514f. For a possible play on the name of Oedipus, see n. 26.

been recognized that the description is appropriate to the fall of Oedipus. But it is *hubris*, or the hubristic man, that falls. Is Oedipus, then, hubristic? And is his *hubris* the reason for his fall?

It belongs to traditional thought[29] that *hubris* is followed by disaster – what is often called *ate*, though the term is not used here. There is a third term which enters variously into the formulations, and that is *koros*; the traditional notion of *koros* must be recalled here by the description of *hubris* as 'vainly glutted with many things that are neither timely nor advantageous' (εἰ πολλῶν ὑπερπλησθῇ μάταν, | ἃ μὴ 'πίκαιρα μηδὲ συμφέροντα). *Koros* is sometimes virtually equated with *hubris*; it is sometimes called the offspring of *hubris* (in which case it means something like 'the misuse of wealth'). But most commonly, as in the well-known lines of Solon,[30] it is spoken of as the parent of *hubris*. Here the expression (ὕβρις, εἰ . . . ὑπερπλησθῇ . . .) is perhaps consistent with any of these relationships, and it is certainly not inconsistent with the last-mentioned to speak of *hubris* as glutted with the *koros* which has brought it into existence. The genetic issue is not raised here, but it is raised by the three preceding words: ὕβρις φυτεύει τύραννον: '*hubris* begets (breeds) the tyrant (a tyrant)', or 'it is *hubris* that breeds a tyrant'. τύραννον must be taken in the bad sense of the word: a tyrannical ruler;[31] and there has been much discussion of the relevance of such 'tyranny' to the character and behaviour of Oedipus in the play. In saying that *hubris* breeds, not *koros*, nor (as in Aeschylus)[32] new *hubris*, but . . . a tyrant, Sophocles will be playing a variation on a traditional theme. Such a variation need not be regarded as unlikely. Nor need the connection of thought with the preceding stanza be obvious: on any interpretation the antistrophe is somewhat tangential to the strophe (just as Ant. β' is tangential to Str. β'). One could say that the Chorus have been praying for εὔσεπτος ἀγνεία, that this quality is eminently lacking in tyrants, and that *hubris*

---

[29] Denniston–Page have a useful note at Aesch. *Agam.* 757–62.

[30] Fr. 5.9f. D (τίκτει γὰρ κόρος ὕβριν, ὅταν πολὺς ὄλβος ἕπηται | ἀνθρώποις ὁπόσοις μὴ νόος ἄρτιος ᾖ). *koros* equals *hubris*: Pindar, *Ol.* 2.95; *Isthm.* 3.2; Aesch. *Agam.* 382. *hubris* breeds *koros*: Pindar, *Ol.* 13.10; Herodotus 8.77.1 (contr. 3.80.3).

[31] 'It is *hubris* that breeds a king' would be a ridiculously untrue generalization. When Müller, *OT*, 287, while retaining the received text, denies that τύραννον has a prejudicial sense and writes: 'Würde der Eingang lauten ὕβριν φυτεύει τυραννίς, so wäre der Sinn der gleiche', I fail to follow his argument. On this whole matter see pp. 192ff. below (and n. 42).

[32] *Agam.* 750ff.

is in contrast (if not the most obvious contrast) with the spirit of reverent purity. And we shall in fact find that arrogance and the reverse of reverent purity are brought together in the third stanza. But the tyrant (as such) is never mentioned again. There is a difficulty here – and a possibility to consider. But it may be useful to turn first to the end of the stanza, when, after describing the fall of *hubris* in non-political terms, the Chorus returns to the political theme with a phrase (τὸ καλῶς ἔχον πόλει πάλαισμα) which demands interpretation. If we can interpret it correctly, it may throw light on the stanza as a whole – and indeed on all aspects of the ode.

There seem to be no really close parallels for *palaisma* in this context. The word must at least imply a struggle, an effort; and it should be a competitive effort. Not rivalry, perhaps, so much as emulation.[33] Emulation is a characteristic Greek motive, avowable and potentially beneficial to the state.[34] This emulous effort, if the stanza is to have any coherence, must be something in which Oedipus is engaged. The scholiast says: ἤγουν τὴν ζήτησιν τοῦ φόνου τοῦ Λαΐου ('the investigation of the murder of Laius'). Kamerbeek, in his discussion,[35] puts all the weight on this, as though the Chorus was genuinely afraid that Oedipus might break off his search for the killers of Laius. But after 859f. they cannot, surely, be preoccupied with such a fear. If, however, this idea is too narrow for the context (as it seems to be), it does not follow that it is irrelevant, since the quest on which Oedipus is now engaged may well be taken as exemplifying his whole conduct during his kingship. Ellendt explains the *palaisma* differently, by reference to the wisdom through which Oedipus gained his kingdom;[36] and this certainly is not to be excluded. His service to the state began when he solved the riddle of the Sphinx, which he was enabled to do by his superior cleverness, which is spoken of in competitive terms. Oedipus himself, wrangling with Teiresias,

---

[33] Does πάλαισμα in any way refer to the quarrel between Oedipus and Creon? Since Creon neither seeks political power nor competes in services towards the state (cf. 584ff.), I had supposed not, but A. A. Long, *Liverpool Classical Monthly* 3 (1978) 49–53, has shown me the possibility that, in describing Oedipus' laudable activities, Sophocles used a word which normally refers to a struggle between parties and so could recall the wrangle, harmful to the city, between him and Creon. τὸ καλῶς ἔχον, taking the stress of the sentence, could well imply its opposite.

[34] Jebb cites Isocrates, *Ep.* 7.7 aptly.

[35] On 879–80, 883, and in the general note on the Second Stasimon, p. 172.

[36] 'πάλαισμα *consilium* intelligo, quo regnum adeptus Oedipus est; cuius imperium cum salutare civitati fuerit, ut maneat, chorus precatur.'

speaks, not only of wealth and kingship as arousing jealousy, but of 'skill surpassing skill' (τέχνη τέχνης ὑπερφέρουσα, 380ff.) and claims proudly that he, not Teiresias, had read the riddle.[37] In the following ode the Chorus sings that 'man may surpass man in cleverness' (σοφίᾳ δ'ἂν σοφίαν παραμείψειεν ἀνήρ) and goes on to sing of Oedipus: σοφὸς ὤφθη βασάνῳ θ' ἁδύπολις—'he was seen as clever and, in the test, a joy to the city' (502ff.). Dramatically, then, the quality of the kingship of Oedipus is shown in two episodes: the riddle of the Sphinx which he read, the quest for the killers of Laius upon which he is now engaged.[38] Between them lies the long story of a good king whom his people love and honour.[39] Now the Chorus prays that the god may not put an end (λῦσαι) to that 'emulation that benefits the city' by which the rule of Oedipus has been characterized. The irony of their prayer (and every prayer in the play is ironical) is that Oedipus' success in his search for the killers, which he conducts with characteristic energy, intelligence and public spirit, will put a final end to the *palaisma;* it will land him in that very plight to which *hubris* is supposed to lead; and this is what the 'protector god' will bring about.

The prayer is ironical, if for nothing else, because the *palaisma* must, in the context of the stanza, be contrasted with *hubris.* It is *hubris* that takes the stress and that has the downfall. What, then, of the tyrant? We must now return to the first three words of the stanza. For ὕβρις φυτεύει τύραννον Blaydes conjectured ὕβριν φυτεύει τυραννίς: instead of '*hubris* breeds the tyrant', 'kingship breeds *hubris*'.[40] It is with some reluctance that I have concluded Blaydes is right. The fact that the conjectural text is in several ways easier automatically confers upon the reading of the MSS the status, so attractive to some critics, of *lectio difficilior.* One should never forget, however, that the expression can also mean 'too difficult a reading'! What, then is the prime difficulty?

The prime difficulty resides in the necessity of taking τύραννος in the bad sense of the word. In Ellendt's *Lexicon Sophocleum* this sense (*iniusti et grauis domini*) is given a separate entry with this one example,

---

[37] 390ff.
[38] The First Episode is largely devoted to this, and particularly the first half of it, up to and beyond the entry of Teiresias.
[39] Cf. Dain–Mazon 104 n. 1.
[40] The emendation is adopted by Dawe. The corruption can be accounted for by the influence of the following ὕβρις. It could be argued that a change of case improves the rhetoric. My interpretation of the stanza and the ode does not of course stand or fall by this emendation.

which is also the only example quoted from Greek poetry by LSJ, other than from Theognis, where the exception proves the rule, since Theognis is writing, not of mythology, but of contemporary politics, at a time when all monarchs in the Greek world *were* tyrants.[41] Everywhere else in the play (where the words occur frequently) and in Greek tragedy as a whole, τύραννος and τυραννίς mean 'king' and 'kingship'. Professor Bernard Knox has a long and interesting discussion[42] of the use of these words in this play. He argues that, since Oedipus' position is ambiguous and his claim to the throne assailable, the terms are themselves used to ambiguous effect. He could be right, at least in some cases: it is certainly unnecessary for me to show that he is wrong. For there is all the difference in the world between (i) using τύραννος in the sense of 'king', with an added overtone suggestive of the unconstitutional and the tyrannical, and (ii) in a play where it is constantly a mere synonym for 'king', and contrary to the normal usage of tragedy, using it, flatly and frankly, in the bad sense – not king at all, but tyrant. I find it almost inconceivable that Sophocles has done such a thing and doubtful whether, if he did, an audience of tragedy would have jumped to this unexampled and anachronistic meaning.

ὕβριν φυτεύει τυραννίς. If a serious difficulty is eliminated, what is positively gained by making this correction? Three things. In the first place, the statement now falls clearly into line with the immediate context in terms of traditional thought. It is *koros* that engenders *hubris* (in the words of Solon), 'when great prosperity attends'. It is a king above all who is attended by material prosperity, by wealth. The notions go familiarly together and have been linked already in a speech of Oedipus (ὦ πλοῦτε καὶ τυραννί, 380). It is thus a small step to say that kingship engenders *hubris,* glutting it with many things – wealth, doubtless also the power which depends on wealth. When it is glutted, it falls from the heights to the depths. *Hubris,* then,

---

[41] The passages (823, 1181) should not in fact have been cited under this heading.

[42] *OTh* 53–6. (For his interpretation of the passage in terms of Athenian imperialism, see *OTh* 102f.) There are certainly passages in other Greek tragedies where the context imports a sinister suggestion, notably in *P.V.*, where Zeus is characterized throughout as a tyrant. Cf. Page on Eur. *Med.* 348. But *in itself* the word never means more than 'king'. Striking examples in our play, prior to the present passage, are 380, 408f. (which recalls 380 and is something which could *not* be said under a tyranny) and, especially, 588; immediately following, we find 925, where the word could carry irony, and 939, where it could not.

in this stanza is a simple concept, linked genetically with kingship, but unconfused with tyranny. The stanza deals only with its genesis and its fate; its characterization, in terms of conventional manifestations, is reserved for the third stanza.

That is one advantage: there is a second. A connection of thought is provided with the preceding stanza which touches on a leading theme of the play. The strophe ended with the greatness of god; it told how the divine laws move on high (are ὑψίποδες) and never come to oblivion. Contrast the 'mortal nature of men'. Contrast human greatness, embodied in a king, which is insecure, which enters up into the high places (where humanity does not belong) only to fall headlong. Such a human king was Oedipus, and he is going to fall. But was his fall due to *hubris* engendered in him by the wealth and power of kingship?

The third advantage is in respect of the contrast between *hubris* and the beneficial *palaisma,* which is greatly elucidated if we read τυραννίς. Royal power, with its wealth, tends to corrupt, to breed *hubris,* in which case the king comes to a bad end. But this need not happen. The king may be emulous, not for his own wicked ends, but (as Oedipus has been) for the good of the *polis.* May this happy state of Oedipus continue! But the terms in which the fall of the hubristic king is described are appropriate, as we have seen, to the fall of Oedipus. Not only so, but, ironically, his fall is accelerated by the very *palaisma* which the Chorus pray 'the god' not to end.

They pray the god not to end it; they sing that they will never cease to hold the god as *prostatēs* (a political term suited to this political stanza). What god do they mean? It might well be Apollo, or at least Sophocles may mean us to think of Apollo, who has set this action in train (and to whom Jocasta will pray at the end of the ode).[43] It is

---

[43] Apollo is προστάτης at *Trach.* 209, προστατήριος at *El.* 637; when Teiresias (who is virtually his representative in Thebes) enters at 300, Oedipus says of him: ἧς [sc. νόσου] σε προστάτην σωτηρά τ᾽ ὦναξ, μοῦνον ἐξευρίσκομεν (303f.), and the lines are followed immediately by the name of Phoebus. The use of words at 284–6 is interesting. It can hardly be accidental that Sophocles uses the word *anax* three times in three lines of three different persons. Apollo is a divine lord, as Oedipus is merely a human lord. Teiresias, though a man and no king, is *anax* in virtue of his religious function. (The presence of two human *anaktes* in Thebes may suggest a potentially difficult relationship, a situation of rivalry which may, on the human level, govern the psychology of the scene. Was there room in Thebes for a Teiresias and an Oedipus?) There are divine and human kings, divine and human saviours (48, 150), divine and human protectors.

natural that the Chorus, when they have been singing about human kings, who may abide in beneficial emulation, but may lapse into *hubris,* should put their trust in a divine ruler. The divine ruler will, they hope and pray, keep the good king good, but he will certainly bring down the bad. The implied contrast between divine and human rulers is taken up again in the last stanza, when the supreme ruler is Zeus. But in the second strophe the Chorus reverts to the hubristic, the arrogant, man. There is hardly a notion in the stanza which does not relate to the facts about Oedipus. But in what relation?

Strophe β', 883–96

'But if a man goes his way in arrogance of hand or word, without fear of Justice or honour for the shrines of the gods, may an evil *moira* take him, on account of his ill-fated pride! If he will not win his gains justly and refrain from impious things – if he will cleave in wantonness to that which should not be touched, what man, in such a case, shall ever boast that he wards off from his life the bolts of the gods? If deeds of that kind are held in honour, why should I dance?'

We return to *hubris:* though the word is not used, the backward reference is unmistakable. If the preceding stanza dealt with the genesis and fall of *hubris,* this stanza characterizes the hubristic man by means (we might say) of a catalogue of traditional offences. The connection of thought is something like this: '*Hubris* comes to a bad end; may god preserve the king's goodness (and so the good king); as for the arrogant man . . .' The arrogant man will suffer – must suffer – at the hands of the gods. That the gods play a role is certain, but there are many difficulties of phraseology; and the language of the whole stanza needs careful examination.[44]

The catalogue falls into two parts, each of which consists of a conditional sentence with protasis and apodosis.[45] In each case both

---

[44] A more detailed examination of this stanza will be found in my *JHS* article (op. cit. n. 1).

[45] The strong stop is generally placed at the end of 891. The reason why this is preferred to 888, despite the tense-structure and other considerations, is presumably twofold. (i) Asyndeton between 888 and 889. This can be defended on the grounds that the second sentence explains the epithet δύσποτμος (cf. Müller, *OT* 276). (ii) The shift of subject. The subject of κερδανεῖ, etc., seems at first to be the τις of 883, but turns out to be the τίς . . . ἀνήρ of the apodosis, which is tantamount to οὐδείς. Since, however, in both cases a hypothetical offender is in question, this is hardly objectionable.

protasis and apodosis have a bearing upon Oedipus. (This is after all a play about Oedipus and this ode a central feature of it.) The bearings differ.

In the first sentence there are three counts against the hubristic man. (i) He walks arrogantly in deed and word.[46] Arrogance in word must be boasting. Did Oedipus boast? No, by Greek standards, he was not a man of arrogant speech; in particular, he was not (like Ajax) overweening towards the gods, nor would he invite (like Creon in Antigone) the great blows with which men pay for their great and boastful words. Was Oedipus arrogant in deed, in a way which might suggest that wealth and prosperity had gone to his head? So to act had not been characteristic of this good king.[47] (ii) The man has no fear of Justice (Δίκας ἀφόβητος). Justice personified is an Aeschylean figure of cardinal importance and the disregard of justice highly characteristic of the offender in Aeschylus.[48] Was Oedipus unjust? Judging rashly by appearances, he was in fact, though not by intention, unjust to Creon: he intended to be just and, in the event, did not carry his injustice into effect.[49] Was he afraid? Words of fear have already been accumulated by Sophocles, for Oedipus now fears that he is liable to punishment as the killer of Laius (towards whose exposure he had prayed for the present help of σύμμαχος Δίκη, 274f.). But the justice he has now begun to fear is merely a forerunner of the terrible justice of time which convicts the unwitting offender (1213ff.); and there is again an accumulation of fear-words.[50] Oedipus has reason to fear – and comes to fear – 'justice'. But no such fear would have saved him from the unwitting acts which he committed. (iii) The man does not reverence the seats of the gods.[51] But Oedipus went to Delphi, which put him on the way to his destiny; he sent to Delphi, which put him on the way to its discovery. It was the irony of circumstance rather than traditional sin that caused Jocasta – and in a measure

---

[46] On Dobree's ὑπέροπλα (which could be right), cf. JHS 91 (1971) 128 n. 43.

[47] But see p. 201 below.

[48] E.g. Agam. 381ff., 772ff., after 763ff.; Eum. 533ff. For fear in Aeschylus, see de Romilly, CA passim.

[49] 552f., 609, 614, 683.

[50] Cf. de Romilly, CA 72 n. 1 on 972ff. The agglomeration of such words in the earlier passage (722, 728, 739, 745–7, 749, 767) is hardly less striking.

[51] Jebb may insist too positively that ἕδη refers to statues rather than to shrines (cf. Kamerbeek ad loc.). But the connection between the cult-statue and the temple is so intimate that the distinction is not perhaps very material.

Oedipus – to doubt the oracle; and still Jocasta, ironically, will pray to a statue of the Delphic god.

Of this offender, whose offences so far listed Oedipus does not share, the Chorus sings: 'May an evil portion (fate, destiny) seize him to itself' (κακά νιν ἕλοιτο μοῖρα, 887). Not the most obvious way of saying 'May he come to a bad end!'; and there must be a reason why this way has been chosen.[52] We know that the *moira* of Oedipus was one of unexampled evil; here an evil *moira* is invoked upon the arrogant man in return for his pride, and destiny seems related to merit. Was it so in the case of Oedipus?

The word for pride is χλιδή; and it is given the epithet 'ill-fated' (δύσποτμος), which looks backward and forward.[53] It looks back to the wish the Chorus has just expressed, but it also looks forward to the following sentence, which explains it in terms not of *moira* but of divine wrath. We have another conditional sentence, this time with future tenses; and the gist of it is that no man who offends in certain ways will escape punishment. The text of the apodosis is corrupt.[54] We can have some confidence, however, that the life of the offender is threatened by 'bolts of wrath' or (more likely)'bolts of the gods' and these he will not be able to boast of warding off. This must be, for, if the gods honour such actions as his, what is the point of dancing in their cult? The sequence of thought is clear.

The protasis amplifies the catalogue of offences, but with a significant difference. Of the offences as expressed in the first sentence

---

[52] Plato, *Rep.* 617d, reverses the use of αἱρεῖσθαι – it is the man who chooses his destiny. Cf. Anderson 49.

[53] On χλιδή, in the sense of intellectual pride, see p. 203 below. If δυσπότμου did not follow μοῖρα, we should not perhaps look too closely into the meaning of the word, accepting it as part of the vocabulary of misfortune. This word, fairly common in Aeschylus and Sophocles, normally means 'ill-fated', of a person or an event. Once perhaps in Sophocles *(Phil.* 1120) it means 'bringing an evil destiny'. Here, is πότμος cause or effect? Does χλιδή arise out of, or bring about, the πότμος? Since an evil *moira* is prayed against the offender, and since the offences of Oedipus arose out of an evil *moira*, the word may be used with a calculated ambiguity.

[54] ἔρξεται (after 890) is intolerable and Musgrave's εὔξεται a virtually certain emendation. βέλη is certainly sound and, in this play, can hardly fail to refer, directly or indirectly, to the bolts of Apollo (cf. 200ff., esp. 203ff., 163, 469). θυμῷ is quite intractable; θυμοῦ (the reading of some codd.) is just tolerable (and accepted by Lloyd-Jones, *JZ* 194 n. 28); the writer who glossed with τὴν θείαν δίκην may well have read θεῶν or θεοῦ. Dawe obelizes, with θεῶν in the app. crit. (cf. *STS* 245).

Oedipus was manifestly guiltless; the second sentence hints at impurities and impieties which we know him to have incurred. There are two counts. (i) Gains got unjustly. Here as elsewhere in the stanza Aeschylus proves the best commentator, when we look, for instance, at *Eum.* 539ff. and find an exhortation to reverence the altar of Justice and not dishonour it at the sight of gain. Oedipus had won a kingdom and a queen. Unjustly? Not as he sees it (383f.), but in fact it was by killing the king (who was his father as the queen was his mother): acts unjust in the eyes of justicer time (1213ff.).[55] But it was not such unwitting acts that the Chorus had in mind. (ii) The man envisaged does not refrain from ἄσεπτα, from impious (irreligious) things. Nor did Oedipus, and when the truth comes out he calls himself impious (ἀσεβής, 1382, 1441). On the contrary,[56] the offender cleaves to things which ought not to be touched (ἀθίκτων). It seems probable that there is a sexual suggestion in this word – and also in ματᾴζων, which the Chorus adds.[57] But the sexual impurity of Oedipus was not the outcome of wantonness: it arose in the course of a long and fruitful union. Yet Oedipus will be shot down by the bolts of the archer god.

Antistrophe β', 898–910

'No more will I go with reverence to earth's untouchable navel or to the temple at Abai or to Olympia, unless the fingers of all men point

[55] Oedipus has the kingdom, 'unjustly', of the man he killed; ironically, he has it also justly by hereditary right.

[56] Disjunctive ἤ must mark a change from negative to positive statement. The righteous man refrains from impiety; this the arrogant man fails to do – or he may actually and positively cling to what should not be touched. The word ἔξεται should by all means be retained. Cf. n. 57.

[57] For the word ἄθικτος a parallel is provided by Aesch. *Agam.* 371. There, since the crime for which Paris has been punished is the rape of Helen, there may be a secondary sexual reference. Is there such a reference here? Kitto, *Poiesis* 227, maintains that, since the word recurs at 898 without it, it cannot be present at 891. This objection is, however, outweighed by the intricate relevance of the content of this stanza to the state of Oedipus. ματᾴζειν is not found of sex, but μάτη and μάταιος are both so found. It could even be a reason for preferring ἔξεται to θίξεται (Blaydes' seductive emendation) that the marriage of Oedipus to his mother was a long and fruitful union, as far removed as could be from a wanton rape. There is a further reason for retention. Whatever we do, we are left with jingling futures. This being so, it is best to maximize the jingling effect within a single sentence: ἔρξεται, ἔξεται, εὔξεται. A naïve play upon the sounds of words characteristic of gnomic speech and appropriate to the traditional themes of the stanza?

to these oracles – that they fit. Zeus the master, if you are rightly so called, lord of all, may it not be hidden from you and your immortal rule! The old prophecies concerning Laius are fading; they leave them out of account; and nowhere is Apollo manifest in his honours. Religion is perishing.'

When the Chorus turn from the punishment of sin to the fulfilment of oracles, the connection of thought is indirect, but perceptible. The failure of oracles to be fulfilled is not indeed the same thing as the failure of sinners to be punished, but both are seen as destructive of religion. (τί δεῖ με χορεύειν is balanced at the end of the antistrophe by ἔρρει δὲ τὰ θεῖα.)[58] In fact neither failure occurs. Fulfilment of oracles and punishment of the offender are both brought about by the disastrous fall of Oedipus, but this is something not yet within the vision of the Chorus.

The content of this stanza is, of all parts of the ode, most explicitly related to the previous action – to the scepticism of Jocasta based, as it was, upon the apparent non-fulfilment of the oracle given to Laius. It is this oracle that is primarily in their minds,[59] though the oracle given to Oedipus may also be in the background of their feeling, as something unseizable, though sinister, with the threat of an awful impurity. The themes of purity and piety (and their opposites) are continued into this stanza by a careful choice of words.[60]

The oracle of Delphi, naturally, comes first and is followed by Abai, a neighbouring seat of Apollo. But Zeus is supreme, in prophecy as in all else,[61] and Olympia also was a prophetic shrine. The mention of Olympia leads up to a prayer to Zeus as supreme ruler of the universe – a prayer which serves as climax to this climacteric ode. Zeus is master (κρατύνων), the lord of all (πάντ' ἀνάσσων), and has an immortal rule (ἀρχάν). But Oedipus too is a king, and all these words are found also of the human ruler. The first words addressed to him by the Priest of Zeus were: 'Oedipus, master of my land' (ἀλλ' ὦ

---

[58] The first link is, however, between τί δει με χορεύειν and οὐκέτι . . . εἶμι – both religious activities.

[59] τάδε (902), cf. 906ff. See the commentaries of Jebb and Kamerbeek.

[60] ἄθικτον, σέβων, both looking back to the strophe (886, 891), keep these notions in circulation.

[61] Cf. 498. For the idea of Apollo's prophecy as dependent upon Zeus, cf. Aesch. *Eum.* 19, 616–18. And this is the point, for the oracle of Zeus at Olympia in the fifth century was of mainly local importance (cf. H. W. Parke, *The oracles of Zeus* (Oxford 1967) 186).

κρατύνων Οἰδίπους χώρας ἐμᾶς, 14); later he is called 'most masterful' (κράτιστον πᾶσιν Οἰδίπου κάρα, 40); the Priest ends his speech with the words: 'If you are to rule this land, as you are now its master, it is better to be master of men than of a waste-land' (ὡς εἴπερ ἄρξεις τῆσδε γῆς, ὥσπερ κρατεῖς, | ξὺν ἀνδράσιν κάλλιον ἢ κενῆς κρατεῖν, 54f.).[62] Oedipus is ἄναξ, naturally; so, naturally, are the gods – Apollo (80, 284), and Zeus.[63] Here, then, the appeal to the supreme divine ruler brings to culmination a theme which has run through the ode – that most Sophoclean theme of the breach between human and divine status, exemplified in the most striking way by the contrast between human and divine greatness. The first strophe stressed the contrast between human nature (θνατὰ φύσις ἀνέρων) and the divine world to which alone greatness belongs. The first antistrophe spoke of the human ruler poised on a dangerous eminence and of the god who alone could preserve him in his goodness. So now too the Chorus pray to the divine ruler. And what is their prayer?

They pray him to be vigilant in his immortal rule (μὴ λάθοι | σὲ τάν τε σὰν ἀθάνατον αἰὲν ἀρχάν, 904f.). It is the oracle given to Laius which they have chiefly in mind (906f.); and they are praying Zeus to do the apparently impossible. If their minds were clear, they would be saying: 'Make the son of Laius to have survived and make his killer to have been that son.'[64] For that – and no less than that – was required to vindicate the truth of oracles; and it was for lack of that that the oracles were losing their force (φθίνοντα), were left out of account (ἐξαιροῦσιν), and that Apollo was in no way 'manifest in his honours' (τιμαῖς ἐμφανής). The τιμαί of Apollo are the Zeus-given prerogative of being a true prophet; and it is no longer manifest that he is performing this function.[65]

[62] An example of ring-composition stressing a significant theme: note the pleonasm of 54f. Still to come are 1197f., 1522f. and (if genuine, which it is probably not) 1525. J. T. Sheppard, on 54, calls attention to the emphasis laid on this theme and speaks of 'the danger of the despotic frame of mind'. Without denying that this notion may be present, I am inclined to think, taking all the relevant passages together, that the contrast between divine and human greatness is more significant.

[63] On 284–6 see n. 43.

[64] And, if they were clearer still, they would be saying: 'Make Oedipus to kill (or to have killed) his father, to marry (or to have married) his mother'. Cf. Kitto, Poiesis 213.

[65] This seems better to suit the word ἐμφανής than to take τιμαῖς of the honours paid to him by men.

It is by a revelation of the truth that Apollo will be τιμαῖς ἐμφανής; and this revelation will come.[66] But, though all the threads are in their hands – the likelihood that Oedipus killed Laius, the prophecy that he would kill his father, the exposure of the child – it is impossible for them, as it was impossible for Jocasta and Oedipus, to make the right pattern. They are in perplexity of mind; and in their perplexity they pray for something which will, in its nature, bring utter disaster upon the king who has earned their loyalty. Upon the fulfilment of their prayer they stake their faith in the gods. For, if oracles are not fulfilled, ἔρρει τὰ θεῖα: the divine order, the divine world, is at an end. They need not have been disturbed. The oracles *were* fulfilled, both the oracle given to Laius and the oracle given to Oedipus; the authority of the divine world *is* re-established. Moreover, the impure man *is* shot down by the bolts of the gods. They can go on with their dances; and the tragic dance is the right dance. But it is the dance of a Sophoclean, not an Aeschylean, chorus.

The foregoing pages have attempted to examine certain trains of thought and association in this complex and difficult ode; if the results of the examination have any validity, they should throw light upon the purposes of Sophocles in writing it and also upon the interpretation of the play of which it forms a striking and central feature. The choral odes of Sophocles, like all parts of the plays but often in a special degree, are a medium to convey his own interpretation of the action, but it is conveyed, obliquely, through a Chorus which is (more or less) involved in that action and limited in its view by the dramatic situation. He uses the Chorus; but he does not use it, undramatically, as his own mouthpiece. We must always seek – and shall always find – a meaning and a coherence of thought which belong to the Chorus in its own dramatic entity. But, like other speakers, they will say more than they know; their words may carry a significance beyond – and even contrary to – their conscious thought. This is the familiar, and characteristically Sophoclean, device of dramatic irony, pervasive in all his plays, above all in the *Oedipus Tyrannus*.

---

[66] A persistent and highly Sophoclean theme. The use of words of sight and appearance in this play deserves a careful detailed study, which would reinforce Reinhardt's interpretation in terms of the contrast between appearance and reality.

It is clear that, in the Second Stasimon, the first stanza was evoked by the suggestions of impurity and impiety that had gathered about Oedipus in the preceding scene; it is equally clear that the last stanza expresses not so much their disapproval of Jocasta's scepticism as their distress of mind at the evidence which seemed to justify it. But why, in the central stanzas, do they sing of *hubris* and its fall? What, in their minds, is the relationship of what they sing to Oedipus and to the dramatic situation? They know that he may be the killer of Laius: Teiresias had said that he was (362) and Oedipus now fears that he may be. But the motive of Oedipus in killing Laius (if he did kill him) can hardly come in question, since they have no reason to doubt his story of the encounter; he did not kill the king to gain his throne, which he acquired quite otherwise. Some interpreters have argued that the act of Oedipus was, nevertheless, hubristic in its wholesale violence. One may doubt whether the conventional Greeks of the Chorus would have seen it in that light and not (as Oedipus presents it in the *Coloneus*) as a justified act of retaliation, indeed of self-defence by a man who found himself one among many and in danger of his life.[67] In any case, even if it were, in the eyes of some, hubristic, this was not the *hubris* bred of *koros* about which they sing; it was the act of an exile, not a king. The theme must therefore stem from a different connection of thought. This connection is far more likely to have been, what has often been suggested, the conduct of Oedipus towards Teiresias and, especially, towards Creon, which was disquieting, just as the suggestions of impiety and impurity were disquieting.[68] Thus the second stanza reacts to the first half of the episode, as the first stanza reacts to the second half. Oedipus is a king, enjoying all the proverbial advantages of kingship. (Once more the sense is improved by reading ὕβριν φυτεύει τυραννίς.) Is he showing signs, by abusing his power, that they have bred *hubris* in him? If so, it will inevitably

[67] There are really two issues: whether Oedipus was culpable, and whether this is what the Chorus had in mind; and opinions will probably continue to be divided on both. (For a formidable catalogue raisonné of views see D. A. Hester, 'Oedipus and Jonah', *PCPS* 23 (1977) 32–61.) Adverse judgements will be found, e.g. in Knox, *OTh.* 57f.; Cameron 131ff.; A. D. Fitton Brown, *CR* n.s. 19 (1969) 308, who makes the point that Laius was on a sacred embassy accompanied by a herald. Contr. J. T. Sheppard xxviiif.; Bowra 193; Kitto *Poiesis* 202f. Impetuous father meets impetuous son – the irony is obvious. The tragic implications of retaliation are not drawn in this play but in the *Coloneus* (cf. *JHS* 74 (1954) 17f. and pp. 260ff. below).

[68] Cf. Gould (1) 594–9.

lead to disaster. Yet they know him as a king who strives for the
common weal: may the gods cause this to continue! In their perplexity they put their faith in the protector god. With the third stanza,
they return to the theme of *hubris* and expatiate upon it. If a man acts
hubristically, may he suffer an evil destiny! If he does so act, he must
suffer at the hands of the gods or religion is at an end. At this point,
perhaps, the thread of thought binding their words to the dramatic
situation has become more tenuous, as they expound a theological
doctrine. If they are thinking of Oedipus at all, they cannot be saying:
'Why worship the gods, unless Oedipus comes to a disastrous end?'; at
the most it can be a feeling rather than a thought – a feeling governed
by all the sources of disquietude – that, if Oedipus becomes hubristic,
then he must fall or religion must fail. But in fact they have been made
to give, proleptically, an explanation of the fall of Oedipus. And it is
the wrong explanation.

It is shown to be the wrong explanation by an elaborate chain of
ironies, to which attention has been called already. The Chorus is
afraid that Oedipus may abuse his royal power and suffer disaster, but
disaster comes upon him through things done before ever he became
king, and things not done out of *hubris*. They pray the god not to put
an end to his striving for the common good, but this striving leads
only towards the disaster. They place their trust in a divine champion,
but it is Apollo *prostaterios* who presides over the downfall of
Oedipus. They characterize the arrogant man in terms of traditional
excesses, impurities and impieties; they call for an evil destiny upon
him and say that, if he is not struck down by the bolts of divine wrath,
there is no point in their religious observances. Oedipus is not that
kind of man at all: yet he *is* caught by an evil *moira,* he does *not* escape
the bolts of Apollo (just as he *does* fall from the heights and accelerate
his own fall). He does not escape divine justice, since he *has* done
deeds[69] which were impure and impious; and to do such deeds was in
fact his evil *moira*.

It was the wrong explanation: yet it was a possible, a plausible, and
a religious, explanation; and it is given in terms of traditional Greek
religious notions. It is given in terms which find parallels in Aeschylus. Dare we say that it is an Aeschylean explanation? The relationship in Aeschylus between the evil destiny of a character and his
willed actions is not altogether simple; it was a problem which

[69] 895 (πράξεις): it is the deed that counts, not the motive.

exercised the poet from the *Persae* to the *Oresteia*. But if one thing is clear, it is that characters collaborate in their own downfall by their own wicked acts. One may look vainly in extant Aeschylus for a divine world which ordains not only the punishment of deliberate sin, but punishment of the unwitting sinner whose punishable acts are part of his destiny from the beginning and are performed in utter innocence. This is what Sophocles gives us in the *Oedipus Tyrannus*. It is likely (though it is perhaps futile to say so) that, if we possessed the *Oedipus* of Aeschylus, we should see a very different hero – a culpable hero who in some way (which we cannot specify) contributed to his own downfall.[70] It is surely not unlikely that Sophocles wrote his play – and wrote this ode – with the Aeschylean treatment of Oedipus in mind.

An innocent Oedipus. But was he innocent of intellectual pride? That sort of pride was of course the last thing that this traditional moralizing Chorus will have had in mind – the last thing they will have meant, when they spoke of χλιδή. The Homeric and archaic worlds knew well that men could be overconfident and, in their confidence, blind to the truth about human status and its relation to the divine government of human affairs. But these were worlds which did not prize intelligence unduly. An arrogant confidence in the sufficiency of human intellect was characteristic, rather, of the fifth century. If there is any sense in which Oedipus is arrogant, his pride is intellectual, not moral. He has too much pride in his keen intelligence: what he must learn – and teach – is that he has been wrong again and again.[71] Which is ironical. The lavish – the almost intolerable – irony of *Oedipus Tyrannus* is justified by this – that the most intelligent of men can be so wrong, that the man who read the riddle of the Sphinx cannot read the riddle of his own appalling destiny.

The acts which drew down on Oedipus the wrath of the gods were not done in pride of any kind, but in simple ignorance. Is there then any moral in his fate? Is there any lesson to be drawn? Yes, if it is

---

[70] There are strong hints in the *Septem* (733, 771, 950) that wealth and luxury may have been significant themes in the earlier plays of the Aeschylean trilogy. Cf. *YCS* 25 (1977) 33f.

[71] This theme has been adequately treated by many writers. O'Brien (8) has recently pointed out that the only quality of Oedipus 'that becomes a major issue is his intelligence' and suggests (10) that, if we are looking for a simple formula, we cannot do better than 'a man matches wits with the gods'.

salutary for men to realize the fragility of human fortunes and the vast sea of ignorance in which they swim. No, if it is meant that Oedipus should have been something other than himself, without the keen energies and the thrusting intelligence which made him great; that he should have been a man like Creon, who always thinks before he speaks and then says less than he means, who is content, parasitically, to enjoy the fruits without the risks of power, a cautious man.[72] Those who consider that Sophocles was the prophet of *sophrosune* should contemplate a world of Creons and wonder whether it would be any place for a tragic poet. There are morals no doubt for those who have the skill to draw them, and there are tragic facts – such tragic facts as the innocence and guilt, the intelligence and blindness, the greatness and weakness, of Oedipus. τί δεῖ με χορεύειν; There was every reason.

---

[72] I have been led into an intemperate judgement upon Creon (who was a good man and behaves generously at the end of the play) by a certain exasperation at those who (almost) make him the hero of the play. Of course, in our prosaic lives, we shall be lucky if we behave as well as he did: as to greatness, we do not aspire to it any more than he. O'Brien (14) has a brief well–balanced statement, calling proper attention to 584ff.–which is an excellent example of how a rhetorical commonplace, a piece of *dianoia*, can be used to make an important dramatic point. Cf. also Gellie 81, 87, 101f.

CHAPTER NINE

Furies in Sophocles

There is no mention of an Erinys or Erinyes in *Oedipus Tyrannus*.[1] Should we find this surprising? True that the curse of Oedipus upon his sons which evoked an Erinys in *Septem* does not enter, even by hint or inference, into this play. Yet Oedipus was a doomed man under threat in consequence of a breach, if an unwitting breach, of the law governing the relationship between parents and children. He had killed his father; and, apart from matricide, it is hard to imagine an act more likely to evoke an Erinys than parricide.[2] But Apollo is the only specific divine power that seems to be concerned with the pursuit of Oedipus. For this absence of Erinyes there could be a reason not unconnected with the way in which the concept of *moira* is introduced into the play. We have already made the acquaintance of Erinyes as punitive agencies closely associated with *moira* and the Moirai.[3] This was one way – and an Aeschylean way – of regarding *moira*. In the *Tyrannus*, however, Sophocles wished to concentrate upon the individual destiny of the hero, upon his unaccountable fate, rather than upon an ineluctable chain of consequences through which, from generation to generation, Erinyes punish breaches of the divine order. It is for this reason that he is unemphatic, if not ambiguous, about the responsibility of Laius; that he ends his play with Oedipus still in Thebes, his exile still undetermined, and with virtually no mention of the sons who will wrong him and be cursed.[4]

---

[1] Nor in *Philoctetes:* see ch. 12 n. 39.

[2] It is not clear from *Septem* whether the notion of an Erinys was introduced into the Aeschylean version at that stage of the story.

[3] See ch. 7 p. 155.

[4] The language of *O.T.* 713f. is equally applicable whether the oracle was given before the begetting of Oedipus (a prohibition on intercourse) or before his birth (a sinister prediction). Lloyd-Jones, *JZ* 119ff., argues against a common view that

He is condemned and punished by the justice of time (1213ff.), but *talio* is not a prominent theme in the play. At the cross-roads we see father and son, dreadfully alike, seeking to retaliate upon one another, a natural Greek reaction in a natural human situation, but the profounder implications of such retaliation wait for the *Coloneus* to reveal.[5]

There are Erinyes in plays we have already considered. In *Ajax* they are invoked by the hero and by his brother against their enemies; in *Trachiniae* by Hyllus against his mother, while he believes her deliberately to have killed his father. In *Antigone* Teiresias speaks of Erinyes in ambush for Creon because of his breaches of divine law. One might say that this is common form; and if, in all cases, there is some reminiscence of Aeschylus, that is natural enough. There are other references to Erinyes in these plays, to which we must return. The question one must ask is whether, until we come to *Electra* and *Oedipus Coloneus,* there is any reason to suppose that Sophocles was powerfully influenced by the Aeschylean conception of these goddesses and the mode in which they operate.

To go behind Aeschylus is a difficult – and perhaps an otiose – task. The whole subject of the nature, cult and functions of Erinyes and similar divinities is one of notorious complexity;[6] and it would be vain to try and identify a general view of the Erinyes held by Greeks of the Homeric or archaic period, since people's notions will have varied so much according to locality and education and other factors. It would be vain and, for our purposes, hardly necessary, since it is widely agreed that Aeschylus could have been the first to impose

Sophocles deliberately 'altered the form of the oracle' and points to the language of 1184f., 1360, 1382f., all of which imply the guilt of the parents. It is the lack of emphasis upon this theme that strikes me as deliberate and significant. As to the sons, there is only *O.T.* 1459–61. Sophocles, who several times opens a window upon fresh tragedy towards the end of a play, hints neither at the offences of the sons nor at the tendance of the daughters, so that the traditional future is excluded. The brief reference to the sons is subordinate to the case of the daughters, who are introduced not merely to enhance the pathos but because they are child-victims (and so balance the child-suppliants of the Prologos). Cf. Gellie 102.

[5] See ch. 11, pp. 260ff.

[6] The evidence is exhaustively reviewed by E. Wüst, *PW* Suppl. viii, s.v. Erinys, who writes about their functions as follows: 'Fast endlos ist die Vielseitigkeit der Aufgaben des Eumeniden, entsprechend der Vielzahl von Dämonen, aus denen ihre Gestalt, und von Ideen, aus denen ihr inneres Wesen zusammengeflossen ist.' See also E. C. Dietrich, *Death, fate and the gods* (London 1965) ch. iv; F. Solmsen, *Hesiod and Aeschylus* (Ithaca, N.Y. 1949) 178ff.

clarity of form and conception upon them.[7] To what extent his great trilogy changed the way in which the ordinary Greek saw Erinyes/ Eumenides we are not in a position to determine, but Sophocles was a tragic poet, never unaware of the work of his great predecessor, least of all in this context (where nearly every Sophoclean reference to Erinyes wakes an echo of Aeschylus); well aware indeed that Aeschylus had made out of these frightening demons a great symbol of tragic process, better aware than many modern critics that this was one of his greatest contributions to tragic thought. So at least I shall argue. It is thus important to identify the main features of the Aeschylean conception as known to us from *Oresteia* and, in a lesser degree, from *Septem*. They can be catalogued as follows.

(i) Erinyes are agents of punishment, called into operation by offences in some area with which the gods are particularly concerned.[8] It was by the sending of Zeus Xenios that an Erinys came against the Priamids for a breach of hospitality.[9] It was for a breach of filial duty that Oedipus cursed his sons with a curse which had the force of an Erinys. But the Erinyes, themselves chthonian, had a special association with the world of the dead, itself powerfully numinous, and a role to avenge those who had been violently slain. So persistent is this association that a view was once popular which saw these goddesses as in effect the vengeful dead themselves within the earth making their power felt to retaliate upon the killer. If *Arai* is one of their names, are they not embodiments of a dying curse? This view has now been generally abandoned, largely because it does not fit the Homeric evidence.[10] In tragedy, however, so much concerned with

---

[7] In some cults Erinyes were horses or horse-like creatures. Horses were no use to Aeschylus: he wanted hounds and, for his chorus, hounds in quasi-human form. How much his description of them (and the costume which went with it) – black-robed, filthy, snake-entwined, with oozing eyes – and his account of their vampirish methods owed to earlier conceptions can hardly now be determined.

[8] The interests of the Erinyes are clearly related, though not exclusively linked, to the great traditional commandments – to honour gods, parents and strangers, on which cf. G. Thomson (ed.), *The Oresteia of Aeschylus* (Cambridge 1938) I 51f., II 269ff., 362ff.; Ehrenberg 167ff.

[9] *Agam.* 58ff., 747ff.

[10] Reviewed by Wüst (loc. cit. n. 6). Among more than a dozen references to an Erinys, very few are connected with death, still fewer with deliberate murder. They are in some cases connected with a curse, but there is more than one reason for cursing. The range covered is wide: for instance, a mother's curse (four times), a father's curse, disregard of primogeniture, the breaking of an oath, a breach of natural law (the horse Xanthus who spoke). Cf. Dodds, *GI* 21 n. 37.

deaths – and particularly in tragedies of revenge – this aspect was bound to be prominent.

(ii) The work of Erinyes tends to be carried out by human beings who resent the injury which, at the divine level, constitutes the ˙ offence. Thus it is the resentful Greeks who avenge the rape of Helen; and in the house of Atreus there was a whole series of avengers. It makes little difference whether we say that divine and human agencies work in parallel or that the human agents are virtual embodiments of Erinyes.[11]

(iii) Ensuring that the offender is punished, that the doer suffers (παθεῖν τὸν ἔρξαντα), they carry into effect a great law of Zeus (*Agam.* 1563f.). We can read in *Eumenides* the horrifying details of an actual physical pursuit by Erinyes, but this is special to a special case, rare as the thunderbolt of Zeus. Gods leave no aftermath, but, when the punishment is carried out by a vengeful human-being, it tends to create a new offence, a new avenger. One death creates another death which demands a third, and so on potentially *ad infinitum*. If the law of *talio* has divine sanction,[12] translated into terms of human life it means a perpetuation of evil in the process of its punishment. The evil past lives on; the dead reach out to assault the living; Erinyes have good memories, they are μνήμονες.[13] And if they remember the past, they determine the future.

(iv) The process is virtually automatic, blind and indiscriminate, since in human situations the innocent tend to suffer along with the guilty, which is why Aeschylus laid so much stress upon the innocent suffering, Greek and Trojan, which attended the punishment of Paris and his city. There is justice, but it is rough and approximate – and it is the justice of Zeus.

(v) Erinyes are chthonian powers, like Hades himself, like the dead still powerful in the earth, but the law which they administer is a law of Zeus – and not the nether Zeus, but the Zeus who wields the thunderbolt. It was all very well for an Isocrates[14] to draw a sharp distinction between two classes of gods: 'those who are the cause of good things to us and are called Olympians; those who are set in charge of disasters and punishments and bear less agreeable names'.

---

[11] On the equation of Helen with an Erinys at *Agam.* 737–49, if (as I incline to believe) she is so equated, see *BICS* 21 (1974) 11–13.

[12] See esp. *Cho.* 306–14, 400–4.

[13] *Eum.* 383; *P.V.* 516; cf. *Agam.* 155.

[14] v. 117.

Valid though this distinction was up to a point, a moment's reflection would have shown the most ordinary Greek that it was too sharply drawn, that the Olympians might be the source of evil and, for that matter, the infernal powers a source of good. To deeper thought there was a problem in these two worlds which refused to be kept apart, the world of light and the world of darkness – a problem for Aeschylus in the fact that Zeus, with his high concern for justice, sends Erinyes, with all the horror and cruelty and indiscriminate suffering which attend them.[15]

(vi) The problem is solved by Aeschylus, insofar as it can be solved, by the reconciliation of the Furies at the end of *Eumenides,* and a change in their role – or, as one should rather say, since they remain formidable, by the assumption of an additional and beneficent role.[16] And this is brought about by the persuasions of Athena. If the implacable Erinyes can be persuaded, then anybody and anything can yield to persuasion. It may well have been the ultimate contribution of Aeschylus to theodicy to reveal these Greek gods of power as exercising it through persuasion and not only by violence.

It has been necessary thus to summarize the Aeschylean view of the Erinyes – and their relation to the Olympian world – before proceeding to a consideration of *Electra* and *Oedipus Coloneus,* two plays which throughout exhibit a close dependence upon the thought of Aeschylus. First, however, let us return briefly to *Ajax, Antigone* and *Trachiniae,* all of which contain references to Erinyes.

In *Ajax* the name occurs four times, twice in the Suicide Speech of the hero (835–42), who summons these all-seeing goddesses to witness and to aid; to destroy the Atridae root and branch as he is destroyed; not only so, but to feed greedily upon the whole Greek army. It is the curse of a dying man upon those who, he thinks, have caused his death; it is a prayer for that retaliation of which he has

---

[15] Cf. 'A religious function of Greek tragedy', *JHS* 74 (1954) 16–24. There has been a tendency to focus discussion of the Erinyes too narrowly upon *Eumenides* and so to miss the degree to which they have been associated with Zeus in the earlier phases of the trilogy. The evidence is set out in my earlier article: see also p. 158 n. 18.

[16] In fact they show themselves 'goddesses of good intent' or 'kindly goddesses'. There is little reason to doubt that the play's title is Aeschylean, but the absence of the new name from the text is surprising. Harpocration asserts that it was given by Athena in the course of the play, and this could have fallen within the lacuna posited by Hermann after *Eum.* 1027.

himself been frustrated. If there are echoes of Aeschylus, it is Sophoclean irony that the prayers will not be fulfilled: Agamemnon will
suffer, but not for this; the army will suffer, but not for this. At the end
of the play (1389–92) Teucer lays a formal curse upon the Atridae;
and this time not only is the Erinys given the Aeschylean epithet
'mindful' (μνήμων) but is associated – and this too is Aeschylean – with the Olympian father and with 'accomplishing Dike'. This
time the offence is the refusal of burial – the will to refuse burial, of
which the Atridae were plainly guilty (it is interesting that Erinyes
should be invoked in respect of an intention and not an act); and
Agamemnon was ultimately punished, though not for his behaviour
towards Ajax (and Menelaus was not punished at all). If there are
implications here, they are not developed.

Perhaps the most interesting reference to an Erinys occurs in a
different context. In a passage (1024ff.) which has already been
discussed,[17] Teucer is searching desperately for an explanation, and
his eye lights upon the sword of Hector. He argues it out, and he is
satisfied: the gods have been at work to destroy the two heroes. The
sword must have been forged by an Erinys (as the belt by Hades). In
the mind of Teucer we may write this down as a piece of primitive
superstition which by-passes the whole question of human motive
and responsibility. But Erinys is not a word used lightly by Sophocles,
nor can he have written of an Erinys forging a sword without thought
of two passages in Oresteia (Agam. 1535; Cho. 646), in one of which
Moira whets, and in the other Aisa forges, a sword in the interests of
justice. In the latter passage indeed it is Dike that sets up the anvil, Aisa
that forges the sword, and an Erinys that introduces the sword-bearer
into the fatal house. Teucer is more likely to have been thinking of the
malice than the justice of heaven. Did Sophocles, who three times
calls our attention to the sword, see some symbolic justice in the
weapon of suicide, some truth in Teucer's ascription of it to an Erinys?
The violent past lives on; the dead reach out to destroy the living; the
chivalrous mitigation of heroic enmity is futile – and Ajax, who
rejects it, ensures that it shall be futile. That is how the Erinys works in
this case.[18]

In Antigone we find Erinyes and an Erinys. Teiresias sees Erinyes as
lying in wait for Creon (1074–6), because he has offended against

[17] See pp. 44, 162 above.
[18] See pp. 18f. above.

upper and nether gods alike, consigning a living creature to a tomb and refusing burial to the dead. Kinship does not enter into it here; the offences are against the gods, and the Erinyes are described as belonging to 'Hades and the gods' ("Αιδου καὶ θεῶν 'Ερινύες).[19] They will retaliate in kind (1076), when Creon's own son pays with his death for the dead who should not have died and for the dead who should have received burial. The function of Erinyes in this case is quite straightforward.

As to the single Erinys at 603, in the Second Stasimon, I have expressed elsewhere[20] some scepticism as to whether Sophocles could have used such an expression as 'Erinys of the mind' (φρενῶν 'Ερινύς), a watered-down 'psychological' Fury, a mere abstraction. The doubt is particularly maddening, since the word Erinys comes at the end of a stanza, closing the first half of the ode, and is immediately followed by the name of Zeus and the description of Zeus's power. The juxtaposition must be willed; and it is a juxtaposition of light and darkness, of two worlds: first the gloom of the nether gods, threatening the one surviving light of the house of Oedipus with extinction, and then the dazzling splendour of the Olympus where Zeus holds his ageless sway; both worlds, it would seem, bent upon the destruction of the doomed offender, whoever that offender may be. The Chorus have in mind Antigone the Labdacid, who is indeed destroyed, but who, in the preceding scene, has claimed to be obeying the eternally valid laws of Zeus and, equally, serving the Justice who dwells with the nether gods.[21]

---

[19] The epithet ὑστεροφθόρος may recall the Aeschylean ὑστερόποινος. 'Hades and the gods'. The latter are unspecified and could be taken either of the infernal or supernal gods, both of whom are offended.

[20] See p. 168 n. 46 above.

[21] The ode is examined in detail in ch. 7 pp. 166ff., where it is observed not only that the two worlds are juxtaposed and contrasted in the second and third stanzas, but that the simile in the first stanza hints at a fusion of the two worlds which, in the context of disaster, is sinister. The ode follows Antigone's great speech (450ff.), which is itself preceded, in the Watchman's description of the Second Burial, by a passage implying a similar fusion. The passage (415–21) is examined in *BICS* 26 (1979) 5f. (Its relation to the Second Stasimon is observed by T. F. Hoey, *Arion* 9 (1970) 342–4.)

Such passages are sinister, because infernal powers are at work to punish an offence against the demands of the infernal world. But the justice of Zeus is also involved. Thus Müller (2) (p. 13) is right to say 'dass die beiden Instanzen, auf die sich Antigone zur Begründung ihres Ungehorsams beruft, Zeus und die ungeschriebenen Gesetze einerseits, Hades und das Recht der unteren Welt anderer-

Of the three earlier plays it is perhaps *Trachiniae* – a play which has
no known Aeschylean prototype – in which we can see most clearly
an Aeschylean conception of the Erinyes. Hyllus, thinking that Heracles has been deliberately murdered by his wife, prays that she may
suffer vengeance at the hands of 'punitive Justice and an Erinys'
(ποίνιμος Δίκη . . . Ἐρινύς τε, 808f.). The words of Heracles at 1050ff.
are richer in implications. 'Never yet has the bedfellow of Zeus nor
the hateful Eurystheus set me an ordeal such as this which the
daughter of Oeneus, with her false beauty, has fastened upon my
back, a woven net of the Erinyes in which I perish.' It is virtually a
cross-reference to *Oresteia*. Later we hear how the Shirt of Nessus eats
away the flesh of Heracles and drinks his blood; and that is how the
Aeschylean Erinyes treat their victims.[22] Both Hyllus, then, and
Heracles see Deianira as a Clytemnestra. Hyllus sees her as a Clytemnestra to be punished by an Erinys, not reflecting that Clytemnestra
was punished and Agamemnon avenged by the matricide of a son,
and not knowing that this was a demand that would be put upon him
by his father; Heracles sees her as bringing Erinyes into operation. Or
rather he does not see what his words imply. For, if the Aeschylean
Clytemnestra was punished by a son serving the function of an
Erinys, she herself, when she slew her husband in the net, was serving
the same function. The reminiscences of Aeschylus thus have implications in respect of Heracles; and these are brought out in a third
passage.

When the Chorus learns that Deianira has taken her own life, they
comment that 'the new bride has borne a child to the house – a great
Erinys' (893ff.).[23] In prosaic terms, the crime brings forth its own
punishment. There follow, first, the account of Deianira's suicide,

seits, nur zwei Seiten derselben Sache sind'. R. Bultmann, 'Polis und Hades in der
Antigone des Sophokles', *Glauben und Verstehen* (Tübingen 1952) II 20–31
(reprinted in *Wege der Forschung* 45 (Darmstadt 1967) 311–24), who is cited by
Müller and criticized by Knox (*Gnomon* 40 (1968) 748), has something similar to
say, but goes too far when he describes Hades as 'die Macht, aus der echtes Recht
entspringt, und durch die alles menschlich-gesetzliche Recht relativiert wird' (p.
314). I had rather say that divine punitive justice, as known to us from Aeschylus,
had deep roots in the frightening chthonian world and owed its problematic
character partly to this fact.

22 For the net, cf. e.g. *Agam.* 1382, 1580; *Cho.* 492f. For Erinyes drinking blood, cf.
Eum. 264ff. and Pearson's note on Soph. fr. 743. The point is made by Perrotta 519
n. 1. See also ch. 10 p. 233, on Soph. *El.* 785f.

23 Cf. Kitto, *Poiesis* 176.

fulfilling the prayer of Hyllus, then the entry of the dying Heracles in the Shirt of Nessus, that 'woven net of the Erinyes'. The fate of Heracles is, like Agamemnon's, the direct result of his own behaviour. That the agent of his punishment is not a virago retaliating, but an exceedingly feminine woman desperately trying to retrieve her position – and destroying herself in the process – is a stroke of Sophoclean irony.

This ironic contrast may in itself have been a reason why Sophocles chose to stress the parallel between Deianira and Clytemnestra,[24] but I would suggest that he also wished to deploy certain ideas, about Zeus and the Erinyes, which Aeschylus had developed in *Oresteia* and make them contribute to the significance of his play. If these three references to Erinyes, closely linked to one another though they are, stood alone, perhaps they could not bear too great a weight of interpretation. But they do not stand alone.

Heracles reaps the consequences of his actions. Now we have already seen[25] that the qualities which led to his downfall were bound up with the qualities which had made possible his great achievements. His whole career had been one of violence, his reaction to every situation the ruthless use of force; his one moral principle was retaliation, what he called punishing the bad ($\kappa\alpha\kappa\text{o}\dot{\upsilon}\varsigma$ ... $\dot{\epsilon}\tau\epsilon\iota\sigma\acute{\alpha}\mu\eta\nu$, 1111).[26] To this principle fall victims not only noxious monsters, not only the

[24] This is well brought out by T. B. L. Webster in *Greek poetry and life* (ed. Cyril Bailey *et al.*, Oxford 1936) 177; cf. also Bowra 139f.; Segal, *YCS* 156.

[25] See p. 89 above.

[26] With 1111 we should surely compare 274ff. Zeus was angry that Heracles killed Iphitus treacherously: $\epsilon\dot{\iota}$ $\gamma\dot{\alpha}\rho$ $\dot{\epsilon}\mu\phi\alpha\nu\tilde{\omega}\varsigma$ $\dot{\eta}\mu\dot{\upsilon}\nu\alpha\tau\text{o}$ | $Z\epsilon\dot{\upsilon}\varsigma$ $\tau\dot{\alpha}\nu$ $\sigma\upsilon\nu\acute{\epsilon}\gamma\nu\omega$ $\xi\dot{\upsilon}\nu$ $\delta\acute{\iota}\kappa\eta$ $\chi\epsilon\iota\rho\text{o}\upsilon\mu\acute{\epsilon}\nu\omega\cdot$ | $\ddot{\upsilon}\beta\rho\iota\nu$ $\gamma\dot{\alpha}\rho$ $\text{o}\dot{\upsilon}$ $\sigma\tau\acute{\epsilon}\rho\gamma\text{o}\upsilon\sigma\iota\nu$ $\text{o}\dot{\upsilon}\delta\dot{\epsilon}$ $\delta\alpha\acute{\iota}\mu\text{o}\nu\epsilon\varsigma$. The *hubris* is that of Iphitus and his family, and the notion is continued in 281 ($\dot{\upsilon}\pi\epsilon\rho\chi\lambda\acute{\iota}\text{o}\nu\tau\epsilon\varsigma$ $\dot{\epsilon}\kappa$ $\gamma\lambda\acute{\omega}\sigma\sigma\eta\varsigma$ $\kappa\alpha\kappa\tilde{\eta}\varsigma$). $\dot{\eta}\mu\dot{\upsilon}\nu\alpha\tau\text{o}$ does not of course imply self-defence against a violent physical attack: Jebb, in his note, is right to translate it 'avenged himself' and to add 'the $\ddot{\upsilon}\beta\rho\iota\varsigma$ of Eurytus would have justified Heracles in challenging Iphitus to open combat'. This was the Heraclean code, and Lichas (who mixes truth with lies, cf. App. B) sees it as endorsed by Zeus. Just because he is (sometimes) a liar, it would be rash to disregard as subterfuge the impressive statements about Zeus that Sophocles has put into his mouth, though we have the difficult task of interpreting them. If Zeus administers his own harsh retaliatory justice, it may be crude, but not without some symbolic truth, to say that he sympathizes ($\sigma\upsilon\nu\acute{\epsilon}\gamma\nu\omega$) with those mortals who act by the *lex talionis*. One is tempted to link the use of $\sigma\upsilon\nu\acute{\epsilon}\gamma\nu\omega$ here, with Hyllus' final comment on the $\sigma\upsilon\gamma\gamma\nu\omega\mu\text{o}\sigma\acute{\upsilon}\nu\eta$ of men, the $\dot{\alpha}\gamma\nu\omega\mu\text{o}\sigma\acute{\upsilon}\nu\eta$ of the gods. What Hyllus could not see was that the justice meted to Heracles by the gods was the same kind of justice he had spent his life in meting to men and monsters.

treacherous Nessus, but Iphitus and the innocent Lichas; and in his agony he called upon his son to help him in retaliating with physical violence upon Deianira. In two of the most unpleasant lines in Greek tragedy, he speaks of spoiling her beauty as his own strength had been spoiled; and the theme is stressed by repetition (1066ff., 1107ff.).[27] He makes indeed a whole series of outrageous demands upon his son which have this in common, that each of them would entail a continuance of evil after his death. First, Hyllus is to participate in the torturing and killing of his mother: from the fate of Orestes (and Alcmaeon) he is saved by the facts of the case. Secondly, he is to burn his father alive, which, as he sees (1206f.), would involve a terrible pollution.[28] From this he is allowed to escape by a compromise; and attention is thus focused upon the third demand which Heracles thinks so trivial, but to which Sophocles devotes more space than to either of its predecessors. Hyllus is to take Iole to his bed. In horror he exclaims: 'Who could choose such a course, if he were not driven sick by avenging spirits?' (ὅστις μὴ 'ξ ἀλαστόρων νοσοῖ, 1235).[29] Hyllus has no choice, but the power which forces this upon him (and destroys his future happiness) is in the nature of an *alastor*. If ἀλάστωρ is a word of the Erinys-connection, so too is παλαμναῖος (1207); so above all are ἀραῖος (1202) and θεῶν ἀρά (1239). A father's curse, whether it is that of Oedipus or of Heracles, has the force of an Erinys, and that is the threat which Heracles brings to bear upon his son.

I would suggest, therefore, that the notion of Erinyes, first introduced at 809, broods over the closing phases of the play. If that is so, there are three divine powers to be considered[30] – not only Kypris, not only Zeus, but also the Erinyes; and Heracles stands in close relation to them all. He acts and suffers for his actions under the influence of Kypris. He is the son of Zeus, but this cannot save him from the justice of Zeus. He is punished by an Erinys, but shows a

[27] 'Perhaps the most savage passage in Greek tragedy' (Kamerbeek). The structure of 1068f. is worth observing. In the mind of Heracles the words ἐν δίκῃ κακούμενον are appropriate to Deianira only, and he associates retributive justice with her alone. But the balance of the sentence compels us to take, not only λωβητὸν εἶδος, but also the concluding words with τοὐμόν as well as with κείνης. Heracles had described himself as the victim of an Erinys without realizing the implications of what he said.

[28] He will be παλαμναῖος if he does, ἀραῖος if he does not. On the text of *Trach.* 1206–9 cf. *BICS* 16 (1969) 47f.

[29] See ch. 4 n. 39.

[30] See p. 88 above.

kinship with the Erinyes by the ways in which he acts.[31] If we are to form a notion of Zeus's world, we cannot exclude from it the devasting power of Kypris: no more can we exclude the pitiless operation of Erinyes as they carry out the justice of Zeus. So Aeschylus saw before Sophocles, but what Aeschylus did with the Erinyes in the closing scene of *Eumenides* is not included by Sophocles in his play, which ends with Zeus, but a Zeus illuminated by the bitter words of Hyllus about the great *agnomosune* of the gods.

The gods are pitiless, and Heracles is pitiless. The final ironical truth is that a ruthless Heracles, administering retaliatory justice, is more like the gods than such human-beings as Deianira and Hyllus who are capable of pity.[32] Perhaps Zeus was not his father for nothing after all. If Heracles became a god (and in one phrase towards the end of the play Sophocles seems to hint at the apotheosis), he earned his status by that same ruthlessness and wrathfulness by which Oedipus in the *Coloneus* earned his status as a *heros*.[33]

For the second time we come back, rightly, to this Oedipus. I have suggested that the two Sophoclean tragedies most closely concerned with Erinyes are *Electra* and the *Coloneus*. They are relatively late plays, and it could be that towards the end of his career Sophocles had given new and deep thought to his predecessor's *Oresteia;* it could even be that this had been stimulated by a revival of the trilogy, in whole or in part, which may – or may not – have taken place in the

[31] It will be argued below that it is characteristic of several Sophoclean heroes to be at once victim and agent of the Furies.

[32] On the god-like characteristics of this Heracles, see Bowra 136.

[33] Critical opinion is sharply divided on this point: cf. Knox, *AJP* 92 (1971) 695; Lloyd-Jones, *JZ* 127f.; Segal, *YCS* 138ff. It seems not unlikely that an audience, reminded by the impressive description of the pyre (1195–9), might think of the apotheosis, when Hyllus speaks of τὰ μέλλοντα (1270). On the other hand, Heracles himself envisages a descent to the world of the dead (1201f.). If there is a hint, it is singularly lacking in emphasis. Why then introduce it at all? Yet it seems to be rather characteristic of Sophocles to introduce, without developing, such a hint towards the end of a play. The most unmistakable – and significant – example is the foreshadowing of the *Antigone*-situation at the end of the O.C. (see pp. 274f. below). But the closest parallel is *El.* 1498, also with μέλλοντα. Sophocles did not wish to treat Electra's story in terms of the pursuit by Furies of Orestes (see pp. 226f. below), but hints at it there. No more did he wish to treat the story of Heracles in terms of apotheosis, despite the kinship of Heracles to the gods. There may have been several reasons for this, and one of them might be that, through the pyre, he became an Olympian god, fit to play his role in the *Philoctetes,* and not, like Oedipus, a *heros*.

last quarter of the century.[34] This cannot be asserted; and our examination of earlier plays may suggest that these notions had long been influential in the mind of Sophocles. What right indeed have we to assert that these two later plays are in fact particularly concerned with the Erinyes? In *Oedipus Coloneus* they are mentioned only twice, in a single scene towards the end of the play. But Erinyes is not their only name: it is to a grove of the Eumenides that Oedipus has come and past which he goes to his final rest. In the first scene and the last the sense of locality is strong, but throughout the play an audience must be aware of the proximity of these ambivalent divinities. Yet interpreters have seldom given due weight to the Eumenides/Erinyes in interpreting the play. What, then, of *Electra?* Has it not been stated again and again that the Sophoclean treatment of the matricide differs from the Aeschylean precisely because Sophocles left the Furies out of account? Nothing could be farther from the truth.

[34] On a possible revival of *Choephori* in the late 420s, cf. H. J. Newiger, *Hermes* 89 (1961) 422ff.

CHAPTER TEN

Electra

The *Electra* of Sophocles might be thought to prove the impossibility of objective literary criticism: so diverse are the interpretations to which it has given rise.[1] The greatest divergence of opinion concerns the poet's attitude towards the matricidal vengeance. At one extreme we have a robust 'Homeric' Sophocles, untroubled by the moral squeamishness of an Aeschylus, and at the other an Aeschylean sensitiveness to the moral implications of the vengeance and a presumption that the Furies are only waiting for the play to end to initiate their traditional pursuit of Orestes. Critics are also divided between those who regard the moral and religious issue as central to the play and those for whom it is either absent or peripheral – incidental, one might say, to an essentially psychological drama. But even here, there is no agreement: for one critic Electra goes mad, for another she reaches the height of human *arete*.[2]

I start from a fact which will hardly be contested: that *Electra* is full of reminiscences of the *Choephori*,[3] which must mean that Sophocles wrote his play with the *Oresteia* constantly in mind. Now it is of course a substantial point of difference between Sophocles, on the one

[1] Cf. Johansen, *C&M* 8–10. This chapter is an expanded version of *PCPS* 183 (1954–5) 20–6.

[2] For some critics the play is grimly serious, while another can write of 'well-staged but shallow melodrama'.

[3] Cf. J. T. Sheppard, *CR* 41 (1927) 2–9, 163–5. 'In the *Electra* of Sophocles there is hardly any touch which in one form or another is not already to be found in Aeschylus' (W. Headlam in G. Thomson (ed.), *The Oresteia of Aeschylus* (Cambridge 1938) II 217). It is unnecessary to list these reminiscences, though many of them are mentioned below. They are testified by a hostile witness in Perrotta, who, being an honest critic, does not fail to note them, but, being committed to the view that matricide is not an issue in the play, tends to qualify them as 'reminiscenze passive', 'una pallida reminiscenza', and so on!

hand, and on the other Aeschylus (and Euripides and the tradition as a whole), that there is nothing in Sophocles about a pursuit of Orestes by the Erinyes of his mother. He is accordingly said to have 'omitted the Furies'.[4] This is not literally true. The word Erinys occurs four times in the play. At 112 Electra prays, among other chthonian powers, to the Erinyes; at 276 she states that Clytemnestra, when she sleeps with Aegisthus, fears no Erinys.[5] At 491 the Chorus sings of the coming of the Erinys; at 1080 that Electra is prepared to die 'when she has destroyed the two-fold Erinys' (διδύμαν ἑλοῦσ' Ἐρινύν) – a remark which could have interesting implications.[6] Furthermore, a reference to Erinyes is universally admitted at 1388, in a short ode full of Aeschylean echoes, where the Chorus describes the avengers as 'inescapable hounds'.[7] Now, if Sophocles had wished to write a supposedly Homeric version of the story or otherwise to by-pass the moral issue, he should scrupulously have avoided a theme so closely associated by his predecessor with the blood-guilt of Orestes. By using this theme, as by all the reminiscences of the *Oresteia*, he insists, on the contrary, upon placing himself in a relationship to Aeschylus and thus himself raises the question: Did he accept or reject or modify the standpoint of the earlier dramatist?[8] This would be true, if the above-mentioned passages stood alone. I shall endeavour to show that the theme of Erinyes is in fact developed by Sophocles in close relation to the thought of Aeschylus and to argue that it is of fundamental importance in the interpretation of his play. (For the Aeschylean concept of the Erinyes I refer the reader to the previous chapter.) It will be convenient to begin with the First Stasimon (472ff.).

The structure of the ode is very simple, the thought determined by the ominous dream of Clytemnestra as interpreted by Electra (459f.). Strophe and antistrophe form a self-contained whole, embraced between *mantis/promantis* at the beginning of the strophe and *manteiai* towards the end of the antistrophe.[9] The strophe says: Justice (Δίκη)

---

[4] Cf. e.g. Whitman 161.
[5] See p. 231 below.
[6] See p. 244 below.
[7] Cf. Segal, *TAPA* 486f. and (on Hermes) 524.
[8] On the relationship of the play to the Euripidean *Electra* (which in my view is much less important) see App. G, p. 342.
[9] On 472ff. Jebb writes: 'The sanguine prediction of the Chorus in *O.T.* 1086ff. has

will come, and the antistrophe says: an (the) Erinys will come (475f., 489ff.). The shift from Justice to Erinys is mediated by a reference to the dead Agamemnon who does not forget (and the Aeschylean Erinyes are *mnemones*). That the Erinys is described (rather unexpectedly) as 'many-handed, many-footed' could be intended to remind us that she will work through a plurality of human agents, already in ambush. The theme of the first two stanzas, then, is justice carried out by an Erinys or Erinyes who are evoked by the resentment of the dead Agamemnon and embodied in the avenging son and his helpers. It is the Erinys that suggests the theme of the Epode. For it is characteristic of Fury-justice that it tends to involve a succession of troubles (πόνοι), and so, since the curse of Myrtilus (implied, not mentioned), the descendants of Pelops had been Fury-haunted, sorrow and outrage have never yet left the house. οὔ τί πω ἔλιπεν: can this fail to prompt the question whether the succession of sorrows will stop now?[10] To this there could be more than one answer, but the question must be asked.

This is, then, an ode about Fury-justice. It is preceded by Chrysothemis saying that it is not sensible for two people to wrangle about 'the just' (τὸ δίκαιον, 466) and followed by a wrangle between Electra and Clytemnestra as to where justice lies.[11]

Everything which has been said about the rhetorical character of this exchange is true or at least contains an important element of truth.[12] A comparison with the notorious 'forensic' debates in Euripides is not unfair, though it should not be pressed too hard, since Sophocles, as we might expect, handles the now fashionable form

a similar preface.' With 499ff. we can compare *O.T.* 897–910. Cf. Johansen, *C&M* 15. In *O.T.* the oracles were true, disastrously; here the dream is true. Is the truth less disastrous? At 502 εὖ could, as so often in *Oresteia*, be ironical. For other passages where a sinister irony has been suspected see pp. 235ff. below.

10 On the text of 513–15 see R. D. Dawe, *Gnomon* 48 (1976) 232, who defends ἔλειπεν ('has never looked like leaving'). πολύπονος is emphasized by repetition (505, 515). Nor is the reiteration of αἰκεία (487, 511, 515) fortuitous, cf. also 102, 191, 206, 216. On repetitions in Sophocles see P. E. Easterling, *Hermes* 101 (1973) 14–34, who examines a number of them and comes to the conclusion that they are seldom undesigned. Unlike Aeschylus, Sophocles takes the story back to Pelops. One reason for this might be that it makes the disastrous series longer, but the wrecked chariot no doubt looks forward to the false story of Orestes' death (on which see p. 236 below).

11 On 466–7 see Stinton 131f.; Dawe, *STS* 180.

12 Cf. e.g. Whitman 157; Woodard (1) 183ff.

with somewhat greater naturalism.[13] As sometimes, if not always, in
Euripides, the form is used – like any other convention – to make
valid dramatic points. But what is the point here? To blacken the
character of Clytemnestra and give Electra an easy dialectical
triumph?

Clytemnestra argues that she killed Agamemnon justly (ἡ γὰρ Δίκη
νιν εἷλεν, οὐκ ἐγὼ μόνη), because he had killed Iphigenia: like a
Euripidean arguer, she exploits 'the rhetoric of the situation'[14] with
over-ingenious arguments. Her tone is vulgar and forfeits sympathy.
In rebuttal, Electra sets out (554f.) to reconcile the cases of Iphigenia
and Agamemnon. But how satisfactory, as argument, is her argumentation intended to appear? When she attributes Clytemnestra's
act to lust for her paramour rather than vengeance for Iphigenia, she is
is taking her stance in an old dispute that goes back to Aeschylus and
Pindar. She could be right or she could be over-simple. In neither case
are we entitled to say that the sacrifice of Iphigenia is presented as a
trivial incident in the story of the much-troubled house. Electra's
account of Aulis, admittedly second-hand (ὡς ἐγὼ κλύω, 566), is the
story she would like to believe; and we can hardly suppose that
Sophocles wishes us to take it too seriously as an explanation of
events.[15] What is more significant is that Electra, who is hoping for
the return of Orestes to kill Clytemnestra (603ff. are quite specific),[16]
uses two arguments without perceiving their implications.

Electra opens her case. 'You say you killed my father. Whether it
was justly or not' (and of course she goes on to say that sex, not justice,
was the motive), 'what statement could there be that brought yet
greater shame than that?' (558ff.) She means that Clytemnestra's
action had shown a lack of *aidos,* of respect for a hallowed relationship. But surely her rhetorical question could be answered, not least
by those who knew the *Oresteia.* If the relationship between husband
and wife was sacred, was it not generally felt in the Greek world that

[13] Opposed speeches in Euripides tend to be of approximately equal length. It may
be worth noticing that, while Clytemnestra is given 36 lines, Electra is given 52,
but the *rational* portion of her speech ends at 594 (37 lines)!

[14] To use A. M. Dale's well-known formulation.

[15] Cf. Kells's note on 566–633, and Segal, *TAPA* 536 n. 84. If Sophocles had been
concerned to give a serious account of Agamemnon's dilemma, he would hardly
have trivialized it in the way he does. The fact remains that Agamemnon did kill
his daughter.

[16] Cf. 1154ff.

the tie binding blood-relations was more sacred still (*ἔτι*)?[17] To kill a mother: justly or not, will that be an honourable thing to avow?

We turn to 577ff. Granted the worst interpretation of Agamemnon's action, was it right that he should die at Clytemnestra's hand? 'By what kind of law? Take care lest, in making this law for men, you make trouble for yourself and a change of heart. For, if we are to kill one in return for another, you (I say) would be the first to die, should you meet with justice.' What kind of law? This question too is easily answered. It is the law of retaliation; the law proclaimed by the Chorus of Libation-bearers (*Cho.* 400ff.);[18] the law which the Erinyes administer, on which Electra and Orestes intend to act, and under which, if the law is generally valid, they will themselves be liable to retaliation.[19]

By making Electra use arguments to which she is not entitled, Sophocles keeps alive the Erinys-theme with which the preceding chorus dealt. But this is far from being the sole relevance of Erinyes to this debate.

In Clytemnestra's speech lines 528–51 form a self-contained whole – her argument about justice. 'Justice slew him, not I alone; and you should have helped Justice, had you been right-minded' (*εἰ φρονοῦσ' ἐτύγχανες*, 528f.). Then, at the end (ring-composition): 'If you think I am wrong-headed, wait till you get right judgement before you criticize your neighbour' (*φρονεῖν κακῶς, γνώμην δικαίαν*, 550f.). She speaks as if there were a right and a wrong conception of justice in this case. *Her* view is right, and Electra would see it as right, if she were not wrong-headed – if, as we might put it, she were open to argument. But she is not. Nevertheless, she affects to meet Clytemnestra on

---

[17] Johansen, *C&M* 18f. It could be that Sophocles has underlined the point with a curious piece of language. *πατέρα φῇς κτεῖναι* 'You say you killed Father.' So translated, it sounds natural enough in English, but as a piece of Greek it invites Jebb's note: 'The sense of *πατέρα* is relative to the speaker, and not (as would be more natural) to the subject of *φῇς*.' A sign of Electra's obsession? Perhaps: but is it not possible that the reference to killing a father might suggest the killing of a mother? The suggestion is not to be pressed.

[18] See ch. 7, n. 15.

[19] 'Electra alla legge del taglione non crede' (Perrotta 310). Did she not, when she sang 245ff.? This is mere rhetoric, like her affectation that Clytemnestra is laying down a *new* law. Cf. Linforth (1963) 98. Whitman is nearer the truth when he says (157) that 'Electra seems to condemn the law of blood for blood while her actions confirm it', though his explanation is unnecessarily complicated. As Gellie says (110), this is 'an awkward principle for a person intent on murder'.

Clytemnestra's terms, and the latter welcomes the more temperate approach. Electra then advances arguments to which Clytemnestra's mind is equally closed. Is not all this argumentation largely beside the point? Yes, because the principle of justice to which they both appeal is the same, while their applications of it are irreconcilable. The principle is that of retaliation, of blood for blood, the law of the Furies; and it is founded not upon reason but upon passion. Actually, Electra's reasonableness does not last long. She sets out to reason with her mother, but she ends (from 595 onward) with an emotional outburst, to which Clytemnestra reacts appropriately. Electra has insulted the mother that bare her (ὕβρισεν, 613); she is shameless (615, 622, 626); Aegisthus will punish her, when he returns (626f.). We are back to the tone and circumstances of 516ff., and it is as though the whole intervening argument had never been. Sophocles was the supreme ironist, and perhaps we can now see that he was making ironical use of the form of a sophistic (or forensic) debate, the entire rational aspect of which turns out to be a sham.[20]

But there is a further point, brought out at the beginning and end of this debate or wrangle. 'You are always accusing me of *hubris*', says Clytemnestra, in effect (520–2), and she goes on: 'It is not insolence on my part, but I speak ill of you because you are constantly speaking ill of me.' 'You cannot say that I began it this time', says Electra at 552f.[21] Both parties are concerned to fasten the responsibility on the other. But clearly an endless process is in operation, in which words and deeds both play their part. Electra states – in a passage to which we shall return (616–21) – that her behaviour is forced on her by the hostility and the deeds of Clytemnestra. To which the latter replies, sarcastically: 'Truly, I and *my* words and *my* deeds give *you* all too much to say.' Then Electra: 'It is you that make the words, not I. For you do the deed; and the deeds find out the words.' To the original deed of Clytemnestra Electra can, for the time being, retort only with words.[22] Clytemnestra replies with deeds, with persecution, but also

[20] 'The debate between mother and daughter . . . has been taken too much at face value' (Whitman 157). Cf. Woodard (1) 183. Woodard's article (on which – and on its sequel – something is said in n. 71 below) contains a valuable examination of the *logos/ergon* contrast in the play.
[21] In view of this I am rather inclined to take ἄρχω with καθυβρίζουσα at 522, in the sense of 'take the initiative' (despite 264 and 597, cited by Jebb in support of the other interpretation).
[22] The position of the Colonean Oedipus, during his debate with Creon, is not

herself with words. κακῶς λέγω κακῶς κλύουσα: the process is reciprocal and potentially infinite, just as the succession of retaliatory deeds is potentially infinite. What we have, then, in this scene is the Furies at work upon the plane of speech. Does this seem far-fetched? Then turn to the great statement of the *lex talionis* at *Choephori* 309ff., to the debt which Justice exacts and the suffering which the doer must endure, to the μέν and the δέ: 'In return for a word of hatred let a word of hatred be brought about (ἀντὶ μὲν ἐχθρᾶς γλώσσης ἐχθρὰ γλῶσσα τελείσθω) . . . In return for a bloody blow let him pay a bloody blow.' As constantly in Greek literature, word balances deed. The tragic process of retaliation has its double aspect.

Of this process Electra in her calmer moments is aware.[23] Such a moment is represented by her speech at 616ff., which provides a general comment on the preceding wrangle. 'Though you may not think it, know that I am ashamed of these things. I am aware that my behaviour is improper and unbecoming to me. But the fact is that your hostility and your actions compel me perforce to act as I do. It is by shameful acts that shameful acts are taught.' The choice of words (ἐξαναγκάζει . . . βίᾳ) is notable, if only because Electra echoes here what she had already said in answer to the friendly criticisms of the Chorus.

We turn back to the long speech of Electra which follows the Parodos (254–309). It begins and ends on the same note. 'I am ashamed, ladies, if you think by reason of my much lamenting that I take things too hard. But you must bear with me, since a violent force compels me to act so' (ἀλλ' ἡ βία γὰρ ταῦτ' ἀναγκάζει με δρᾶν σύγγνωτε, 254–7). She goes on to describe all the outrageous circumstances of her life within the palace. She ends her speech with these words: 'In such a case neither moderation nor piety is possible' (ἐν οὖν τοιούτοις οὔτε σωφρονεῖν, φίλαι, | οὔτ' εὐσεβεῖν πάρεστιν), 'but in the midst of evils one is utterly bound to follow evil ways' (ἀλλ' ἐν τοῖς κακοῖς | πολλή 'στ' ἀνάγκη κἀπιτηδεύειν κακά). Which is just a different way of saying that shameful acts are taught by shameful acts

---

dissimilar (see p. 252 below). It has often been pointed out that in our play the tragic hero takes no action which directly influences events (cf. Perrotta 331; Segal, *TAPA* 532; Ronnet 205–7), but, in view of the function of words in the retaliatory process, perhaps one should not lay too much stress on the 'passivity' of Electra.

[23] Having made Clytemnestra angry, she becomes calmer herself?

(αἰσχροῖς γάρ αἰσχρὰ πράγματ' ἐκδιδάσκεται). Taking these passages together – and noting such words as *bia* and *ananke*[24] – it is surely permissible to say that Sophocles is laying a great deal of stress on the notion that evil in the past sets up a process, compulsive and inevitable, determining evil in the future. And that is, in the most general light, how Aeschylus conceived the action of Furies, perpetuating evil in the course of its own punishment.

Moving backwards again, we find that this notion, which we have traced in Electra's speech (254ff.), in the First Stasimon and in the debate between Electra and Clytemnestra, is already prepared in the Parodos. Electra's monody and the ensuing *kommos* together constitute the longest lyric passage in Sophocles.[25] The force of the pathos is extreme; and it might appear at first sight that the scene is designed for nothing else than to convey the grief, the courage and the despair of Electra, counterpointed by the moderate counsels of a sympathetic but unheroic Chorus. But this is not quite so. Electra and the Chorus sing alternately; and, while she expresses and rouses emotion, they raise questions – or Sophocles raises questions through them. In terms often reminiscent of the *Oresteia,* they raise questions not irrelevant to the themes we have been considering. The crimes of Clytemnestra and Aegisthus are, naturally, in the forefront of their imaginations. A convergence of divine powers will, they trust, bring about the punishment of those crimes through the human agency of Orestes. But, when they sing: 'whether it was a god or mortal that did these things' (εἴτ' οὖν θεὸς εἴτε βροτῶν ἦν ὁ ταῦτα πράσσων, 199f.), they are singing, not of the vengeance of Orestes, but of the killing of Agamemnon; and earlier they had used language which was likely to suggest (my witness is Jebb, not given to fanciful interpretations) the slaying of Iphigenia by her father.[26] In these, and in other, ways the Chorus provides the perspective in which to view the closing words

---

[24] Cf. 221 (δείν' ἐν δεινοῖς ἠναγκάσθην – or whatever one should read).

[25] 86–120 are not strictly a monody, but include passages in sung anapaests, along with (for the most part) 'recitative' anapaests. Cf. Kamerbeek on 86–120. For an examination of the Parodos see App. D.

[26] On 157 Jebb justly remarks that 'ζώει has more point when it is remembered that *one* sister had perished'. Why has Sophocles resurrected the epic Iphianassa as a living sister only to re-inter her at once? Can he have had any other motive than, by the similarity of names, to remind the audience of Iphigenia? For a different view see A. D. Fitton Brown, *PCPS* 12 (1966) 20f.

of the *kommos*,[27] when Electra, who in her monody had appealed to the powers of the chthonian world – an Aeschylean set, including chthonian Hermes, *potnia Ara,* and the awful Erinyes – ends with these words: εἰ γὰρ ὁ μὲν θανὼν γᾶ τε καὶ οὐδὲν ὢν | κείσεται τάλας, οἱ δὲ μὴ πάλιν | δώσουσ᾽ ἀντιφόνους δίκας – if, that is to say, the chthonian power of the dead is to count for nothing, if the just law of blood for blood is not to be applied, then – ἔρροι τ᾽ ἂν αἰδὼς ἁπάντων τ᾽ εὐσέβεια θνατῶν (245–50). 'All regard for man, all fear of heaven, will vanish from the earth.' So Jebb translates, with his customary skill in bringing out the implications of the Greek: and he comments: 'αἰδώς is respect for those opinions and feelings of mankind which condemn wrong-doing; as εὐσέβεια is reverence for the gods'. But this is a particular kind of wrong-doing, in which – and in the punishment of which – the gods have a particular interest.[28] And, if the children do not avenge their father, where then is *eusebeia?* It is this emphatic statement that leads into Electra's speech: and that speech ended with words already quoted. 'In such a case neither moderation nor piety is possible, but in the midst of evils one is utterly bound to follow evil ways' (307–9). Neither moderation as generally understood nor the god-sanctioned reverence for a parent is possible. Electra is thinking of words, but between words and deeds, in this connection, no difference of principle exists. Thus, unless the murder is punished with ἀντίφονοι δίκαι, there can be no *aidos*, no *eusebeia.* Yet the mind – and the actions – of the blood-avenger are such as to exclude *eusebeia.*[29] Inevitably so: πολλή 'στ᾽ ἀνάγκη. This dilemma may be cardinal to the interpretation of the play.

It has been my purpose so far to call attention to Sophocles' employment of an Aeschylean theme (or set of related themes) and to suggest that it must be taken fully into account in interpreting the play. The question still remains as already put. Did Sophocles accept, or reject, or modify, the standpoint of the earlier dramatist?

Sophocles might be saying – and this is how many have interpreted the play: 'I know that matricide is a terrible thing, but I have made this mother so utterly bad that, on a choice of evils, the children were justified in killing her. I know that retaliatory justice – Fury-jus-

---

[27] Cf. Linforth (1963) 93.
[28] Cf. *Eum.* 508ff. (*both* parents).
[29] Sophocles may have had in mind *Cho.* 122, 140f.

tice – is grim, but at least it *is* justice. Were Clytemnestra and Aegisthus to get away with their crime? I know that deeds of violence tend to breed successors, but in this case it really was the end, as Orestes and Electra and the Chorus believed it to be. Study (he might say) my use in the closing stages of words which imply finality.'[30] A plausible case can be made out for this line of interpretation, though with Sophocles of course we must always be on the look-out for irony: he might be making his characters say τέλος just because it was not – and in the nature of the case could not be – the end. In Aeschylus it was not the end. There is a salient difference, often remarked, between the Aeschylean and Sophoclean treatments of the plot. *Electra* ends with the imminent death of Aegisthus; in the *Oresteia* Orestes is pursued by the Furies of his mother and there is a sequel. About this difference something further must now be said.

The pursuit of Orestes was an established part of the legend.[31] If Sophocles had wished to rule it out, he could hardly have done so specifically, but he could at least have avoided anything which would positively suggest it to the minds of his audience. This he has not avoided. The Aeschylean reminiscences and the theme of retaliation may perhaps be thought inconclusive on this point, but, if Sophocles wished his audience to forget or disregard the pursuit of Orestes, he was surely unwise to use the metaphor of hounds, when Orestes and his friends entered the house to avenge; and I suggest he was unwise to make his Chorus (837ff.) refer to Amphiaraus, Electra to Alcmaeon, of whom the one thing most certainly known was that, for the killing of his mother, he was pursued, again and again, by Furies.[32] But we forget all this at the end of the play? Perhaps; or perhaps Sophocles has written a line to make sure that we do not, when he makes Aegisthus speak of 'the ills of the Pelopidae, present and to come' (τά τ' ὄντα καὶ μέλλοντα Πελοπιδῶν κακά, 1498) and throw doubt on the capacity of

[30] τελεῖν (et sim.): 1344, 1397, 1399, 1417, 1435, 1464, 1510 (if genuine – Dawe deletes with Ritter).

[31] Cf. Letters 244f., who writes (a little too positively perhaps) that 'everybody in the theatre knew that Orestes would be tormented' by the Furies. Knox, in his review of Ronnet, *AJP* 92 (1971) 694, points out that the Athenian public was familiar with the fate of Orestes not only through literature but through the ritual of the Choes.

[32] Cf. Kells 1 n. 1 for the two Sophoclean tragedies on this theme (Pearson 1 68ff., 129ff.). Cross-reference is always possible. The plays, of which *Epigoni* (probably identical with *Eriphyle*) seems to have been particularly famous, cannot be dated but are quite likely to have been earlier than *Electra*.

Orestes to foresee the future. That Aegisthus means by μέλλοντα κακά – and that Sophocles intended to convey–something over and beyond his own death would seem obvious, though it has been denied.[33] The only question is what weight, if any, should be attached to the remark.

What did happen after the play was over? Critics are of course rash to ask such a question, but ask it they sometimes do. One critic remarks very sensibly that 'there is absolutely no reason to suppose that Orestes and Electra were imagined as living happily ever after'; another suggests that, after a difficult period of adjustment, they did probably attain to peace and satisfaction![34] But where does one stop asking such questions about matters which Aristotle might have described as 'outside the drama'? The sooner the better, it may be said (as in the notorious case of Lady Macbeth's children). But the subsequent fate of tragic personages can be a part of the drama, not least when it was a well-known part of the legend. This was a theme which Sophocles had to handle with tact. He could not deny and, for a reason which will appear, did not wish to assert that Orestes was pursued by Furies. I would suggest that he deliberately indicates it as a possibility inherent in the system of justice which Orestes has successfully applied. So much and no more. Which is not to deny the paramount importance of the Furies, and of what they represent, in the play. It is not the future fate of Orestes (and Electra) which matters; it is not what the Furies may do when the play is over that matters, but what they have done and do before and during the play. It has sometimes been assumed (oddly) that, because the play ends without a pursuit of Orestes, the ending is 'happier' than in the Aeschylean version.[35] The reverse is true. No pursuit by Furies; then no Delphi, no Athens, no Areopagus, no acquittal, and – above all – no reconciliation of the Furies by the persuasions of Athena. The difference of approach between the two dramatists might be stated,

[33] Cf. Johansen, *C&M* 29 n. 36 (who calls attention to the normal limiting force of γοῦν); Méautis 250; Linforth (1963) 124, who remarks on 1500 that 'in this there is the suggestion that, as Agamemnon could not foresee his fate, so there may be in store for Orestes a fate that he is unable to foresee'. Contr. Bowra 258; Ronnet 215.

[34] D. W. Lucas, *The Greek tragic poets*[2] (London 1959) 153; Bowra 256.

[35] Linforth (1963), recognizing (n. 33 above) that Sophocles hints at the future ordeals of Orestes, suggests (123) that the poet 'relies on the spectators' remembrance of how it was settled in *The Eumenides*'. This seems very like wanting to have it both ways.

rather crudely, by saying that Aeschylus, without detracting from the sufferings of the past and present, has his eyes upon the future, while Sophocles concentrates upon the present as generated by the past. This corresponds to a difference of form – the difference between trilogy and single play – and to a difference in the attitudes of the poets towards their leading characters. The more strongly the light is focused upon the individual caught up in the workings of the Furies, the more emphasis there is likely to be upon their unpersuaded grimness. And the leading character in *Electra* is the heroine.

The reader may indeed be surprised that I have not already mentioned a main dramatic reason why Sophocles did not wish to lay stress on the pursuit or non-pursuit of Orestes by the Furies.[36] The play is about Electra, who is central to its interest as to its form. The skill with which the dramatist presents his heroine and manipulates the structure of the play to this end has been so greatly, and so rightly, admired that some critics have tended to write off the whole religious and moral issue as mere background – or framework – to a primarily psychological drama. If this issue refuses to be so written off, we would appear to be confronted with an interpretative dilemma. Is this a play of ideas or a play about a person?[37] The ideas concern matricide as an act of just retaliation and, in other dramatic treatments, have been focused upon Orestes as the matricidal son, upon his responsibility and his ultimate fate; the person is Electra. The dilemma is more apparent than real, but it is only eliminated if we appreciate that Electra is in fact conceived and drawn as at once the victim and the agent of the Furies. At this point a word or two must be said about the characters.

They are all involved in a central situation; they are all in some sort of relationship to Electra. They are all members or adherents of the Pelopid house; and the play is framed between a description of the palace as *poluphthoron* (10) and a reference to the ills of the Pelopidae, present and to come, which the palace must see. The Chorus ends the First Stasimon by singing of *poluponos aikeia* which has never left the house. Within the house have been living Electra and Chrysothemis

[36] Segal, *TAPA* 476.
[37] Perrotta in particular has argued most forcefully for the view that ideas are unimportant, the character of Electra all-important, in the play.

and Clytemnestra, with Aegisthus. From outside comes the exiled Orestes, with Pylades and the Paedagogus.

To say, with one critic,[38] that Orestes is simply 'une machine à tuer' doubtless goes too far, but he is from the start purposeful and efficient, given to military language,[39] committed to an intrigue about which he feels (except in one particular) no scruple. Bred by the Paedagogus to avenge his father, he had no need to consult the oracle except upon the means.[40] Towards the end of the first scene, he hears the cry of a woman who may be Electra, but will not allow himself to be diverted from the course dictated by Apollo. We do not see him again until he enters with the urn, to play his part in one of the great emotional scenes of Greek tragedy.[41] And what part is that? It is Electra who is moving, and Orestes is moved. This is not a treatise but a play; Orestes is a person, not a formula. Naturally he is moved; and some critics have found a deep significance in the scene, with a change of role for Orestes: the man who came to avenge his father remains to liberate his sister.[42] This would be an interesting development, but I doubt whether it was an interest intended by the dramatist, and there is little in the text to support such an interpretation. Surely the most striking feature in the episode is that, when Orestes joins his sister in her song of joy, he does not sing[43] and contributes little except words of caution. Emotion is rebuffed, if less harshly than by the Paedagogus, who now enters to summon them to the task. All is now cruel

---

[38] Ronnet 208f.

[39] Cf. Kells 81 (on 23–38). Woodard (1) 165f. speaks of 'a mind that exists only in external action, and only for external action'.

[40] If we accept the traditional attributions of 80f. to Orestes and 82–5 to the Paedagogus, we must say that it is the latter who refuses to allow the former to respond to human feeling and shall compare his more brutal interruption at 1326. (Cf. Reinhardt 151f.) Recently, however, F. H. Sandbach has argued powerfully (*PCPS* 23 (1977) 71–3) that 80f. belong to the Paedagogus and 82–5 to Orestes. I find his argument irresistible.

[41] On this scene see Perrotta 353ff.; H. Diller, *Göttliches und menschliches Wissen bei Sophokles* (Kiel 1950) 7f.; F. Solmsen, *Electra and Orestes: three recognitions in Greek tragedy* (Amsterdam 1967) 25f.

[42] Adams 78; Bowra 249ff. Contr. Linforth (1963) 107 n. 4; Ronnet 214 n. 2; Gellie 122f. See also Segal, *TAPA* 513–15.

[43] Unless in the epode τί μὴ ποήσω; (1276) and τί μῆν οὔ; (1280) rank as singing. I take it that Orestes declaimed rather than sang his trimeters. (On similar phenomena in late Euripidean Recognition Duos see A. M. Dale in her edition of Euripides' *Helen* (Oxford 1967) p. 106.)

and practical. Electra's joy has flowered only to wither in the cold wind of a vindictive killing.[44] 'Strike twice, if you can.'[45]

Orestes the exile erupts into a life of which he has not been part:[46] how he lived from the time of his father's murder to the time of his return is, dramatically, blank. Not so the life which Electra led in the company of Clytemnestra and Chrysothemis, under the rule of Aegisthus, and which made her what she is. 'I am used to her words', says Chrysothemis (372f.). 'You will not say that I began it this time', says Electra to her mother (552f.). The revelation of Electra's state of mind, which is begun with such poignancy and pathos in the Parodos, is carried forward in her long speech which follows (254ff.), which has all the importance that speeches so placed tend to have in Sophocles. Set between words of compulsion (ἀναγκάζει and ἀνάγκη), we have a picture of her life. Her lyrics in the Parodos were dominated by the thought of her dead father, and here she begins by speaking of 'a father's woes' (258), and of course he is in the background of her thought and feeling throughout, but now in the foreground stand her mother and Aegisthus. Her mother hates her (261f.). Aegisthus sits on her father's throne, wears his robes, pours libations at the hearth where he killed him. The final outrage: he is in her father's bed sleeping with a mother who does not deserve the name *(ἐν κοίτῃ πατρός . . . τῷδε συγκοιμωμένην)*. So brazen is she that she has intercourse with the defiler, 'fearing no Erinys' (275f.).

44 Ronnet 222: 'liberée du malheur, elle reste prisonnière de sa haine'. On 1309–11 see Segal, *TAPA* 504f. This has rightly been taken to refer to Electra's mask of sadness which could not be changed in mid-play. A concession to realism? Cf. *Arethusa* 2 (1969) 130. It would perhaps be characteristic of Sophocles, in making such a concession, to derive dramatic profit from it. Electra's hatred *is* engrained in her and remains uppermost in the closing scene. Cf. Gellie 122.

45 Linforth's suggestion (109 n. 5) that these words (1415) are addressed to Clytemnestra must be rejected, not least because they are immediately followed by her ὤμοι μάλ' αὖθις (the two blows being of course Aeschylean, *Agam.* 1343f.). See Kells ad loc.

I say nothing in the text about 1487f. (Electra on the burial of Aegisthus), which have become a matter of controversy. With Jebb, Kaibel and many others (e.g. Kitto; Ronnet 212 n. 2), as against e.g. Bowra 255; Knox, *JHS* 88 (1968) 157; Johansen, *C&M* 28 n. 34, I believe that the 'buriers' she has in mind are dogs and birds. Quite apart from the possible reference to *Od.* 3.259f., I cannot see why Sophocles should have brought in the burial of Aegisthus at all – with specific mention of 'buriers' – unless he, the writer of *Ajax* and *Antigone,* meant to suggest what the scholiast thought he did. Cf. Gellie 291 n. 25. None of Knox's objections strikes me as really cogent: of course it depends on whether we think Electra's hatred capable of such an action.

46 Cf. Whitman 155. We hear nothing (apart from 602) of that common theme – the miseries of exile. See also App. D p. 336.

It is not surprising that Electra should be outraged by the sexual aspect of the situation.[47] Nor is it surprising that she should complain of her own state, long deprived of marriage and children (164f., 187f., cf. 961ff.). One might, however, hesitate to relate these things, if the *Electra* of Euripides had not been preserved. Euripides, with his ingenious device of an unconsummated marriage, presents us with a sex-starved Electra, jealous of an easy-going 'sexy' Clytemnestra; the portrait approaches caricature (or perhaps the case-book). If, as I incline to believe (the matter is beyond proof),[48] Euripides wrote first, then perhaps Sophocles has taken a hint from his predecessor, but has, as one would expect, handled the theme with more restraint. In any case it would seem perverse to deny that there is a sexual component in the Sophoclean Electra's hatred of her mother, her hatred of Aegisthus. Interesting, if so, as part of the poet's realization of Electra's state of mind.[49] But interesting also, if we notice a new factor which Sophocles has introduced into the conception of an Erinys.

Clytemnestra 'fears no Erinys', when she sleeps with Aegisthus. He is qualified as *miastor*, which might simply refer to the blood-guilt which she shares with him; and the Erinys might simply be the blood-avenger.[50] But look back to Electra's opening anapaests and the first reference to Erinyes: 'awful daughters of the gods, who look upon those who unjustly die and on those whose bed is stolen' (112ff.). And look at the language of the second stanza of the First Stasimon, immediately following the Erinys (492f.). The marriage which calls out the Fury is bloody *(μιαιφόνων)*, but it is also unlawful *(ἄλεκτρ' ἄνυμφα . . . οἷσιν οὐ θέμις)*.[51] This seems not to be Aeschylean.[52] There is adultery in the *Oresteia*, and it has its consequences,

---

[47] Little is said on this score by most interpreters, but cf. John Jones 149–53; Segal, *TAPA* 493f.

[48] See App. G p. 342.

[49] On the whole I should prefer not to use the term 'neurotic' of Electra as some writers have done: I feel it is both lacking in precision and provocative!

[50] There may be a notion similar to that of *O.T.* 821f., where Oedipus sees a pollution in sleeping with the widow of the man he has killed.

[51] The language of 136ff. is fruitfully examined by Long 136ff. See also Segal, *TAPA* 494.

[52] Does this go too far? Jones (149) certainly goes too far in the other direction, when he says that the Greeks believed 'the Furies exercised a general jurisdiction over wrongdoing within the family – over sexual offences as well as crimes of blood'. Wüst, PW Suppl. viii, s.v. Erinys, cites no instance of Erinyes punishing '*Ehebruch*' prior to our play: his other references are to Quintus Smyrnaeus and Ovid.

but the Erinyes went against Paris and Troy, not because of adultery,
but because of a breach of hospitality. For Electra – and presumably
for Sophocles – breach of marital relationship has become one of
those crimes which evoke the Fury-process. And since such crimes
tend to generate their own punishment through the resentment they
cause, it may not be too far-fetched to see the virginal Electra as an
appropriate agent for punishing the unchastity of Clytemnestra.

Clytemnestra is a wicked woman; and it is commonly held that
Sophocles has made her so bad in order to palliate the matricide.
There are indeed melodramatically bad characters in Sophocles:
Menelaus in *Ajax*, Creon in *Oedipus Coloneus*. What are we to think
of a woman who celebrates her husband's murder with a monthly
festival (277ff.)?[53] We might certainly ask how she came to hate her
husband so much and whether it was merely because he stood
between her and a lover. We might remember that the case against
her is made by a bitter woman with whom she has been for years in
mounting conflict; and that Agamemnon *did* sacrifice Iphigenia.
(Something has been said above about the artificial rhetoric with
which this theme is handled in the wrangle between mother and
daughter.) But what are we to think of a woman who prays for the
death of her son (655ff.)? When she hears the 'news' of his death,
maternal feelings return: she is sincere in what she says (766ff.), and it
is a master-stroke of Sophocles, not merely as 'a touch of psychology',
but because the brevity of their return brings out the tragic character
of the situation, when they are stifled by an over-mastering relief
from fear.[54] This is a woman who, seen in the perspective of the total

But Jones is right to refer to *Agam.* 1191ff. If the children of Thyestes owe their
status as Erinyes to a kindred murder, the adultery does have its penal consequences in which they are concerned. Aeschylus, thus, goes some way towards
the doctrine which Sophocles makes explicit. For Sophocles' interest in the tragic
aspects of sex, see chs. 4 and 5 and (for Erinyes in *Trach.*) ch. 9 pp. 212ff. It may be
worth noting that in *Electra* he has made Clytemnestra's dream specifically sexual,
her husband returning from the dead to claim his conjugal rights. (Not that I
would be bold enough to deny all sexual reference to the Aeschylean snake: any
snake today comes under suspicion, particularly in dreams!)

[53] Cf. 444–6.

[54] On Clytemnestra's feeling for Orestes Perrotta (350) has one of his not infrequent
perceptive comments: 'un rancore che è, in certo modo, sentimento materno
ricacciato dentro a forza nell' animo, snaturato e convertito in odio, ma in un odio
doloroso'. Is this one of those psychological subtleties which we are so often
exhorted to deny to Sophocles? G. Thomson, *Aeschylus and Athens* (London 1941)
356: 'her depravity too has a history'. Electra, in her urn-speech, naturally puts the

history of the house, had been brought to hate her husband and to fear her son.

The punishment of Clytemnestra did not await the sword of Orestes. For all her bravado she lived in fear. 'Fearing no Erinys': it is not true.[55] She is telling the truth when she says (780ff.): 'Neither by night nor day could sweet sleep cover my eyes, but time in its forward movement kept me living ever in the thought of death' (ἀλλ' ὁ προστατῶν | χρόνος διῆγέ μ' αἰὲν ὡς θανουμένην). She was already being punished, in the course of time, by the absent Orestes and by the all-too-present Electra – punished by fear (and fear, in Aeschylus, is an emotion which the Erinyes inspire in their victims).[56] About Electra Clytemnestra goes on to make a most revealing remark, when she says (783ff.): 'On this day I am rid of fear from her and from him. For she was the greater plague that shared the house with me, ever drinking my blood – my soul's blood – unmixed' (τοὐμὸν ἐκπίνουσ' ἀεὶ | ψυχῆς ἄκρατον αἷμα).[57] The mythological Erinyes drank the physical life-blood of their victims: Electra had been acting the Erinys to Clytemnestra, upon the mental plane, over all the long stretch of time between the murder of Agamemnon and the action of the play; and during that same stretch of time had been suffering a degradation of which she was herself aware.

worst construction (1153f.): μαίνεται δ' ὑφ' ἡδονῆς μήτηρ ἀμήτωρ, but immediately adds: ἧς ἐμοὶ σὺ πολλάκις | φήμας λάθρα προὔπεμπες ὡς φανούμενος | τιμωρὸς αὐτός. We may recall 293ff.: πλὴν ὅταν κλύῃ τινὸς | ἥξοντ' Ὀρέστην· τηνικαῦτα δ' ἐμμανὴς | βοᾷ παραστᾶσ', οὐ σύ μοι τῶνδ' αἰτία;

55 The sequence of references to divine powers at 275ff. deserves close consideration. 276: Clytemnestra fears no Erinys. 280f.: she sacrifices θεοῖσιν . . . τοῖς σωτηρίοις, i.e. to Olympian gods, especially perhaps to Zeus and Apollo. (In Aeschylus she made sacrifices to the Erinyes, *Eum.* 106ff.; spoke blasphemously of a Zeus Soter of the dead, *Agam.* 1386f.) 289ff.: she addresses Electra as δύσθεον μίσημα. The epithet is Aeschylean (cf. esp. *Cho.* 46, 191, 525, of Clytemnestra). 'δύσθεον, because Clytaemnestra thinks Agamemnon's death was a good thing, of which the σωτήριοι θεοί (having helped to bring it about) approve' (Kells). But Electra's lamentations were addressed to the nether gods, and Clytemnestra therefore prays, impudently, that they may never give her relief from those lamentations. Those gods will, however, answer her prayers with the return of Orestes. Thus the transition to 293ff.: the mad fury of Clytemnestra when she hears of Orestes. Cf. n. 53.

56 Cf. de Romilly, *CA* passim. At 447, it is worth considering whether we should not read φόβου for φόνου (cf. 427, 635f.). For confusion of the two words in MSS, see H. D. Broadhead, *Tragica* (Christchurch, N.Z. 1968) 69 n. 1.

57 Sophocles may well have had *Cho.* 577f. in mind:

φόνου δ' Ἐρινὺς οὐχ ὑπεσπανισμένη
ἄκρατον αἷμα πίεται τρίτην πόσιν.

Time.[58] There is the stretch of time which has created the situation; there is the point of time which is the moment of crisis and dramatic action. We have seen how these two aspects of time are brought together in *Ajax*. It is perhaps characteristic of the art of Sophocles to integrate them with the same skill with which he integrates character and action – if indeed a distinction can be made, since character is created by time and action occurs at a point of time. The point of time, the moment of crisis, belongs particularly to Orestes. Hence the emphasis on *kairos* in the Prologos. They have come to a point, says the Paedagogus, at which the time (*kairos*) for hesitation is past, the time for deeds is ripe (*akme*).[59] 'We shall go forward', says Orestes, 'for it is now time (*kairos*), which is the chief ruler of every action among men' (75f.). Orestes comes and acts and hopes that that is the end of it. Electra belongs to a different dimension of time, but she too is part of a drama: for her too things have come to a climax. She is at breaking-point. 'Send me my brother', she prays to the chthonian powers (117ff.), 'for I have no more the strength to bear up alone against the load of grief that weighs me down' (Jebb). And Chrysothemis tells us that the patience of her governors is now exhausted (374ff.). The time is ripe for the tragic action. First Clytemnestra, and then Aegisthus, are killed.

Why has Sophocles reversed the Aeschylean (and Euripidean) order of the deaths? Obviously, it has been said, because Aegisthus was the tougher proposition, the greater obstacle to the liberation of Electra and the house; and this has been taken as evidence that Sophocles regarded the killing of Clytemnestra as less important, the matricide as a minor issue or no issue at all. If the foregoing examination of the play has any validity, this is a view which can hardly be accepted; nor would I have thought that the episode of Clytemnestra's killing, brief though it is, and Electra's reaction to it were anything less than horrifying. Electra's 'Strike again, if you can' is enough! And is there no irony, when the Chorus immediately sings of curses (or Curses) and the vengeance of the dead? Or when Orestes comes out of the palace, his hand dripping blood, and says: 'All is well within the house, if Apollo's oracle was well' (1424f.)?[60] Horrifying

---

[58] On time in Sophocles see ch. 2 pp. 39ff.

[59] It is uncertain what we should read at the end of 21, but the point is unaffected.

[60] I would not suggest, with Bowra 253, that Orestes' own confidence in the rightness of his action is shaken, but a question could be raised. καλῶς occurs in

enough as it stands, if Clytemnestra's death had come last, it would have had to be followed by an ampler reaction and the more difficult it would have been to avoid (as Sophocles wished to avoid) more specific reference to the future, with an acceptance or a rejection of the traditional fate of Orestes. The mere fact that, in this long play, the dramatist deals so late and so rapidly with the climax of action may, moreover, indicate that he was less interested in the critical decisive moment when the Furies strike physically than in the long process of time during which, equally, they were at work.

I have spoken of ironic ambiguities in the aftermath of Clytemnestra's killing and so entered an area in which subjective judgements can hardly be avoided. Clearly, however, the more ambivalent are the reactions intended by the poet the less interested we should be in such a crude question as whether he *approved* the matricide. It can still be argued that he thought it better on the whole that Aegisthus and Clytemnestra, who could not be punished except through Agamemnon's children, should be punished even at such a cost; and that, when the Coryphaeus, seeing the hands of Orestes dripping with his mother's blood, exclaims: 'I cannot blame it' (οὐδ᾽ ἔχω ψέγειν, 1423),[61] she is speaking for the poet. Fury-justice is just: the malefactors are punished. But what of the human punishers? I have spoken of Electra as being at once the victim and the agent of the Furies; Orestes operates upon a different emotional plane, but he too, if the train of argument is valid, must be their agent, which is Aeschylean. And in Aeschylus he is their victim, which is traditional. For reasons which we have already explored Sophocles has left this traditional theme on

two of those clusters which tend to be significant in Sophocles. (i) 790, 791, 793, 816; (ii) 1305, 1320f. (bis), 1340, 1345 (bis), 1425 (bis). (i) is associated with the false news of Orestes' death, (ii) with the killing of Clytemnestra. The relationship of the two situations is brought out saliently by the corresponding prayers to Apollo (cf. Segal, *TAPA* 525f.). Clytemnestra's prayer at 637ff. is for the death of Orestes and is apparently answered by the false news from Delphi (just as, in *O.T.*, the news from Corinth seems to answer Jocasta's prayer). At 766ff., for a sincere moment, she realizes the tragic nature of the (supposed) situation, until relief from her fears swamps every other emotion; and this is what governs the irony of the repeated καλῶς. Electra prays at 1376ff., and her prayer is answered by the death-cry of Clytemnestra, followed by the double καλῶς. 'It is well within the house, if Apollo's oracle was well given.' The irony could be simple or complex, but we should at least recognize the art with which Sophocles has related the two situations.

61 Erfurdt's correction – ψέγειν for λέγειν – seems indispensable.

the margins of his drama. It can, however, be argued that, by various means, including an elaborate use of double irony, he has not only insisted upon Orestes' chthonian role but represented the punitive act as bringing disaster upon its agents; and this argument, hard though it may be to evaluate, must be presented.

I do not begin where Sheppard began, with a wrong question to the oracle.[62] If Orestes asked about means and not ends, we are given no reason to suppose that the god did not approve the end or, for that matter, that the gods of Sophocles are not behind the *lex talionis*. Later in Orestes' speech, however, there is a passage which has attracted some attention, in which he asserts, at what might seem gratuitous length (59–66), that there is really nothing sinister in the false report of his death which is to be made. Sophocles does not waste lines.[63] Was it his intention to make the mission of Orestes appear sinister – so that a cloud, we might say, comes over the bright early morning sun?[64] The passage is, in any case, preparation for one of the most striking features of the play.

The false report is duly delivered by the Paedagogus. It is a *tour de force* of a Messenger speech, rivalling the most elaborate efforts of Euripides in that kind; and it is devoted to the presentation of a lie![65] The speech is heard by two women, whose contrasted reactions constitute a powerful dramatic effect. It is also heard by us the audience. And how do we react? Orestes rejects the notion that it might be ominous to be spoken of as dead: when his 'death' is described with all the power of Sophoclean rhetoric, what do we forebode? 'As we listen', writes one sensitive critic, 'we realise that he is doomed.'[66] Audience-reactions no doubt differ, but it is worth

---

[62] Kells also takes this view, but cf. Bowra 215–18.

[63] Eight lines to make a point which, if it accords with Greek attitudes, hardly seems to be demanded. Sophocles had become interested in Shamans and drags them in? This will not commend itself to those who appreciate the economy of his writing. (Eur. *Helen* 1050–2 is similar, and A. M. Dale suggests that it cross-refers to our play.)

[64] Cf. 17–19. Day and night constitute a structural theme in *Oresteia*. In *Agam.* the day belies its promise: how will it be in this case? As Jebb writes in his note on 17f.? Perhaps; perhaps not. On the *dolos*-theme, cf. Segal, *TAPA* 510ff.

[65] 'Nicht viel mehr als ein Virtuosenstück' (Reinhardt 161, though he does not leave it at that). We must certainly allow its virtuosity, while hesitating to conclude with Ronnet (217f.) that 'le morceau est un intermède, destiné non aux person-nages, mais aux spectateurs, qui laisse à penser que Sophocle ne prend pas sa pièce tout à fait au sérieux'!

[66] G. Thomson (op. cit. n. 53) 357. One has heard it stated and denied with equal

considering whether Sophocles may not have wished to convey an impression that Orestes really did suffer disaster through his Pythian associations.

If Orestes rises from the dead, it is to play a chthonian role as the avenger of his dead father – by an act of matricide. The scenes which intervene between the Messenger speech and the Recognition can be seen as full of an elaborate double irony, the truth being more horrible than the tormenting lie.[67] The joy of recognition, when it comes, is cut short by the necessity of ruthless action. Rejoicing is postponed till success has been won (1299f.): but what promise of happiness is held by the nights and days which await Electra and her friends (1364–6)?[68] There is much talk of finality: but can there be an end to the Fury-process?

We have seen that the murder of Clytemnestra is attended with Aeschylean echoes. Nor are they absent from the closing scene with Aegisthus, in which nothing is more striking than the exchanges when he unveils the corpse (1475–80). Orestes taunts him. Aegisthus exclaims: 'Who are these men into the midst of whose net I have fallen?' Not men, but Furies: it is the Oresteian metaphor. 'Do you not see that you are bandying words with the dead?' 'I read the riddle', replies Aegisthus, using the very words which Clytemnestra had used (*Cho.* 887f.) in answer to a similar riddling equation of the living and the dead. It is Orestes; it is a Fury; it is the dead.[69] Orestes

vehemence by spectators (and readers) that disbelief is involuntarily suspended by the power of the narrative, i.e. that they react emotionally as though it were true. The matter is not worth arguing: some people react one way, some the other. Were the Greeks, with their ready response to rhetoric, more likely or, with their strong sense of reality, less likely than some members of a modern audience to be so carried away? He would be a clever man who could answer that question.

If we ask why Sophocles set the false story in Delphi (with that anachronistic updating of the Pythian games which worried Aristotle's generation so much), it may not be the sole and sufficient reason that this brings out the irony of Clytemnestra's prayer (see n. 60).

[67] Cf. nn. 9 and 60.

[68] Nights and days: 86ff (Electra's); 78off. (Clytemnestra's); 1364ff. (Electra's again).

[69] The significance of these lines was pointed out to me by Professor Thomas Gould in private correspondence. Nets and snares abound in *Oresteia*: note esp. *Agam.* 1580, spoken by Aegisthus over the body of Agamemnon, where there is a strong case for reading πάγαις with Nauck (ὑφαντοῖς ἐν πάγαις Ἐρινύων), cf. *Trach.* 1050–2. The text of 1478 is disputed. Tyrwhitt's popular emendation ζῶντας is rejected, rightly, in favour of the received text (ζῶν τοῖς) by G. A. Longman (*CR* 6 (1954) 192–4) and Dawe; Kells and Kamerbeek are dubious. The prefix ἀντι- with a verb of saying can hardly connote anything but speaking in reply, in turn,

taunts him with his failure as a prophet ($\mu\acute{\alpha}\nu\tau\iota\varsigma$). But we are not done
with the theme of prophecy. At 1497ff. Aegisthus asks whether the
house need see the ills of the Pelopidae, present and to come; and
Orestes, claiming to be a first-rate prophet, limits those future ills to
the death of Aegisthus. He could be right, but he could be wrong.
Aegisthus has the last word: it was not from Agamemnon that
Orestes had inherited his gift of prophecy. Prophets and prophecy:
we may recall the First Stasimon, where the coming of Justice, the
coming of the Erinys, was embraced by a twofold reference to this
theme.[70] We may remember that this was followed by the story of
Pelops and a chariot-wreck – and the question whether since that day
torment and trouble have ever failed in the house. Have they failed
now?

We are left wondering, and on many of these points there will
never be agreement between critics.[71] On one point, however,
Sophocles has surely left us in no doubt, which is that we cannot
understand the action and the personages without regard to the
Aeschylean conception of the Furies. If this is a grim play, it is because

or in opposition, cf. 1501 below and (with $\emph{ἴσα}$) *O.T.* 409. 'You, though living, are
bandying words with the dead on equal terms'. On equal terms (*pace* Dawe, *STS*
202), because he is himself virtually a dead man. τοῖς θανοῦσι refers to Agamemnon and to the son, his surrogate, who has risen from the 'dead' to avenge him. In
so far as we need to pin down the highly suggestive language, this seems the
simplest way of doing it.

[70] See p. 218 above.

[71] Two of the most stimulating recent contributions to the criticism of the play came
from the United States in the 1960s: by T. M. Woodard, '*Electra* by Sophocles: the
dialectical design', Part I, *HSCP* 68 (1964) 163–205; Part II, *HSCP* 70 (1965)
195–233, and by C. P. Segal, 'The *Electra* of Sophocles', *TAPA* 97 (1966) 473–545.
Both articles investigate the language of the play in considerable detail. I have
referred elsewhere to Woodard's valuable examination of *logos, ergon,* and similar
words, though this leads him along paths which I cannot always follow. In
general he casts an eye of almost unqualified favour upon Electra and Orestes: it
only needs a combination of their respective virtues to provide the perfect team
for a completely laudable action. Segal's article, written with knowledge of
Woodard's, takes (as I see it) a much better balanced view of the play, which he
regards as essentially 'a play of inversions and reversals'. Exploring the ambiguities, bringing out the sinister reverse of the bright surface, he arrives at a view
which is not very different from that which I have tried to present; and it may be
simply for this reason that his article strikes me as a notably successful application
of the critical methods he employs. Though he has a good deal to say about
retaliation, I feel, however, that perhaps he misses the clue provided by the
Aeschylean conception of the Erinyes, which itself involves the tragic duality he
finds in the Sophoclean play.

Furies have been and are at work with the result that only deplorable alternatives are open. Which brings us back to Electra, with whom any consideration of the play must end. And we must face a crucial issue central to Sophoclean heroism, here focused on yet another controversial choral ode.

We have seen Electra as victim and agent of the Furies. She is also a Sophoclean hero, with all that courageous idealism and preoccupation with honour which we associate with such heroes. For some these two notions may not lie too happily together in the mind. We must return to Electra – and to Chrysothemis, with whom she shares two important scenes. The deplorable alternatives are action and inaction. Electra acts (or would act), her sister refrains from action; Electra is heroic, her sister is unheroic. It is not only that Sophocles is, *more suo*, illuminating his heroine by a character-contrast: it is largely through the two Chrysothemis-scenes that he presents the issues of heroism and its reverse. It may be important to observe the terms in which they are presented. We have already seen how, in the exchanges between Electra and Clytemnestra, the semblance of rationality proves to be illusory and irrelevant. The exchanges between Electra and Chrysothemis turn largely upon the significance to be attached to *sophrosune* (and its equivalents), to *nous* and *gnome*. The contexts of the two debates are different. In the first, the point at issue is Electra's excessive lamentation, already censured by the sympathetic Chorus. It is a matter of words. But words can be a form of action, or so Electra thinks (256, 258, 350, 357f.), though her sensible sister is contemptuous of seeming action which does no actual harm (336). (But would Clytemnestra agree? Does not the word of hate have its place along with the bloody stroke?)[72] Electra, who had admitted (307f.) that *sophrosune* (as generally understood) was ruled out by circumstances, tells Chrysothemis that neither would she, if she were *sophron*, desire the privileges she gained by compliance (365). Chrysothemis later rejoins (394) that Electra's life might have been a good one, if only she had known how to be sensible[73] But was not the sister's life too good, her moral position undercut by the practical advantages she enjoyed? Electra is extreme, but not outrageous. Chrysothemis admits the justice of her case. At the end of the

---

[72] See p. 223 above.
[73] Cf. 343, 345f. (where I follow Jebb), 384, 390, 398.

scene, with the matter of Clytemnestra's offerings, the moral issue takes a twist. An action is required. Will Chrysothemis throw them away? She will do it, says the Coryphaeus, if she means to be *sophron* (464f.); and choruses are good judges of *sophrosune*. She passes this minor test, though with misgivings.

By the second scene circumstances have changed. Orestes is 'dead', and Chrysothemis is confronted with Electra's resolve to kill Aegisthus. Now words of more specifically intellectual import proliferate.[74] When Chrysothemis has made her first speech in reply, the Coryphaeus says to Electra (1015f.); 'Be persuaded; there is no better gain for men to win than forethought ($\pi\rho o\nu o i a s$) and a wise mind ($\nu o \hat{u} \sigma o \phi o \hat{u}$).' Chrysothemis uses her brain, and it is she for the most part who employs rational terms, while the only folly Electra admits is that which she would show if she attempted to persuade her sister. But there is a logic in her position, if a logic which has nothing to do with argument. If we take the two debates together – one concerned with words and the other with deeds, we must recognize that Electra's new decision to act, mad though it may be in the eyes of Chrysothemis and of the world, was the only decision fully consistent with her earlier attitude. It is in the nature of a hero to maintain such a consistency in the teeth of facts and regard it as true wisdom.

It is in the nature of a hero to sacrifice everything, even life, to the pursuit of a noble design; and this is a point of honour. This theme emerges strongly in the second Chrysothemis-scene where Electra tries to persuade her sister that by killing Aegisthus they would not only show piety ($\epsilon \hat{v} \sigma \epsilon \beta \epsilon \iota a$) but also win *eukleia* (973ff., 984ff.).[75] Her final eloquent appeal ends with the words: 'To live basely is base for the nobly born' ($\zeta \hat{\eta} \nu$ $a \hat{\iota} \sigma \chi \rho \grave{o} \nu$ $a \hat{\iota} \sigma \chi \rho \hat{\omega} s$ $\tau o \hat{\iota} s$ $\kappa a \lambda \hat{\omega} s$ $\pi \epsilon \phi \nu \kappa \acute{o} \sigma \iota \nu$, 989). So Ajax felt. And Electra, like Ajax (*Ajax* 479f.), feels that the only permissible alternatives are honourable success or an honourable death: 'Even alone, I would not have failed in both – I would have saved myself honourably or honourably perished' (1319–21).[76] The theme had been picked up in the choral ode which follows the exit of

---

[74] Between 1013 and 1057 there are no fewer than seventeen terms which imply (more or less) rational consideration.

[75] The point is answered (with some confusion of thought?) by Chrysothemis at 1005f., when she says there is no advantage $\beta \acute{a} \xi \iota \nu$ $\kappa a \lambda \grave{\eta} \nu$ $\lambda a \beta \acute{o} \nu \tau \epsilon$ $\delta \nu \sigma \kappa \lambda \epsilon \hat{\omega} s$ $\theta a \nu \epsilon \hat{\iota} \nu$.

[76] $\dot{\omega} s$ $\dot{\epsilon} \gamma \grave{\omega}$ $\mu \acute{o} \nu \eta$
          $o \dot{\nu} \kappa$ $\ddot{a} \nu$ $\delta \nu o \hat{\iota} \nu$ $\ddot{\eta} \mu a \rho \tau o \nu \cdot$ $\ddot{\eta}$ $\gamma \grave{a} \rho$ $\ddot{a} \nu$ $\kappa a \lambda \hat{\omega} s$
          $\ddot{\epsilon} \sigma \omega \sigma^{,}$ $\dot{\epsilon} \mu a \nu \tau \acute{\eta} \nu$, $\ddot{\eta}$ $\kappa a \lambda \hat{\omega} s$ $\dot{a} \pi \omega \lambda \acute{o} \mu \eta \nu$.   (1319-21)

Chrysothemis. For Electra had converted the Chorus: if the Coryphaeus had commended the rationality of the sister, the ode expresses not only sympathy but admiration and support for the heroine.[77] 'There is none of the *agathoi* that deigns by living a cowardly life to shame his fair repute and let his name perish' (οὐδεὶς τῶν ἀγαθῶν ζῶν κακῶς εὔκλειαν αἰσχῦναι θέλει νώνυμος, 1082ff.). 'As you too, my child, . . .' – and so on, in a corrupt text![78] A little later, at the end of the ode, they sing that, evil as her fate may be, she is, in regard to the greatest laws that grow, winning the noblest prize by piety towards Zeus (1093–7).[79] She is, that is to say, obeying the law which enjoins respect for parents.

We think of Antigone; and Sophocles, when he wrote *Electra*, must have thought of that earlier play about two sisters, one of whom was heroic. Where he seems to repeat an effect, the difference is often instructive.[80] Electra and Antigone are alike formidable, alike in their lonely and obstinate courage, alike in their single-minded devotion to a duty imposed, as they see it, by kinship. Of the two principal differences between the persons, the first is a matter of time-scale. Antigone is little more than a child; and though she too has been moulded by a past of unexampled horror (so that she is half in love with death), she has not suffered from long eroding years of hatred like Electra; and her concern is with love.[81] And that brings us to the second difference. The duty imposed upon Antigone is that of burial, and humane feeling goes alone with it (if 'political' sense demurs); she

[77] Whether we must always look for complete consistency between a Coryphaeus addressing trimeters to the actors and the Chorus as a whole functioning on the lyric plane is a big question which cannot be explored here. In this case it may be noted that, if dedicated to *sophrosune*, they are also dedicated to the cause of Electra. Immediately after the opening *kommos*, the Coryphaeus had said: 'I came in pursuit of your welfare no less than my own. If I do not speak well, do you prevail. We will follow you' (251–3). On the change of attitude, see also Gellie 120.

[78] On the text of 1085ff., which is almost certainly corrupt, see *BICS* 26 (1979) 9f.

[79]
ἐπεί σ᾽ ἐφηύρηκα μοί-
ρᾳ μὲν οὐκ ἐν ἐσθλᾷ
βεβῶσαν, ἃ δὲ μέγιστ᾽ ἔβλαστε νόμιμα, τῶνδε φερομέναν
ἄριστα τᾷ Ζηνὸς εὐσεβείᾳ.   (1093–7)

[80] There is nothing in Chrysothemis to compare with Ismene's tormented affection for her sister. Perrotta 338: 'Fa maraviglia, anzi, che qualche volta i critici abbian preferito Crisotemi a Ismene.' I share his astonishment: see p. 239 above. See also Pohlenz II 91f. (for detailed correspondences); Reinhardt 155ff.

[81] See p. 135.

causes the death of herself alone. Electra's task is to kill or abet a
killing – and to kill a mother, against which humane feeling revolts,
but out of passionate grief and resentment for a father's death, to
which humane feeling responds. Antigone's dilemma, of which she is
oblivious, disappears in the course of the play, as state authority comes
to be identified with the ill-judged decision of a tyrant; Electra's
dilemma, of which she is not totally unaware, is inherent in the *lex
talionis* as applied to the extreme case of a father and a mother.

We revert to an area of controversy. The matricide: does it matter
to Sophocles, as it mattered to Aeschylus, that in avenging a father the
children are killing a mother? Or did he make the mother so bad in
order to mitigate the matricide? We might expect guidance from a
choral ode, not least from an ode so placed as the Second Stasimon. It
is in fact one of the most difficult choruses in Sophocles to interpret;
and we are not helped by a defective textual tradition.

The ode lies between the desperate resolve of Electra and the appearance of Orestes, between the wrangle with Chrysothemis over 'wisdom' and the sequence of events which leads up to the murders. As we
have seen, the Chorus picks up a theme from Electra, when they
praise her for the nobility of her resolve. They also pick up the theme
of wisdom, on which the dispute between the sisters had turned. They
pick it up at the beginning of their song, when they refer to the
'wisdom' of birds shown by their filial piety (we shall return to this);
and at the end they sing of Electra as winning a reputation for *sophia* as
well as *arete*.[82] She is truly wise; she is living up to a code of honour;

[82] How can the Chorus now be attributing *sophia* to Electra, when the Coryphaeus
had commended the *nous sophos* of Chrysothemis? Kells feels this difficulty so
strongly that he advances an ingenious new interpretation of this difficult passage.
Reading τὰ μὴ κάλ' οὐ καθοπλίσασα, he interprets the statement as saying that
Electra, in rejecting the dishonourable prudence of her sister, has *rejected* the
ambition to be called 'clever' as well as 'good'. His trump card is *Phil.* 117–19,
where Odysseus tries to persuade Neoptolemus that this combination is precisely
what he can achieve; and it is a fact that, to judge by Euripides, the standards by
which conduct should be judged – the modern *sophon*-standard and the traditional *kalon*-standard – were in the late fifth century a matter of strong debate (cf.
Arethusa 2 (1969) 139 n. 5). Nevertheless, I find it hard to suppose that the Chorus
is in fact denying *sophia* to Electra, particularly as this would by implication deny
that it was *sophon* to obey the 'greatest ordinances' and show *eusebeia* towards
Zeus. It seems more likely that, having answered Chrysothemis' claims to τὸ
φρονεῖν by reference to the φρονιμώτατοι οἰωνοί, they now go farther by
attributing *sophia* to Electra.

she is pious. The ode closes with the words 'piety towards Zeus'.

And her piety is shown by observance of the greatest of all ordinances (ἃ μέγιστ᾽ ἔβλαστε νόμιμα). We think of Antigone, rejecting the man-made decree of Creon as not emanating from Zeus, preferring to observe 'the unwritten and unfailing ordinances of the gods'.[83] In both cases the law imposes a duty upon the kin and towards kin; in both cases it comes to be applied in a context of death. Antigone's duty is to bury, and the interest of the nether gods is involved. Electra's duty is to kill and, in this passage, Zeus is the only god who is mentioned. But this is not the first reference to Zeus in the ode.

'No, by the lightning-flash of Zeus, by heavenly Themis, they shall not long be free of trouble' (ἀλλ᾽ οὐ τὰν Διὸς ἀστραπὰν καὶ τὰν οὐρανίαν Θέμιν δαρὸν οὐκ ἀπόνητοι, 1063–5). It has been strangely supposed[84] that the commonplace Chrysothemis, whose good sense the Coryphaeus had praised at 1015f., is now being threatened with the weapons of divine vengeance, supernal and infernal! The clue will be found, if we look back to 823ff., the first choral reaction to the news of Orestes' 'death'. 'Where are the thunderbolts of Zeus, where is the blazing sun, if they can look on these things and, inactive, let them lie hidden?'[85] Here, as there, like simple people they are thinking such wickedness is *bound* to be punished, the bolt of Zeus *must* enforce heavenly Themis. But how often does he punish homicide with the thunderbolt? Does he not rather work with and through the nether powers? So now the thoughts of the Chorus turn to the dead and they send a message, reminiscent of the great *kommos* in *Choephori*,[86] to the Atridae in the world below (τοῖς ἔνερθ᾽ Ἀτρείδαις, 1068). This plural has caused undue concern: 'the refer-

---

[83] *Ant.* 450ff.

[84] Not, however, by Σ or Dain–Mazon p. 176 n. 2 or Kells p. 180. The connection of thought at 1063 is through an unexpressed middle term, which is 'vengeance'. Unexpressed, but implied, since they see this as part of the duty of children to parents, which the instinctive 'wisdom' of Electra has perceived. The figurative terms, however, in which they are made to express the notion are such as to remind us of the complex web of child–parent relationships which the total situation has involved. (See text below.)

[85] It is the function of the sun to reveal, not to hide. For the over-seeing Zeus, cf. 175.

[86] With ὀνείδη (1069), cf. *Cho.* 495.

ence', says Jebb, 'is to Agamemnon only'.[87] Certainly there can be no thought of Menelaus. But what of Orestes, who, as they now believe, has joined the family dead in Hades. And from Hades an answer does come; and the answer is Orestes returned from the 'dead' to execute a justice which is, as in Aeschylus, that of the dead, of the Furies, and of Zeus.

To say that it is wrathful and violent invites the reply that it is deserved, as indeed it is. To say that it is, in its nature, reproductive of evil – that Orestes and Electra are taking over the roles which, in the earlier phase, were played by Aegisthus and Clytemnestra – may seem to beg a question. But, in this ode, the Chorus sings of Electra that 'she has no thought for death, she is ready to quit the light, if only she could destroy the twin Erinys' (1078ff.). Clytemnestra as well as Aegisthus, they are twinned as an evil spirit plaguing the house. But could Sophocles have meant so little by so big a word? Could it mean less than that they had themselves been instruments of divine punishment as Orestes and Electra were to be?[88] Could it be that Electra has inherited her mother's role? That is not what the Chorus sing: they sing 'Who could be born a truer child of her father?' (1081).

Parents and children. Birds have a wisdom in this matter, the old caring for the young, the young for the old. The opening sentence of the ode has caused some surprise. Why birds? Why call them 'wise' or 'sensible' (φρονιμώτατοι)? Clearly, the word cannot be dissociated from the φρονεῖν, φρονεῖ of Chrysothemis' last speech (1056) and the whole theme of the preceding stichomythia; and the point must be to indicate that Electra shows a wisdom in her filial piety which, like that of birds, is instinctive rather than rational. Perhaps the matter can be taken a little further. It is generally assumed that the birds' 'care to nourish' (τροφὰς κηδομένους) is in respect of parents only, but this suits neither the facts nor the *topos* nor the structure of the sentence.[89]

---

[87] Jebb's parallels (*El.* 1419; Aesch. *Cho.* 49) are vague masculine plurals without a name. Kamerbeek remarks that 'σφιν 1070 makes Jebb's interpretation dubious'. The latter's note on *O.C.* 1490 is illuminating on the possibility of singular σφιν. The form is normally plural, but there are cases where it might be natural to take it as singular, though in several of these it could be taken of 'X and his associates'. Here, after τοῖς 'Ατρείδαις it is naturally taken as plural, though Agamemnon is principally in mind. I have little doubt that plurals were used because of the supposed presence of Orestes in the lower world.

[88] On 199f. see discussion in App. D p. 337.

[89] The *topos,* i.e. reciprocal obligation as between parents and children, is illustrated from the behaviour of storks at Arist. *Birds* 1355f. It is generally assumed that the

The relationship is, or should be, reciprocal: parents nurture their children in infancy and in return are cared for in their old age. Basic to Greek family ethics, this relationship had been breached again and again in the sad history of the house of Atreus, in which parents and children had been constantly at variance. Agamemnon had sacrificed his daughter and Clytemnestra has prayed for the death of her son. Now at last, in the reverse relation, there seems to be a clear issue, when Electra and Orestes set out to repay a debt to their father. This, however, they can only do by destroying the life of the other parent. They are repaying the debt of nurture: but who, if not the mother, is the child's immediate source of *trophe?*[90]

The dilemma is Aeschylean. It is the primary point of controversy in the interpretation of this play whether it is Sophoclean also, whether in obeying the law of Zeus they are not inevitably breaching it. Electra considers one parent only as worthy of the name, as the source of her nature and the object of her emulation. She would be *eupatris,* and is called so by the Chorus in this ode (1081).[91] Electra no doubt thinks that she derives from her father the courage and loyalty which she also demands of her brother. *Phusis* is said to be – and to some extent is – an important notion in Sophocles:[92] not particularly prominent in this play, it does occur. It occurs, doubly, at 608f., to close Electra's long speech which began with reason and ended with passion – and an avowal that she has raised Orestes to avenge.[93] Therefore, she goes on, let Clytemnestra call her villainous or terma-

---

entire phrase ἀφ' ὧν τε βλαστῶσιν . . . εὕρωσι refers to parents, but the form of expression ἀφ' ὧν τε . . . ἀφ' ὧν τε is strongly against this, being proper to two sets of persons. (According to Kamerbeek, the repetition lends urgency to the words, but this is not quite convincing.) Kells points out that ὄνησις and similar words are commonly used of the benefits derived by parents from children (though I cannot follow him when he suggests that the Chorus has in mind a breach of duty on the part of the dead Agamemnon, who should not come into the stanza so early). ἐπ' ἴσας, at 1062, is generally taken to refer to an equality between humans and birds: may it not rather refer to the reciprocal relationship of parents and children?

[90] Cf. Segal, *TAPA* 488, 499f.

[91] With her new role Electra assumes the epithet (εὔπατρις) which both the Chorus and she herself had applied to Orestes in a variant form: 162 (εὐπατρίδαν), and, in the negative context, 857 (εὐπατρίδων).

[92] See ch. 13 p. 308.

[93] As a *miastor* (603). This, like certain other words, has a sort of reciprocal sense: it is used normally of one who pollutes by an act of bloodshed – and seems to be so used of Aegisthus at 275, but may also be used of one who avenges such an act (cf. Aesch. *Eum.* 178). Should one see an ambiguity here?

gant or full of shamelessness. 'For if I am by nature (πέφυκα) knowledgeable of such deeds, I can scarcely be said to disgrace your nature (φύσιν).'[94] Is not Sophocles here – and perhaps in the whole of the scene – bringing out a dreadful similarity between mother and daughter? Could it not be that the violence and extremism of Electra are part of her inheritance in the female line? That heredity as well as circumstance has contributed to making her what she is? It is, then, a mother whose *phusis* she shares whose life she is determined to take.

If this is a right way of looking at it, we have an example of the depth and complexity in which Sophocles envisaged the people and situations of his dramas. And it should discourage us from giving glib answers to crude questions. Was Electra right or wrong? Right or wrong to abandon *sophrosune* in lamenting her father, to disregard reality in her plan to kill Aegisthus, to disregard the sacred tie of blood between herself and her mother? If Electra was wrong, then Chrysothemis was right; and even the Chorus of ordinary women do not reach this absurd conclusion. Or are they both wrong? If so, it is not that the wit of man can discover some just point dictated by wisdom and moderation between the excess of Electra and the defect of Chrysothemis.[95] It is that, in the tragic circumstances, there is no mode of conduct which can be truly salutary and truly laudable.

Electra is *eupatris, euklees, sophe, ariste, eusebes*. She is also a woman (like her mother) of violence in word and deed; she is a Fury, a wrathful agent of infernal powers; she is a willing matricide. She is a Sophoclean hero. And she operates within a world of Sophoclean gods: an Apollo who recommends a vengeance of Aeschylean craft, and a Zeus who demands a vengeance which, as in Aeschylus, is itself a crime against the law it follows, a Zeus who, as in Aeschylus, stands in close relation to the Furies.[96]

This is a grim play – grimmer perhaps than *Oedipus Coloneus*. For, though that play too deals with the activity of Furies, there is

---

[94] Segal, *TAPA* 499.

[95] This is brought out by the rather absurd comment of the Coryphaeus at 369–71. For what would be the programme of such a compromise? Only at the end of the scene, on one particular issue, does a compromise become possible, when Chrysothemis is urged to throw away or bury Clytemnestra's offerings. This course is commended as *sophron* by the Coryphaeus and accepted, though with qualms, by Chrysothemis. (See p. 240.)

[96] On Sophoclean heroes and Sophoclean gods, see ch. 13.

Antigone, with her noble failures; there is Theseus, who represents a land where the Furies are, with some right, worshipped as Eumenides; there is the solemn passing of Oedipus, with its mysterious hints of reconciliation. Nevertheless, there is a common background of ideas to the two plays; and this background is Aeschylean. It may be that, in his last phase, Sophocles, brooding over the thought of his great predecessor, as he never ceased to brood, brought his own tragic thought to its most mature expression. But this view of *Oedipus Coloneus* must now be justified.

CHAPTER ELEVEN

Oedipus at Colonus

The play has been seen in many lights: as a re-treatment, perhaps a re-thinking, of the Oedipus story, and so in some sense a sequel to the *Tyrannus*;[1] as an Athenian play, first and foremost, glorifying Athens in her traditional role as protector of the oppressed; as a study in the nature of a *heros* and the process of becoming one; as the final testament of a poet on the threshold of death. Perhaps all these ways of looking at the play have a legitimate basis, even those which might appear somewhat remote from one another. It is indeed full of clashes and seeming contradictions: between the love of Oedipus for his daughters and his hatred for his sons, between the beauty of the grove of the Eumenides and the terror which it inspires, between Justice and Pity; above all, between the miseries of Oedipus, past and present, and the destiny which awaits him when he goes, attended by the king of Athens, 'to keep a strange appointment with heaven'.[2] This last has been recognized to be the central mystery. What does it mean? And how is it related to the entire action of a lengthy play? This action – of the longest extant tragedy – is sometimes said to be episodic, which is, I suppose, a polite word for rambling. That the play unfolds with a certain amplitude, a lack of hurry, can hardly be denied, whether or not we choose to attribute this to the old age of a nonagenarian poet.[3] The structure, however, may be tighter and more symmetrical than has always been observed. We must look for the points of rest, and we shall find that they do not often correspond to those points at which

---

[1] Whitman 203; Letters 285; Burian 429 n. 48 (on the symmetrical, but inverse, design of the two plays). This chapter repeats much of what I have said about the play in *JHS* 74 (1954) 16–24 and in Anderson (ed.), 31–50.

[2] Kitto, *GT* 393.

[3] See Jebb's sceptical remarks at p. xliii.

episodes are separated by stasima.[4] As I see it, the play falls into five main movements.[5]

In the first movement, Oedipus enters, led by Antigone – a blind beggar. Antigone describes the grove[6] and seats her father upon a rock. A man of the neighbourhood approaches and bids Oedipus leave his seat, for he is on ground sacred to the Eumenides. Oedipus refuses to move; the stranger goes to consult his fellow-villagers, who will be the Chorus. But Oedipus, when he heard that he had come to a seat of these awesome goddesses, remembered an oracle of Phoebus that in such a place he would end his troubles and his life. He prays to them and then, as the villagers approach, he and Antigone enter the grove. The Parodos takes the form of a *kommos* and falls into two halves. The first half is concerned with the unlawful presence of Oedipus in the grove; and at the end of it Oedipus agrees to return to profane ground, on the advice of Antigone, who guides his faltering steps to a new seat. Then comes the revelation of his identity, which strikes the Chorus with such horror that they threaten to expel him from their land. First Antigone pleads in song (237ff,); she evokes pity, but no concession. Then Oedipus speaks, and his speech is a claim to be guiltless. He argues the case, and he chides the Chorus; and so impressed are they that they agree to leave him where he is and send for the king, for Theseus. This is a point of rest, and it ends the first movement of the play (309), which has been concerned with Oedipus and the Eumenides, with Oedipus and the men of Colonus. It contains a striking double action which is the entry of Oedipus into the grove and his retreat from it. There is a strong sense of locality: the grove, Colonus – and Athens.[7] For at the end Oedipus, who has

---

4 Cf. Linforth (1951) 153 on the Creon-sequence.

5 Bowra, 311, prefers to see it as three movements, taking my first and second, my third and fourth, as each being one, but this obscures the balance between the second and fourth. Linforth (1951) 189f., shows a feeling for the structure of the piece, in which he sees a resemblance to sonata form in music.

6 Clearly this serves a double function: to inform the audience and to emphasize the blindness of Oedipus.

7 Cf. J. Jones 222ff.; Vidal-Naquet 168; Gellie 160. The sense of locality is also strong in *Philoctetes* (not so much, *pace* Jones 219, in *Electra*). In the present play its explicit importance is limited to the opening and the close, but once established it will no doubt stick in the mind of the audience, with the help of the stage-picture. Appendix E studies the employment of words of locality in the opening scene and other aspects of the theme.

already hinted at the benefits which he can confer upon Athens, is in a fair way to winning protection when Theseus comes. There is nothing, on the other hand, about Thebes or the circumstances of his banishment, other than the well-known horrors of his career.

The entry of Ismene (in mid-episode) changes this. Instead of the narrow local concentration and the religious atmosphere, the horizons expand and politics enters the field. While Antigone was tending her blind father in his wanderings, Ismene had remained in Thebes to watch his interests there. Now she comes with important news. The sons of Oedipus, who had at first left the throne to their uncle Creon, have now become rivals. Eteocles, the younger, has driven Polynices into exile; and Polynices is bringing an army from Argos against his native city. This is not all. An oracle has come from Phoebus about Oedipus: 'In life as in death he shall yet be sought by the men of Thebes for their welfare's sake' (389f.). Old emotions stir in Oedipus, but when he learns that the intention is merely to bring him under Theban control and not even to bury him, when dead, upon Theban soil, his reaction is terrible and he curses his sons (421ff.); or, if he does not actually curse them, he prays, terribly, to their disadvantage. He is confident that, with the help of Athens and the Awful Goddesses, he will bring suffering upon his enemies (457ff.). The Awful Goddesses: and now the Chorus bids Oedipus make his peace with them by a rite of purification, which is described in detail; the tone is solemn, quiet, harmonious. Ismene goes to perform the rite on behalf of Oedipus.[8] The Chorus breaks into song and questions him about his terrible past; and once again he maintains that he is guiltless. Then Theseus enters. This part of the play is full of strong contrasts: the threatening prayer against the sons, the austere beauty of the sacrifice, the passionate lyric dialogue about Laius and Jocasta, the entry of Theseus, noble and humane. It is not episodic, for (as we shall see) the contrasts are carefully designed; and it is the function of this part of the second movement to bring back in a new context the themes of the first. With Theseus there is no need for Oedipus to plead or argue. He

---

[8] This is a dramaturgical necessity: it could be something more. 498f. (after 488) are strangely impressive and seem to relate to the role played by Antigone and Ismene in the play. It is wholly appropriate that a rite intended to secure the *eumeneia* of the Eumenides should be performed by one of those who are themselves characterized by *eunoia*. Was the rite actually carried out before Ismene was seized by Creon? We are not told. The description of the rite is more important than its performance.

makes his simple request, a grave in Attica, through which he will himself confer a benefit, since the possession of his grave will protect Athens against Thebes, when the time comes that it is needed. Theseus places Oedipus in charge of the men of Colonus and leaves the stage. Once again, we have reached a point of rest, with Oedipus now firmly under the protection of the king of Athens. Here at this major pause in the action, Sophocles places the most famous of his songs. It separates the second and third movements of the play.

The third – and longest – movement includes the whole episode (in the modern sense) of Creon. It had already been hinted that Creon would come, on behalf of Thebes, to secure the person of Oedipus; and immediately after the ode he enters with an armed escort. Creon is a character of unrelieved badness – as bad as Theseus is good. Creon is an old man, as Oedipus is old; and, as we shall see, the quality of the scene between them is partly determined by this fact. Creon tries to persuade Oedipus to return to Thebes, but Oedipus knows the offer is not sincere. Creon then reveals that he has already seized Ismene and proceeds to seize Antigone also. The Chorus is powerless to prevent her removal, but they so anger Creon that he now threatens to lay hands on Oedipus, who curses him. Then, in the nick of time (the cliché imposes itself), comes Theseus. He sends a force to rescue the women and upbraids Creon with his lawless conduct. Creon affects surprise that Athens should harbour the polluted Oedipus and so evokes from him the third, the last and longest, of his pleas of guiltlessness. Theseus leaves the stage, taking Creon as his guide perforce. Oedipus is left alone with the Chorus, who sing of the armed clash which they imagine to be taking place between the forces of Creon and those of Theseus.[9] At the close of the ode, Theseus

---

[9] 1044ff. What actually happened? 'The poet has left the details of the rescue indistinct' (Jebb on 1055); and the last thing he wished was to encumber his play with a messenger-speech at this point or a long account by Theseus. This was a problem often faced by the Greek dramatists and handled in different ways (cf. *Arethusa* 2 (1969), 134, with n. 52). Here Sophocles uses the imagination of the Chorus to present the struggle which Theseus (1148) declines to narrate. Did he also wish his audience to remember an occasion in 407 B.C. in which Athenian cavalry had defeated a Theban force, in the neighbourhood of Colonus? This has been a matter of debate (cf. Rosenmeyer, *Phoenix* 100 n. 34). On the whole it seems likely there had been such a skirmish, and not unlikely that, among other motives, Sophocles, writing in the closing years of the Peloponnesian War, wished to encourage his fellow-countrymen with the idea that they had divine

returns, bringing Antigone and Ismene back to their father, who greets them with passionate relief and gives thanks to their liberator. So ends the third movement. It is a miniature drama, and on a traditional theme, which is Athens protecting the suppliant. It is a melodrama: the villainous Creon, the exemplary Theseus, the abduction, the father's curse, and the rescue. In form a melodrama, it also deals with issues of political conduct, and in it Theseus and his Athenians play the fine role. And of course Oedipus is far more than the victim of a melodramatic intrigue. At least he is a victim who can strike back, if only with words – with curses and with arguments. If the action is melodramatic, the words are tragic. At the close of the movement, Oedipus is again at rest, secure in the protection of Athens, now proved effective. What more can befall him, before the end?

The fourth movement begins (in mid-episode) when Theseus mentions (1150) a suppliant who sits at the altar of Poseidon seeking an interview with Oedipus. It is Polynices, the hated son, and at first his father refuses to receive him, until he is persuaded by Antigone to do so. While Polynices is being fetched, the Chorus sings an ode, about old age and its sorrows,[10] about Oedipus, who is compared to a rock upon which the waves beat from all quarters. Enter Polynices, in tears; penitent and asking his father to show mercy (*aidos*). (To this scene we must return.)[11] Oedipus maintains a stubborn silence; and in this discouraging atmosphere Polynices makes his plea. He tells of the wrongs he has suffered at his brother's hand, of the great army he has gathered to assert his rights. For himself and for the army he implores the favour of Oedipus, on whom he knows all to depend; and in

---

support in their struggle against Thebes, so that the protective value of Oedipus as *heros* (not of course exemplified in this particular episode) had a topical relevance.

[10] 1211ff. Sophocles was a very old man when he wrote this ode and may have felt some of the emotions about old age he makes his Chorus express. But Ronnet 288f., is right to say that we should interpret the ode in relation to Oedipus rather than to Sophocles. To Oedipus and to the dramatic situation. The ode should be – and is – relevant to what immediately precedes and immediately follows. It is about youth and age. It is preceded by the appeal of the youthful Polynices. What is said of youth (1229ff.) relates to Polynices (and his brother); what is said of age is true of Oedipus. The epode is particularly significant. Bowra, 351, says that it is concerned 'with praise for Oedipus' endurance'. Does it not also suggest his hardness? Polynices will make as little impression on his father as the waves beating on a rock.

[11] See pp. 275ff.

return he will restore Oedipus to Thebes, to his home. Now at last Oedipus speaks. To Polynices he ascribes responsibility for all his sufferings, even for his death. In words that chill the blood, he curses both his sons with the doom of mutual slaughter. Polynices recognizes – or half-recognizes – the finality of this sentence, but even so cannot bring himself to abandon the expedition. Antigone pleads with him, but to no purpose: he merely begs her to give him burial, if he should fall. With a prayer for his sisters he leaves the stage, and the fourth movement ends. It ends with dialogue between Polynices and Antigone, with the young, with the future – a tragic future for both of them. It is the only time, prior to his final exit, when Oedipus loses the centre of the stage. Antigone, who had made her one long speech towards the beginning of the movement, becomes important.

Now comes peal after peal of thunder, as a sign to Oedipus that his end is near. Theseus is summoned, to fulfil his promise and receive the promised reward. He alone will know, and will transmit to his successors, the secret of the grave of Oedipus, which will be worth more to Athens than many shields and a host of allies. Then the blind Oedipus himself, with slow but unfaltering steps, leads his daughters and the king of Athens off the stage and past the grove of the Eumenides to an unknown destination.[12] An effect so simple and yet by its contrast with the opening of the play the greatest *coup de théâtre* in Sophocles.[13] There is a short ode, before an attendant returns as Messenger, with a tale of wonder (1586ff.). He tells of the preparations of Oedipus for death; more thunder; the loving farewell to his daughters; the summons by an unearthly voice; the dismissal of all but Theseus; the look back which shows Oedipus vanished and Theseus shading his eyes with his hand. Antigone and Ismene return, lamenting: they have lost their father and even the last consolation of tending his grave, which is forbidden, gently but firmly, by Theseus out of respect for the commands of the dead. That, surely, is the end of the play. But no. To Antigone one wish remains (1770), to go to Thebes to prevent, if she can, the mutual slaughter of her brothers. Theseus promises her safe-conduct, and on this note the play ends.

The broad design has thus an Aeschylean symmetry. The five

---

[12] See App. E, p. 340.
[13] Taplin 31f., shows that 1450–1504 is, as it were, a 'mirror-image' of 831–90: not only, therefore, in sharp contrast with the opening scene but also with the Creon-scene in the middle of the play.

movements are of approximately equal length (the third being the longest). It has been widely recognized that the fifth corresponds to the first, being concerned with Oedipus and the holy place to which he has come and in which he will find rest; and in the fifth we come to realize that his entry into the grove in the first was in the nature of a rehearsal and that his retreat from it was only temporary. No less does the fourth movement correspond to the second in so far as it is concerned with Oedipus' relationship to his sons (and to his daughters); and the two are in fact linked by many reminiscences in the text. The centre of the design is formed by the scenes with Creon and Theseus. This symmetrical design is handled and modified with a Sophoclean flexibility (I have already drawn attention to the elaborate series of contrasts in the second movement). It is unified by the central figure of Oedipus, to whose nature and destiny every part is relevant. This relevance must now be examined.

Oedipus, the blind beggar, the polluted man who killed his father and lay with his mother, is summoned by the gods and (in some sense) taken to them, in circumstances of a mysterious solemnity; it is made clear that, after his death, he will be powerful for good and for evil, to aid his friends and to harm his (and their) foes; he will, that is to say, be a *heros,* one of that class of beings, intermediate between gods and men, whose worship was common throughout Greece, many of whom had in fact been great figures of myth granted after death a special status corresponding to the exceptional powers they had displayed in life. That a man, even a polluted man, should be thus destined was not without parallel in Greek cult. But a dramatist must extract significance from his theme: not least Sophocles, who had already made of Oedipus in the *Tyrannus* a great symbol of human destiny. If the heroization of Oedipus after death is a mystery, it follows upon the mystery of his destiny in life. It is the pre-eminent victim of the gods who is (in some sense) raised by their grace. Do these mysteries throw light upon one another? And what can we see in that light about the nature of gods and the fate of men?

That the heroization of Oedipus is a salient theme in the play has been widely recognized; and no critic has laid more stress upon it than Bowra, who writes (349): 'At the end of the *Oedipus at Colonus* no unresolved discords remain, no mysteries call for an answer . . . The justice of the gods is no longer revealed in a half-light as something not wholly explicable; its workings are shown and its rightness emphasized.' For Bowra, and for some others, the gods show their justice by compensating Oedipus in full for his past sufferings.[14] But we must be careful here, or we may assume something that Sophocles does not tell us: we may assume a belief which has played a dubious part in some Christian theodicy, namely that sufferings in this world may be compensated by eternal bliss. Neither Sophocles nor popular belief tells us much about the mental state of a *heros* after death,[15] except that he can be angry. What Oedipus craved was rest; what he tells us is that his cold corpse, sleeping and hidden, will drink the hot blood of his enemies (621f.). It is not bliss, but honour and power that await him in the chthonian realm to which he is summoned. An impossible calculus between sufferings and honours is beside the point and beneath the argument. Oedipus is raised to power and not to happiness.

'No unresolved discords remain': and yet Antigone walks straight out of the play to meet her tragic destiny in *Antigone,* a tragedy which is the direct – and unforeseen – consequence of Oedipus' curse upon his sons. 'No mysteries call for an answer': yet is there nothing mysterious in the juxtaposition of Oedipus' solemn assumption to that awful curse? Not, I suppose, if we accept the absolute justice and justification of the curse and regard it as issuing from one who already speaks with more than human authority. Which, in a sense, Oedipus does. If he is grim and passionate, so is a *heros*; and *heroes,* themselves half-divine, may be ministers of divine justice. That the conception of a *heros* might itself be a mystery, itself discordant, does not enter into Bowra's calculations. If Antigone, in the goodness of her soul, pleads for mercy, it is because 'she does not see the truth in its right perspective'.[16]

Antigone has her importance, but the characterization of Oedipus is fundamental – and disputed, perhaps because in itself it involves one of those apparent contradictions which complicate the interpretation of the play. That he is superhuman from the start – larger than life – has been denied, but is, surely, true. His entry into the grove of the Eumenides has a rightness which is finally established in the closing scene. His authority is felt and acknowledged by the Chorus (292ff.).

[14] Bowra 314f., 349; Letters 299. Contr. Perrotta 564; Linforth (1951) 115f.
[15] Cf. Linforth (1951) 99ff., Ronnet 310.
[16] Contr. Perrotta 610, for whom the heart of the poet is with Antigone.

Yet this awful figure is drawn with some realistic human psychology. In his portrayal there is a deliberate polarization of weakness and strength, of fear and confidence; and it may not be without significance that his confidence always seems to grow with his anger.[17]

The *Coloneus* is a sequel to the *Tyrannus* in the sense that not only events of the earlier play but, in some measure, the characteristics of the earlier Oedipus are taken for granted. Years of suffering, of blind beggary, have intervened; time has passed and Oedipus is old. The effects of time are a staple Sophoclean theme. What did time do to Ajax, to Electra, to Philoctetes? What did it do to Oedipus? It gave him long hours of brooding. At the end of the *Tyrannus* he was overwhelmed by the sense of pollution and guilt. This he has not entirely lost (how could he have?),[18] but reflection has convinced him of his essential innocence (and that he was wrong to put out his eyes). Three times in the *Coloneus* he protests this innocence and argues it, to convince his auditors and perhaps himself. (We shall return to this.)[19] What else has he learnt? Has he learnt patience? So he tells us in his first speech. 'For my sufferings and the long time that has been with me teach me to be patient – and thirdly my nobility' (στέργειν γὰρ αἱ πάθαι με χὠ χρόνος ξυνὼν | μακρὸς διδάσκει καὶ τὸ γενναῖον τρίτον, 7f.).[20] If indeed we are going to see a patient Oedipus, that will be an astonishing thing. But perhaps there is here, as sometimes in prologues, a deliberate misleading of the audience. If he has learnt to endure hardship, if he has learnt to bow to the will of strangers (12f.)

---

[17] Ronnet 298f.; Perrotta 582 ('ogni contrasto lo rende aspro e violento; poi ritorna il cieco, l'infelice, il rassegnato'). Linforth passim lays a great stress upon the human aspects of Oedipus. Lesky, *TD* 133, does well to emphasize that the *heros* has the same characteristics as the man, that he undergoes not a *Verklärung* but an *Erhöhung*.

[18] Linforth (1951) 142f. is good on 510–48: 'its purpose is to lay bare the abiding horror in his soul'. See p. 261 below. On 1132ff. cf. Linforth (1951) 108, 152. This reminder is carefully placed between a moment of joy and the first news of the presence of Polynices, between the daughters and the son of the incestuous marriage.

[19] See pp. 261ff. below.

[20] χρόνος ξυνών: the notion of a companionship between man and time is characteristically Sophoclean (cf. Jebb on 7 and p. 33 n. 66 above). τὸ γενναῖον: it is incumbent on an *agathos* to endure hardship. On στέργειν Jebb cites *Phil.* 538. Philoctetes, whose situation has something in common with that of Oedipus (see p. 257), does not claim *arete* explicitly at this point (but cf. 535, 537): it is Heracles at the end of the play who links *arete* with the endurance of *ponoi* (1419ff.). On the theme of teaching and learning see n. 49 below.

like any blind beggar, we shall see – and before very long – that he has no patience with those to whom he attributes his misfortunes.

This we begin to see when Ismene first speaks about his sons and, before he hears her news, he breaks out into a diatribe against them for their neglect. Their neglect of his *trophe,* of his maintenance. This word (or *tropheia*) occurs five times in thirty-three lines. Such accumulations are, as we have often seen, a characteristic Sophoclean technique; and the purpose is, I think, not merely to bring out the offence of sons who have neglected their sacred duty (similar language will recur in a later scene),[21] but to reveal the preoccupation of one who has lived for years at or below the level of subsistence. The *Coloneus* was written near in time to *Philoctetes,* and many similarities between the two plays have been observed. One similarity is this: that in both plays a man of noble rank is reduced to destitution. The skill of Sophocles in conveying Philoctetes' preoccupation with the sheer business of existence has been freely admired. Is it an inadmissible intrusion of 'psychology' to see a similar preoccupation in the old Oedipus?[22]

This old Oedipus had been a king. Ismene gives her news about the oracle: Oedipus the exile will be sought after (ζητητός). 'They say', she says, 'that their power (κράτη) is coming to be in your hand (ἐν σοί)' (392). Is it inadmissible to say that old emotions stir in the once masterful king of the *Tyrannus?*[23] At any rate Sophocles now reiterates *kratos* and *kratein* (392, 400, 405, 408). It is a matter of Oedipus coming under the mastery of Thebes and not even finding a grave on Theban soil. And so he moves from the bitter grumble of his earlier speech (337ff.) to the quasi-curse of 421ff. 'May the gods not quench their fated strife': and is it not always a terrible thing to pray that strife may continue? 'And may the decision (τέλος) concerning their warfare come to be in my hand (ἐν ἐμοί).' If the power, the mastery, cannot be his in one way, then let it be in another.[24] Words may be as powerful as deeds.

No one, I think, has denied that the Colonean Oedipus is characterized by passion, by wrath, by *thumos;* or that this characteristic is connected with his future destiny as a *heros.*[25] Kitto observes[26] that

---

[21] See p. 276 below.

[22] The tone of 3–6 may involve a little more than mere exposition of circumstance.

[23] See n. 79 below.

[24] The climax of this theme comes at 1379–82.

[25] Cf. e.g. Pohlenz I 365, II 102; Perrotta 562, 606ff. [26] Kitto, *GT* 393.

the rhythm of the play is that of a growth of power in Oedipus, as he approaches that destiny. True as this may be, it is no less true that the rhythm is that of an intensification of a wrathful passion rooted in human motive. We see the first stages in the scene with Ismene. In the scene with Creon the passion of Oedipus increases still further; and it is one of the functions of that scene so to increase it. He curses Creon; and of his sons he says, curse-like, that 'this is their heritage, room enough in my realm to die in' (789f.). It is the first reference to their deaths. The climax is reached in the scene with Polynices, when he lays upon his sons the curse of mutual fratricide.[27] This is indeed a growth of power (including prophetic power), and at the same time a gradual dramatic revelation of destiny. But it is also a crescendo of human passion. When Oedipus curses Polynices, he is beyond himself. 'I shall ever think of *you* (σοῦ) as of a murderer; for it is *you* (σύ) that have brought my days to this anguish, it is *you* (σύ) that have thrust me out; to *you* I owe it (ἐκ σέθεν) that I wander begging my daily bread from strangers' (1361ff.). Commentators are worried. Oedipus here places upon Polynices a degree of responsibility which seems inconsistent with what we are elsewhere told about the shifting political situation at Thebes.[28] At the most Polynices had failed to speak against the original sentence of exile (427ff.), had failed to take advantage of the new oracle, if indeed it was known before his own exile, to secure his father's restoration. Argue as we like about the guilt of a neglectful son and the sincerity of his repentance,[29] it was no part of Sophocles' intention that Oedipus should be fair and reasonable towards his son. Oedipus speaks not as a dispassionate judge but as an ill-used man brimming over with *thumos*.[30] He speaks so upon the very threshold of heroization.

How should we judge the *thumos* of Oedipus? In a *heros* certainly an

---

[27] On the sequence of 'curses' see Linforth (1951) 109–12. Oedipus curses Creon in due form at 864ff.; the formal curse upon the sons is reserved for the scene with Polynices (on 1375 see n. 50 below). 787ff., on Creon and the sons, are in the form of (prophetic) statements. The tone, however, approximates to that of a curse, and Oedipus speaks of his *alastor* dwelling in Thebes. The locality of his dwelling-place, present and future, is so much a theme of the play (see App. E) that this use of ἐνναίων is worth noting. Where will he dwell? There seem to be two answers: in Attica as a *heros*, but also through his *alastor* in Thebes.

[28] C. Robert, *Oidipus* (Berlin 1915) 469ff. The apparent inconsistencies are real. Cf. Rosenmeyer, *Phoenix* 97f., Ronnet 300, Gellie 165ff.

[29] See pp. 275ff. below.

[30] 'An explosion of wrath and hatred without parallel' (Burian 425).

awful wrath against an offender is (if we can understand the nature of a *heros*) understandable. But in a man? It so happens, but not surely by chance, that the play contains two comments on the *thumos* of Oedipus which are so similar that we may be justified in taking them together. When Theseus hears that Oedipus is set against returning to Thebes, 'Foolish man', he says, 'temper (θυμός) in misfortunes is not expedient' (592). Coming from the king who is so courteous and sympathetic, the rebuke is strong. But of course he does not yet know the facts. 'Wait till you learn', says Oedipus, 'and then admonish me[31] . . . I have suffered terrible evils upon evils' (593ff.). No, it is not the ancient misfortune of his race. 'What then is your sickness that passes human measure?' (τί γὰρ τὸ μεῖζον ἢ κατ' ἄνθρωπον νοσεῖς;).[32] It is exile, says Oedipus, at the hands of his own children. Theseus does not pursue his criticism: he is given other things to think of.

But when Antigone pleads with her father that he should give Polynices a hearing, she makes explicit what is only implied by the words of Theseus. 'Let him come. Other men too have bad sons and a sharp temper (θυμὸς ὀξύς) but they hear advice (νουθετούμενοι) and are charmed out of their nature (φύσιν) by the gentle spells of friends' (1192ff.). 'What', said Theseus, 'is your sickness that passes human measure?' 'Other men', says Antigone, 'have bad sons and a quick temper.' The two sentences form virtually a single argument. What Theseus says, and what Antigone says, are important in themselves: when they say the same thing, we should doubly take notice. Yet to Oedipus the behaviour of his sons is so outrageous as to justify the cruellest retaliation.

This – Antigone's longest speech[33] – could well be one of the most important in the play. She is, on the face of it, pleading only for an

---

[31] See n. 49 below.

[32] By this Theseus means no more than that, to justify his attitude, Oedipus' sufferings must indeed be extraordinary (he does not yet know what they are). It may, however, be worth noticing *Ant.* 768, where Creon uses a similar expression. 'Let Haemon be as angry as he likes' may be all he means, but the phrase he uses is ironical, since his son is in fact under the spell of a daemonic passion (see p. 94 above). νοσεῖν could be ambiguous: 'to be in mental anguish' (cf. *O.T.* 1061) or 'to suffer from a mad (and daemonic) passion' (which is how Aeschylus saw the cursing of the sons at *Sept.* 781). Moreover, how valid is the distinction Oedipus seems to be drawing between the behaviour of his sons and the παλαιὰ ξυμφορὰ γένους?

[33] Its length is all the more impressive after the stress laid at 1115–18 on the brevity appropriate to her age and sex!

audience, but what she says goes far beyond the immediate issue. After the lines already quoted, she goes on (1195ff.). 'Look to the past, not the present – to all you have suffered through father and mother (πατρῷα καὶ μητρῷα πήματα). If you look at that past, I am sure you will understand that bad is the end which waits on a bad wrath (γνώσῃ κακοῦ | θυμοῦ τελευτὴν ὡς κακὴ προσγίγνεται). You have no small food for thought, you who have lost the sight of your eyes.'[34] Oedipus had blinded himself and to this act of his he had indeed given thought. 'After a time', he said (437ff.), 'when all my anguish was already assuaged, and when I was beginning to understand that my wrath had run too far in punishing those past errors . . .' (κἀμάνθανον τὸν θυμὸν ἐκδραμόντα μοι | μείζω κολαστὴν τῶν πρὶν ἡμαρτημένων). It is hard to see how Sophocles could have suggested more clearly that the self-blinding and the curse upon the sons (not yet delivered in its final form) were actions of the same order and significance. (Aeschylus saw them as twin acts of madness, *Sept.* 778ff.) Oedipus had come to understand how excessively his *thumos* had operated against himself; Antigone hopes, in vain, that he will understand the nature of his *thumos* as directed towards his sons. Creon, an evil man and an old man,[35] knows more about *thumos* than Antigone. 'Anger', he says, 'knows no old age till death comes' (θυμοῦ γὰρ οὐδὲν γῆράς ἐστιν ἄλλο πλὴν | θανεῖν) (954f.). It was true of Oedipus. And, when death came, the gods took this man of wrath to themselves.

What has been said so far is preliminary, but an essential preliminary, if we are to see Oedipus and his fate in true perspective. It is particularly important, if obvious, to note how the wrath of Oedipus

---

34 It is striking – and hardly accidental – that at 1195ff., Antigone is made to use two words of sight immediately before the reference to her father's blindness. (This is observed by the Budé translator, p. 128 n. 1.) Is it that we should *expect* the blind man to have mental vision?

35 Great stress is laid on the age of both Oedipus and Creon. The theme is prepared by three words of age at 724–7. There follow 733, 735, 744, 751 (youth), 804f., 870, 931, 954f. (cited in text), 959, 961, 1008. Naturally the theme recurs on the entry of Polynices: 1255f., 1259, which are themselves prepared by the ode upon old age, e.g. 1235ff.

Creon also says (852–5) that, now as in the past, Oedipus is not doing well but is damaging himself 'by giving in to anger, in despite of friends' (βίᾳ φίλων ὀργῇ χάριν δούς). The past reference Jebb explains, perhaps rightly, in terms of certain episodes in the *Tyrannus*. As to the present, Creon by *philoi* means, presumably, himself and Eteocles, but his words may look forward ironically to Oedipus' rejection of Antigone's persuasions.

is grounded in his past experience. It is provoked by suffering; and it issues in retaliation. The theme of retaliation is perhaps more prominent in the *Coloneus* than has always been observed.

Oedipus proclaims and argues his innocence on three separate occasions.[36] The arguments are to some extent repeated from passage to passage; and one wonders at first why Sophocles should have handled the topic in this way and at such length, especially since the acceptance of Oedipus by Theseus is not conditioned by any argument as to his guilt or innocence. It has been suggested that the guilt of Oedipus had become an issue since the *Tyrannus* or a source of misunderstanding, or that Sophocles, like his Oedipus, had rethought the question.[37] This is not inconceivable but hardly accounts for the way in which Sophocles has written. The passages differ of course in situation and in tone. The first and the third are evoked by attack: the first by the superstitious fear the Chorus feel at the name and history of Oedipus so that they wish to drive him out, the third by Creon's hypocritical debating-point, his feigned surprise that Athens should tolerate the presence of a polluted man. Creon speaks of the Areopagus, and Oedipus argues at length as though he were defending himself before that court.[38] The second passage is quite different. Here the defence of Oedipus is evoked by the cruel, if natural, curiosity of the Chorus. It is sung not spoken; it is passionate affirmation rather than reasoned argument; and it reveals, surely, that the emotions of the end of the *Tyrannus* are, despite all reasoning, still alive in the aged Oedipus[39] – so much alive that he can call the daughters on whom he depends and whom he loves, the daughters who are also his sisters, 'twin disasters' (δύο ἄτα, 532). With its tense lyrical evocation of unimaginable horror, it takes its place, as we have seen, in a series of sharply contrasted episodes.

In it Jocasta is more prominent than Laius; and the argument – for there is an argument – is the only plea that is relevant to the case of Jocasta. The plea is ignorance. When he killed his father and married his mother, he acted in ignorance that they were so. 'With no knowledge did I come to this' (ἄιδρις ἐς τόδ' ἦλθον, 548),[40] a plea

---

[36] This series of arguments has been much discussed: cf., e.g., Linforth (1951) 108, 142f., 152; Knox, *HT* 157ff.; Rosenmeyer, *Phoenix* 97; Ronnet 305.

[37] Cf. Gould (1) 603.

[38] Cf. Knox, *HT* 157f.

[39] See n. 18 above.

[40] Of Laius, cf. 521–3, 538ff.

which would have absolved him in Attic law. But the first argument
he employs on the first occasion – and it is also the last that he
employs on the third occasion, so that the total defence of Oedipus is
framed by a repetition of the theme – is different. Speaking of the
killing of Laius, he says: 'Even if I had acted with knowledge
(φρονῶν), I should not have proved myself base (κακός): I was
requiting a wrong' (271f.). The Greek expression here used is
παθὼν . . . ἀντέδρων. Oedipus had asked: 'How was I base by nature'
(κακὸς φύσιν)? And the answer implied is that it was in his nature to
retaliate a wrong, which was the mark of an *agathos*. The reference is,
clearly, to the narrative in the *Tyrannus*, when father and son met at
the place where three roads joined, when Laius aimed the first blow,
Oedipus retaliated and killed him. Oedipus has just said that his
actions (ἔργα) were a matter of suffering rather than doing (πεπονθότ'
ἐστὶ μᾶλλον ἢ δεδρακότα, 266f.). He goes on to say that, while he came
where he came in ignorance, those at whose hands he suffered
(ἔπασχον) destroyed – or sought to destroy – him in knowledge. And
here he must be thinking of the parents who knowingly exposed their
son to die. That they should suffer at his hands by incest and parricide
was indeed an ironical kind of unconscious retaliation but that is not
what Oedipus meant when he said παθὼν ἀντέδρων and so modified
his claim to be patient rather than agent. This becomes clear when we
turn to the third passage. The argument seems already to be concluded on the now familiar plea of ignorance, when Oedipus rounds
on Creon and says: 'Answer me. If, here and now, someone were to
come up and seek to kill you . . . , would you ask if the killer was your
father or retaliate forthwith? I think, if you love your life, you would
retaliate' (991ff.).[41]

Reasonable enough – in law, in recognised Greek morality, and in
common sense. And we should be making altogether too much of
this ground of Oedipus' defence, if it were not that the theme of

---

[41] The argument at 270ff. actually goes farther, implying that it would have been
permissible for a son to retaliate upon one whom he knew to be his father.
Oedipus will in due course retaliate upon his sons; and Antigone, seeking to
restrain him, in effect reverses the argument of 270ff., when she maintains
(1189–91) that it is *not* permissible for a father to retaliate against a son even if he
has suffered terribly at his hands. Dover, *GPM* 274 (with a wrong reference)
comments that this is 'a note unusual for the fifth century'. The more remarkable,
therefore.

retaliation is otherwise prominent in the play, and that it has implications of the first importance for tragedy and for religion.

It is, like the theme of wrath, particularly prominent in the scenes
with Creon. Justifying himself before Theseus for his assault on
Oedipus, Creon says (951ff.): 'This I should not have done, if he had
not been calling down bitter curses upon me and upon my race. For
which, having suffered, I thought right so to retaliate' (ἀνθ' ὧν
πεπονθὼς ἠξίουν τάδ' ἀντιδρᾶν). Creon actually misrepresents the
facts: the curse (864ff.) came after, not before, the threat of violence
(860).[42] It was Oedipus who, not for the first time, had suffered and
retaliated – with the words which were his only weapon: ἔργοις
πεπονθὼς ῥήμασίν σ' ἀμύνομαι (873). Still, Creon's quibble signifies
little. For the two old men are striking blow for blow as each can, in
the same spirit of wrath. Oedipus cursed Creon, as he will curse his
sons. But between the scene with Creon and the scene with Polynices
comes that speech of Antigone's already quoted, in which many
threads meet. One could almost have predicted that the theme of
retaliation would recur in it; and recur it does in a most interesting
way. Immediately before the passages already quoted (1192–200),
Antigone had said: 'You are his father (ἔφυσας αὐτόν), so that, even if
he is doing you the most impious among the worst of wrongs, it is not
right (θέμις) that you, of all people, should wrong him in return'
(1189–91). (The words here are δρῶντα and ἀντιδρᾶν.)[43] A great
breach opens up, not simply between strict justice and a pity or mercy
which could be attributed to a woman's soft heart, but between two
irreconcilable views of retaliation within the context of the family.
Clearly, the scope here goes far beyond the mere question of an
audience for Polynices. Antigone maintains that a father, of all
people, should not retaliate upon a son for whose *phusis* he is responsible, not even if that son commits the most impious of crimes (which
is neglect of duty towards a father). For Oedipus, on the other hand, it
is precisely that neglect of duty which impels and justifies the most
terrible retribution, when he retaliates with a final curse on both his

---

[42] Or is he thinking of 785–7? It is a minor point.

[43] 1201–3 are carefully phrased to bring out the converse and complementary
principle of returning good for good. (For τίνειν in the context of evil, cf. 994,
996.) Oedipus in fact acts upon both principles (cf. 1489f.).

sons.[44] Having done so, he then goes on, at the summons of a divine power, to assume the status of a *heros*.

I have said that the theme of retaliation has tragic implications. Retaliation was, of course, regarded by the ordinary Greek as a right, if not a duty. Whether Sophocles, as a man and a citizen, accepted this morality is beside the point. What matters is how he saw retaliation as a tragic process. An offence is committed. Someone suffers, and retaliates. By his act, the first doer suffers; and this suffering, in its turn, evokes retaliation (by the sufferer or by his representative). So there is set up a sequence of action and passion which appears to have no end. Offence and retaliation; crime and counter-crime. It is nothing short of a formula for tragedy. It is certainly the formula to which the *Oresteia* of Aeschylus is constructed.[45] Now the divine powers which, in the *Oresteia*, preside over this apparently interminable series of crimes and punishments are the Furies, the Erinyes, who, at the end of the trilogy, come to be known as Eumenides. There are Eumenides (and Erinyes) also in the *Coloneus*.

When Oedipus learns that he has come to a sanctuary of the Eumenides, he recognizes that he has found his final resting-place: the wanderer has found a *hedra*.[46] How the grove was indicated we cannot say, but indicated it must have been, the entry into it of Oedipus and his departure from it must have been clearly marked. It was part – and an insistent part – of the visual background of the piece, compelling the attention of the spectator, even when little was being said about the goddesses, and becoming once more the focus of action at the end of the play.

The goddesses are called Eumenides, for that was their cult-title at Colonus, though, as the villager says: 'In other places other names find favour' (43). At Colonus, however, and generally throughout the play, their name is Eumenides – that is 'well-disposed', 'goddesses of good will'. When Oedipus hears their name, he prays (44): 'Graciously, then, may they receive the suppliant' (ἀλλ' ἵλεῳ μὲν τὸν

---

[44] On the curse see further n. 50.

[45] To the παθόντα ἀντιδρᾶν of the *Coloneus* corresponds the δράσαντα παθεῖν of the *Choephori*. The principles are complementary and between them give a perfect expression to the *lex talionis* (on which see ch. 9 pp. 208f.).

[46] On ἕδρα see n. 7 above and App. E.

ἱκέτην δεξαίατο), anticipating the prayer which is later dictated by the Coryphaeus (486ff.). 'Pray that, as we call them Eumenides, so with hearts of good will (ἐξ εὐμενῶν στέρνων) they may receive and save the suppliant.' These prayers are answered, not only perhaps by the protection which is afforded Oedipus, jointly, by the goddesses and by the city of Athens (to this we shall return), but in a more mysterious way by the divine grace[47] which summons Oedipus to take his place among the powers that dwell in the earth.

The name Eumenides is paradoxical – and is presented as a paradox in the play. First, Antigone describes the quiet beauty of the grove: the laurels, vines and olives, the song of the nightingales. Then the villager: 'Depart from this place . . . for it belongs to the fearful goddesses (ἔμφοβοι θεαί), daughters of Earth and Darkness' (39f.). Later, when the Chorus enter, they sing of 'the Invincible Virgins, whose name we tremble to speak, whom we pass by with eyes averted, without voice or word' (127–31). But the paradox had already been expressed most sharply in the prayer of Oedipus (84ff.): at the beginning, 'Queens of dread aspect (ὦ πότνιαι δεινῶπες), show yourselves not without sympathy towards Phoebus and towards me';[48] and then, strikingly, at the end: 'Come, sweet daughters of primeval Darkness, . . . have pity (οἰκτίρατε).' This to the implacable powers of the nether world!

When, during the second movement of the play, shortly before the entry of Theseus, the Coryphaeus instructs Oedipus how he (or one on his behalf) should make sacrifice and prayer to the goddesses, the passage is quiet and harmonious: it has a certain beauty corresponding to the natural beauty of the grove. And it is a calm, enquiring and

---

[47] On the notion of χάρις see Gellie 182.

[48] The word ἀγνώμων has slightly different senses in relation to Phoebus and to Oedipus: if they refuse to harbour Oedipus, they will be hard-hearted towards him, but they will be at cross-purposes with Apollo who has given the oracle. There might be a reminiscence of the hostility between Furies and Apollo in the *Oresteia*. How important a role does Apollo play in the *Coloneus*? He enters into it of course as the source of the oracles on which Oedipus relies: 86ff., 102, 412–14, 456, 623, 665, 793. He does not, however, brood over the play as over the *Tyrannus*. There could be several reasons for this. The role of Athens directs attention rather to the second half of *Eumenides*. Towards the end of the play Zeus emerges into prominence (see p. 271), and *his* relationship to the nether powers is (as ultimately in the *Oresteia*) more important than that of Apollo. Possibly also it is because (cf. Knox, *HT* 193 n. 11) Oedipus seems to acquire a growth of prophetic power in his own right.

almost humbly receptive, Oedipus who listens and obeys.[49] But we
have already observed where Sophocles has placed the passage. He has
placed it between the first prayer of Oedipus against his sons and that
gratuitous haling-back of Oedipus into his terrible past by the curiosity of the Chorus. It comes, that is, between the tragic future and the
tragic past. Now, in the Aeschylean view (so far as we can see it), both
that past and that future were determined by the operation of Furies,
of Erinyes. In between future and past come the details of ritual and
the prayer, already quoted, to the Eumenides to justify their name.
And, in some mysterious way, they did justify it. They show themselves, they are, Eumenides, but – and could Sophocles have emphasized this more clearly than by the sequence of scenes to which I have
just referred? – that did not save Oedipus from a life-time of suffering
or Polynices (and for that matter Antigone) from the consequences of
a father's curse. The word *Erinys* occurs twice in the play, the speaker
in each case being Polynices: once he speaks of the past (1299), and by
'your Erinys' he means the malign power which has pursed Oedipus
and his race (for as yet he knows nothing of a father's curse),[50] but by
1434 the Erinyes of Oedipus have already determined the future.

[49] Words of teaching and learning are fairly common in the play but, *more Sophoc-
leo*, tend to appear in clusters. One such cluster follows the entry of Theseus. From
the king three businesslike imperatives: 560, 575, 594; of the king 580, 593. Finally
654: Theseus needs to know the facts, but not how he should act upon them!
There is no direct relevance to Oedipus. The first cluster is different: 8, 12, 22f.,
113–16 (ring-composition?). There is stress on the great age of Oedipus. What has
his long experience taught him? How great is his readiness to learn? These may be
important questions. Thirdly, at 461ff. (the sacrifice to the goddesses) we have
468, 480 (cf. 464, 485, 504). Knox, *HT* 151f. speaks of 'the hero's docility and
eagerness to be instructed in matters of religion' and calls attention (194 n. 16) to
words usually associated with a hero's intractability which here emphasize his
willingness to cooperate. He adds that this attitude of docility 'will be sharply
contrasted with his growing assertiveness and intractability in his relations with
men'. On the central issue, will he learn the lesson of which Creon speaks at 852ff.
and Antigone at 1195ff.? He will not: his *thumos* will determine all for ill.

[50] On the interpretation of 1375 (τοιάσδ' ἀρὰς σφῷν πρόσθε τ' ἐξανῆκ' ἐγώ) opinions
differ. Most critics, with Jebb, take this as a reference to such curse-like utterances
as 421ff. (or 789f.). Campbell had suggested that it refers to a curse or curses
pronounced before Oedipus had left Thebes (and therefore known to Polynices);
and he is strongly supported by Knox, *HT* 194 n. 14 (cf. also Rosenmeyer,
Phoenix 109 n. 70). It would certainly throw an ironical light backwards over the
earlier phases of the play, if we now learn that Oedipus had long ago cursed his
sons with the doom of mutual slaughter. I feel, nevertheless, that this is the wrong
sort of irony, which spoils rather than enhances a carefully designed effect of
cumulative wrath. Certainly, in the second movement, Oedipus gives no indica-

Some critics have wished to minimize the importance of the Eumenides within the play; to deny, in Sophocles, their Aeschylean identity with the Erinyes; to deny any significant relationship, at a deep level, between them and Oedipus, his fate and his destiny.[51] Yet, when Sophocles made the villager say: 'In other places other names find favour', he must have meant us to think of some of those other names.[52] And of all names we might be expected to remember, if not Arai, at least Erinyes. No other name would be more surely called up by words of fear in the minds of those familiar with the *Oresteia*. And is there not a kinship between Oedipus and those goddesses to whose seat he has come and makes it his own? Returning once more to his prayer, do we not see how Oedipus himself feels such a kinship? He knows that the omen is faithful. 'For otherwise I should not have met with you, first of all, in my travelling – I, the sober one, with you who receive no wine[53] – or taken this awful ($\sigma\epsilon\mu\nu\acute{o}\nu$) seat not shaped with tools' (98ff.). The seat is awful, and it is that of Oedipus no less

tion of having delivered such a curse, though he sees the strife of his sons as predestined (421f., $\tau\grave{\eta}\nu\ \pi\epsilon\pi\rho\omega\mu\acute{\epsilon}\nu\eta\nu\ \acute{\epsilon}\rho\iota\nu$). At 789f. he has come to see that his sons will die, using language which recalls a version of the Aeschylean curse, but without indication that he has previously so cursed them. The language of 1370 ff. is still a little vague. What is the *daimon*? The Erinys-curse, the *alastor*, of a father? Or just destiny (cf. the fatalism of Polynices at 1443)? It is as though his mind is moving towards the great climactic curse of 1383ff., which I cannot believe to be a mere endorsement of a years old imprecation. Nor do I believe that Polynices, when he approached his father, knew that he was under precisely such a curse or that, when he saw the wrong inflicted on him by his brother as due to his father's Erinys ($\tau\grave{\eta}\nu\ \sigma\grave{\eta}\nu\ {}^{\prime}E\rho\iota\nu\acute{\nu}\nu$, 1299), he was thinking of more than what is elsewhere (369) called $\mathring{\eta}\ \pi\acute{a}\lambda\alpha\iota\ \gamma\acute{\epsilon}\nu o\nu\varsigma\ \phi\theta o\rho\acute{a}$, of which Oedipus was the prime exemplification. One could, I suppose, take up a compromise position and say that Oedipus had, as in the general tradition, cursed his sons before going into exile but Sophocles has reserved the specific curse of mutual slaughter to be the climax of his play. But this seems too nice.

[51] Notably Linforth (1951) 92–7, whose single-minded efforts (in a work which has so many merits) to deny significance to the Eumenides – and indeed to the whole theological theme – sometimes approach the ludicrous. Cf. Adams 165. Contr. Knox's good note at p. 194 n. 12. Rosenmeyer, *Phoenix* 106 says of Oedipus: 'His merger with the Furies may well be the most profound and at the same time the most obscure symbol of the play.' A rather extreme statement of a very important aspect of the drama.

[52] The name *Semnai* is suggested by the use of the epithet at 41, followed by 89f., 100. Cf. Aesch. *Eum.* 1041.

[53] For a different interpretation see A. D. Fitton Brown, *LCM* 1 (1976) 103–5. As it is generally taken, the comparison, which is in point of austerity and fairly superficial, seems to have no purpose except to insist on a kinship between Oedipus and the goddesses.

than of the goddesses; and rightfully. He had addressed the goddesses
as *deinopes*: dread of visage. When the Chorus first see him in the
grove, they exclaim: 'Dread to see, and dread to hear' (141); when
they hear his name, they are full of fear, and Oedipus says: 'Have no
fear of what I say' (223). If, as Jebb suggests in his stage direction, they
are 'holding their mantles before their eyes', this would be a splendid
stage-effect, which would show that they were in effect reacting to
Oedipus as they reacted to the goddesses themselves they dared not
look upon. This is the man who will end the play as himself one of the
nether powers, but he is also the man whose destiny it was to be
cursed and to curse, to be the victim and agent of Erinyes.[54] The
mystery of Oedipus merges into the background of the mystery of
the Eumenides and the paradox of their name.

With this mystery Aeschylus dealt in the *Oresteia*, for it was he who
dramatized the transformation of the Erinyes into Eumenides. In the
Oresteia (and in other plays) he explored, dramatically, the relationship between Furies and Fate (or the Fates), and between both of them
and the ultimate power of Zeus. (I refer the reader to earlier discussions.)[55] Sophocles, for reasons of his own, though he had used the
Aeschylean concept of Erinyes in previous plays, excluded Furies
from the *Tyrannus*. He wished there to concentrate upon the evil
destiny of Oedipus in relative isolation and with minimal reference to
past and future generations. The destiny of Oedipus is still a theme in
the *Coloneus*,[56] but now the Furies return, bringing with them the

---

[54] Like Electra? See p. 228 above.

[55] See n. 57.

[56] Cf. esp. 144ff. 'Who is the old man?' 'Not wholly of the best fortune, that ye
should envy him' (οὐ πάνυ μοίρας εὐδαιμονίσαι πρώτης), as Jebb translates the
untranslatable with his usual ingenuity. The language speaks of *moira* and hints at
daimon; and the evidence is the blindness. 'Were you blind from birth?' The text of
150ff. is uncertain, but it is fairly clear that that is what the Chorus ask, followed
by a double reference to his *aion*. Why are they made to ask this question which is
not answered? Oedipus' blindness was self-inflicted, yet he cites it as evidence of
his *moira/daimon*. It is hard to believe that Sophocles did not recall a certain passage
in the *O.T.* (1299ff., on which see pp. 174f. above).
    The language of 229f. is interesting. The Chorus argue that they were trapped
into making a promise on false pretences. It is a natural and defensible point, but it
is expressed at considerable length and in difficult language. Can an expression
such as μοιριδία τίσις be used, in the context of this play, merely to convey the
retribution which might fall on them if they break their promise? Two points
seem to arise: (i) unwittingly, they are anticipating the line of defence of Oedipus

whole question of the nether world, its role in justice, and its disquieting relation to the government of Zeus.

I have argued elsewhere[57] that for Aeschylus – and also for Sophocles – a fundamental religious problem which presented itself, in and through tragedy, was precisely this: what was the relationship between Zeus on the one hand (and along with Zeus the other bright gods of the heavenly Olympus) and, on the other hand, the dark, primitive, infernal powers that dwell in the earth. It was natural – and all too easy – for the Greeks to distinguish between *chthonioi* and *ouranioi*. They were distinguished by many details of cult, but equally by the emotional attitude of the worshippers. The cult of the Olympians was cheerful – the sacrifice was a festival, in the benefits of which the worshippers had their share; the worship of the *chthonioi* was attended by fear which cannot be better illustrated than by the attitude of the villagers of Colonus towards the Eumenides. Clearly the Greeks worshipped the Olympians in the hope of good, the chthonians in the fear of evil. Isocrates[58] – and who could be better evidence for conventional Greek attitudes? – divides the gods into two classes: 'those who are the cause of good things to us and are called Olympians: those who are set in charge of disasters and punishments and bear less agreeable names'. Every Greek knew, of course, that the distinction was not absolute – that they had cause to fear the Olympians as a source of evil and, for that matter, that the earth and its powers promoted the fertility of the land. But, broadly, a distinction held good, which was also the distinction between light and darkness, between day and night, between hope and fear, between good and evil.

Upon the tragedians this contrast forced itself with a unique insistence. The terror which attended the worship of the *chthonioi* derived above all from association with the dead. The earth, if it was

on the charge of parricide (cf. 270ff., which is thus prepared?); (ii) nothing could be less true than what they say, witness the history of Oedipus and his race – retaliate for your sufferings, and the inevitable result is a continuance of the process. Cf. Gellie 161: 'they are borrowing from the play's major theme'. It is a standing question whether, in the case of words which form part of the common vocabulary of misery, their etymology is ever felt. Thus *dusmoros* (but equally *athlios*) is of frequent occurrence in the play: 224, cf. 327, 331, 347, 365, 557, 559, 749, 804, 1109. In any or all of these cases is a notion of *moira* present?

[57] See *JHS* 74 (1954) 16–24.
[58] v. 117. Cf. p. 208.

the source of fertility, was also the dwelling of the dead; the powers of
the earth were representative of the interests and influence of the dead.
Now the Greek tragic myths tended to deal with violent deaths and
the consequences of such deaths. For those who died by violence did
not rest in the earth: they demanded vengeance, and their Erinyes
secured it. And this was a form of justice. But Aeschylus had inherited
a conception of Zeus as the supreme ruler of the universe and the
upholder of just order. Therefore he must stand in some relationship
to the powers of the dead, though his bright home in the sky was the
very antithesis of the nether gloom. Indeed, according to one early
formulation, the latter was not part of Zeus's realm at all, but
belonged to his brother Pluto or Hades, who might also be called the
nether Zeus (Ζεὺς χθόνιος). For Aeschylus, however, there could not
be two Zeus's, but only one Zeus. In his world there could not be a
divided responsibility for good and evil: Olympians against
chthonians, one Zeus against another Zeus – or for that matter Zeus
against Moira or the Moirai. The world, human and divine, if it was
to be understood at all, must be understood as a whole, the dark with
light, the evil with the good. To do so was a function of tragic poetry.

What right have we to say that Sophocles saw the same problem in
a similar way? Some evidence to this effect has already emerged from
our examination of earlier plays.[59] It might seem, however, that the
Coloneus is heavily concentrated upon the nether world: it opens with
the arrival of Oedipus at the grove of the Eumenides and ends with his
passing to become himself a chthonian power. To this destiny he is
summoned by the thunder of Zeus. ἔκτυπεν αἰθήρ, ὦ Ζεῦ, exclaims
the Chorus (1456); and thunder is an attribute of the Olympian Zeus.
'This winged thunder of Zeus', says Oedipus, 'will shortly bring me
to Hades.' But as the Messenger heard it, it was from Zeus Chthonios
that came a thunderous noise (κτύπησε μὲν Ζεὺς χθόνιος, 1606). If, as it
would seem, Sophocles is establishing a mysterious relationship
between Zeus and the other nether powers, then that relationship is
symbolized by the joint act of worship which Theseus was seen to
perform when the Messenger looked back and saw that Oedipus had
disappeared from view and Theseus, who had been screening his eyes
with his hand, made adoration simultaneously to earth and to the
Olympus of the gods: ὁρῶμεν αὐτὸν γῆν τε προσκυνοῦνθ' ἅμα | καὶ τὸν

---

[59] Cf., e.g., p. 211 n. 21.

θεῶν "Ολυμπον ἐν ταὐτῷ λόγῳ (1654f.). Doubtless a familiar ritual gesture,[60] but the phrasing is emphatic (ἅμα . . . ἐν ταὐτῷ λόγῳ). Jebb has a percipient note: 'The vision which [Theseus] had just seen moved him to adore both the χθόνιοι and the ὕπατοι. The touch is finely conceived so as to leave the mystery unbroken.' The mystery, that is, of the passing of Oedipus. 'By what doom he perished no mortal man could tell save Theseus. For neither did a fiery thunderbolt of the god bring about his end at that time nor a whirlwind set in motion from the sea, but either there was a messenger from the gods or the base of earth, the nether world of gloom, parted in friendship.'[61]

It might be said that Zeus gradually comes into prominence – and into relationship with the nether powers – as the play proceeds.[62] In the course of the Polynices-scene – and no part of the play more clearly reveals the sinister side of the Erinyes (only there given that name) – the name of Zeus occurs three times. And each reference is striking. At 1432ff., Polynices, recognizing that his course is doomed by the Erinyes of his father, immediately prays that Zeus may grant good (or a good way) to his sisters – if they accomplish his burial.[63] In fact Antigone will be involved in his evil fate precisely if she fulfils the condition which he lays down for Zeus's granting her good. Most striking of all, however, are two passages so closely similar and so strongly contrasted that the second must be a deliberate riposte to the first. Appealing to his father, Polynices says: 'Zeus, in all he does, has *Aidos* for the sharer of his throne: so let her stand also at your side' (1267ff.).[64] But Oedipus claims (1380ff.) that his curses prevail, 'if indeed Justice, proclaimed from of old, sits with Zeus according to

---

[60] Cf. Aristophanes, *Knights* 156, where the Sausage-seller is bidden to adore earth and the gods.

[61] The scholiast's ἀλάμπετον is on the whole preferable to the ἀλύπητον of the codd. (1662), which could have been suggested by the following line (where, however, the γάρ is adequately justified by εὔνουν). A word of darkness is admirable here, and the contrast of εὔνουν . . . ἀλάμπετον could be compared with the enigmatic γλυκεῖαι παῖδες ἀρχαίου Σκότου at 106.

[62] Cf. *JHS* 74 (1954) 21 n. 31.

[63] 1435: εὐοδοίη codd., Jebb, Dain; εὖ διδοίη Burges, Pearson. The point is unaffected.

[64] Easterling, *PCPS* 6f. finds 'a deliberate ambiguity of association here: the self-seeking of the sons is recalled in θρόνων and yet with it the suppliant state of Polynices (σύνθακος)'.

primeval laws'. The issue could not be more clearly put or in a more fundamental context; and to it we shall return.

The problem of divine justice – of the relationship between Zeus and the Furies, between Olympians and chthonians – was solved (if that is the right word) by Aeschylus through those developments which enabled him to bring the *Oresteia* to a joyful close. The joy derives from a sure hope of good, now at last replacing the fear of evil which has brooded over the trilogy. It is as though Aeschylus was affirming that the divine government of the world leads in the end to a triumph of good over evil and to hope for mankind. And this is symbolized above all by the reconciliation and (in some sense) transformation of the Erinyes, which also means that Aeschylus can make his Chorus sing that 'Zeus and Moira have come together'.[65] This is no facile optimism or dramatic sleight-of-hand. The Erinyes have not ceased to be frightening; they still dwell in the earth; they are still ministers of punishment (*Eum.* 950ff.). The great law – that we must suffer for our actions – has not been abrogated; and the divine powers still exercise their awful sovereignty, if need be, by force or violence. But to this principle has been added another – the principle of persuasion, embodied in Athena. The antithesis of force and persuasion – of *bia* and *peitho* – is as fundamental to the thought of Aeschylus as it was natural to the Greek mind. What is significant in the closing stages of the *Oresteia* is that we see the divine persuasion applied to the very representatives of divine violence. It was this transforming, reconciling power of reasonable persuasion that made the difference between primitive Argos and the new Athens of Athena, and it was because of this difference – and the revelation of divine nature which it implied – that Aeschylus was able to end his trilogy with a confident faith in the victory of good.[66]

When we turn to Sophocles, we find what perhaps we should expect to find. Both Greeks, both Athenians, both tragic poets, both confronting the same world of good and evil – and Sophocles with the example of Aeschylus constantly before him – it is not surprising if the tragic thought of both shared much in common. The Furies are 'Eumenides' at Colonus, and they show their good will towards Oedipus. Their transformation is, in some degree, assumed – and

[65] See p. 158.
[66] See ch. 9 p. 209.

their transformation at Athens. More than once in the play, Athens and the Eumenides are significantly linked as saviours of Oedipus, first and most strikingly in the Prologos in his prayer for pity (106ff.).[67] If the poet saw some special meaning in the fact that the Furies were worshipped in Attica under that title, we should find that meaning in the role of Theseus. Unlike the Chorus, who all but drive their benefactor away, Theseus shows no fear either of Oedipus or of the goddesses.[68] Ruling in a city where law prevails at home, which respects the rights of others, practises fair dealing (τοὐπιεικές)[69] and keeps its word, perhaps he has no need to fear them. His pity springs spontaneously from his humanity and, when he uses force, he does so without passion, in defence of the weak.[70] Theseus in the *Coloneus* preserves what Athena in the *Oresteia* had ordained. Goddess and king, both represent an ideal for Athens: the more nearly it was attained, the less had Athens to fear the harsh retributive forces and the more would the Furies justify the title under which they were worshipped at Colonus.[71]

But Theseus, being an ideal, is a little remote. He acts towards

[67] Cf. 457ff., 1010ff.

[68] Contrast their caution at 490ff. with the attitude of Theseus at 560f. Not until 1650ff. does Theseus show fear.

[69] An ill-defined characteristic something like 'decency', on which the Athenians prided themselves, cf. Dover, *GPM* 191, J. de Romilly, *La douceur dans la pensée grecque* (Paris 1979) 53ff.

[70] Cf., e.g., 658ff., 904ff.

[71] To ask whether Sophocles believed that this ideal had been fully embodied in the Athens he knew is probably as futile as to ask whether Aeschylus believed that the reconciliation of the Furies and the triumph of persuasion over violence had been achieved once and for all at a fixed point of mythological time. Nor does the Colonus-ode help us to answer such a question. If I say little about this famous song, it is mainly because Knox, *HT* 154–6 has given such a penetrating account of it, showing how the poet 'recreates for us the landscape as [he] knew and loved it', how 'every detail of the landscape recalls some aspect of the city's greatness', and how the complex and subtle fabric of the ode includes a 'deep strain of sadness'. His reference to Pericles' last speech in Thucydides is apt – a speech of which J. de Romilly has recently said (*Ancient Society* 4 (1973) 39–70) that it is 'une sorte d'oraison funèbre pour Athènes'. So Knox: 'The Athens Sophocles knew in his youth is to die, but be immortal; he sings of it as he remembered it in its days of greatness and beauty, and this is how we remember it still.' Sophocles loved his birthplace and his land, their landscape and their cults, their arts and their joys, and saw them threatened with imminent destruction. It is likely enough that the friend of Pericles found admirable features in Athenian society and deplored the corruption which a long war had brought about: how the tragic poet judged that society does not emerge from the ode, but must be hazardously inferred from the whole theatre of the dramatist.

Oedipus with a generous humanity, but is not really involved in his tragedy, which he cannot fully understand.[72] He has no need to be persuaded nor to persuade. The role of persuader belongs to Antigone. Caught, like her father and brothers, in the harsh workings of destiny, she has, it would seem, the function of mitigating the harshness. With what success? It is her triumph that she (along with her sister) has evoked a great love from the embittered soul of Oedipus. Fruits of the incestuous Fury-haunted marriage, to whom he refers with horror when he is questioned by the Chorus (532), they receive from him those most moving words with which he bids them farewell (1617ff.). Is this not a triumph of good over evil? Antigone plays her role with love, with devotion, with wisdom, with a gentle persuasion in the face of passion. She has made her father love her and depend on her, with a dependence that is more than material: in the first scene with the Chorus he seeks and takes her advice. Yet at the grand climax she cannot, for all her eloquent pleading, prevail with him. 'It is not right for you of all people to retaliate upon him.' Oedipus consents to see and hear Polynices, only to curse him with a curse which might not otherwise have been pronounced.[73] If Antigone represents the power of persuasion, she fails: fails with the Chorus in the Parodos, fails with her father, fails with Polynices, fails (as we know) in the task she sets herself at the end of the play.[74] She fails to prevent terrible events, but by her love and pity mitigates the gross evil of them.

She fails, and she dies. Her death, which is certain, lies beyond the limits of the play, but Sophocles has ensured that we shall remember *Antigone,* first, when Polynices pleads with his sisters to give him burial 'if this father's curses are fulfilled, and a return home is granted you' (1407ff.), and then – which is how he chose to end his play –

---

[72] The terms of 1633–5 may be worth noting (the passage is closely recalled at 1773ff.). Theseus is made to promise that he will not willingly (or wittingly, ἑκών) leave Oedipus' daughters in the lurch, but carry out all that, φρονῶν εὖ, he is likely to do to their advantage (ὅσ' ἂν μέλλῃς φρονῶν εὖ ξυμφέροντ' αὐταῖς ἀεί). Jebb notes: 'as a well-wisher will do *his best,* φρονῶν εὖ thus practically means, "to the best of thy judgment"; but that is not the first sense of the words.' Actually he sends Antigone to Thebes.

[73] Linforth (1951) 163. This is no doubt controversial: cf. n. 50 above.

[74] 254ff.: she moves the Chorus to pity only (it is the awe-inspiring Oedipus, 292, who influences their action). 1181ff.: despite her limited success in obtaining audience for Polynices, Oedipus remains unmoved as a rock in the sea and the force of her arguments (esp. 1189ff.) is lost. 1414ff., 1770ff.

when Theseus promises her safe-conduct to Thebes in order that she may perform a service of love, the futile service of attempting to prevent the deaths her father had imprecated on his sons (1769ff.). Those deaths she cannot prevent, but she will bury Polynices at the cost of her own life. Thus, through a curse the effects of which he could neither limit nor, for all his prophetic power, foresee, Oedipus came to destroy the daughter he loved along with the sons he hated.[75]

Polynices did well to speak of his father's Erinyes, for it was such a blind passionate sweeping justice, involving the innocent along with the guilty, that the Aeschylean Erinyes administered – based upon retaliation and using human resentments as the means of punishment. Is it too much to say that Oedipus earns his status as a chthonian power by acting like the unpersuaded Furies of the *Oresteia*? Many will shrink from such an interpretation. It is, however, a standing problem, perhaps the central problem for the interpreter of the play. Oedipus is so angry, so apparently vindictive. Some critics have been content to judge the character and behaviour of Oedipus purely on the human level without considering its religious implications, except in the most superficial way. Others have been more deeply exercised; and they have been exercised not merely by the fact that the assumption of Oedipus seems to confer a divine sanction upon his curse but also by the great beauty and pathos of his loving farewell to his daughters. Could a man who loved so much also hate so much? The temptation to interpret or reinterpret the scene with Polynices in the light of its immediate sequel becomes irresistible. To that scene we must briefly return.

It is a major scene, but Polynices is not, of course, a major personage, though Sophocles has given him that plausibility of motive and character that his role requires.[76] He is not a Creon; and

---

[75] The more significance we attach (with Knox) to the growth of prophetic power in Oedipus the more significant this limitation upon his foreknowledge.

[76] The character is well studied, with close attention to the language of the scene, by Easterling, *PCPS* 1–13, who concludes that the curse of Oedipus 'is both just and psychologically plausible and, though appalling, not vindictive'. She speaks of him as retaining 'a nobility and consistency in his rage which seems . . . to be a far cry from mere vindictiveness'. This suggests to me that the last word, though I have used it once above, is better avoided, since in our post-Christian civilization it has acquired a strongly pejorative sense and a connotation of petty-mindedness which is, I should have thought, completely absent from corresponding words in Greek. It is better to speak of retaliation – a notion fundamental to Greek morals and a fundamental theme of the play.

the poet has no intention to deprive him of sympathy or deny him all
sincerity. It could be that, like the young Neoptolemus confronted
with Philoctetes, he had never fully realized his father's plight until he
saw him: still, one critic may be right to find a 'tastelessness and
artificiality' in his remarks at 1256–63.[77] One might say that in him
are combined a weak pity for Oedipus and a strong ambition for
himself (which comes out clearly at 1342f.). But the psychology of
Polynices is far less important than the themes that are developed in
this scene. It has been observed, rightly, that the theme of nurture
(with words such as *trophe*), so prominent in the second movement of
the play, returns in this scene to bring out the heinousness of the sons'
neglect of their father.[78] This duty Polynices has sacrificed to his
ambition, to the sceptre and the throne (1354); and that too is an echo
of the same earlier scene (418, 448f.). What might also be observed is
that, in that scene and prior to the story of the brothers' quarrel, the
accumulation of nurture-words had, on news of the oracle, been
followed by a similar accumulation of words of 'mastery'. If the
nurture-words stress the offence of the sons, they reveal the long-fostered resentment of Oedipus; if the words of mastery prepare the
theme of kingship, they show perhaps that he remembers he was once
a king. The stress on royal power which follows may be more than an
objective statement of fact.[79]

In judging this later scene we should not forget that Sophocles was
an ironist. It is preceded not only by the touching reunion of father
and daughters but also by the great speech of Antigone. In that
remarkable speech the most remarkable thing she says is that
Oedipus, who begat Polynices (gave him his *phusis*), had therefore no

---

[77] Easterling, *PCPS* 6.

[78] Easterling, *PCPS* 3f., 9.

[79] On the 'mastery'-group, which belongs to 392–408, see p. 257 above. It should
perhaps be considered in relation to the language used in the same context about
the ambitions of the sons. (This language is studied by Easterling, *PCPS* 4f.) First,
a simple reference to 'thrones' (368, 375); then – from Oedipus – 'tyranny' (419),
'sceptres and thrones' (425), followed at 448f. by the elaborate pleonasm of
'thrones' and 'sceptres' and 'tyranny'. I cannot help wondering whether this does
not cut both ways: not only stressing the ambition of the sons and their offence in
preferring power to filial duty but also indicating a revival of power-feelings in
Oedipus. I notice also – though this is a more hazardous region of speculation – that, in this context of power, at 427 and 448 Oedipus is ὁ φύσας, i.e. the
notion of *phusis* is introduced. (At 1293 a striking expression of Oedipus' royal
power is immediately followed by two *phusis*-words.) On the text of 367 see
BICS 26 (1979) 11.

right to retaliate upon him even for the most impious of offences. Are we not thus invited, when father and son meet, to see a likeness in *phusis* between them?[80]

There is certainly a likeness in situation, on which Polynices seeks to play (1335ff.).[81] But it goes farther than that. What is the suppliant's prayer (1326ff.)? That Oedipus will relax his heavy wrath (μῆνιν βαρεῖαν) in favour of one who has set out to take vengeance on a brother (πρὸς κασιγνήτου τίσιν), one who has been thrust out of his land, deprived of his power and dishonoured. But that heavy wrath itself sprang from the same fount of emotion, for a similar offence: Oedipus too had been dishonoured, thrust out, reduced from royal status to beggary. Polynices' plea by analogy misfires, because he does not know that that other suppliant had found a protector, that other exile a new home and citizenship. He has transferred his allegiance from the city that had wronged him. If Polynices is going to attack his native land, Oedipus looks forward to the day when his cold corpse in the grave will drink the hot blood of Thebans.[82]

No doubt to put it in this way is to over-simplify. Equally, it is an over-simplification to miss the irony of those resemblances, to which Oedipus in his passion is blind; to miss the whole passionate unreflecting character of his imprecation, which is the brimming-over of long-pent resentments. Yet Oedipus goes on to bless his daughters and become a *heros*.

Why should it ever have been supposed that there is an inconsistency in this? The depth of love which he feels for his daughters, the depth of hatred he feels for his sons, are two sides of the same coin. He loved his daughters because they were his benefactors, hated his sons because they had wronged him. To do good to your friends and harm to your enemies was the old *arete*, the newer justice; this is the code we have so often met and which Oedipus follows – and being a man beyond the common measure carries both his love and his hate

---

[80] 1369: ὑμεῖς δ᾽ ἀπ᾽ ἄλλου κοὐκ ἐμοῦ πεφύκατον. Antigone knew better than that (1189).

[81] Burian, in his interesting study of O.C. as a suppliant drama, brings out (p. 422) the parallelism between the suppliances of Oedipus and Polynices, remarking that 'Antigone pleads on behalf of a suppliant, but this time to a reluctant Oedipus, not for him'.

[82] Contr. Letters 303: 'Of course it would be irrelevant to charge Oedipus with lack of patriotism here.' Perhaps; perhaps not.

beyond the common measure. There are perhaps three things to be said.

(i) Since here, as in *Antigone*,[83] benefit and injury, love and hate, arise within the context of the family – a context which imposes duties paramount in the Greek moral scheme – the emotions generated have a peculiar intensity and poignancy.

(ii) Time has been at work, but it works in two ways. It can bring ease:[84] Oedipus came to understand that, in the self-blinding, his *thumos* had run too far. It was time – and Antigone – that had taught him such patience as he had learnt. But time, in its other aspect, was too strong for him. The past lived on; his *thumos* lived on and grew. For time brought with it a long life of hardship which, if it bred a love for his devoted daughters, bred also an accumulating resentment against his sons. It is a function of Creon to hale him back into the past: the two old men are terrible, because the past has made them so. It is a function of Polynices to show the evil past determining an evil future and destroying the young.

(iii) The gods are at work. Oedipus claims that his curses will overmaster the suppliance – and the ambitions – of Polynices, 'if indeed Justice proclaimed of old sits beside Zeus in accordance with primeval laws' (1380ff.).[85] The laws are ancient, Justice is as she was anciently proclaimed. We may recall the opening of the great *kommos* in the *Choephori*, when the Coryphaeus puts into the mouth of Dike a striking formulation of the *lex talionis* and adds: 'It is a thrice-ancient saying that gives voice to this' (τριγέρων μῦθος τάδε φωνεῖ, *Cho*. 314). It is indeed an ancient principle that 'the doer must suffer'; and the Chorus of the *Agamemnon* sang that it would abide while Zeus abode upon his throne (*Agam*. 1563f.). It is a principle upon which men act and which the gods sanction: it is particularly associated with the Erinyes. But there is a complementary principle – that good must be returned to those who do good. Jointly, the two principles were the basis of traditional Greek morality. *Herões* were quasi-divine exemplifications of this principle, being powerful in their graves to help their friends and harm their enemies. It was thus altogether appropriate that an Oedipus who loved and hated with such intensity should go on to heroic status. But what did this mean to Sophocles?

---

[83] See pp. 129 ff.
[84] Cf. *El*. 179 (εὐμαρὴς θεός).
[85] Easterling, *PCPS* 10 has interesting remarks on this passage.

What truth about the gods and about the world in which he had lived for some ninety years did it embody? That it embodied an important truth – and a grim truth – we can hardly doubt. So much of his tragedy is concerned with divine wrath. With divine wrath, but also with human pity. We must return to this.

CHAPTER TWELVE

Philoctetes

A play of extraordinary brilliance and power, *Philoctetes* is here taken outside the chronological order, in which it lies between *Electra* and the *Coloneus*. There were special reasons for taking those two plays together. Are there features which, as some feel, separate *Philoctetes* from other extant plays of Sophocles? After all, if (unlike *Electra* and the *Coloneus*) the play has no Erinyes, yet the lasting effects of a cruel act are displayed. There is a hero who shares many characteristics with other Sophoclean heroes; the pathos – and the rhetoric – are unsurpassed; there is human pity, and irony, and other Sophoclean themes in plenty. If the ending is 'happy', so in some strange sense are the endings of *Electra* and the *Coloneus,* though it may be remarked that here the final solution is not marred by an ambivalent matricide or a parental curse. The absence of death and disaster from the outcome do not necessarily deprive the play of tragic quality, though they affect its tone.

Odysseus, and with him the young Neoptolemus, have been sent to bring Philoctetes to Troy. Philoctetes, inheritor of Heracles' infallible bow, had been jettisoned by the Greeks ten years before upon the desert island of Lemnos, but a prophetic utterance has now revealed that his presence is necessary if Troy is to be captured. How is he to be brought? By force? By persuasion? By craft? Odysseus, for good reasons, opts for craft and enlists the services of Neoptolemus. But is it Philoctetes who is needed or merely the bow? What *did* the prophet say? While Philoctetes holds the bow, the question is academic, since the bow cannot come without its owner. But circumstances separate the bow from Philoctetes and it passes into the possession of Neoptolemus, whereupon the question becomes a real one. Neoptolemus returns the bow to Philoctetes, and the original situation is restored.

280

The bow-question thus has three phases, which are essential to the economy of the play. The question has been debated for decades, one might have said *ad nauseam*, but the criticism of the play has recently been refreshed by a series of valuable contributions from which one thing at least emerges, which is the skill of Sophocles in inviting the attention and maintaining the suspense of his audience.[1] Information is withheld and released as it will be dramatically effective. There are dramatic reversals. There are false starts and, above all, false endings, so that the audience is kept in a state of uncertainty,[2] never quite sure what the characters will do or even in some cases what they are trying to do. The trick fails; force is hardly tried; persuasion fails. In the end – or what seems to be the end – bow, Philoctetes and Neoptolemus are leaving, but not for Troy. With the appearance of Heracles, there is a final reversal.

It does not of course follow that, because Sophocles has developed and maintained an interest of this kind with great dramaturgical skill, he is not simultaneously exploring serious issues. Other recent writers have taken the play very seriously as an expression of the poet's tragic vision, particularly in relation to the divine plan, to the refusal of Philoctetes to conform, and to the role of Heracles.[3] These are matters to which we must return, when we have considered the course of the action, and when we have considered the characters. For character and action are no less closely meshed in this than in other Sophoclean plays: indeed it might be fair to say that in no other play is interest in character so absorbing, not only in what the personages are and how they have become so, but also in what they *should* do and what they *will* do, which, largely because of the uncertainties already mentioned, is a far more open question than in most Greek tragedies. We become absorbed in the characters and problems of three men, in their relationships and in their communication with one another.[4]

Three men: Odysseus, Neoptolemus and Philoctetes. One could look at Neoptolemus as the focus of a struggle between the other two, both fighting for the soul of the young man; and it is true that he is under

---

[1] Esp. Hinds (1967); Steidle (1968); Robinson (1969); Taplin (1971); Garvie (1972); Seale (1972). The revised picture which emerges is well summarized by Easterling, *ICS*.

[2] Seale, in particular, shows how Sophocles uses visual effects for this purpose.

[3] Alt (1961); Avery (1965); Erbse (1966); Poe (1974); Rose (1976); Segal (1977).

[4] 'It is a play of relationships and communication, not of great deeds' (Taplin 26).

pressures from both which come to be tormenting. This does not, however, represent the true balance of the play.[5] It is not simply that the appearances of Odysseus are brief: he dominates the Prologos and participates in two vital scenes at the climax of action. Nevertheless, he remains a subordinate character. He is a political man, of a type which may have been recognizable to the fifth-century audience,[6] but not primarily what we call a 'self-seeking' politician. He is an agent: he sees himself as such and wishes Neoptolemus to be one – a *huperetes* (15, 53). He is the agent of the Greek army and its leaders and even represents himself as the agent of Zeus (989f.).[7] He has no personal stake, except that stake in success (1052) which is common to the Greek world, and no decisions to make, except on tactics, where he is unfeeling, unscrupulous and cunning – with a cunning which seems to over-reach itself.[8] He undergoes no change whatever in the course of the play; and, when we see him in his last scene hovering on the outskirts of the action, that is where he belongs. A prudent man and a realist, who sees no point in getting himself killed, he cuts his losses and goes away, leaving the stage to the two personages that matter.[9]

We are already familiar with plays of Sophocles which have two characters of central importance; here too there has been the usual dispute as to which is primary.[10] No doubt, insofar as the question is interesting, we must put Philoctetes first, not because he has given his name to the play, but because he is the great hero whose story is being told, and because he is so Sophoclean in his 'heroism'. Well and good, provided we do justice to the balance Sophocles has maintained between the man and the boy; provided we observe how each is brought in turn – first Neoptolemus, then Philoctetes – to the point of decision, to the cry of 'What am I to do?', and how their answers jointly create the situation in which the gods must intervene. Both

[5] See n. 11 below, on Vidal-Naquet.
[6] Cf. Kitto, *FMD* 109; Poe 23; Gellie 138. Accounts of Odysseus in modern writers do not differ greatly, though some are slightly more sympathetic than others. Gellie, 132, says aptly that he is 'the real professional'. In his concentration on the bow Linforth (1956) 103–5, sees 'his concern for the impersonal instrument and his disregard of the man'.
[7] Cf. Kitto, *FMD* 122f.
[8] Cf. Garvie 216.
[9] Taplin 37, seems right to detect a whiff of Old Comedy – the discomfiture of an *alazon*? – in his reappearance and rapid dismissal at 1293ff. Cf. also his 28 n.8.
[10] See p. 75 above.

Neoptolemus and Philoctetes are striking creations of poetic imagination and psychological insight.

Neoptolemus is a young man, little more than a boy,[11] son of a famous father, newly come from Scyros to the society of famous warriors; he is sent on an important mission in the company of a man of outstanding fame, by whom he is impressed and whom no doubt he wishes to impress. When he hears that his role is to be one of deception, he jibs: that is not in the Achilles-tradition, not consonant with his *phusis*. Take Philoctetes by force, yes; by lies, no. (The feelings of Philoctetes do not enter into it one way or the other.) Odysseus, who knew that this would be the difficulty, handles the situation with skill; and he has a strong card to play. Neoptolemus has been promised that he will have the honour of taking Troy (as even his great father failed to do). For this, however, Philoctetes and his bow will also be needed and, Odysseus argues, can only be obtained by craft. He tempts the boy with the prospect of a twofold reputation, both clever and valiant (a combination of Odysseus and Achilles?); and Neoptolemus falls (116, 119f.). If his conscience is still not easy, he conducts his deceitful role with competence, if not with zest. But, from the entry of Philoctetes onwards, he is subject to a long cumulative pressure which results in his returning the bow to its owner in defiance of Odysseus; and, finally, he agrees to take Philoctetes home – an agreement he is about to fulfil when Heracles intervenes.

The process is intriguing – and was meant by Sophocles to intrigue his audience – since, in the nature of the situation, Neoptolemus having to preserve the façade of deception, it is not until the pressure has become fully effective that we are allowed to see its effects at all. We cannot *know* how he is reacting from moment to moment. The audience does not know, but, having seen and heard him in the Prologos, is bound to ask; and the critic is equally entitled to wonder and to guess. When the truth comes out, Sophocles can tell us by a word of retrospect (*palai*) something of what has been going on in the

---

[11] For Vidal-Naquet's suggestion that Neoptolemus is to be seen as an ephebe who graduates into a hoplite in the course of the play, and who, being *qua* ephebe associated with wild nature, serves as a link between Philoctetes and Odysseus, see *BICS* 26 (1979) 1of. In the same article I consider a very different view of Neoptolemus taken by W. M. Calder, *GRBS* 12 (1971) 153–74, for whom he is from first to last a consummate villain. I find this quite unconvincing, but his argument raises an interesting point about the winds, which I discuss.

mind of his character.[12] The word occurs four times in this connection. But what does it signify? It can be used of comparatively recent
events. When Neoptolemus uses it (806) during the agonies of Philoctetes, which commenced at 730, it might refer to those agonies alone,
the effect of which upon him is crucial. Yet, at 759f., when Philoctetes
has appealed for pity (756) – and it is Neoptolemus' first expression of
pity in the play, he calls him 'hapless in all manner of woe' (διὰ πόνων
πάντων). When did he begin to pity? When did he begin to feel
ashamed? We cannot say. The word recurs three times in the confes-
sion-scene: first at 906, and this immediately follows words (902f.)
which recall the Prologos; then at 913, which also refers to the trick;
and, finally, after Philoctetes' scathing attack, the climax comes in
two splendid lines. 'In me a terrible pity has come to lodge and has
long been there' (ἐμοὶ μὲν οἶκτος δεινὸς ἐμπέπτωκέ τις | τοῦδ' ἀνδρὸς
οὐ νῦν πρῶτον ἀλλὰ καὶ πάλαι, 965f.).[13] The process which produced
this state may well have begun with the first sight of Philoctetes.

The entry – the sight – of Philoctetes is prepared by the Parodos of
a Chorus of sailors; and Sophocles uses it, among other things, to
show his young hero in a new relation which brings out at once his
youth and his responsibility. The relationship is very natural and
rather touching. They ask for his instructions, deferring to the greater
skill and judgement of one who holds the sceptre from Zeus. Immediately they call him 'child', but say their duty is to serve (*hupourgein*)
him. Very flattering to the young man who has just been freed from
the overwhelming presence of Odysseus, but an Odysseus who had
promised him a reputation for cleverness! The *kommos* is, naturally,
about Philoctetes. Where is he? 'It's quite clear to *me* (ἔμοιγε, 162)',
says Neoptolemus, that he is out after food;[14] and he describes his life
objectively. The Chorus is moved to pity (169, 186, cf. 161) at such a
life for one who had been a great man. 'Nothing surprising in all this
to *me* (ἐμοί)', says the young man; 'if *I* (κἀγώ) have any judgement',
Philoctetes is suffering at the hands of the gods for their good reasons.
Neoptolemus is right of course! But it is rather glib, the cocksureness

[12] Cf. Kirkwood, *SSD*159.
[13] Steidle 181, points out that the expressions with *palai* are 'alle verschieden
nuanciert'. The translation of 965f. attempts to bring out the force of the perfect
tense.
[14] Neoptolemus is in fact repeating – and appropriating – what Odysseus said at 43!
For the use of stressed personal pronouns, see Select Index.

of youth.[15] Older men, with their experience of life, may pity Philoctetes, but Neoptolemus lacks the experience and imagination to realize his plight – until he sees him and hears him. Philoctetes appears,[16] and the long process begins.

Well described by several writers, it need not be described in detail here. There is the joy of Philoctetes at hearing a Greek voice; his love and admiration for Achilles; his generous sympathy for Neoptolemus in his supposed wrongs (336ff.). This leads into an enquiry about the fates of various Greeks, the 'good' who have died, the 'bad' who have survived.[17] Here Neoptolemus is proper, if a little evasive: any light thrown is upon Philoctetes. Now the former feigns to be going away, and the latter launches his moving appeal in terms which remind us of the Prologos and must have reminded Neoptolemus of the standards Odysseus had persuaded him to abandon.[18] But the play-acting goes on.[19] Neoptolemus will take Philoctetes on board his ship and carry him – 'whithersoever we wish to sail' (529). The plan is working; and we are not *told* how the young man is feeling, either then or when,

[15] Kitto, *FMD* 112, maintains that Neoptolemus is here on the defensive, but this seems less probable.

[16] A sudden dramatic appearance with the bow at the mouth of the cave. Robinson, 39ff. argues ingeniously that Philoctetes is seen, by the audience *and* by the Chorus, trailing across from a Parodos (and that this influences their language in the final antistrophe). But it is precisely the language of 201ff. on which the argument falls down: an accumulation of words of sound, not a word of sight. How often does a chorus *see* a character approaching and not *say* so? On Sophocles' purpose in giving the the cave a double entrance Dale was right, cf. *WS* 69 (1956) 104ff.

[17] See App. F below.

[18] Neoptolemus is promised *eukleia* by Philoctetes and by Odysseus (119) on different grounds. Both lay stress on the brevity of the countervailing disadvantage: ἡμέρας τοι μόχθος οὐχ ὅλης μιᾶς (480), ἡμέρας μέρος βραχύ (83). Both call on him to endure – Odysseus a brief dishonour, Philoctetes a brief inconvenience. If this is an intentional parallel (as I think it is), 477 might be invoked to support Housman's εἰς ὄνειδος at 83, which has other merits. When, at 519ff., Neoptolemus and the Chorus do their play-acting, the leader asking if they can really put up with Philoctetes' noisome disease and the Coryphaeus replying that *that* is a reproach which he will never be able to bring against them, the stress on τοῦτο, which is not strictly required, may suggest the possibility of *other* reproaches (τοὔνειδος . . . ὀνειδίσαι).

[19] Some interpreters find a positive zest in Neoptolemus' playing of his deceptive role, others find signs of reluctance, notably Steidle, who, in the course of a close analysis, points to the possibly ambiguous tenour of e.g. 431f. and 436f. Judgements here are so subjective that agreement may never be reached, but see my text below on the language of 671.

after the untimely intervention of the 'Merchant', he is to be allowed
to handle the famous bow – because of his *arete* (669). 'It was', says
Philoctetes, 'for a good service that I myself acquired it' (670). In
other words, the boy will take him home and in return will be lent the
bow.[20] Neoptolemus' reply is, again, proper. 'I am not sorry to have
seen you and gained your friendship. No possession is more valuable
than a friend who knows how to requite a benefit.' He might seem the
apt pupil of Odysseus. There are, however, two features of the
language which invite attention. There is οὐκ ἄχθομαι: a characteristic
Greek understatement which Jebb translates, quite legitimately: 'I
rejoice.' But the verb can mean 'to be embarrassed', being in fact the
word which Neoptolemus is going to use at 970 of his embarrassment. And there is ἰδών, which Jebb translates: 'to have found thee'.
But is it not the actual visible presence of Philoctetes which is making
all the difference to the feelings of Neoptolemus? 'It is no embarrassment to me to have seen you.' Could this not be the precise opposite
of the truth?[21] Particularly with the addition: 'to have made a friend
of you'? This from a young man who had been brought up to a world
in which friendship and loyalty to friends was a part of *arete*.

The man and the boy enter the cave together; the Chorus sings. At
the end of the song they reappear, but, as they are leaving for the ship,
Philoctetes is struck down by his agonizing pain. 'Pity me', he
exclaims (755); and for the first time words of pity come from the lips
of Neoptolemus (759f.).[22] The agony passes, and Philoctetes falls
asleep, having entrusted the bow to the care of his companion. The
Chorus, in famous words, sing a hymn to Sleep.[23] 'Sleep, stranger to

[20] Neoptolemus does not at this point handle the bow, which must not go to and fro,
the transfers when they occur being of prime dramatic importance. 667f. are a
promise for the future, but both the giving and the giving back will take place in
circumstances not envisaged by the speaker. 668f. are wrongly athetized by
Fraenkel, *Sem*.62f.

[21] A far-fetched hypothesis? Perhaps, but – the action having reached a point of rest
– the Chorus starts singing, and the first line they sing – they are about to cite
Ixion as a parallel for the miseries of Philoctetes – runs as follows: 'I have heard
said, but I have certainly never seen . . .' Why this stress on seeing, except that
Neoptolemus has now *seen* Philoctetes and is about to see him in agony?

[22] When Neoptolemus says τί δῆτα δράσω; at 757 he means 'what can I do to help?',
but perhaps it already hints at his dilemma (Taplin 33).

[23] At 830f. J. Diggle, *CR* 16 (1966) 262, argues powerfully for τοῦδ' αἴγλαν ὅς . . . He
might have added that, as the text stands, ὄμμασι has to be understood of the eyes,
not of the only persons mentioned (ἡμῖν), but of someone who is not mentioned
at all.

anguish . . . come, I pray, with power to heal.' It is very beautiful – and lasts for half a stanza only, being followed by one of the harshest discords one could find in Greek poetry.[24] The sleep they pray to visit the suffering Philoctetes is something to be *used*. Now, they think, is the time to make off with the bow. These are plain, practical men.[25] They have heard the 'Merchant's' report of the words of Helenus, but for them the important thing is the bow; and, when Neoptolemus 'corrects' them, they make a plain, practical answer. 'The god will see to that' (and indeed before the end of the play the gods will have to see to more than that!). What the sailors want to know is whether Philoctetes is *really* asleep.

It is the words of Neoptolemus that matter: just four hexameters declaimed between strophe and antistrophe. The form and the metre are arresting; the words must be important, and it has been suggested that the hexameters are oracular to express a new insight on the young man's part into the true significance of the prophecy. If that were true, if he were taking the 'Merchant's' words to heart (and why should he?), one might expect him to speak of persuasion. Far from this, his words are hard, even brutal. No, he replies, the bow by itself is not enough; the prey and the prize is Philoctetes himself.[26] The metaphor of the hunt is resumed from the Prologos.[27] The purpose of the deceit was success, the glory of taking Troy; now the man Philoctetes is spoken of as the garland-prize of an agonistic contest. But of course it is the fourth hexameter which counts. To boast (as huntsman or as competitor) of an uncompleted task is a disgrace and a reproach: κομπεῖν δ' ἔστ' ἀτελῆ . . . αἰσχρὸν ὄνειδος. The language is subtle and, again, takes us back to the Prologos. The lies were felt by Neoptolemus to be αἰσχρόν (108), but for the sake of success he would put aside all shame (120); and it is probable that the word ὄνειδος

---

[24] Cf. Segal, *Hermes* 146.

[25] Recent writers have pointed out, correctly, that Greeks of the classical period did not necessarily put a simple faith in the terms of oracles and prophecies. Cf. Robinson 47.

[26] Cf. *BICS* 16 (1969) 48–50, where I hope to have shown that στέφανος refers, not to a victory of Philoctetes at Troy, but, by an agonistic metaphor, to him as the prize for which Neoptolemus is now striving; and I suggest that hexameters are used as a heroic, not as an oracular, metre.

[27] On 'hunting' in the play, literal and metaphorical, see Rose 83f. The word θηρᾶν is first used by Neoptolemus (116) – of the bow, but he had already spoken of 'taking' Philoctetes by force or by cunning (90f.).

should be read at 83.[28] What is shameful? What is a reproach? Failure is both; deceit is both; to combine failure with deceit is doubly reprehensible. The ambiguity which cloaked Philoctetes and the bow, while Philoctetes still held the bow, can no longer be maintained, and Neoptolemus now realizes that he must take the man whom he has begun to pity and with whom he has, deceitfully, promised to stay. Is he not embarrassed?

With the recovery of Philoctetes, with his joy to find Neoptolemus still in attendance, all comes out into the open. Neoptolemus cries out loud; and it is no accident that his cry (παπαῖ) echoes the cries of Philoctetes: he is now in mental agony.[29] 'What am I to do next?' (895). He is in a state of *aporia* (897f.). What is he to say? What should he do? (The whole short dialogue is a network of words of saying and words of doing.)[30] He has abandoned his *phusis* to do what is unseemly (902f.); he will be found base (αἰσχρός, 906), and that has *long* been distressing him. What shall he do? (908). As to saying, he will tell the truth; as to doing, he will stick to his duty, he will obey authority.[31] So the truth comes out, and Philoctetes reacts with a devastating speech. 'What are we to do?' says the Coryphaeus; it is for Neoptolemus to decide (963f.). 'Me? In me a terrible pity for this man has come to lodge and has long been there.' (Not shame this time, but pity.) Philoctetes seizes on the word. 'Pity me, my son, for the gods' sake, and do not let men reproach you (ὄνειδος) for having cheated me.' 'Alas, what shall I do?' Then a nice touch: 'I wish I had never left Scyros, so embarrassed am I by the situation' (969f.). It is no good, he cannot revert to childhood; and it is no good now saying to his sailors (974): 'My men, what are we to do?', since the responsibility is his. At this point he must have moved towards Philoctetes with the bow, for Odysseus interrupts in mid-line to prevent him. 'You worst of men, what are you doing?'[32]

The scene is now played between Odysseus and Philoctetes, while

---

[28] See n. 18 above.

[29] Knox, *HT* 132

[30] Between 895 and 924 we find δρᾶν eight times and ten words of saying. For similar accumulations of words of saying at 1267ff. and 1373ff. see n. 46.

[31] Like more than one Thucydidean speaker (cf. 3.40.4; 1.34–5, 42–3), Neoptolemus claims (925f.) that justice and self-interest coincide. Such claims were no doubt a feature of contemporary oratory and reflect sophistic thought.

[32] On the staging of this – and of the corresponding scene at 1291–6 – see Taplin 27–9. (Neoptolemus certainly does *not* give Odysseus the bow at this or any other time.)

Neoptolemus stands, miserably, holding the bow and listening –
listening, among other things, to Philoctetes, who now understands
the position so well, as he accuses Odysseus of using the boy and
perverting his true nature (1007–15). Neoptolemus is silent (for more
than 100 lines) till near the end of the scene, when he and Odysseus are
about to leave together with the bow and Philoctetes appeals to him.
He makes no answer: Odysseus sees to that. 'Come on', he says, 'Stop
looking at him,[33] noble though you are, lest you mar *our* luck.'
Philoctetes turns to the Chorus; the Coryphaeus replies that their
captain must tell them what to do; and at last Neoptolemus speaks.
Odysseus may or may not be bluffing, when he proposes to leave
Philoctetes behind on the island to starve to death (the matter is
controversial), but Neoptolemus is certainly temporizing, only too
happy to leave the Chorus with him for a time, in the hope that they
will bring him to see sense. Even for this he excuses himself. 'I shall be
told by Odysseus that I am full of pity' (1074f.); and so he is. To what
will the pity of Neoptolemus lead?

It leads to his dramatic reappearance pursued by Odysseus and his
return of the bow to Philoctetes. A weight is off his mind (εἶἑν, 1308),
but he still has a job to do. Trickery is out, force no longer possible,
only persuasion remains. Philoctetes must go to Troy; it is in his
interest and in that of Neoptolemus, and it is the will of the gods.
Neoptolemus sets out to persuade him and fails, partly because his
generous change of heart cannot easily undo the harm which the false
approach dictated by Odysseus had done. It is sometimes said, truly,
that in Greek tragedy we do not see development of character, as
though this were surprising – and regrettable – in a drama which
preserves the unity of time. But there are, in human life, cases in
which maturity is forced upon a young man within a short space of
time. This adult Neoptolemus we now see – is he a little too mature,
too wise a counsellor? One may well doubt whether Sophocles was
much interested in portraying the mature Neoptolemus through the
rhetoric and argumentation which is given him.[34] The interest has
shifted. Always divided between Neoptolemus and Philoctetes, it is
now concentrated upon the latter. Neoptolemus has solved his moral
problem and taken his decision; Philoctetes must face his.

[33] The present imperative at 1068 must be given its proper force: Odysseus does not
say, e.g., μὴ προσίδῃς.
[34] Rose 77, has some interesting remarks on the argumentation of 1314ff.

Philoctetes was first introduced to us through the inanimate objects
which Neoptolemus saw in the cave (32ff.): the bedding, the home-
made cup, the tinder, the noisome rags. (The originality, even the
modernity, of this is typically unobtrusive.)[35] To Neoptolemus they
are mere objects, the last a nasty one, but we can see a life behind
them. We come to the Parodos. Where is Philoctetes? Clearly, says
Neoptolemus, he has gone after food, shooting wild creatures, for
that is the 'nature of his way of life' (162ff.). The Chorus expresses
pity: he is alone with no one to care for him, no ξύντροφον ὄμμα, sick
with a cruel disease and in every kind of need. 'Noble perchance as
any scion of the noblest house' (Jebb), he lies apart from others 'with
the dappled or shaggy beasts of the field'. What happens to a hero of
noble birth, friend of Heracles and recipient of his bow, when he is cut
off from human society for ten years, living with and like the beasts?
To what state of mind is he brought? To answering these questions
Sophocles has devoted his imagination and the resources of his art.
The answers are not quite so simple as has sometimes been supposed.

Can such a man revert to a normal relationship with his fellow-
men, and on what terms? When Philoctetes begins to speak, greeting
his fellow-Greeks, overjoyed to learn the identity of Neoptolemus
and entering into courteous conversation with a fellow-noble, it
seems there will be no problem. He tells them not to be scared by his
wild appearance (ἀπηγριωμένον, 226), and there is as yet no sign that
he is 'brutalized' in mind as well as in looks. Philoctetes tells his story;
he even tells it with a touch of pride, so ingenious, so courageous has
he been.[36] That he feels a bitter resentment at the way he has been
treated is only natural (and this resentment dominates the long
dialogue in which he cross-examines Neoptolemus about the fates of
various Greeks). His hatred for the Atridae and, above all, for Odysseus comes into greater and greater prominence. The language at the
beginning and the end of his first long speech (254ff.) deserves
attention. He feels his misery aggravated by the fact that, as he has
been led to believe, no news of it has reached Greece; with his own
plight he contrasts the prosperity of his enemies. And who are they?
He sets them out with a formal *men* and *de*. They are the Greek leaders
who cast him forth and now mock him in silence – and, coupled with

---

[35] It is perhaps more what one would expect to find in a novel by Conrad than in a
      Greek tragedy.
[36] 533ff. Cf. also 285ff., on which see Linforth (1956) 110.

them, his disease which ever flourishes and grows in strength. At the end of the speech he tells of his ten years of hunger and misery. 'That, my son, is what the Atridae and the violent Odysseus have done. May the Olympian gods give them some day themselves to suffer in requital for me!' (311–16).[37]

Sophocles knew – how we cannot say – that a man in solitude must make his own companions; and we come to realize that Philoctetes has peopled the island with personifications. There is his disease – the beastly sickness (265), 'in whose company' (ξὺν ᾗ, 268) he had been abandoned, and which, like a greedy animal, he has to feed (313).[38] It is a personal enemy; and no less is true of the viper who made him lame (631f.). His foot takes on an existence independent of himself (786). 'You bays and headlands, you beasts on the mountains who dwell with me, you precipitous rocks, to you – for I have no one else to whom to speak – to you my wonted companions (παροῦσι τοῖς εἰωθόσιν) – I bewail my treatment by the son of Achilles' (936ff.). Philoctetes apostrophizes the natural scene – and his cave (952f.); he apostrophizes the birds who have been his prey and whose prey he will become (1146ff.). He apostrophizes his bow, a friend now wrenched from his loving hands, and calls upon it to look with pity upon its change of masters (1128ff.).

But closer to him than any of these companions is the hatred he has so long cherished for the Greeks, for the Atridae and for Odysseus; and it becomes a question whether this is a companionship which it is psychologically possible for him to relinquish. When the agony comes upon him (782ff.), after the address to his foot, as the pain redoubles, he cries out: 'My friend from Cephallenia, would that this anguish might pierce *your* breast.' More cries of agony. 'You two generals, if only you instead of me might cherish this malady for so long.' We realize, with horror, that we are witnessing an oft-repeated scene, that again and again for ten years not only has he prayed for death (ὦ θάνατε θάνατε, 797), but has derived a kind of horrible consolation from imagining that such sufferings might befall his enemies. His passionate hatred, his longing for revenge, have come to

[37] A little later we have the well-known passage (410ff.) about the living and the dead upon which much has been built by some interpreters. Too much? It is given detailed consideration in App. F, where I conclude that its main function is to feed and elicit Philoctetes' hatred and contempt for his enemies.

[38] For the wound as a beast, see J. C. Kamerbeek, *Mnem*. sér. 4.1 (1948) 198–204.

outweigh every other emotion that he feels. 'Land of my fathers, gods who watch over me, take vengeance, take vengeance on them all, late in time though it be, if you have any pity upon me. My life is pitiable, but, if I saw them dead, I could think that I had escaped from my disease' (1040ff.). [39] This is the man who, with a promise of healing, will be asked to help the Greeks. It is against this emotional background, and in this state of mind, that Philoctetes has to make his decision.

Philoctetes must go to Troy; he must be persuaded to go (612); he must go willingly (1332). Our knowledge of the prophecy is of course dispensed by Sophocles according to his dramatic convenience. In the Prologos, where Odysseus rules out persuasion meaning a direct appeal to Philoctetes, it is not mentioned at all. The 'Merchant' quotes Helenus as saying that Philoctetes should be 'persuaded by speech'. But the 'Merchant' tells lies; moreover, there are more ways of persuading in words than honest suasion.[40] Still, the lines sound like a genuine prophecy and stick in the mind. (We do not know quite where we are.) Neoptolemus is convinced – we need not ask precisely how – that Philoctetes must be brought and not the bow alone, but his language is far from being that of persuasion. It is not until a late stage that we have a full, though not a verbatim, account of the prophecy. It is preposterous to suppose that it is not authentic, being confirmed by Heracles; it is no less preposterous to belittle the importance of the persuasion-theme. The audience is not being asked to read a riddle, but to contemplate a theme of Aeschylean dimensions which comes to dominate the closing phases of the play.

Five attempts are made to persuade Philoctetes, three while he is

---

[39] It may be worth looking at 1035ff. a little more carefully. May they perish, he says; and, having wronged him, they *will* perish, if the gods care for justice (ἠδικηκότες, δίκης). He finds evidence that they do so care in the fact that the Greeks have come to him. By κέντρον θεῖον he means, not the prophecy, but their ill-success. But the punishment is incomplete – and long-delayed. He calls on the witnessing gods to take vengeance at last upon them all. (By ξύμπαντας αὐτούς he presumably means the whole Greek army, and we can compare the sweeping curse of Ajax at *Ajax* 843f.) He then introduces the notion of divine pity. Belated justice is often associated with the Erinyes, but Sophocles preferred not to introduce those goddesses in this play, nor does he, as in *O.C.*, explore the relationship between divine justice and divine pity. The important thing here is Philoctetes' own passionate longing for retaliation, which takes priority over his desire for cure.

[40] Linforth (1956) 115; Garvie 218 n. 16; Gellie 144.

deprived of the bow, two after its return to him.[41] While Neoptolemus, acknowledging his lie, still withholds the bow, little can be
effected. Philoctetes, he says, *must* sail to Troy 'to the Achaeans and
the army of the Atridae' (915f.). There is brief reference (919f.) to
saving him from his troubles and to his share in the sack of Troy, but
Philoctetes is only interested in what Neoptolemus has done and will
do (921, 924). When Odysseus takes control of the situation, his
persuasions, if they can be so described – he speaks of force (983) and
uses it (1003) – were bound to fail and he may not have believed in
their efficacy.[42] Having failed, he changes his tack and creates a new
situation. 'Let him stay' (1055).

There has been much argument about the intentions of Odysseus at
this point; and it could be that Sophocles did not intend his audience
to be certain of them. That he would have preferred Philoctetes to go
to Troy is evident from the forcible prevention of suicide; that he was
prepared, if necessary, to go without him is probable enough; that, at
the least, he was happy for the sailors to remain is also probable. Let
Philoctetes realize what it means to be left alone without the bow, let
him reflect that, if he does not come, the famous bow will be used by
Teucer or, worse still, by Odysseus himself, and, so thinks Odysseus
(who is a rational man and knows nothing of the force of blind
emotion), he will see sense and change his mind.[43]

The *kommos* (1081–217) is a big set-piece which bulks large in the
play. Like many lyric scenes in Euripides, it has great pathos: does it
advance or affect the action? It is primarily directed to revealing the
mind of Philoctetes. Will he go to Troy? Yes, the legend said so; and
that was something Sophocles could hardly change. Will he go of his
own accord? Odysseus perhaps thinks that he will, now that he has
lost the bow, and when he has had time to reflect. The *kommos* shows
that he will not – not on those terms, not in response to blackmail.
The Chorus – sympathetic realists – reason with him, and a reason-

[41] Kitto, *FMD* 121ff.

[42] At 994 πειστέον suggests obedience rather than persuasion. When he *is* treating
Philoctetes like a slave (995), it is no good telling him that he is a noble hero
destined to sack Troy.

[43] Sophocles does not invite us to ask whether, if this failed, Odysseus would have
been content with the bow or whether, as he could well have done, he would have
returned and taken Philoctetes by force. The essential point is that, as Sophocles
has chosen to tell the story, the audience must believe Philoctetes will go to Troy
and cannot see how this is to be brought about.

able man would go to Troy.[44] But can he be reasonable after all that he has suffered at the hands of the Greek leaders? He is back where he was before, living in a world of his own, peopled with birds (which he can no longer shoot), a bow (which is no longer his), his cave, his painful foot – all vividly personified.[45] It is the same, except that it is worse for the frustration of his hopes, the treachery of Neoptolemus, and the loss of the bow. Without the bow he is unable to live (1081–115). Does this lead to a change of mind? No, but to his old psychological refuge, a curse on Odysseus (1113–15). The bow is in hostile hands (1123–39). Does this lead to a change of mind? No, but to more vilification of Odysseus. His mind dwells with the birds (1146–62), but the Chorus wants him to come back to men. 'For the god's sake, if you have any respect for a stranger who comes close to you in all good-will, come close to him' (1163f.). Again the reaction is unfavourable, but, when they begin to move away, his feeling for society revives. He apologizes to them, using a very social word: 'you must not be angry (νεμεσητόν, 1193)', he says, 'if a man who is distraught with pain speaks frantically'; but, when they renew their advice and say 'come', his response is more violent than ever, approaching blasphemy, and once more he curses those who have rejected the cripple. Philoctetes retires into his cave.

Of the two tests to which the heroic obstinacy of Philoctetes is exposed he has passed the first: he has faced the prospect of a lingering death and preferred it to compliance. The second test – once more in possession of the bow, to withstand the persuasions of a generous Neoptolemus – will be subtler and more difficult. For with the return of Neoptolemus and Odysseus the situation changes dramatically. At the end of their brief altercation, the former calls Philoctetes out of the cave. Naturally, he thinks he is going to be taken perforce to Troy, and the persuasive words spoken by Neoptolemus, with the bow still in his hands, go for nothing. They are mere words; and words have been used before to his detriment.[46] But now comes a deed (τοὔργον,

---

[44] *Pace* Rose 75, we should not regard the pity of the Chorus, here any more than at
      169ff., as hypocritical. Their attitude – a combination of weak pity and strong
      self-interest – does not vary, and by not varying provides, as it were, an axis
      against which we can plot the movements of their captain's emotions. Their line
      at 1178 is perfectly natural in people arguing with a stubborn man: 'All right, if
      that is what you want, it suits me.'

[45] Cave: 1081ff. Bow: 1128ff. Birds: 1146ff. Foot: 1188f.

[46] There are three notable accumulations of words of saying in the play. (i) 895ff. (see

1291), as Neoptolemus hands back the bow. Now, surely, he has created the circumstances in which Philoctetes can be persuaded. It is in this situation that the fourth – and penultimate – attempt at persuasion takes place. And it fails. (The audience, though it knows that Philoctetes will ultimately go to Troy, does not know whether it will succeed or fail.) Neoptolemus has one great asset, which is the good-will he has so dramatically established, and he has powerful arguments of self-interest to which a rational man might well respond: not only the promise of glory but – something which has been carefully reserved for this climax – the promise of cure. Both promises are confirmed by reference to Zeus Horkios (1324) and restated with the utmost clarity and emphasis at the end of Neoptolemus' speech (1344–7). Now Philoctetes is faced with *his* dilemma; it is now his turn to say 'What shall I do?' (οἴμοι, τί δράσω; 1350);[47] and, as Neoptolemus at a moment of decision wished he was back in Scyros, so Philoctetes wishes he were dead. He makes a speech of some length (1348–72), which is followed by a brief conclusive dialogue. It is from this point onwards that the interpretation of the play becomes difficult.

Philoctetes states his dilemma. How can he reject the words of one who had advised him in good-will (εὔνους)?[48] But how can he give way (εἰκάθω)? It is not the speech but the dialogue that makes clear why he cannot do so – makes clear that it is precisely the polarity of friends and enemies which creates his dilemma, when a friend urges him to help his enemies (1384f.).[49] Leave Lemnos with a friend

n. 30 above). (ii) 1267–90 (fourteen cases), leading up to an action (1291). (iii) 1373–96 (ten cases), leading up to an action (1399). This is a characteristic Sophoclean technique. Podlecki provides a useful inventory of the relevant vocabulary as an Addendum (246–50) to his article on 'The power of the word in Sophocles' *Philoctetes*', *GRBS* 7 (1966) 233–50. He speaks of the play as 'a case study in the failure of communication', which, provided we do not put too narrow an interpretation on 'communication', is a useful way of looking at it. Of course the characters in this play, as in all Greek tragedy, are articulate and comprehend the surface meaning of what is said to them; and to this degree are in communication, the 'wild' Philoctetes no less than the others. But words differ in respect of truth and falsehood, of success and failure to persuade. (There is also the contrast between word and action.)

47 If this echoes Neoptolemus' 969, it might also be thought to echo Philoctetes' own 1063, when he faces the first of the two tests mentioned in the text above.
48 He is stung by the severe rebuke of Neoptolemus (1322f.)?
49 'The just man hates his enemies as he loves his friends. This principle the gods themselves approve, as he believes, and he adheres to it in spite of the bright

(1375), yes; go to Troy and the most hated son of Atreus, no. His friend is wanting to betray him to his foes (1386). 'Please', says Neoptolemus, 'learn to be less stubborn in misfortune.' But Philoctetes will not understand (1389); even with the prospect of salvation, he will not join those who cast him out; enmity wins out over friendship. What, then, do we make of Philoctetes' long speech, in which he argues rationally, and in which he denies that his refusal was dictated by his past sufferings? Much has been made of it by some interpreters.

When Neoptolemus comments (1373) that his arguments are 'reasonable' (*eikota*), we should bear in mind that he is made to use a word associated with the rhetorical theory of the late fifth century;[50] and this is perhaps a sign that we should look carefully at his argumentation (as indeed we should always look at such argumentative passages in Greek tragedy). Philoctetes is making a case. His final argument – an *argumentum ad hominem* – is ironical. How, he asks, can Neoptolemus go to Troy and help those who have outraged him (1363ff.)? It is ironical, because the young man cannot disabuse his friend without raking over his lies, of which he is still the prisoner, and so damage his new credit. The fact remains that *this* evidence for the villainy of the Atridae is spurious and Philoctetes is trying to turn his friend against his enemies on non-existent grounds. What does he say about them on his own account? The Atridae have destroyed him, the son of Laertes is *panōlēs* (1356f.). After this emotionally charged language – indeed after the long build-up of the theme of resentment and hatred – it is hard to accept from him that 'it is not *algos* for the past' that stings him or even (a typical argument from probability) the thought of how they will treat him now, though that might have more truth, being a plausible emotional reaction – and one whose plausibility has been established by the remarkable words which have preceded. 'How, if I do this', he asks, 'shall I come into the light of day? To whom shall I speak?' And this is followed by perhaps the most astonishing of his personifications, when he addresses his own

---

promises which are held out to him if he will be false to it' (Linforth (1956) 148). At 1383 Jebb's objection to ὠφελούμενος is well based; Buttmann's ὠφελῶν φίλους, though quite uncertain, is attractive, fitting into the sequence 1375, 1377, 1385f. (See also Fraenkel, *Sem.* 75.)

[50] On arguments from probability – of which 1358–61 is a typical example – see W. K. C. Guthrie, *A history of Greek Philosophy* III (Cambridge 1969) 178f.; G. Kennedy, *The art of persuasion in Greece* (Princeton, N.J. 1963) 30f. and elsewhere.

eyes and asks them how they will tolerate his association with the sons of Atreus (1354–6).[51]

With this we return to an old question. What happens to a man – a great hero – when he has been cut off from human society for ten years? Rebuking Philoctetes, Neoptolemus used the word ἠγρίωσαι (1321): 'you have been brutalized'. But isolation amid the sole company of beasts (183ff.) has not turned him into a 'wild man' snarling like an animal at anyone who approaches. With a Neoptolemus he can resume a social relationship easily enough and even, subject to a difference of status, with the Chorus: not, however, with those who have wronged him so cruelly. Is this from a detached moral judgement that they are bad (as indeed they did act badly)? Is it the rejection of a world from which true heroism has departed? There is no hint of this in the decisive dialogue which ensues, which turns not on virtue and villainy, but on friendship and enmity, on benefit and harm. But these latter were fundamental categories of the heroic code in which Philoctetes was bred. We can now see that Lemnos, with all its loneliness and agony, has not turned him from a hero into a beast: what it has done is to intensify – and render wholly intractable – that heroic resentment of injury and hatred of enemies which we have seen to dominate the play. It has caused the negative aspect of the code to occupy the whole of his emotion, so that he is bound to reject the plea of Neoptolemus' friendship – and even the prospect of heroic glory. We wait for Heracles.

The words of Neoptolemus go for nothing, as they went for nothing while he still withheld the bow.[52] Once again, Philoctetes requires an action – and receives it.[53] 'If you will', says the other, 'let us go' (1402). As they move to sail for Malis, the audience will have mixed emotions of relief and regret:[54] they will also be puzzled. They know

---

[51] 'These are the words of one who has brooded for years on every aspect of his own wrongs – wrestling with misery in solitude. His own faculties are his comrades' (Jebb). But his eyes come close to being his very self.

[52] See n. 46 above.

[53] On the 'promise' (1398) of Neoptolemus cf. Taplin 38. 'Sophocles makes us feel that morally Neoptolemus is committed to this undertaking after everything that has gone before.' He had promised (810ff.) to stay with Philoctetes. One might say that this promise could only be fulfilled by taking him to Troy (ruled out), remaining with him on the island (absurd), or taking him back to their homelands.

[54] Knox, *HT* 139: 'Philoctetes' victory is a terrible defeat. He will go home, a prey

that Troy did fall, and they have heard the prophecy that it will fall to two specific heroes. The action has, however, now worked itself out upon the human plane in such a way that, given the nature of Neoptolemus and the experience of Philoctetes, given their respective decisions, the latter cannot, willingly or unwillingly, be brought to Troy. Each has faced a dilemma and made his decision. Neoptolemus cannot have it both ways: he cannot both respond to pity and serve his leaders, both maintain his standard of honour and win martial glory. Philoctetes cannot preserve his resentment *and* win cure, glory and happiness. Their combined decisions seem to be frustrating the intentions of the gods. We must now consider briefly how, and with what emphasis, these intentions enter into the play.[55]

That Troy is to fall, but not for ten years, are facts given without hint of a motive behind the dispensation. It is also given that Troy will fall to Philoctetes; and, in order that it may not fall to the inerrable bow of Heracles too soon, Philoctetes must be held on Lemnos. So said the young Neoptolemus in the Parodos (191ff.), in words which, if glib, were presumably true. Does this mean that the gods were responsible for the callousness of the Greeks? The issue is not raised in such terms, but Neoptolemus again, in the closing scene, attributes Philoctetes' sufferings to the gods (1316f.), just as the Chorus had told him to blame, not human trickery, but *potmos daimonōn* (1116ff.). If both speakers had a motive for taking responsibility off the Greeks, the fact remains that Philoctetes had, like other Sophoclean heroes, a given divinely appointed fate. On the other side of the balance-sheet are cure and glory. But it is no easier to speak of compensation here than in the case of the Colonean Oedipus.[56] No easier, and far less important, since nowhere in the play are we invited to judge – or even speculate about – the purposes, motives or methods, of the gods. As for Troy, we are not concerned that Troy shall fall, or why it should fall, but how, in view of the dramatic situation presented, it can fall.

This, to some extent, governs the tone of the play, beneath the brilliant surface of which, with its shifts and tantalizing uncertainties, there are deep and poignant emotions, though whether we are to call them tragic is no doubt a matter of definition. It may be tragic that a

---

still to the monstrous pain of his sickness, to rot in idleness in Oeta as he did on Lemnos'; Easterling, *ICS* 36f.

[55] For a different view, cf. Segal, *Hermes* passim.

[56] See p. 255 above.

man like Philoctetes is subjected to such a fate, but that is not the central dramatic issue. The pious Sophocles constantly surprises us; the ironist operates at the divine level also. It is ironical that Neoptolemus, by behaving well, should endanger the designs of the gods;[57] and the very prophecy has its ironical aspect.[58] Philoctetes must go to Troy as a free agent, yet it is, apparently, what the gods – and not merely the Greeks – have done to him that makes this virtually impossible. Can the gods have it both ways? Of course they can: they are gods. They send Heracles.

Everything that has been said so far about the divine world of the play could be disproved by Heracles in a couple of sentences. It is therefore important to consider what he says and what he does not say. Indeed one must consider his role, which is twofold: he performs a double function, as spokesman of Zeus and as a persuasive friend. That he is the last – and the successful – persuader has been denied, presumably because he speaks with authority and Philoctetes complies with a word of obedience (1447).[59] But the personal relationship is stressed from the beginning, when Heracles says he has come for the sake of Philoctetes (he does not say at the command of Zeus). The compliance of Philoctetes is preceded by a touching greeting (1445f.), and in his last words (to which we shall return) he attributes his being brought to Troy, in part, to 'the advice of friends'. Not only was it necessary that this should happen, but it was psychologically plausible that Heracles should succeed where Odysseus, the Chorus and even Neoptolemus had failed.[60]

But what does Heracles say? First he speaks briefly in anapaests, calling his utterances *muthoi* (1410, 1417) – a more dignified term which may be thought to contrast with the ineffective *logoi* of Neoptolemus; and the word is picked up later by Philoctetes (1447). He has come, he says, to expound the counsels of Zeus and to stop the

---

[57] 'Neoptolemus is now acting honestly, which raises the presumption that he is doing what the gods would have him do' (Kitto, *FMD* 126). But this perhaps takes too favourable – or at least too simple – a view of the Sophoclean gods. Cf. Adams 18, answered by Poe 25 n. 52.

[58] The point is made by Alt, 153f., whose intelligent examination of the play retains its value, even if one cannot accept all her conclusions. Cf. also Segal, *Hermes* 142.

[59] But see Easterling, *ICS* 31.

[60] And Sophocles has given an unobtrusive demonstration of how the deus-ex-machina convention could be used without that discontinuity of tone we find so often in Euripides.

journey on which Philoctetes is setting out; he tells him to listen. He
then moves into the normal dialogue metre and a less formal tone.[61]
He tells Philoctetes, in future tenses, what is going to happen; with his
greater authority he ratifies the prospects of cure and fame that have
already been held out. That is what the prophecies of Helenus have
always been – not commands as such but statements of what is bound
to happen. It is not *incumbent* upon a mortal to confirm divine
foreknowledge, but the wise man recognizes that he has no option.[62]
The last words of Philoctetes recognize that, along with the *gnome* of
friends, he is being brought to Troy by the power of Moira, by the
all-subduing *daimon* that has ratified these things.[63]

The *gnome* of friends plays its part in persuading Philoctetes to
accept his inevitable destiny. What, then, does Heracles say? What
does he *not* say? He says nothing about the fall of Troy as an end in
itself, as a Greek – or a divine – 'cause'. Nothing? Yes, he says that the
guilty Paris will be killed by his arrows. That is all. And Paris is the
only combatant on either side who is mentioned. He says nothing
about Odysseus or the Atridae, whether they were good or bad, and
nothing, in praise or in blame, about the resentment of Philoctetes.[64]
But he does speak about toil and tribulation (πόνοι). Much has been
built upon the lines in which Heracles draws an analogy between his
own case and that of Philoctetes.[65] If any man had suffered labours

[61] Jebb, on 1424f., speaks of 'the somewhat careless writing which appears in this
speech'.

[62] It was not incumbent on Oedipus to seek out his father and kill him. An oracle or
prophecy can of course take the form of a command. In this play, like many
things, the prophecy's status tends to be left a little vague. The two main
statements (610ff., 1329ff.) are both conditional, until Helenus adds (1339f.) that
these things *must* be. (841 could be conditional, and 915 is vague.) With one
exception, the notion of a specific design of Zeus waits for Heracles (1415). The
exception is at 989f., where Odysseus – the least impressive witness – claims the
authority of Zeus. Events, ironically, prove him right.

[63] The familiar nexus of fatality and human motivation is brought out (1466–8) by
an ABA arrangement. *moira* and *daimon* are often closely associated. Here, if Moira
is personifed, the *daimon* is still more personal. Who is he? Certainly not Heracles
(though Campbell, *Paral.* 231, adhered to this view), but probably Zeus (cf. 1415).
The poet has, however, made a choice of words which stresses the fatality to
which the hero's stubborn will has yielded.

[64] Garvie 225.

[65] Erbse 200, expands the analogy as follows: the whole life of Heracles had been toil
in the service of a worser man for the good of mankind, a constant self-conquest;
equally Philoctetes must not refuse to associate with his moral inferiors for the
general advantage. One feels that Sophocles could have made this point, if he had
wished to do so.

and survived, it was Heracles; and through them, as he says, he had gained 'immortal *arete*' – an expression which may combine the notions of deathless glory and that glorious immortality which is now visible. A similar debt of glory is owing to Philoctetes. This is the speech of a fighting man to his former comrade-in-arms. *arete*, as virtually always in Sophocles, means supreme valour or the reputation for it, nothing less and nothing more.[66] Heracles is saying in effect: '*ponoi?* You make too much of them. I endured them: why cannot you? Through them you are offered *eukleia*, which is something no friend of mine can refuse.' He cannot refuse to be picked out of the army as 'first in *arete*' (1425), to receive the *aristeia*, the prize of valour (1429), to win the spoils from which he must make a dedication at the pyre of Heracles. He – and Neoptolemus – must be lions, like Homeric warriors. The wind is set fair for Troy: then hurry! It is to this martial Heracles – and to this positive aspect of the heroic code – that Philoctetes responds.

It is unlikely that interpreters will ever agree about the precise tone of the play's close. To leave the scene even of desolation and agony may be a poignant thing, and the emotions of Philoctetes, as he apostrophizes – these are his last personifications – the 'house' that has shared his watches, the mountain that has echoed his cries, and all the natural features of the island, are deep and complex.[67] But how do we, the audience, react to his sudden acceptance of destiny? The riddle is solved – the riddle of how Philoctetes can be brought to Troy – and not by mere fiat of the gods, since we can see why he should respond to the friendship of Heracles. But is this more than the sleight-of-hand of a consummate dramatist? Do we say that tragedy has yielded to mythology, to history? After all, the callous Greeks do get the help of Philoctetes, Odysseus – a cynical realist who will not care how the desired success is brought about – gets his way. I doubt if Sophocles invites us to think along these lines. Do we say that the gods, despite all appearances, have ordered everything for the best?

The play has two 'endings'; and it would contradict its whole trend and the whole artistry of Sophocles, if the 'second ending' deprived

---

[66] See p. 309 n. 16.

[67] Knox, *HT* 141. I cannot accept the suggestion of Vidal-Naquet, 179f., that the natural world of the island is now presented under a different – and pastoral – aspect.

the 'first ending' of all its value. It remains that Neoptolemus, out of
pity and a scrupulous adherence to a concept of honour, was prepared
to sacrifice his own interests; that the calculations of Odysseus were in
the way to be defeated; that the cruelty of the Greeks was faced with
an apparent nemesis. Philoctetes, against his own interests, is to
preserve his heroic resentment; and we are both glad and sorry, since
the prospect before him is still a miserable one. We are glad and sorry
for them both. And if tragedy is to be found anywhere in the play, it is
in the tragic consequences of a cruel act and in the tragic implications
of a heroic code. The question which arises is whether the 'second
ending' is more than a mechanical negation of these consequences.

Philoctetes is to be cured at Troy, and can only be cured at Troy.[68]
It has been suggested that he is not only cured physically but, by his
reintegration into society, cured mentally as well. Is it emotionally
valid for the audience that he is to resume relations with the Greek
community as a whole? Heracles is careful to say nothing about the
Greek leaders, but he speaks of the *strateuma* (1425, 1429) as the
context of Philoctetes' future glory. He will be back in the army. Do
we say more – that, having found a friend of like mind, he forms with
him a new heroic community and with him enters upon a heroic
enterprise?[69] These are questions not easily answered, but there is one
passage which Sophocles wrote which ought not be ignored.

'Bear this in mind, when you lay waste the land, to show piety
towards the gods. All else is of less account in the sight of father Zeus.
Piety does not die with men: it does not perish, whether they live or
die' (1440–4). The subsequent history of Philoctetes is of no legendary
interest, but Neoptolemus had a future. The young man who, in the
play, shows a pity which was not obviously a part of the Achillean
tradition was destined to kill, at the altar, an old man whom his father
had respected and spared. The reference is utterly clear: it seems
gratuitous, but Sophocles, the most controlled of playwrights, does
not deal in the gratuitous. More than once, towards the end of a play,
he opens a window upon a tragic future.[70] This was not a quirk of his;

---

[68] The 'inconsistency' between 1437f. and 1333f. is not only harmless (cf. Jebb) but
deliberate. Neoptolemus can only promise the services of the Asclepiads, who
were members of the Greek army and so suspect to Philoctetes: Heracles can send
the god himself!

[69] Cf. Steidle 187; J. U. Schmidt, *Sophokles Philoktet, eine Strukturanalyse* (Heidelberg 1973), 246f.; Easterling, *ICS* 37f.

[70] The three clear examples all occur in 'happy ending' plays.

it was not a quirk that at the end of the *Coloneus* he sent Antigone to Thebes or (I believe), in *Electra,* that Aegisthus was made to refer to future ills of the Pelopidae. The references are ironical and relevant to the tragic themes of the plays. It may be suggested, then, that in *Philoctetes* the poet has introduced these impressive lines as a hint of what is waiting for Neoptolemus at Troy, of the world in which martial heroes live and the temptations to which they are liable. Before we become sentimental about that pair of lions, we should remember that lions are fierce predators and owe their force in metaphor to their ferocity; before we acclaim the joint mission of the two heroic friends, we should reflect, momentarily, upon what precisely they are going to do, that not only Paris but old Priam will be among the victims, that the pity and scruple of Neoptolemus will disappear in the heat of battle and sack.

No two assumptions have more persistently bedevilled the interpretation of Sophocles than these: (i) that the values for which his heroes stand, destroying themselves and others, are, simply and necessarily, right in the eyes of the poet; and (ii) that the will of the gods is not only just but also benevolent and must be seen to be so. The pietists and the 'hero-worshippers' are equally below the measure of the poet's tragic vision, which owes its character both to the limitations of the heroes and to the conditions which the gods impose upon them. To these matters we must now turn.

CHAPTER THIRTEEN

Heroes and gods

Professor Bernard Knox, in *The heroc temper*, has studied Sophoclean heroes with great skill and, largely by a careful examination of the language which they use and which is used of them, has brought out a number of characteristics which they tend to share in common. 'Such', he writes (op. cit. 44), 'is the strange and awesome character who, in six of the Sophoclean tragedies,[1] commands the stage. Immovable once his decision is taken, deaf to appeals and persuasion, to reproof and threat, unterrified by physical violence, even by the ultimate violence of death itself, more stubborn as his isolation increases until he has no one to speak to but the unfeeling landscape, bitter at the disrespect and mockery the world levels at what it regards as failure, the hero prays for vengeance and curses his enemies as he welcomes the death that is the predictable end of his intransigence.' These characteristics are displayed in a situation and in relation to other people; and therefore what the heroes do and suffer throws light not only upon them but upon a world – *their* world and perhaps *the* world. If *the* world, governed by the gods, is one and the same, *their* worlds – their circumstances and companions – differ so widely that, similar as their reactions may be in some fundamental respects, generalization becomes hazardous. Sophocles was, after all, writing individual plays on specific subjects, not a series of exemplifications of heroic character, though his handling of heroic character was partly determined by a certain – and, it seems, a remarkably stable – view of the world.

[1] Knox excludes Heracles from consideration. Does he not, however, share characteristics with Ajax and the Colonean Oedipus, not least self-centredness? King Oedipus, on the other hand, until the course of the action forces him to concentrate upon himself, is the least self-centred of Sophoclean heroes (see below) and must be treated with reserve.

To say that the situations of his heroes are striking and sometimes astonishing might seem merely a comment upon Greek mythology as such. Famous figures of myth, they are seen in situations provided by the myth. But the handling and the emphasis are Sophoclean. We are familiar with the idea that Euripides looked at such figures and asked himself – and invited his audience to ask – how they might appear in a more or less contemporary light. Sophocles, remaining firmly within the mythical frame, sometimes seems to be asking a rather different question, which is: what happens to a hero, to a man or woman of heroic background and standards, when he is exposed to certain pressures, particularly over a long period of time. Time, and the effects of time, are indeed a staple theme in Sophocles.

The Sophoclean hero is lonely: isolated from men, he may feel himself also abandoned by the gods; *monos* and *eremos* are key-words.[2] Of all the heroes this is most literally true of Philoctetes, who has been alone on Lemnos for ten years; and it is an essential interest of the play to discover what happens to a great hero when he is thus cut off, an outcast from human society. What has time done to him? Since *Philoctetes* is a late play, we might be tempted to suppose this a late and sophisticated exploration on the part of Sophocles.[3] Yet, turning to the relatively early *Ajax,* we find a hero who, in a different and equally extraordinary way, is alone, isolated (as the Chorus sees) in his own mental world (φρενὸς οἰοβώτας) – isolated even from his friends, not so far from what we sometimes call the 'private world' of a madman. He too broods over a wrong; he too has a malady. Where the malady of Philoctetes is objective and physical, that of Ajax is his own megalomaniac pride. Both are the victims of time, but the time-span in the case of Ajax is shown in the receding perspective of the play, to be longer. Both cases belong in their different ways to the pathology of heroism.[4]

Here are two extraordinary conceptions within the heroic world, separated (probably) by some thirty years or more of the dramatic

---

[2] Cf. J. Jones 214. On the vocabulary cf. Knox, *HT* 32f.

[3] Cf. Rose n. 17.

[4] The statement is provocative, but (I trust), as regards Ajax, substantiated by the examination of the themes of madness and disease in an earlier chapter (ch. 2 passim). It is the *pathe* of Philoctetes that so intensify his heroic resentment that, despite all advantage and short of the persuasions of Heracles, it is impossible for him to aid the Greeks. On the difference between the two cases cf. Poe 17 and n. 41.

career of Sophocles. Fairly close (probably) in time to Ajax, nearer to Ajax than to Philoctetes, comes the Heracles of *Trachiniae*; and he is another amazing phenomenon. He was the hero *par excellence,* not merely for the Dorians but for the whole Hellenic world. And how is he shown? He is not lonely in either of the ways in which Philoctetes and Ajax are shown to be lonely, but still he *is* lonely. He is rootless;[5] he has no settled home, belongs to no community. Nor can it be said that he has any real human relationships other than those of sex: even his wife he visits rarely, and to beget children. His son Hyllus he seems to regard as a mere extension of his own person, even of his sexual person.[6] If there is a sense in which he belongs to the Hellas which he has liberated from monsters, it is those monsters that have constituted his formative past. At the human level he is absorbed in himself and in his limited but overwhelming prowess.[7]

Little need be said about the loneliness of the two great heroines: Electra alone with her obsessive grief in a household of enemies and timorous friends – alone until her brother comes; Antigone alone in her task, her friends already in the nether world to which she is drawn, rejected by – and then rejecting – the sister who remains, deprived (by the dramatist) of the consolation which a sympathetic chorus might have afforded, deprived, one might add, of a knowledge of Haemon's loyalty. There remain the two Oedipuses. The Colonean Oedipus bears a certain similarity to Philoctetes. Here too a great hero finds himself in a situation which invites a similar question: what happens to a man, to a king, when not only has he done – and discovered himself to have done – appalling actions in the past, but has also spent years as a blind beggar on the margin of subsistence. Resentment against those who have wronged him accumulates and issues in a wrath which is as terrible as that of an Ajax or a Heracles. But Oedipus is *not* alone: he has Antigone (and Ismene), he finds Theseus and Athens and the grove of the Eumenides. The outcast finds a home.

We turn to the *Tyrannus,* to find a paradox. We are accustomed to think of it as the typical Sophoclean tragedy and of Oedipus as the typical Sophoclean hero. Yet he is the one hero who, at the beginning of the play, is to all appearance in a normal situation. Isolated only by

---

[5] Cf, *BICS* 16 (1969) 45.

[6] Cf. ch. 4 p. 85.

[7] In his moment of despair he apostrophizes his own body (1089ff.), cf. 83 n. 32.

his kingly status, he is a well-loved king, standing in a warm relationship to his grateful subjects and, no less, to his wife and children.[8] All of which is to be destroyed, ironically, by the discovery of the past: his wife is his mother, his children are his brothers and sisters, and by his presence he is causing his subjects to die of the plague. It was a past of whose true nature he was unaware and which had therefore not created in him those obsessive hates and loves which characterize so many Sophoclean heroes. There is indeed a sinister background of apprehension which will be re-activated by the words of Teiresias,[9] but we are not to think of an Oedipus whose states of mind, during his career of success, have been dominated by such fears. He is a man of action, with full confidence in his powers and his intelligence. He feels no guilt about killing the unknown stranger, until he begins to suspect, first, that it was the king, and then his father. If he is under threat from the oracle, he thinks that his precautions have been adequate, and there is no reason to suppose that the Corinthian drunkard's insults continued to rankle after he had left Corinth.[10] It is indeed essential to the whole point of the play that Oedipus should feel himself secure, that he should be unaware of the true past. Since the past has moulded his fate and not his mind, he stands apart from other Sophoclean heroes, as the *Tyrannus,* in its treatment of fate, stands somewhat apart from other extant plays of Sophocles.[11]

This review of the heroes, in point of their situations and of their relations to society, should at least warn us against supposing that we can catalogue them in accordance with some simple scheme or, for that matter, easily identify a typical Sophoclean attitude towards the world of which they are members. At least the generalizations and categorizations must be carefully tested.

The notion of a 'Homeric' Sophocles, turning away in disgust from a degenerate world to enjoy the congenial company of heroes,

---

[8] Cf. Gould (1) 590.

[9] 'Go in and think it out', says Teiresias (ταῦτ' ἰὼν | εἴσω λογίζου, *O. T.* 460f.). And so Oedipus has been doing during the following ode. This leads him not to a realization of the truth but to a state of anxiety which, far more than any tendency towards tyrannical arrogance, accounts for his emotional reactions in the Creon-scene. I cannot accept Vellacott's hypothesis (*Sophocles and Oedipus* (London 1971) passim) that Oedipus is aware of his parentage throughout the play.

[10] See p. 177 n. 73.

[11] See pp. 205f.

would hardly find adherents today. It is, however, often said that his
personages are 'aristocrats' (which in some sense they are), and that he
was concerned, like Pindar, to promote aristocratic ideals.[12] In this
delicate field of enquiry, beset by the dangers of subjectivity and even
sentimentality, semantic studies of individual words and groups of
words can be valuable. It is said, for instance, that, again like Pindar,
Sophocles was a strong believer in hereditary excellence. *Phusis* (and
related words) occur not infrequently in his plays, if not quite so
prominently as is sometimes suggested; and there is no doubt that he
did believe in the significance of heredity, as aristocrats did, though
not only aristocrats.[13] The theme is more prominent in some plays
than in others: notably so in *Philoctetes,* where it is much stressed that
Neoptolemus derives his *phusis* from Achilles, betrays it and then
redeems himself: acting in accordance with his *phusis* (though also
out of pity), he does, within the terms of the play, act well. Ajax
derives his *phusis* from Telamon, whom he is bent on equalling or
surpassing, and hopes that he has transmitted it to Eurysaces (who
must still be schooled), but that play is concerned with the hard and
potentially destructive aspects of heroism. Antigone takes after a
father who is largely unknown to us, but the quality she owes to him
(so the chorus sees it) is one of hardness or harshness. Electra, it would
seem, owes her *phusis* to both parents: explicitly to her mother, as in a
bitter moment she admits, and by implication to her father (whatever
that connotes).[14] The notion is virtually absent, like some other
Sophoclean features, from *Oedipus Tyrannus,* except for the scene at
the cross-roads in which father and son may be thought to show a
likeness (but Laius is not otherwise characterized in the play). It enters
into the *Coloneus* in a surprising way, when Antigone questions the
right of a father to retaliate upon a son for whose *phusis* he is
responsible.[15]

---

[12] In which case one might perhaps have expected a Pindaric view of the Ajax/
Odysseus situation, cf. *Nem.* 7.24–7.

[13] On heredity in popular thought from the late fifth century see Dover, *GPM* 88ff.
A comprehensive review of *phusis*-words in Sophocles will be found in C. E.
Hajistephanou, *The use of ΦΥΣΙΣ and its cognates in Greek tragedy with special
reference to character drawing* (Nicosia 1975) 9–54.

[14] *El.* 608f. (Clytemnestra); 1081 (Agamemnon), on which see p. 245 n. 91. What do
we learn about Agamemnon in the play except that he was a great general,
sacrificed his daughter, was hated and murdered by his wife?

[15] See also – though this is more speculative – p. 276 n. 79.

It may be doubted whether, if *Philoctetes* had not survived, so much emphasis would have been placed by critics on this theme. If a study of *phusis*-words does not carry us very far, perhaps we shall have better luck with *arete,* a word which has been much employed in the interpretation of Sophocles. It would certainly be rash to deny that Heracles, for instance, in *Trachiniae* is a supreme exemplification of *arete.* The word is, however, rare in extant Sophocles; and it is employed almost exclusively of martial prowess, which was in fact the *arete* of Heracles.[16] But critics who speak of the *arete* of Sophoclean heroes generally mean something more than martial prowess. The corresponding adjective *agathos* is used, unqualified, of persons rather more often (being, with its superlative, slightly more amenable to the iambic trimeter) and with a rather wider spread of meaning – not only good at fighting, but loyal to friends.[17] The superlative *aristos* is even more common: sometime the context is military (as with *aristeuein, aristeia*), but the word, used three times of women,[18] tends to have a general complimentary sense, with a class-overtone. The *agathos/aristos* is one who lives up to the heroic code in its various aspects; the *agathoi* as a class are the nobles. We find this plural at *El.* 1082, where it follows the word *eupatris*. When Philoctetes speaks sarcastically of the 'good' (the brave) generals, who could not put up with his cries and his offensive odour, he contrasts them with Neoptolemus, who is prepared to do so: 'for his *phusis* is well-born and of well-born stock' (εὐγενὴς γὰρ ἡ φύσις κἀξ εὐγενῶν, 874). Clearly *eugenes* – and to a lesser degree *gennaios* – are words to be taken into consideration.[19] In common Greek usage – the former word less frequent in prose – they were, among other things, part of the vocabulary of compliment; and a good many of the Sophoclean cases are complimentary, or commendatory in a very general way. In some

16 Pointed out by Torrance (272). The one exception is *Phil.* 669 (on which see ch. 12 p. 286). On *Phil.* 1420 see ch. 12 p. 301: seen in the light of 1425, here too *arete* is essentially martial. On the survival of this narrower sense, cf. Dover, *GPM* 164.
17 Of eleven cases five are in *Phil.* Three are sarcastic: *Ant.* 31(cf. ch. 5 p. 129), *Trach.* 541 (cf. ch. 4 p. 82), *Phil.* 873. Strictly, *O.T.* 687 should not be counted, since ἀγαθός is qualified by γνώμην. Though there may be some notion of honesty or loyalty, the intellectual sense is carried through into παραφρόνιμον and φρόνιμα (691) and would comport well with the reading προνοουμένῳ at 685 (but contr. Dawe, *STS* 238).
18 Seventeen cases. Of women: *Trach.* 1105, *El.* 1089 (cf. ch. 10 p. 242), *O.C.* 1693.
19 For a useful review, cf. Dover, *GPM* 93–5.

cases, however, the words are used with specific reference to an issue of conduct; and of course it is these which are important and (especially with *eugenes*) raise the question of inherited excellence. It is particularly striking, for instance, when Ajax says (*Aj.* 479f.) that the man of noble birth must either live nobly (καλῶς) or be noble in his death and Tecmessa replies with a persuasive re-definition of *eugeneia* (524).[20] The same word is heard on the lips of Antigone (*Ant.* 38) and of Electra (*El.* 257), in their respective situations and of their respective parentage. Ajax was once *gennaios*, says Odysseus (*Aj.* 1355); and it is followed by a reference to *arete*.[21]

The purpose of this summary review, if it inspires a little caution, is certainly not to deny that the notion of inherited excellence is present in Sophocles. His personages are heroes, to whom heredity is important; they have standards and principles to which they are prepared to sacrifice everything, even life; and this is a point of honour. To say that they belong to the heroic world is true, but not enough. Sophocles did not retreat into that world, nor did he re-create its personages as an exercise of the historical imagination. And if we say (what is obvious) that the doings and sufferings of his heroes are relevant to his own time, it is insufficient to point to the broad general categories, pervasive though they are in Sophoclean drama, such as the fragility of human fortunes and the pathetic fallibility of human knowledge and judgement. The issues, the standards and the principles, are also relevant. But how, precisely?

Several questions present themselves. Are these heroes, with their pride of ancestry, their sense of honour, their 'idealism' and obstinate courage, recognizable as 'aristocrats'? Before answering that question, we must be sure that these values and virtues are not simply those of a traditional morality, first heroic, then aristocratic, but which by the fifth century have percolated downwards to become part and parcel of Greek morals. Or is Sophocles taking sides? Taking sides with the conservatives, with those who wished to maintain certain (allegedly) aristocratic values and virtues? And before we answer *that* question, we should reflect that, when these heroes put their principles into action, the consequences are tragic; we should wonder

---

[20] See ch. 2 p. 29.
[21] It can be a 'class-term', so linking (in the *Coloneus*) an Oedipus and a Theseus, cf. 76, 1042, 1636. At *Phil.* 1402 the *gennaion epos* of Neoptolemus is something more than a splendid utterance.

whether perhaps tragedy is inherent, not only in the human condition and the individual destiny, but in the very standards of heroism. We should perhaps ask ourselves why, when a form of serious drama arose in Greece, it had that character, recognizable if hard to define, rare in the world's literature, of being *tragic*. Despite the notorious contradictions and deficiencies in the evidence, it is possible to give a more or less plausible account of how drama may have arisen in the Greek world; and we can see that, using myth, it was likely to be serious and heroic. But need it have been tragic? Granted that for one reason and another it was religious, need the theodicy have been so tormented? Or was there something in the Greek experience which led in the direction of tragedy?[22]

The Greeks were emulous and competitive people with a passion for success; and by success they tended to judge their fellows and themselves. They were proud and sensitive to their status and privileges, which it was a main purpose of their lives to maintain. An injury or affront was intolerable until it had been avenged. These are the characteristics of nobles in a heroic age, and they are familiar to us from the Greek epic. But the emotional attitudes of this shame-culture did not disappear with the heroes but survived tenaciously, if with modifications, into the archaic period and the world of the city-states; they survived the end of aristocratic domination to be still powerful in a democratic Athens.[23] If we find them in tragedy, it is because the issues, the motives and the emotions were still real in the present.

The moral experience of the Greeks led towards tragedy by at least two routes. The more society valued success the greater was the temptation for individuals to pursue it beyond bounds. The admired quality becomes a social menace; and a tragic tension is built up. Success confers power, and power invites abuse. The Greek for abuse of power is *hubris*, with which this competitive society had a bitter acquaintance and against which, as against a poison in the body-politic, it had developed an antidote in the countervailing ideal of moderation or *sophrosune*. In support of this ideal they invoked the gods. For when power destroys itself through its own excess, its downfall is marked with gratification and awe, since it is believed that

[22] On the problematic origins of Greek tragedy see my chapter in the *Cambridge History of Classical Literature* I (forthcoming).

[23] Cf. Adkins, *MR*.

the gods either grudge human success when it is over-great or punish it when it has been obtained in disregard of justice. All these ideas are familiar to us from Aeschylean tragedy: if they are less evident in Sophocles, they play some part in *Ajax* and *Antigone*, and (negatively) in *Oedipus Tyrannus*.[24]

But there is another route. That a man should seek to avenge a wrong is natural and, by the standard of honour, laudable. When he has retaliated successfully, he has, from his point of view, restored the position, but, from the point of view of his adversary, he has created another wrong, which in its turn requires redress. The typical example of this is the blood-feud or vendetta, which is a potentially endless process, crime breeding counter-crime, yet both demanded by the code. In the case of the vendetta it is *philoi* – the kinsmen – who seek vengeance, but there are *philoi* in a wider context; and it is characteristic of these honour-situations that each party has its friends and its enemies – a polarity fundamental in Greek ethics, yet dividing the society into warring groups. There is a notion which constantly recurs in Greek literature, namely, that virtue, or justice, consists in doing good to your friends and harm to your enemies.[25]

Each play of Sophocles exists in its own right, with its own situation, its own pattern, its own subtle variations upon common themes. The critic's primary task is no doubt to try and understand the individual play. Yet every play reveals a view of the world – and a view of heroes in that world; and a poet who saw the world in a certain way.[26] The term 'Sophoclean' is not an empty one, though its definition, because of the variety of the plays – and because they are so few and were selected for survival by a process largely irrelevant to the issues we are discussing, is a matter of extreme difficulty. Perhaps the surprising thing is that this small selection of plays does in fact contain so many common themes. The themes are social and religious.

The hero suffers a wrong, or what he regards as a wrong, done to himself or to those who are bound to him by kinship. This wrong he resents, in many cases to such a degree that it totally dominates his

---

[24] For the negative bearing in *O.T.*, see ch. 8.
[25] See p. 129 above.
[26] It was not for nothing that Webster prefaced his *An introduction to Sophocles* with a quotation from Proust: 'Les grands littérateurs n'ont jamais fait qu'une seule oeuvre.'

mind; moreover, it divides his world into friends and enemies who for him constitute, or should (he feels) constitute, irreconcilable camps. In one way or another he seeks to retrieve his position, to restore his honour or the honour of his kin; and in the process he is, or is like to be, destroyed. This pattern is clearest in *Ajax, Antigone, Electra,* and *Philoctetes*; it is an important aspect of *Oedipus Coloneus,* a minor feature in *Trachiniae,* and in *Oedipus Tyrannus* virtually absent. It will be convenient now to take the plays out of their (hypothetical) chronological order and, briefly, examine their themes, beginning with two plays which, separated by decades, unfold in a context of war.[27]

Ajax might seem a simple matter of honour. 'The man of good birth must either live nobly or be noble in his death.' Ajax has no way of retrieving his honour in life, and so he kills himself. Honour is conferred by society. Ajax thinks it has been unjustly withheld from him by the Judgement of the Arms, which he resents to such a degree that he goes out to murder the Greek leaders as they sleep. He is frustrated by Athena; and this is the second and ultimate blow to his honour which necessitates his suicide. Sophocles has been at pains to show that the pride of Ajax is so hypertrophied as to be irreconcilable even with heroic society, a mental sickness, grown pathological in the course of time. Attempts have been made to extract a milder, wiser Ajax from the famous Deception Speech, even to represent his suicide as an act of *sophrosune*: on the contrary, it is the final assertion of his pride and his difference, the final rejection of a society whose values he has carried to an intolerable extreme. He dies calling upon the Erinyes to avenge him not only upon the Atridae but upon the whole Greek army – upon those who should have been his friends but have proved enemies. With Ajax is contrasted Odysseus, the 'enemy' who ends by acting as a friend, refusing to accept that rigid polarity of friendship and enmity which was part of the creed of Ajax; a man of different temper who perhaps foreshadowed a different age;[28] a man who, knowing the fragility of human fortunes, was capable of pity.

Philoctetes, like Ajax, had come to hate the Atridae and Odysseus. If Ajax had fought for ten years only to be cheated (as he thought) of his just reward, Philoctetes had spent those same ten years upon a

---

[27] The following account assumes the results of detailed analysis in the preceding chapters, by which it stands or falls.

[28] See ch. 3 pp. 71f.

desert island in company with a foul disease. As the action of the play
unfolds, he is confronted with a dilemma. Not to mention the cure of
his wound, this once mighty hero is offered the prospect of sharing
the supreme honour of taking Troy, a thing which Achilles and Ajax
and Diomede and the rest had failed to do; and, hero though he is, he
rejects it. Some critics have argued that he rejects it because of the
moral inferiority of the remaining Greek leaders, being unwilling to
associate his heroism with their baseness, but the seductions of this
hypothesis must be resisted. He rejects it, because it conflicts with
another part of the heroic code, which is to resent an injury and
pursue a grievance to the extreme point. And the reason why this
prevails over the prospect of glory is to be found in the circumstances
of the ten years' solitude during which he has brooded over his
wrongs. Hatred of his enemies has become something he cannot
abandon; he cannot benefit himself, if this means benefiting them.
With him is contrasted Odysseus, who, as in *Ajax*, belongs to another
world, but in its most repugnant aspect: a man of adaptable standards,
who will be just and pious when he can, but will sacrifice everything
to success. More important is Neoptolemus, who shares the main
interest of the play. He has inherited a heroic – or if you will an
aristocratic – code which does not reject violence but rejects deceit.
For a time he is seduced by Odysseus, but repents, not simply because
the deceit revolts him, but because he turns out to be one of those who
are capable of pity – and of acting on it, even to his own detriment.[29]

Antigone and *Electra,* also separated in time, fall to be considered
together: both 'family' plays, each with a formidable heroine who
owes a duty derived from kinship. Antigone's duty is to bury, with
humanity and decency on her side; Electra's to avenge by matricide.
For Electra it is a point of honour first to lament and then to avenge
her father, and no consideration of caution or moderation weighs
with her; when she believes her brother dead, she urges Chrysothemis
to join with her in killing Aegisthus (and by implication Clytemnestra) and so win honour in life and in death. 'For those who are nobly
born it is shameful to live shamefully' (989); and the Chorus sings that
'none of the good, by living a base life, is willing to shame his fair
repute, leaving no name' (1082ff.), and that Electra is winning the
noblest renown for observing the greatest natural laws, for her piety

[29] And will, alas, go on to kill Priam at the altar. On the vexed interpretation of the
final scene, see ch. 12 pp. 301ff.

towards Zeus – the laws being those which demand filial piety.[30] But piety towards one parent demands the sacrifice of the other, about which Electra has no qualms: indeed she is consumed with hatred for her. What is certain, in a play of vexed interpretation, is that her obsessive grief and obsessive hatred are the product of a long process of time which precedes and prepares the matricide. They are the work of Furies, of whom she is both the victim and the agent.[31]

Antigone is rendered complex by the contrasted tragedies of Creon and Antigone – tragedies of different type of which Antigone's is typically Sophoclean. There is also a contrast of principles and of character. She acts out of an emotion which is at once narrow and generous: she is no reasoner, and the other side of the case simply does not exist for her. That other side is put by Creon, but the poet deliberately undercuts his position and shows his rationality as more apparent than real. He is crude and insensitive, and the sympathies of poet and audience are with Antigone, who, however, could not have done what she did, if she had not been hard, with a hardness inherited from her father. She too is made by her past, but the intensity of her emotion is the product, not (as with Electra) of long eroding time, but of a brief experience of unimaginable horror which has given her an obsession with the world of the dead. It is to this world that her 'friends' belong; and it is in and through that world that, by a heroic resolve, she would cancel the hatreds which have dogged the house, retrieve its honour, declare peace and the restoration of love.[32] Seeing things always in terms of 'friends' and 'enemies', she claims that it is her nature to join in friendship rather than in enmity, but, when her sister, who had failed to share her heroism, seeks out of mere affection to share her death, she casts her out into the ranks of the enemy. The heroic polarity prevails, as it will prevail in *Oedipus Coloneus*.

The work of time; heredity; friends and enemies; resentment and retaliation; the return of good for good and evil for evil; pity and the absence of pity. In the *Coloneus* all these familiar Sophoclean themes are present, woven into an intricate fabric: what marks it out is the ultimate destiny of an Oedipus who had seemed to be the paradigm of human fragility, of the breach between gods and men. Oedipus becomes a *heros*. Unlike the man of the *Tyrannus,* whose past is

[30] See ch. 10 pp. 242f.
[31] See ch. 10 p. 228.
[32] On the central importance of *Ant.* 508–25, see ch. 5 pp. 131ff.

essentially personal to him, whose future is left in uncertainty, and in the treatment of whose destiny there is no word of the Erinyes, this Oedipus comes to a sanctuary of the Eumenides, which he recognizes as his final resting-place, and goes on, at a divine command, to assume himself the status of a chthonian power – powerful to benefit his friends and harm his enemies. What is the principle to which, inflexibly, he adheres? It is the principle of wrathful retaliation: so far from waning with time, his *thumos* grows into the gigantic curse upon his sons which foreshadows his role in the nether world. Pity belongs to Antigone.

A different Antigone; and a different Oedipus, if one which the masterful king of the *Tyrannus* might – in time – have become. What, then, was the principle to which the latter adhered to the point of destruction? The contrast between appearance and reality, the fallibility of human knowledge, the late learning of truth, are common themes in Sophocles. One of the functions of time is to conceal and then to reveal; and one of the functions of those oracles whose terms are known but whose significance waits to be disclosed is to emphasize the breach between divine and human knowledge. Such oracles are prominent in *Trachiniae,* a highly ironical play, but, if there is one play in which irony runs riot, it is the *Tyrannus*; and, if there is one characteristic which marks out this Oedipus, it is his intellectual assurance and, one must add, his intellectual integrity, his determination to know the truth which blasts him by its discovery. It is this, not his character as a man of action, not his duty as a king, that marks him out as a Sophoclean hero.

We are left with *Trachiniae,* which moves in a different context from the other plays, being a tragedy of sex. Deianira, a wife of conventional virtue, a human-being who recognizes human status and is, like Odysseus in *Ajax* and like Neoptolemus, capable of pity, and who has therefore, it might seem, the qualities to safeguard her against tragedy, is led by the power of sex to perform an unscrupulous act with a consequence to be expected of a wicked woman. Which is ironical; it is no less ironical that the hero who has vanquished monsters – and has taken women as a requirement of his strong body – should be destroyed by his lusts and by the conjunction of two women. The only victor is Aphrodite, to whose power it is the fate of both Heracles and Deianira to fall victim. She is the force working within them that has inspired the actions for which they must pay.

Yet they were deliberate actions, and in both cases they were the product of a past way of life, though in Deianira's case a paradoxical product. There is paradox and irony too in the case of Heracles. His career had consisted in a series of ordeals by which he had benefited humanity, freeing the Greek world of noxious monsters. If we look for a guiding principle of his life, he gives it to us, when he says: 'Both living and dead, I have retaliated upon the evil' (1111); and it seems that this theme – of retaliation and the perpetuation of evil through *talio* – is given some prominence in the later stages of the play.[33] The irony is that his final ordeal, which Lichas invited us to see in terms of revenge, turns out to have been performed in pursuit of a lust; it is the monster that has his revenge.

This summary should have brought out two things: the frequent recurrence of certain themes and issues closely bound up with the heroism of the heroes, but also the variety of circumstance and tone and implication with which the themes are treated. The recurrences are important if we would form some general notion of the heroes and what they stand for; the variety, which involves the whole richness of the individual plays, should be cautionary when we come to generalize. One generalization at least is valid. The heroes have a dimension of greatness beyond the measure of normal humanity: they go on where ordinary men would stop. It is a kind of excess, and excess is dangerous. About their greatness there are two things to be said. It is just because they have this almost superhuman capacity of holding to their principles that the poet, through extreme cases, is able to unfold the tragic implications of those principles. Secondly, this kind of greatness does not comport with the conditions of mortal existence and tends towards disaster. If this is no world for them, as it is not, we are bound to ask how Sophocles saw the world in which they suffer their tormented destinies; and if it is governed by divine powers, as for Sophocles it was, to ask how he saw the gods at work in it.

Sophocles was a religious man. He held the priesthood of a minor deity. When a cult of Asclepius was being introduced into Athens during the Peloponnesian War, he took the god – or at least the sacred snake – into his house while a shrine was being prepared. The cult of the Eumenides at Colonus, where he was born, is described in loving

33 See ch. 9 pp. 212ff.

detail, and all the sanctities of the place are celebrated in an ode. That he believed in the gods is certain, but how, precisely, he envisaged the anthropomorphic pantheon we are in no position to say. Nor is the question very important.[34] Crude anthropomorphism was only one expression of Greek religious experience; and polytheism was the more acceptable that the gods were a part of nature and, being gods of power, reflected, as the Greek gods did, those aspects of life – physical, social, and emotional – where power resided and some impulse outside man was felt, feared or desired.

The personal religion of Sophocles is a matter of pure speculation: how religion and the gods enter into his tragedy we can attempt to discern, but must bear in mind that conventional piety need not imply untroubled acceptance of everything and anything attributable to the divine world. Greek polytheism represents the world as it impinges upon men. And as it is it must be accepted? A good pagan position, but even pagans are strangely reluctant to accept paganism. Are the gods just? Are men free? Greeks, like others, wrestled with these questions. The anxious wrestlings of Aeschylus, in particular, are reflected in the work of Sophocles at every point.

In the extant plays gods are seldom seen upon the stage. We have Heracles in *Philoctetes,* but it is essential to his role that he was recently a man and much of what he says is at the human level: indeed *qua* spokesman of heaven he says very little. We have Athena in *Ajax;* and of her function something has been said in earlier chapters.[35] Her role in the Prologos may be thought ambiguous, but is clarified by the words of Calchas, so that we see why she makes that pronouncement of the grounds of divine favour and disfavour: we see that her 'wrath', which Ajax rightly recognizes without understanding its cause, was the appropriate penalty for his pride. Constantly, however, there are gods in the background, generally and specifically.

There is Aphrodite (with Eros). Athena punishes, but does not cause, the nature and action of Ajax: Aphrodite has worked power-fully within both Heracles and Deianira. It may be a misleading

---

[34] People today who have a firm belief in a personal god do not in fact envisage him as an old man with a long white beard. Iconography is one thing; theology is another. Sophocles may have thought the Apollo at Olympia a worthy represen-tation of the god; he may have seen something of Athena both in the ancient *bretas* and in the cult-statue by Pheidias (which cannot have been quite so hideous as late copies suggest).

[35] See ch. 2 pp. 41f.

accident that this power is prominent in two of the extant plays and hymned in both.[36] We must, however, take what we are given and recognize an aspect of the divine world of Sophocles which is seldom stressed, but should not be ignored. The power of sexual passion operating on, and in, the human mind is generative of tragedy because men may break under the strain and perform disastrous acts. There is some reason to suppose that Sophocles, like Aeschylus before him and like Euripides, saw another god of overwhelming emotion, Dionysus, as a potentially disastrous power.[37] Both these powers are divine and part of the given world in which men have to play out their destinies. They are given, like the individual fates, and men have not asked for them.

There is Apollo, who enters particularly into the story of Oedipus, prominent in the *Tyrannus,* less so in the *Coloneus.* In the *Tyrannus* one gets the impression that Apollo is working against Oedipus, which is how the latter sees it (1329ff.). What, then, is Apollo's interest?[38] Like Athena in *Ajax,* to punish a deliberate offence against divine law? The Chorus uses language of the unknown offender which might suggest such a thing (463–82), in an ode which immediately follows the all but explicit revelations of Teiresias. But Oedipus was not a deliberate offender. He was, however, deeply polluted; and Apollo was a god much concerned with pollution and purification. Or do we say that, as the god who knows what is to be and has foretold it, he has an interest in the fulfilment of his oracle? So stated, this sounds rather jejune. Better, perhaps, to remember that in Greek thought he was associated with the notion of self-knowledge (γνῶθι σαυτόν). This Oedipus is to acquire and becomes a symbol of human ignorance as Apollo and his oracle are symbols of divine knowledge.[39]

Above and beyond Apollo, in point of knowledge and in point of power, stands Zeus. As in Homer, as in Aeschylus, he is the supreme authority, the divine king.[40] The Chorus of the *Tyrannus,* when they think (how wrongly!) that oracles are not being fulfilled, pray to Zeus

---

[36] Though it can hardly have failed to be prominent in *Phaedra* among other plays.

[37] See ch. 5 pp. 110ff.

[38] See ch. 7 p. 178.

[39] See ch. 8 p. 181 n. 4.

[40] The search for unity amid polytheism, which was a natural development of thought, was facilitated by the essentially anthropomorphic conception of a patriarchal family.

as ruler and king of all things (*O. T.* 903ff.). 'There is none of these
things that is not Zeus', says that Coryphaeus at the end of *Trachiniae*.[41] If the prominence of Zeus in a play about Heracles owes
something to his fatherhood, he looms in all the extant plays, and in
some he looms larger as the play draws towards its close.[42] The ways
in which he enters into a play can be problematic. The prayer in the
Tyrannus comes at the end of an ode whose tendency is to show that
the fate of Oedipus was *not* the consequence of traditional wickedness.
The choral comment in *Trachiniae* follows – and cannot fail to recall –
the bitter complaint of Hyllus about the heartlessness of the gods. In
Antigone Zeus is at once responsible for the troubles that have beset the
house and also the authority to which the heroine appeals in defence
of her action. There is no reason to suppose that for Sophocles he was
a simpler and less troubling concept than he was for Aeschylus. As in
Aeschylus so in Sophocles, he stands in an enigmatic relationship to
the nether powers, to fate and the Erinyes.

Divine power bears upon the heroes in more than one way. Each of
them comes into the world of human action and passion with a *moira*:
he is of such-and-such a kind and will find himself in such-and-such a
situation; and there is not a great deal that he can do about it. This is
true of them, and it is true of us. To the question Why? there may be
no ultimate answer or, if an answer is sought, it recedes into a
vanishing distance. Sophocles wrote one play – and it is his most
famous – which provides the paradigm of this aspect of human
existence. It was the *moira* of Oedipus to kill his father and lie with his
mother; and it is no good asking what the gods had to gain by this
horror.[43] That was what was going to happen to him and it did:
everything stems from that. The story is given the greatest possible
dramatic impact, because it did not happen, as it might have happened, to you or to me, but to a man of high station who fell into the
depth of misery and so illustrated the precarious condition of
humanity; it happened to a man of high intelligence, against his
expectation, and so revealed the limitations of human knowledge.
The world is such a world in which such a thing can happen. We
cannot call the gods to account.

[41] On Zeus in *Trach.* see the good remarks of Segal, *YCS* 154f.
[42] See ch. 11 p. 271.
[43] Except an object-lesson. On the issue of hereditary guilt see Lloyd-Jones, *JZ* 119ff.
      and p. 205 n. 4 above.

It was the *moira* of Philoctetes to be bitten by a sacred snake, receive a noisome wound and be in consequence abandoned by the Greeks. Here indeed there is some kind of divine purpose in the background, but it is neither very specific nor much stressed; it is an arbitrary datum, but it needs Philoctetes as a victim, it even needs him to forego his heroic resentment.[44] This is of course a very different kind of play, in which the factor of destiny is hardly in the forefront and the consequences of the destined situation are worked out largely in terms of human psychology and social relationships. But the surd factor of an unaccountable destiny enters into all the plays in one way or another. Ajax has his *moira* no less than Oedipus; Antigone and Electra have theirs. It seems cruel to the sufferer who may cry out against it: so Oedipus speaks of a *daimon* which is *omos* and of himself as *echthrodaimon*.

We cannot say with what emotion, other than pity, Sophocles saw the dice loaded against his heroes in a pitiless world or contemplated, for that matter, the forces to which they were exposed. For if they have their individual fates assigned to them, they share – and exemplify – the general vulnerability of man, and this in many ways. Among those ways, they are subject to the forces of passion which assault the human mind, and which Sophocles, as a Greek, attributed to a divine origin, to an Aphrodite or a Dionysus, who, if they represent the irrational in man, are yet themselves gods. Nothing in the Greek conception of the divine is more characteristic or more revealing than these gods who work within the human *psyche* for delight or for tragedy. We may count it as a stroke of luck that mere chance has preserved two plays of Sophocles which exhibit Aphrodite in her tragic guise, in one of which she is protagonist. When she emerges sole victor from the destruction of Heracles and Deianira, she is not, as in *Hippolytus*, avenging a slighted divinity: she is merely being herself, nor is she responsible for the ironical fact that the physical strength which made Heracles a hero made him also her victim.

In the exposure to such forces, as in the individual *moira*, there is an arbitrariness which defies explanation, but this does not mean that Sophocles saw the divine dispensations as arbitrary – or wholly arbitrary. In an earlier chapter we saw that he had inherited from his

[44] Cf. *Phil.* 1466–8.

predecessors – and indeed from early strata of Greek thought – two notions of *moira*;[45] that, along with that of personal destiny, to all appearance arbitrary, there was a notion of *moira* as order, divinely sanctioned and entailing, by inexorable law, the punishment of offences against that order. It is a kind of justice and thus naturally associated with that clamant demand for justice in the gods which had led to the moralization of Zeus and so to all the problems of theodicy. It is in this connection that the relationship between the heroes and the gods becomes most difficult to determine and, thus, most interesting.

The gods represent – are responsible for – the world as it is and as it is governed. The heroes are obviously, in some sense, up against the world, hence their intransigence, hence their loneliness: they feel not only isolated from their fellow-men but (often) abandoned, even victimized, by the gods. Are they right to feel so, or are they wrong? If we apply to our old acquaintances, the pietists and the 'hero-worshippers',[46] we receive different answers. The gods of the pietists order all for the best; their harsh justice is in the interests of men, for whose welfare they care; learning comes by suffering, and those who lack the saving grace of *sophrosune* are taught a lesson; the intellectual pride of an Oedipus is humbled no less than the traditional heroic pride of an Ajax (the only matter in dispute being whether he learns his lesson or not). It follows that those who behave differently are right and favoured by the gods, Creon in the *Tyrannus* and Odysseus in *Ajax*. Of Odysseus this seems, broadly, to be true, but *Ajax* is a relatively early play, and there is nothing in later Sophocles quite so explicit as the motto-couplet of Athena (132f.) which relates the love and hatred of the gods to the presence or absence of *sophrosune* in men. We turn to Antigone. What has she to learn, except that by being pious she has earned the reward of impiety?[47] In that play Creon acts badly and, amid echoes of Aeschylus, is punished, learns – or half-learns – a lesson, but he does not share the typical attributes of a Sophoclean hero; Antigone, who does, claims to be acting in accord with divine law and is destroyed. Do we, then, go into reverse and say, with the hero-worshippers, that this is a bad world; that what the heroes do is great and right and exposes the badness of a world unworthy of them? We then take another look at Ajax; we bring

45 See ch. 7 p. 155.
46 See ch. 1 p. 9.
47 See ch. 5 p. 146.

Heracles and Electra into the picture; we begin to wonder, and we wait for the Colonean Oedipus.

The generalizations founder upon the variety of the heroes and of the situations in which they are placed, and extreme views can only be defended by interpretations which defy the text of Sophocles. Do we say the heroes are *per se* admirable? Or do we, rather, lay stress on their lack of *sophrosune*, that spirit of moderation and control which keeps men safe (as indeed it does), for which they suffer (as indeed they do), adding perhaps that they show their greatness above all in the moment of defeat?[48] Are they approved or disapproved? But tragedy is not about approval and disapproval, which is why Ajax and Antigone can both be tragic figures, though no one could approve of the action of Ajax in seeking to kill his generals or (one might have hoped) disapprove of the action of Antigone in burying her brother; nor, for all they have in common, do we respond in the same way to those formidable heroines, Antigone and Electra. Indeed the engagement of our sympathies with these different figures varies notably in degree and in kind. These great and often terrible personages are neither models of how human-beings should behave nor models of how they should not behave. They are tragic figures who find themselves in tragic situations. Plato and Aristotle are bad guides. Aristotle encourages us to look for a *hamartia*, by which he presumably meant something different from the divine distraction, *ate*-produced and *ate*-producing, of early Greek thought (the kind of thing he was not interested in), but he does not make it clear how wide his conception of *hamartia* was (factual? moral?) nor, wisely perhaps, does he give examples. Of course tragic heroes make their tragic mistakes, but, if we seek in each case to identify a specific *hamartia*, we may end up discovering one of the least interesting things about them. For Plato it was a primary purpose to acquit the gods of responsibility for evil, in which he departed from the main stream of Greek thought, and by which he was led to banish tragedy.[49] Can the gods of

---

[48] How does this popular cliché stand the test of Sophocles? Ajax dies with courage and with bitter hatred in his heart; Antigone dies with her obstinate will unbroken, uncomprehending that her piety has met such a reward; King Oedipus we see with his intelligence unimpaired and his spirit beginning to surge back after the overwhelming blow of fate; Electra has won her battle at the cost of a corruption of soul which will remain with her; the other Oedipus becomes a *heros*.

[49] On Plato and tragedy, see Anderson 48–50. Recently, on Aristotle, see T. C. W.

Sophocles, responsible for the conditions of human life, be so acquit-
ted? May it not be that the gods whom the Chorus of *Oedipus
Tyrannus*, appropriately, wished to worship[50] were tragic gods, with
whom the tragic heroes have an awful kinship?

There is a point of junction between the heroes – many or most of
them – and the gods. (i) We have seen how frequently these plays turn
on the sequence of injury, resentment and (as a matter of honour)
retaliation. This is not a mere accident of mythology, or random
selection. The emotions and motives involved belong to traditional
Greek morals; and I have argued that the Greeks were taught to write
tragedy (beginning of course, as Aristotle saw, with Homer), in part,
by observing the consequences which followed when the code was
carried inexorably into effect. (ii) We have seen how there is a justice
of the gods, whether it is viewed in terms of *moira* or of Zeus. It is a
penal justice, a matter of retribution, of the past offence exacting
payment in the present and laying up further retribution in the
future.[51] And this, too, for those who believed in divine justice, led in
the direction of tragedy. Indeed, (i) and (ii) are meshed together. For
it is the way of the gods to punish, not with thunderbolt or plague
(though these may be used), but through human agency. Human
retaliation is matched, in the proliferation of evil, by a divine law
under which actions carry their inevitable penal consequences; divine
talio is the sanction behind human *talio*; wrathful men are the agents of
wrathful gods.[52]

Talio was a preoccupation of all three tragedians. No theme is more
persistent in Euripides: always it is exposed as a false basis for human
morals, always, when it appears within the divine world, it is the
object of satire or abhorrence and beyond the scope of theodicy,
which was not his concern. For Aeschylus it was, precisely, a problem
of theodicy; and *Oresteia* is essentially a dramatic exploration of *talio*

Stinton, '*Hamartia* in Aristotle and Greek tragedy', *CQ* 69 (1975) 221–54, and
Suzanne Saïd, *La faute tragique* (Paris 1978). I would suggest that Aristotle, having
his own problem to solve (about the fall of the 'tragic hero' from good fortune to
bad), found the concept of *hamartia* a useful tool: it does not follow that it is much
use to us. Nor is the *Poetics* the best starting-point for an understanding of Greek
tragedy – not Aristotle, but Homer.

[50] See ch. 8 p. 200.

[51] Kitto, in his valuable discussion of *dike* in Sophocles (*SDP* 47ff.), tends to play
down the legal or quasi-legal associations of the word. This seems particularly
unwise at *O.T.* 1213f., where legal language is accumulated.

[52] I owe something here to discussion with Professor Thomas Gould.

on the divine and human levels, the pursuit of a solution to an apparently insoluble problem, moral, social and religious. Given a human world in which men resent and avenge their wrongs, given a divine world which ordains that wrongs shall be punished, how is it possible to break a chain which leads from one crime to another in a theoretically endless series of violent acts. The solution which he finds is partly in terms of society, and of the evolution of society.[53] But there is a deeper dimension. Aeschylus had made of the Erinyes the great symbol of *talio*. At the end of the trilogy they remain, still retaining their primitive and punitive function, but having added to it an attribute of benevolence. The Aeschylean solution is found in terms not of pity but of good-will; and, above all, of persuasion. The most astonishing thing in *Oresteia* is that the inexorable Furies should be persuaded, as Athena persuades them; the ultimate religious insight of Aeschylus was that persuasion as well as force could be a mode in which the divine will operates. This was known to Sophocles.

In earlier plays of Sophocles Erinyes appear in their traditional role of avengers, as symbols of the dead reaching out against the living. It is not until two late plays, *Electra* and *Oedipus Coloneus* (so I have argued), that the Aeschylean concept of Erinyes comes near to dominating the dramatic thought of Sophocles. In *Electra,* which repeats a situation from *Oresteia,* Sophocles parts company from Aeschylus, not by omitting the Furies (which he does not do), but by omitting their transformation at Athens.[54] In the *Coloneus,* which takes place at Athens, does he part company from Aeschylus? And if so how?

Whether Sophocles knowingly wrote *Oedipus Coloneus* as a final tragic testament we cannot tell, but it is inevitable that we should see the play in that light, particularly as it gathers together so many themes from earlier plays. It takes Oedipus, who may already have become the most famous of his heroes, and makes a god of him. Which is not quite true: he makes of him a *heros*. The Erinyes, now worshipped as Eumenides, are important, but still more important is the coming hero-status of Oedipus. Both are chthonian. This is not the Oedipus, simply, of the *Tyrannus,* though it bears a resemblance to him. He is still obsessed with his polluted state, but has given thought to his past and come to see his actions as innocent, and in particular the killing of Laius innocent because it was an act of

[53] For some discussion of this matter, see *JHS* 74 (1954) 16–24.
[54] See ch. 10 p. 227.

justified retaliation. (Which should make us think.) The self-blinding had been an act of immoderate passion; his exile is no longer the desired refuge from a scene of horror, but an injury inflicted on him by his own kin. Resentment has built up in the blind beggar who was once a king – resentment, and a will to retaliate upon his sons. But he has daughters who have served him; and he loves them no less than he hates the sons who have wronged him. This is the reverse of the medal: benefits evoke love as injuries evoke hatred. So Oedipus responds to the generous reception which he received from Theseus, which is also, mysteriously and paradoxically, a reception by the Eumenides who, as Erinyes, have dogged his tragic career. The play has a double climax, curse and assumption, but also a coda. If the passionate curse of Oedipus upon his sons is followed by his reception into the divine world as a *heros,* at the end we realize that Antigone is involved in the fate of Polynices, which puts the final emphasis upon the wrath rather than upon the love of Oedipus. The play ends with pity failing to persuade and with the ironical certainty of violence. Persuasion, pity and irony: these are perhaps the three words with which this chapter should close.

Oresteia ends with a victory of persuasion (and the same seems to have been true of the Danaid trilogy).[55] To say that Sophocles parts company with Aeschylus – that, as in *Electra* there is not even a forward-looking hint at the ultimate persuasion of the Furies, so in the *Coloneus* there is no significance in the name under which they were worshipped at Colonus – goes too far. Theseus did not fear these awesome goddesses; and (as I have suggested)[56] he – and that ideal Athens for which he stands – did not need to fear them. But Sophocles is not writing his play about Theseus or any men who, by luck or virtue, succeed in living immune from the operation of Furies. He is writing about Oedipus, pre-eminent among their victims, about his sons and his daughters. What, then, did it mean that he found favour with the Eumenides and an end of his sufferings in their grove? He did not find a life of happiness, but a place in which to die and, in death, to join them as himself a chthonian power, mighty to help his friends and harm his enemies. It is an astounding conception. It is a conse-

---

[55] On the Danaid trilogy see *JHS* 81 (1961) 141–52. The *bia/peitho* contrast is also prominent in *P.V.*, and there seems a strong likelihood that persuasion prevailed in the sequel. On the authorship of this play, see p. 158 n. 19.

[56] See ch. 9 p. 273.

cration at the divine level of that polar reaction towards friends and enemies which haunts the theatre of Sophocles, an endorsement of that notion of justice which is closely involved with friendship and enmity.

This polarity is rejected, in their very different ways, by both Antigones. The first Antigone refuses to admit the continuance of hatred beyond the grave and determines by her own heroic act to end it: she loves, but does not pity or persuade (which is not her nature), and she comes to hate the living sister who loves her (which is ironical). The second Antigone is the all-loving creature the first Antigone thought herself to be. Her love extends to the brother who had wronged her father, whose right to harm his harmful sons she denies. She seeks to persuade, and she fails, and the tragic process continues until it culminates in her own death. She fails, because her pity beats upon a rock.[57]

Pity is a common theme in Sophocles. Who has it? We tend to concentrate attention upon the great unyielding heroes and regard them as being typically Sophoclean. Pity, we may say, is shown by minor characters, by a Hyllus or a Creon (O.T. 1473). This is hardly true. Odysseus (in *Ajax*), Deianira and the Colonean Antigone, are not to be written off so simply. The pity of Odysseus is structural to its play. Deianira has equal rights with Heracles in *Trachiniae*. If Antigone is a 'minor character' in the *Coloneus,* she is present almost throughout the play, has her moment when she holds the stage, and confronts us with her fate at the end. A pitying character is as Sophoclean as a hero. Pity is an attribute of men rather than of gods. Do the gods approve it in men? They do indeed seem to demand that human-beings recognize the inferior status which they share in common, the recognition of which makes them capable of pity, though this, if it wins the favour of Athena for Odysseus, does not save a Deianira or (in the *Coloneus*) an Antigone. Hyllus, seeking the sympathy of his fellow-men, asks them at the same time to recognize the great *agnomosune* of the gods. He is hardly an impartial witness, but the fact remains that pity is sought from men and not from gods, with one notable exception. Knowing that he has come to a sanctuary of the Awful Goddesses, Oedipus prays to them, addressing them as 'sweet daughters of ancient Darkness', to have pity on him. Which

---

[57] *O.C.* 1239ff. See ch. 11 p. 252 n. 10.

they do, by receiving him on his way to become a pitiless, yet loving, *heros*.

That pity was for Sophocles a supreme value need hardly be argued. Pity inspires every work of his that has come down to us – pity and *suggnome*, that capacity to enter into the feelings of another which made possible every aspect of his dramatic creation. But what response to human pity did he find in the divine world?[58] Polynices urged his father to show *aidos* towards him, saying that Aidos shares the throne of Zeus in all he does. *Aidos* from Oedipus to Polynices means that he should respect a claim, the claim of a suppliant, of a blood-relation; and it is doubtful whether Polynices by his own conduct had the right to make such a claim. But what does it mean to say that the goddess Aidos is the assessor of Zeus? Is it merely a reference to Zeus in his function as Hikesios, protecting the suppliant? But Polynices says ἐπ᾽ ἔργοις πᾶσι, 'in all his works': the reference must be wider. There must be some suggestion of mercy or compassion, some tempering of justice. Oedipus has his answer (1381f.), when he in his turn asserts that primeval Justice sits with Zeus in accordance with ancient laws; and that therefore his curses will prevail. And they do. And Oedipus becomes a *heros*.

It might seem that, at the end of his life and of his long concern with tragic events, Sophocles looked at the divine world and saw a profound significance in the concept of a *heros*,[59] meting out with a rough justice good to friends and harm to enemies. It is a just world, but the divine justice turns out to bear a sinister resemblance to that kind of retaliatory justice in pursuing which men themselves bring about tragic events. The resemblance is ironical. The gods, themselves immune from disaster, exercise their awful sovereignty at a distance, but the heroes are in the midst of things. Born with arbitrary destinies for which they have not asked, placed in situations which preclude any outcome which is not tragic, they pursue their god-like code with a consistency and energy which is more than human, but, being men and not gods, they come to grief. It is not, however, their fallible humanity alone which is responsible for the disasters and the ironies, but something deep-seated in a world where human nature and society mirror – or are mirrored by – the dictates of the gods.

[58] On *Aj.* 756f., where the further wrath of Athena is limited to one day, see ch. 2 pp. 41f. It is not said, or necessarily implied, that the goddess had pity on the hero.
[59] On Sophocles and hero-cult, cf. Knox, *HT* 54ff.

Sophocles is recognized as the supreme ironist, which is something not to be forgotten when we seek to understand his heroes and his gods. Irony in Sophocles goes far deeper than an effective, if obvious, use of language.[60] There is irony of situation. It is ironical that the faithful and sensitive Deianira should produce a result to be expected from the 'pitiless woman' of Aeschylus; that the admirable monster-slayer should be destroyed by the women he despises. But the world is like that! It is ironical that the man who read the riddle of the Sphinx should fail to discern his own parentage, until (more irony) his sheer intellectual integrity accelerates the discovery of the awful truth. It is ironical that Antigone, heroically determined to end the hatreds of her house, should reject her own sister's love. It is ironical that the other Oedipus should not realize that, in cursing his sons, he has signed the death-warrant of his daughter. But the world is like that! The ways of the gods no less than the ways of heroes tend to such ends.[61]

This kind of irony can have no seat except in a flawed world: we find little response to it among the adherents of any optimistic philosophy.[62] Irony responds to disharmony and imperfections which it accepts for what they are, which it exploits and does not deny or explain away. In comedy it becomes the source of a subtle pleasure; in tragedy, which itself owes its existence to the flaws in the world – what they do to men and what men do amid them – it is bitter and terrible and pitiable: it is a mode of the expression of pity. It comports with gods who, like the Greek gods, are in the last analysis reflections of the conditions of human life. Sophocles saw human life as tragic and ironical.

---

[60] 'Word play is the lowest level of dramatic irony': Kirkwood, *SSD* 247, in his chapter on 'The irony of Sophocles'.

[61] It is argued in ch. 12 p. 299, that the divine purpose which required the sufferings of Philoctetes has its ironical aspect.

[62] I prefer not to be more specific, but creeds – religious, political and social – which are resistant to irony will no doubt spring to the reader's mind.

APPENDIXES

The Parodos of *Trachiniae*

In the Parodos the alternation of joy and sorrow is symbolized by the great alternating process of nature, day and night. It is the consoling argument of the Chorus that sorrow cannot last for ever, but will give place to joy as night gives place to day, and Deianira should therefore not reject good hope. This they have in mind as they sing, but the words which Sophocles gives them may suggest that she is right not to be so consoled. The handling of this theme, particularly in the first stanza and the last, is a striking example of the lyric subtlety of Sophocles.

In the first stanza, overtly, the Chorus appeal to the sun as the source of knowledge, to tell them where Alcmena's son may be. The sun is λαμπρᾷ στεροπᾷ φλεγέθων and κρατιστεύων κατ' ὄμμα. The first word in the stanza refers to the sun, but is a colourless relative (ὅν), the antecedent of which is still unspecified. The first subject, the first noun, is νύξ. (Compare the twofold νύξ at 29f., there too with two verbs and the idea of succession, but a succession of πόνοι.) Night which gives birth to the sun and puts the sun to sleep. Thus the notion of alternation is introduced at the outset. Not only so. If there is a double process, sunrise and sunset (and the stanza is rounded off by a reference to the regions of sunrise and sunset),[1] night is made the grammatical subject and ‚ operating force of both, so that, as it were, the sun is put under the control of night; and this is a counterpoise to the brilliant description of the sun as the source of knowledge. In fact, the blazing light of the sun, in which and to which all is visible, is first heard of as extinguished by the action of night (κατευνάζει . . . φλογιζόμενον).

The epode begins with μένει, as though a positive statement were coming, but this is followed by οὔτ' αἰόλα νύξ, which – noun and epithet – recall the opening of the first stanza (and its aesthetics). Despite the negative – and aided perhaps by the positive μένει – the emphasis is upon night, the more strongly so that the alternative (day or sun) is not expressed. Instead of

---

[1] Ring-composition. I accept Lloyd-Jones' interpretation of 100f. at *CQ* 4 (1954) 91–3, contr. Stinton 127–9.

330

following οὔτ' αἰόλα νύξ with, e.g., οὔτ' ἦμαρ, the sentence continues with
οὔτε κῆρες: 'calamities' (recalling πῆμα in 129). Then, surprisingly, we have
οὔτε πλοῦτος. Surprisingly, because wealth is not otherwise a theme in the
play nor is it apparently relevant to Deianira. But wealth is the obvious
proverbial example of the transitoriness of good fortune. And that is why it
is here introduced, as one 'good' thing (πλοῦτος) after two 'bad' things (νύξ,
κῆρες), all involved in a process of alternation. But there is one respect in
which wealth differs from the earlier examples of the transitory. It involves
two human parties: the man who loses and the man who gains. Hence τῷ δ'
ἐπέρχεται (which is appropriate only to πλοῦτος). Wealth, when it is lost by
one man (to his grief), passes to another, who rejoices, though he too may in
turn be deprived of it. It was necessary to introduce the notion of joy coming
to a man (since it is the argument of the Chorus that joy may come even to
Deianira), and this is done by τῷ δ' ἐπέρχεται. But the force of χαίρειν is
immediately cancelled by στέρεσθαι. For it was also necessary to introduce
the idea of deprivation (not implied by νύξ or κῆρες). Kamerbeek rightly
refers to 176f. (εἴ με χρὴ μένειν | πάντων ἀρίστου φωτὸς ἐστερημένην, where
μένειν may recall μένει at 132). Deianira has been deprived of her husband by
his absences and would be by his death, did she not forestall it with her own.
But there will also be a question of deprivation by a rival, though a rival who
has no joy in him. Deianira's ἐστερημένην (177) is immediately followed by
the entry of a messenger garlanded and bringing news of joy: 179, πρὸς
χαρὰν λόγων (where χάριν should by no means be preferred). He brings joy
even to Deianira: ὦ Ζεῦ . . . ἔδωκας ἡμῖν ἀλλὰ σὺν χρόνῳ χαράν (200f.). She
greets Lichas on the same note, and the theme of joy is brought out by a play
on words (227f.). Yet the captives who seem to provide evidence to support
her new-found joy in fact bring the evidence of her deprivation. Joy and
deprivation are as closely linked in the experience of Deianira as in the lyric
phrase: χαίρειν τε καὶ στέρεσθαι.

As to the 'argument' of the whole Parodos, there are two things to say. It is
obvious that such an argument is reversible: that, if the alternations of nature
are a just analogy and prove that sorrow is transitory, the same must also be
true of joy. But it may be more significant to ask whether the analogy of
natural process is not fallacious when applied to human life, at least to
Deianira's life, which (in Mrs Easterling's words) 'violates the natural
rhythm' whereby day follows night and night follows day. (Easterling,
BICS 59f., with her excellent comment on 175–7.) Her joy is a fallacious
false dawn, and the tenour of her life – her αἰών (2) – remains dark to the
end. The emphasis is rightly on νύξ; and Deianira belongs as surely to the
realm of night as Ajax shows himself to belong (see ch. 2 p. 55).[2]

___

[2] 'As the play begins, night dominates'. Cf. Segal, *YCS* 107f., 143f. (from which I
quote). His view of the aesthetics of the Parodos is broadly similar to mine, but he

APPENDIX B

Trachiniae 248ff.

There are features in Lichas' narrative which are extremely obscure; and it is not enough to say that we ought not to demand complete clarity from an embarrassed liar. It has long been recognized that what is impossibly obscure to us may have been relatively clear to the original audience or to a large section of it. What sources of information could Sophocles count on their knowing? The epic Οἰχαλίας ἅλωσις, no doubt. Panyassis' epic on Heracles? Sophocles himself may well have known this, if only through Herodotus, but one cannot assume that it was widely known in Athens. The notion that a recent stage treatment, e.g. the Eurytidae of Ion, lies behind the passage is attractive (cf. T. B. L. Webster, Hermes 71 (1936) 267), but neither Ion's tragedy nor his satyric Omphale can be dated. Since none of these sources is available to us, it is perhaps hardly worth speculating.

The basic lie of Lichas is about motives, not about facts. Heracles *was* thrown out when drunk (Lichas would never have invented so discreditable a story); he *did* kill Iphitus and *was* in servitude to Omphale – both traditional features. But (351ff.) it was not his servitude to Omphale in Lydia, i.e. his resentment of it, nor the death of Iphitus which led to it, that motivated his attack upon Oechalia, but his passion for Iole. When was that passion conceived?

The Messenger tells us, i.e. Lichas had said, that Heracles asked for Iole as a concubine (359f.), unsuccessfully. When? Hardly subsequent to the events of 262ff., including the slaying of Iphitus. We get the impression that the attack followed immediately upon the end of his servitude, which was also a year of purification (258ff.). (The petty pretexts of 361 are presumably implied in 254–8, 281ff. The Messenger knows nothing Lichas did not tell, and that these were mere pretexts must therefore be the impression that Lichas gave.) It is natural to suppose that Heracles' passion for Iole was conceived, and expressed, during the original visit to her father's palace.

There is an odd feature in the story at 262ff., a great hiatus. A guest arrives, a ξένος παλαιός. Immediately we hear of a quarrel, and a drunken Heracles is thrown out of the palace. Odd, if quite gratuitous. Lichas of course wishes to

carries his examination of the themes further than I have done or, in some cases, should care to do. T. F. Hoey, 'Sun symbolism in the parodos of the *Trachiniae*', Arethusa 5 (1972) 133–54, also brings out the association of Deianira with night (p. 146), but I find his attempt to make an equation of Heracles with the sun less successful. Nor am I convinced that the notion of cyclicity has that importance in the development of the play which he attaches to it.

suggest that Eurytus and his sons were impossible hubristic people on whom Heracles was quite justified in taking vengeance (cf. 278–80 and ch. 9, n. 26). And this indeed they may have been (and there may have been epic and dramatic substantiation of this). But one cannot help thinking that the lost sources may have linked the quarrel and the drunkenness with Heracles' lustful demand for Iole.

There is other evidence to link the drunken and the amorous Heracles. He can of course get drunk (as in *Alcestis*) without becoming amorous. In Ion's *Omphale* the Lydian queen tried to seduce him when he was drunk, cf. frs. 26, 27, 29, but this is a satyr-play. In Euripides' *Auge* (frs. 265, 268) he ascribes his rape of Auge to the combined influences of lust and wine; and this may have been traditional (cf. Alcidamas, *Odyss.* 14–16). Is it not possible, then, that his pursuit of Iole lay behind the whole fracas? Did he ask for her company in bed as an agreeable sequel to the dinner-party? One is reminded of the Persian envoys in Herodotus 5.18–20. One is reminded of the centaurs, who 'intoxicated at the wedding feast, behaved very similarly'. I quote from Susan Woodford, 'More light on old walls', *JHS* 94 (1974) 158–65. The point is that Nessus was a centaur. I quote from Woodford again (pp. 161f.): 'Representations of Heracles fighting the centaur Nessus who has attempted to carry off Heracles' wife convey something of the same message about the difference between civilisation and savagery. They also portray the contrast between self-control and self-indulgence, responsible guardianship and irresponsible passion, lawful marriage and lawless rape, and they may have pointed the way to the development of the theme of centauromachy at the feast in art.' If there was such an iconographic tradition of the Heracles–Nessus story, it could have been in the mind of Sophocles, to ironic effect. Heracles is in fact betrayed by a lust comparable to that of the centaur he killed.

This speculation is, however, complicated by the reference at 265–8 to the *hoplon krisis*. There was a tradition which associated this contest with Iole (Apollodorus 6.1.2), but, in default of further evidence, we can hardly hope to bring it into relation with our passage. Another obscure feature is why Heracles should have killed Iphitus by treachery, when he could have done so by force. And there were several versions of the episode of the wandering cattle. We can only envy the original audience for their superior knowledge. (The textual difficulties of 262–9 are discussed by Stinton 133f.).

APPENDIX C

Prometheus Vinctus 511–20

The authenticity of *P.V.* has long been under suspicion. A careful and unprejudiced examination of this problem by Mark Griffith (*The authenticity of 'Prometheus Bound'*, Cambridge 1977) – and particularly the metrical evidence which he adduces – has made it hard to believe any longer in its Aeschylean authorship. Whoever wrote it, it remains, however, an important document closely related to Aeschylean thought; and it contains a passage closely relevant to the themes discussed in chapter 7.

Prometheus, rebellious against Zeus, has said (103ff.) that he must bear his fated destiny (τὴν πεπρωμένην αἶσαν) as easily as he can, recognizing that the force of *ananke* is irresistible. At 511ff., in reply to the facile optimism of the friendly Chorus, he states that his release from bondage is not predestined until he has suffered a myriad torments. The language used is actually very difficult, the basic difficulty being that the verb πέπρωται is appropriate to the 'portion' (cf. the common πεπρωμένη μοῖρα / αἶσα), whereas the verb κρᾶναι and the epithet τελεσφόρος are appropriate to the 'apportioner'. There is a sort of conflation of μοῖρα πεπρωμένη with Μοῖρα τελεσφόρος. It is difficult, but not perhaps unintelligible: 'an accomplishing *moira* has been given so as to bring about these things so'. (Whether Aeschylus did, or could have, written this Greek might be a matter of debate.)

In any case, the notion, as at 103ff., seems to be that of a rigid individual fate; and, when Prometheus adds that 'art' (τέχνη, meaning his inventive powers) is weaker far than *ananke,* we may recall 103. The passage continues as follows. The Coryphaeus asks: 'Who then moves the tiller of *ananke*?' The answer comes: 'The triformed Moirai and the mindful (μνήμονες) Erinyes.' 'Is Zeus then weaker than these?' 'He could not escape his destined fate (τὴν πεπρωμένην).' 'What is fated (πέπρωται) for Zeus except to rule for ever?' To which question no answer is given, but we shall learn that Zeus might have begotten a son more powerful than himself who would have put an end to his rule. Ed. Fraenkel, who has discussed the passage so well, is no doubt right to say (*Aeschylus Oresteia* III 729), following Wilamowitz, that 'no more than any other being can he escape the consequences of his actions'. There appears to be thus a shift in the point of view, with the introduction of Erinyes, whose association with the Moirai is one of punishing breaches of order; and *ananke* is now the rigid operation of cause and effect by which punishment follows crime. Should we say that, in this passage, the writer has conflated two different conceptions of *moira*? (In which case the question whether Aeschylus did, or could have, done this might be a matter of debate.) The evidence is insufficient; and in the *Luomenos* (which I am convinced was written by the author of the *Vinctus*) and in the third play (if there was one) the theme may well have been taken up and developed.

APPENDIX D

The Parodos of *Electra*

A full analysis of all the trains of thought and emotion, of all the aesthetic relationships, in this subtle *kommos* would be lengthy and difficult. I wish only to pick out certain features, particularly those which seem to reflect the Aeschylean background.

The main theme of the first two stanzas (121–52) is Electra and her excessive lamentation, the Chorus' appeal to her to be moderate (which is to say not Electra, not heroic, not tragic). Electra uses a strong word of distraction at 135 (ἀλύειν); the chorus pick it up with τῶν δυσφόρων (144), which may carry a suggestion of mental sickness (see above p. 20 n. 28 on *Ajax*). To this she replies with νήπιος ὅς ... ἐπιλάθεται. The claim that her apparent breach of *sophrosune* or mental balance is the only true wisdom is characteristic and will be carried further in the scenes with Chrysothemis.

121–7 (Chorus) contains a clear reference back to 37 (δόλοισι), the Pythian instruction to Orestes. (Note, therefore, ἀθεώτατα intervening between δολερᾶς and ἀπάταις.) That one crafty killing is to be avenged by another is a theme prominent in the *Choephori* (cf. esp. 555–8). Segal *TAPA* 475 remarks that 'treachery and deceit ... seldom come off well in Sophocles'. Whether there is any special significance in the fact that Electra is addressed as daughter of her *mother* rather than of her father (contr. 1f. of Orestes) each reader must decide for himself. In so far as the reference to trickery suggests the vengeance as well as the crime, it may be worth noting that the chorus are made to use the masculine: ὁ τάδε πορών (suggestive of Aegisthus only). Change this to the feminine, and εἴ μοι θέμις τάδ᾽ αὐδᾶν might take on a different tone.

137–44 (Chorus). That you cannot raise the dead is a commonplace prominent in the *Oresteia*. But the γόος in the *Cho.* was a way of mobilizing the power of the dead; and Electra has prayed to the chthonian powers at 110ff. (cf. 184, 245f. below). And the dead man returns in the ominous dream of Clytemnestra (cf. 453ff.).

145–52 (Electra). Electra compares herself – her state of mind – to two great legendary types of lamentation: Procne and Niobe. Electra laments a parent (γονέων), Procne and Niobe their children. Procne had killed her own child, as we cannot fail to remember after 107 (τεκνολέτειρα . . . ἀηδών); Niobe had caused the deaths of her children, and her sons had been slain by Apollo. Parents and children. (Segal 495.) There is little to pin down, and we should not say at this stage that there is any thought of Agamemnon who killed his child (and Clytemnestra has not yet prayed for the death of hers), but the passage hints at the web of parent–child relationships and so leads into the next half-stanza of the chorus: about Electra, her sisters and her brother (cf. τέκνον, 154). First, however, note the rather surprising description of the nightingale as 'messenger of Zeus'. 'The harbinger of spring' (Jebb); and the seasons are sacred to Zeus. How odd, though, of Sophocles to break the tension with this apparently irrelevant association and to introduce Zeus into the play in this apparently trivial fashion! If any bird is the messenger of Zeus, it is the eagle. (Compare *Cho.* 258f. I would not assert that Sophocles had that passage in mind, though the young of Agamemnon are there seen as eagles.) Perhaps the point is that the lamentations of this human nightingale are harbingers, not of spring, but of vengeance, when Orestes returns Διὸς εὔφρονι βήματι (162f.). (Cf. Segal 493 n. 25.) Another lead into the following stanza.

153–63 (Chorus). Kells quotes aptly from *Hamlet*: 'Why seems it so particular with thee?' At first it sounds general (οὔτοι σοὶ μούνᾳ), but is immediately given a more particular reference. Electra and her sisters: Chrysothemis and Iphianassa. The latter, who plays no further part, seems to have been introduced merely in order to make us think of Iphigenia (see ch. 10 n. 26). Iphianassa lives; Iphigenia is dead, killed by her father. Then Orestes, though the name is at first withheld. Chrysothemis and Iphianassa are moderate in their grief; Orestes is – ὄλβιος. A surprising word, explicable of course by the following relative clause, by the return to glory which awaits him (as son of his father, εὐπατρίδας). But there is a progression – or regression – from the extreme grief of Electra, through the moderation of her sisters, to an Orestes who is quite outside the domestic situation (see p. 230. (Not a miserable exile but, if the false story is plausible, living the life of a wealthy prince.) Which may be a good reason for taking κρυπτᾷ ἀχέων ἐν ἥβᾳ (159) as Hermann took it: 'in his youth hidden from griefs' (cf. Kamerbeek and Kells ad loc.). No wonder Electra (ἄτεκνος, ἀνύμφευτος) thinks he has forgotten (164–72).

173–84 (Chorus). The Chorus consoles. There is a third mention of Zeus (in quick succession). She must assign her excessive grief to Zeus (who is still great in heaven, over-seeing and ruling all things), herself neither hating overmuch nor forgetting. 'For time is a god that gives ease' (179). εὐμαρής is, again, a somewhat surprising word, in the context. A passage in *O.C.*

(437ff.) is relevant: time reduced the suffering of Oedipus so that he felt his passion had run too far. That would be the normal connotation, but that is not how time works on Electra nor how the situation is to be resolved. Not by a gradual running-down of emotion, but by catastrophe; and the catastrophe is implied by the next explanatory γάρ and what it goes with. This is one of those cases (cf. *Ajax* 182ff.) in which two reasons are given, each with its own γάρ, but here the reasons are, emotionally, contradictory. For how will Zeus, to whom Electra must commit her grief, punish the offence? Time will bring, not an easing of emotion, but action on the part of two agencies, neither of which is heedless (182): Orestes, now (as they think) an exile at Crisa and the god that rules in the underworld, to whom Electra had prayed (110). A human agent and a divine power. So here, in this stanza, we find that Aeschylean conjunction of powers: at the beginning Zeus in heaven, at the end 'the god that rules beside Acheron', and in between Orestes, the human agent, so described as to remind us of his association with Apollo.

185–92 (Electra). Electra remains inconsolable: hopeless, desperate, childless, husbandless, a drudge, ill-clothed, ill-fed.

193–200 (Chorus). 'Moved by Electra's misery, they join with her in bewailing its cause' (Jebb). With them we return, vividly, to the moment of Agamemnon's death – to his piteous death-cry, when the axe struck. 'It was craft that plotted, lust that killed.' (Craft again, which will be answered by craft.) And then we get some more remarkable phrases. Craft and lust 'had engendered, terribly, a terrible shape' (198f.). The shape of what? 'The act of murder', says Jebb, 'embodied in the image of a supernatural ἀλάστωρ.' The μορφή does indeed indicate a personification, an embodiment, an *alastor*, a *daimon*, an Erinys. They go on to sing: 'whether it was a god or some mortal who was accomplishing these things'. They are not singing of the deed of Orestes and Electra, but the deed of Clytemnestra and Aegisthus. The killing of Agamemnon was, in Aeschylus, the work of an Erinys or Erinyes (*Agam.* 1433, 1580); and it was in consequence of a crime or crimes. The same ambivalence, the same relationship between deity and human agent, holds good of the vengeance of Orestes. (The εἴτε . . . εἴτε here is in fact an antithesis strictly comparable to the οὔτε . . . οὔτε of 180ff., about Orestes and the god of the nether world.)

201–12 (Electra). Day and night again. The night of disaster following the day of hope, which is therefore, in retrospect, the most hateful of days. Electra returns to her own plight and prays for vengeance on the murderers. She prays that the great god of Olympus may punish them (209f.). θεὸς ὁ μέγας Ὀλύμπιος picks up 174f. *(μέγας οὐρανῷ Ζεύς)*, so enclosing the reference to Hades at 184 and the Erinys implied at 198ff. between two mentions of Zeus. ποίνιμα πάθεα παθεῖν πόροι (210), Zeus works through Erinyes (*Poinai*), embodied in human avengers: it is Zeus who, with good will (εὔφρονι), is going to bring Orestes home (162f.). 'May they not enjoy their splendour, having accomplished such deeds!' (211f.). It is, as Jebb says, 'the external splendour of their life' (ἀγλαΐας); and this is what Electra so much resents in its contrast to her own life of misery (189–92). The word might perhaps recall ὄλβιος (160). What glory and prosperity await Orestes (and Electra) τοιάδ' ἀνύσαντες ἔργα?

213–32 (Chorus, Electra). Frightened by this explicit prayer for vengeance (their own similar prayer, in the singular, 126f., had been qualified by εἴ μοι θέμις τάδ' αὐδᾶν), the Chorus return to their warnings, which are once more rejected by Electra. She is aggravating her present plight, bringing *atai* upon herself (οἰκείας εἰς ἄτας, 215). *Ate* is a strong word which will be repeated. She replies that she can do no other (ἠναγκάσθην, 221): δεινά give rise to δεινά. (On the theme of *ananke*, evil inevitably creating fresh evil, see pp. 223ff.)

233–50 (Chorus, Electra). The Chorus return to their warning and to the word *ate* (οἰκείας εἰς ἄτας, 215; and, after Electra's 224, μὴ τίκτειν σ'ἄταν ἄταις, 235), which is now doubled. They advise her, in goodwill, like a faithful mother (which is just what Electra does not have). Kells points out that they end their contribution to the *kommos* as they began it (ring-composition) with the mother-theme. And they use the metaphor of birth (τίκτειν). But Electra's own mother that bare her is the actual cause that she herself bears *atai* from *atai*. The verb is followed by ἔφυ and ἔβλαστε, with suggestions of heredity and natural process. (Cf. Segal 487ff.) Electra replies by asking, indignantly, what measure (μέτρον) there can be of, or in, κακότης. The precise sense may be doubtful, but she is certainly (one would suppose) rejecting the notion that in her plight there is a point at which one can, and should, stop. So much and no more, as the Chorus seem to think. Is this in nature? Disregard the dead? How can this be *kalon*? In what human being is this inborn? If there are any such (preparation for Chrysothemis), she rejects their approval, as she rejects a quiet enjoyment (like Chrysothemis) of advantage. She will continue to honour parents (γονέων) with unfettered wings of lamentation. Parents, but she is thinking of one parent only. She passes on to that lucid statement of the duty of revenge which has been examined in the text (see p. 225), without which, she claims, there can be no *aidos*, no *eusebeia*. ὁ μέν: her father; οἳ δέ: the murderers, but the masculine plural pronoun conceals the fact that one of the murderers is her mother.

Not everybody will find in the words of the *kommos* every suggestion that I have put forward, and I would not dare to assert that they were all present to the mind of the poet. This is Sophoclean lyric at its most complex and elusive. I hope, however, that there is enough to justify my statement in the text that, along with the expression of poignant emotion, there is a deployment of ideas, and of ideas closely related to the thought of Aeschylus, which must at least raise questions, however they are to be answered, about the quality of the act of matricide to come.

APPENDIX E

Locality in *Oedipus Coloneus*

Words of locality are frequent in the opening scene. The matter is first raised in 1f., with the twofold enquiry of Oedipus: what places (χώρους), what city of men? This is answered, in reverse order, by Antigone at 14ff.: the city afar, which she knows to be Athens (24), and the χῶρος (16, 24) which she only knows to be holy. When the villager enters, Oedipus asks (38): what is the χῶρος? And the first answer is: ἄθικτος οὐδ' οἰκητός (39, cf. 37). It may be accident that this follows ἐξοικήσιμος, οἰκητός (27f.) of the τόπος (26), but, when Oedipus repeats apparently the same question at 52 (τίς ἐσθ' ὁ χῶρος δῆτ' ἐν ᾧ βεβήκαμεν), the answer is different: no longer that this is a dwelling of the fearful goddesses but that 'this whole χῶρος is holy' (54) – it is Colonus with all its sanctuaries and with its people (60f., 64). The distinction between Colonus itself and the grove which it contains (as localities) may not be very significant, but it exists; and the people of Colonus, represented by the Chorus, have their own attitude to the grove and their own (conflicting) reactions to Oedipus. The main localities, however, are Athens and the grove; and the relations of each to the other and of Oedipus to both have prime importance in the play.

Oedipus is a wanderer: 3, 50, 123f. (πλανάτας . . . οὐδ' ἔγχωρος), 165. He is a foreigner (13). As a foreigner he finds a new citizenship (χώρᾳ δ' ἔμπολιν κατοικιῶ, 637) in Athens, but chooses to remain in 'this χῶρος' (644), as *themis* demands. As a wanderer he finds a settled resting-place, which is also a seat of supplication: a ἕδρα. The word is insistent, cf. 45, 112. The villagers will allow Oedipus to settle on profane ground (ἑδράνων, 176, cf. 195), but, when they hear who he is, they take this back (ἑδράνων, 233), bidding him leave their land and not embarrass their city. But Oedipus was still on holy ground when he made his prayer at 84ff. He prayed to the ladies of terrible visage, 'since now I have come to rest first with you in this land' (it is not perhaps quite clear whether ἕδρας here should be taken of Oedipus or the goddesses). This is at 84f.; at 89f. he says Phoebus had foretold that *this* would be his rest after long time, when he had reached his goal in a land where he would find a seat (ἕδραν) of the Awful Goddesses and a halt for strangers (ξενόστασιν). This is their ἕδρα, and it is his. The relationship which subsists between Oedipus and the Eumenides is a vital element in the play (see p. 267 above).

Finally, yet another locality will acquire dramatic importance as the last resting-place of Oedipus; and this is the place of his grave (or whatever we should call it). This too is a χῶρος (1520, 1540). Its precise location is *ex hypothesi* unknown to the audience, but various topographical indications are given in the Messenger's speech which the poet of Colonus must have expected his auditors to recognize (Rosenmeyer, *Phoenix* 104 n. 48 is altogether too sceptical), if they are mostly lost on us. One point is clear: the brazen steps of which the Messenger speaks at 1590f. cannot be dissociated from the Brazen Threshold of 56f. The final resting-place of Oedipus was in the general area sacred to the goddesses.

APPENDIX F

Philoctetes 410ff.

Having heard Neoptolemus' narrative of his supposed wrongs, Philoctetes is led to enquire after a number of eminent Greeks. It emerges that the 'good' are dead (or powerless), only the 'bad' survive. Great significance has been attached to this passage by some interpreters, who use it to explain, in part, the refusal of Philoctetes to go to Troy. The true heroes, they say, have departed leaving a corrupt world with which a Philoctetes cannot bear to be associated. Cf. 1348ff. (on which see pp. 296f. above). But can the episode really carry this weight of interpretation? It is worth considering who, precisely, are the living and the dead in question.

First, then, for the living bad. They are Odysseus: and who else? The sequence of names is as follows: Diomede and Odysseus (416f.), Odysseus (429f.), Odysseus (441) – but no, it is Thersites (442)! Diomede, who is on the whole an attractive character in the *Iliad,* is introduced, very briefly, as known to have been associated with Odysseus in more than one crafty action (and possibly with a cross-reference to the *Philoctetes* of Euripides). The function of Thersites is simply and solely to provide the crowning insult. The *Aithiopis* story is beside the point: what an educated man in the audience would remember was *Iliad* 2 (Jebb refers to 212, 222) and how Thersites for speaking out of place was soundly thrashed by Odysseus!

By contrast, the good are dead, or, in the case of Nestor, powerless. Philoctetes selects for enquiry those who might have been expected to protect Neoptolemus against his (non-existent) injury. Patroclus was an obvious case. The reference to Nestor and Antilochus is obscure, and we may be missing a point here through ignorance. The first – and most interesting – figure is Ajax (410–15). Since the Judgement of the Arms and the suicide of Ajax had been suppressed in Neoptolemus' fictitious narrative, this enquiry may have been particularly embarrassing to him. It is, moreover, ironical that in his reply Ajax is made, hypothetically, to play such an untraditional role in relation to the arms. If any of the older listeners remembered *Ajax* and (what Sophocles may have had in mind) the hero's avid desire for those arms in that play (cf. *Ajax* 444 and p. 28 above), he might not be so sure that Ajax would have surrendered them as readily as the cool realist Odysseus evidently did.

Ajax at the beginning and Thersites at the end make it difficult to attach profound moral significance to a passage which was intended to feed and elicit the hatred and contempt of Philoctetes for his enemies – a theme with which it is introduced (405–9).

APPENDIX G

The chronology of the plays

Of the seven extant plays two only have firm production-dates: *Philoctetes* was produced in 409, *Oedipus Coloneus* (posthumously) in 401. *Antigone* is said to have been responsible for Sophocles' election as general in 440, which, true or false, would not have been said unless the play was known to have been produced shortly before that date. The chronology of the four remaining plays is disputed. The following notes aim only to set out, without much argument, the assumptions made in the foregoing discussions. For fuller treatment of these complex matters the reader is referred to standard editions of the plays, to Lesky, *TD*, and to specialized monographs, some of which are mentioned below.

Ajax. This has often been assumed, on inconclusive grounds, to be the earliest extant play. There are, however, stylistic and technical reasons for placing it relatively early. I say relatively, since Sophocles first produced in 468, and there is no good ground for supposing that any of the extant plays belongs to the earliest period of his work.

Trachiniae. The dating is highly controversial, but recent opinion concurs in placing it early rather than late, cf. Kamerbeek 27–9; Lesky, *TD* 118–20;

Johansen, *Lustrum* 257f.; Segal, *YCS* 103 n. 18. 'Der Bau des Stückes schliesst eine Spätdatierung aus' (Lesky); and one may observe the collocation of long speeches, with little or no dialogue, in the centre of this play (749–812, 899–946, 1046–1111) as of *Ajax* (646–92, 748–83, 815–65). Metrical evidence also seems to exclude a late dating. H. A. Pohlsander, *AJP* 84 (1963) 280ff., seeks to show, by an analysis of the lyric metres, that *Trachiniae* is closer to *Oedipus Tyrannus* than to *Ajax* and *Antigone* (cf. also D. S. Raven, *AJP* 86 (1965) 225ff.). Pohlsander's argument is criticized by L. P. E. Parker, *Lustrum* 1970/15, 96; and T. C. W. Stinton, *CQ* 27 (1977) 67–72, adduces other metrical evidence which could indicate that *Trachiniae* is the earliest extant play. E. R. Schwinge, *Die Stellung der Trachinierinnen im Werk des Sophokles* (Göttingen 1962) argues for a date in association with *Ajax* and *Antigone*; and F. R. Earp, *The style of Sophocles* (Cambridge 1944) reached the same conclusion on stylistic grounds. That is perhaps as far as we ought to go.

Oedipus Tyrannus. Alleged parodies in Aristophanes' *Acharnians* (425) and *Knights* (424) are dubious, but the play has commonly been assumed later than the great plague at Athens (430 onwards). This assumption was first placed on a solid basis by B. M. W. Knox, *AJP* 77 (1956) 133–47, who pointed out the addition of *nosos* to the traditional blights incurred by pollution and the (otherwise puzzling) attribution of responsibility for the plague to Ares. This important article has been unjustly neglected (except by Kamerbeek). Knox argues further for a date after the reappearance of the plague, i.e. after the autumn of 427 and, preferably, the summer of 426, giving 425 as the most likely date for the play. This argument is plausible, but less compelling.

Electra. Jebb gave reasons for placing this play relatively late, i.e. not earlier than *c.* 420; many would wish to put it far closer to *Philoctetes* and *Oedipus Coloneus,* with which it shares characteristics of form and spirit; and A. M. Dale, *Collected papers* (Cambridge 1969) 227–9, argues for 413. The vexed question of priority as between the *Electras* of Sophocles and Euripides would only help us if we could (i) settle the priority, (ii) establish a firm date for the Euripidean play, neither of which we can do. It is doubtful if (i) can ever be done on internal evidence, since all the main points of contrast between the two plays can be equally well explained on either hypothesis of date. As to (ii), Euripides' *Electra* was once confidently assigned to 413, on evidence which has now been assailed; and it is rash to disregard the metrical evidence which points to 420–17. This earlier dating would not of course rule out the priority of Sophocles, but renders it much less likely. A. Vögler, *Vergleichende Studien zur sophokleischen und euripideischen Elektra* (Heidelberg 1967), should be read together with H. Lloyd-Jones' review in *CR* 19 (1969)

36–8. Both incline towards the priority of Sophocles, but Lloyd-Jones repeats his salutary warning (*AC* 33 (1964) 372) that 'people who confidently claim to know the date of Sophocles' *Electra* or *Trachiniae* are living in a private world'.

The picture which emerges, then, is a group of relatively early plays, the order of which cannot be determined; *Oedipus Tyrannus* in the early or mid-420s; and a group of relatively late or very late plays, one of uncertain date.

SELECT INDEX